Praise for

1938

"Historian Giles MacDonogh chronicles Adolf Hitler's consolidation of power over the course of one year. Until 1938, Hitler could be dismissed as a ruthless but efficient dictator, a problem to Germany alone; after 1938 he was clearly a threat to the entire world."
—*Washington Times*

"A fine book . . . well-written, combining its diverse sources with elegance and skill, and painting an engaging canvas of the disaster that was developing in Germany and was soon to engulf Europe as a whole. . . . [Giles MacDonogh's] searing descriptions of the fate endured by Austrian Jewry—from expropriation, casual cruelty, and exile, to calculated persecution and murder—are especially impassioned and moving. . . . It ably conveys the growing desperation and alarm felt by many that year, as Germany began to flex its muscles internationally and stepped up its persecution of its perceived enemies."
—*BBC History Magazine*

"In 1938, MacDonogh writes, Hitler hadn't yet become the all-powerful Führer who would soon march through Poland and send six millions Jews to the death camps. . . . There's no real answer to MacDonogh's "What if?" question, but one thing is clear: Hitler's extremism grew steadily stronger each time the rest of the world feigned blindness and looked the other away."   —*New York Post*

"[MacDonogh] is able to mine dozens of sources in German . . . [which] help us understand the roots of genocide. The book is excellent on the details of how the Nazis turned on the Jews."
—*Literary Review*

"[MacDonogh] uses new sources to flesh out his narrative and within each month he includes verbal snapshots showing different events unfolding. He is particularly good when discussing the Nazi takeover of Austria and of Vienna in particular. He also sheds much new light on the role of the Church of England's parishes in Austria. Poignancy is added to this superb book because Mr. MacDonogh's maternal grandparents were Viennese Jews."   —*Contemporary Review*

"Adolf Hitler was a natural gambler, and this book graphically describes the critical year of 1938 when his winning streak took off. . . . Harrowing." —*Edinburgh Evening News*

"This micro-focus is chillingly effective. . . . The author is at his best when interweaving individuals' experiences with the incremental machinery of Nazi persecution. . . . This is a scholarly, highly readable work which makes a fresh and valuable contribution . . . " —*The Journal of Military History*

"An accessible chronicle of crisis and atrocity that should especially interest readers who want to review the gathering storm of World War II." —*Booklist*

"This well-researched, fine-grained study sketches the moral rot that made possible Hitler's rise." —*Publishers Weekly*

"This is not a traditional history based on dry archival sources or details about who said or did what and when. . . . Interesting and easy to read, this is recommended for avid general readers of World War II history." —*Library Journal*

"[A] careful, thoughtful and wholly fascinating month-by-month account of the countdown to war." —*Jewish Journal of Los Angeles*

"A powerful, disturbing and invaluable analysis of the events in 1938 that enabled Hitler to unleash the full force of his insanity and destruction on the world." —*Shelf Awareness*

"A chilling examination of a critical year in European history." —*Kirkus*

"Giles MacDonogh is quickly becoming a must-read historian for me. . . . His great writing style draws the reader into the horrible events he is discussing. His research, to my inexperienced eye, seems top-notch, and he brings it all together to create a powerful book. *1938* is well worth your time." —*Curled Up with a Good Book*

1938

Hitler's Gamble

GILES MACDONOGH

BASIC BOOKS
A Member of the Perseus Books Group
New York

Hardcover first published in 2009 by Basic Books,
A Member of the Perseus Books Group
Paperback first published in 2011 by Basic Books

Designed by Brent Wilcox

The Library of Congress has catalogued the hardcover as follows:
MacDonogh, Giles, 1955-
    1938 : Hitler's gamble / Giles MacDonogh.
      p.   cm.
    Includes bibliographical references and index.
    ISBN 978-0-465-00954-1 (alk. paper)
    1. Hitler, Adolf, 1889-1945.   2. Germany—History—1933-1945.
  3. Germany—Politics and government—1933-1945.   I. Title.
    DD256.5M23 2009b
    943.086—dc22

                                                    2009036684

Paperback ISBN: 978-0-465-02205-2

10 9 8 7 6 5 4 3 2

For Augi
Wiedergefunden

Ich ging dann nach draußen, wo die Sterne funkelten und die Abschüsse am Himmel wetterleuchteten. Die ewigen Zeichen und Male—der Große Wagen, der Orion, die Wega, das Siebengestirn, der Gürtel der Milchstraße—was sind wir Menschen und unsere Erdenjahre vor diesem Glanz? Was ist unsere flüchtige Qual? Um Mitternacht, bei Lärm der Zecher, gedachte ich lebhaft meiner Lieben und fühlte, wie auch ihre Grüße durchdrangen.

—ERNST JÜNGER,
DECEMBER 31, 1942

Contents

Introduction

The year 1938 was one of cataclysmal change for Germany. On January 1, the Reich was administered by a right-wing coalition led by the chancellor, Adolf Hitler, and dominated by members of the Nazi Party. The army had sworn a personal oath of allegiance to Hitler, but its commanders had managed to retain a degree of independence. The country lay confined within borders decreed by the Treaty of Versailles nearly twenty years before. Hitler so far had contented himself with policing his own house and grabbing back the Demilitarized Zone in the Rhineland. He had yet to pursue any foreign adventures. Although stripped of their roles in German public life, Jews were still allowed to possess their own property, and many continued to lead relatively normal lives. They were evidently in no hurry to leave.

By New Year's Day 1939, everything had changed: The non-Nazis had been purged of all but a few insignificant roles in government; Hitler had assumed total control of the armed forces; Germany had invaded Austria and the German-speaking areas of Czechoslovakia; Jews had been robbed, beaten, and imprisoned, and many had been driven into penurious exile. Hundreds had been killed. Hitler emerged *deus ex machina*, with all the powers of the Nazi regime consolidated in his own person. And worse was to come. That Germans felt an increase in stress and anxiety during those twelve months is borne out by one telling statistic: Their consumption of strong alcohol doubled in the course of the year.

We now remember 1938 above all for the Munich Agreement, that moment at the end of September in which Western leaders apparently gave in to the Führer's demands. Peace was hanging by a thread: Hitler had launched his second foreign "gamble," and French and British statesmen met their Fascist counterparts in a bid to avoid war. Czechoslovakia was sacrificed for the sake of détente.

We are also painfully aware of the condition of much of Europe by May 1945: a collection of smoldering ruins filled with fresh or festering corpses. In the intervening years between 1938 and 1945, some 50 million people died violent deaths. There is, however, a danger in hindsight; it would be unfair to seek to draw a direct line between the two, for the line is not straight at all. Before the outbreak of war in 1939, no one could have accurately predicted the depths to which Nazi Germany would sink by the end.

Nonetheless the events that took place in 1938 make it easy to reach the conclusion that Hitler had already mapped out the entire series of conquests by which he had regained the old imperial German borders in the east and more besides. We need to avoid racing to conclusions. Hitler could be more pragmatic than his writings and public utterances suggest, and rather than conducting his activities based on a master plan, he was probably simply hoping to get as much as he could without fighting the great powers. If all went well, and the West made no trouble, other territories might fall into his lap. It was only in the spring of 1939, for example, that he began to make plans to take the Polish Corridor by force, after the Poles refused to concede the territory of Danzig to the Reich.

It is similarly tempting to connect the injustice and violence directed against Austria and Germany's Jews in 1938 with the industrialized slaughter of the Final Solution. Nazi antisemitism certainly took a new turn in 1938, but it would be difficult to argue that by then plans had been drawn up to murder the Jews in specially created camps in east-central Europe. Some would say that Hitler had already made up his mind by January 30, 1939, when he delivered a notorious speech to celebrate the sixth anniversary of the Nazi takeover. Nevertheless, he had to find a means of putting his thoughts into action, and even then, German leaders were remarkably sensitive to foreign opinion. It is more likely that the speech, with its prophecies of Jewish suffering, was a warning to the United States that there would be trouble for the Jews if they continued to stifle German trade and rob the country of the foreign currency it so desperately needed to survive.

Words like *vernichten* (exterminate) and *ausrotten* (wipe out) came easily to Hitler's lips. As a frontline soldier in the Great War, he had personally experienced the effects of poison gas, but even by the end of 1938 it was unlikely that he had considered using it on his racial enemies. Wartime conditions vastly accelerated the Nazis' as yet unformulated projects, and only when the smoke was thick enough to obscure the activities of the zealots in the extermination camps did massive troop deployment, inadequate communications, inurement to violence and death, together with casualties on an unprecedented scale, all help remove the last moral barriers to genocide.

Yet 1938 was *the* crucial year in the history of Nazi Germany before Europe tumbled into war. Every month resounded with shocks or sensations: the Blomberg-Fritsch crisis in January, which shook faith in the armed forces; the end of cabinet government in February; the Anschluss in March, which melded Austria to the Reich; the plebiscite in April, which revealed overwhelming support for the Führer; Hitler's trip to Rome in May, which laid the keel of a proper alliance with Mussolini; the Evian Conference in July, which revealed that the countries opposing Hitler's racial policies were not prepared to put their money where their mouths were; the Kendrick Crisis in August, which destroyed the British intelligence network in Germany; Chamberlain's visits to Berchtesgaden and Bad Godesberg in September, followed by the notorious Munich conference; the occupation of the Sudetenland in October and, later that month, the expulsion of the Polish Jews from the Reich; Goebbels's re-creation of a medieval pogrom in November's Reichskristallnacht. While the Jews repaired their broken homes and shops in December, the kindertransports began to ferry their children to safety.

In 1938, the blood was scarcely cold on the battlefields of the Great War, and few people were ready for more—yet in the course of those twelve months, Hitler, Hermann Göring, and Joachim von Ribbentrop prodded the West's defenses and found out how thin they were. They gambled, and with each easy victory they decided they could push even further. Hitler's eyes were already searching, but for the time being he was looking to the southeast. In his mind, Germany required *Lebensraum* (living space), raw materials, and industry. It was Austria and Czechoslovakia that appealed to him at the beginning of 1938, not right-wing Poland, where many people abhorred the Jews as much as he did and which was still a useful bulwark against Bolshevik Russia.

In 1938 the deportation of the Reich's Jews began in earnest. Germany gained experience in forcible expulsion: with the October eviction of the Polish Jews and with Reichskristallnacht two weeks later. Following the pogrom of November 9–10, as many as 30,000 Jews were shoved into the concentration camps, which Himmler had been extending and expanding all year. This was the first large-scale, organized strike against the Jews of the Altreich—as Germany north of the former Austro-German border on the river Inn was now called. A few thousand rich Austrian Jews had been languishing in Dachau and Buchenwald since April. The aim was to speed up emigration, but it also oiled the cogs of a machine that would be used again and again once war began. And when that happened the end result was mostly murder.

It is as well to remember, nevertheless, that although 1938 was a grim year for Germany's Jews, many ordinary people reaped the benefits of the "racial community" or *Volksgemeinschaft*. Both the proletariat, purged of its left-wing allegiances, and the peasantry in particular enjoyed the benefits of social welfare organizations such as Kraft durch Freude (Strength through Joy). For the German poor, there was the possibility of a holiday for the first time in their lives, and there was the chance to place a down payment on a Volkswagen Beetle. Distractions came in all shapes and sizes, such as the many sparkling parades and festive occasions orchestrated by Joseph Goebbels at the Ministry of Propaganda. Only slowly did they realize—if they noticed at all—that the Führer was leading them to war.

PROLOGUE

On November 5, 1937, in the course of a two-hour monologue at the Reich Chancellery, Hitler set out his new vision for Germany, proposing to smash the shackles of Versailles. No notes were to be taken at the top secret session, which lasted from 4:15 to 8:30 PM. Hitler's aim was to test his service chiefs and see how ready they were to subscribe to his more radical plans. Present at the meeting were Field Marshal Werner von Blomberg, Colonel-General Werner von Fritsch, Admiral Erich Raeder, and Hermann Göring (representing the Luftwaffe), together with the foreign minister, Constantin von Neurath. Blomberg's adjutant, Colonel Friedrich Hossbach (who was also present) thought the discussion might interest his mentor, the chief of staff, Colonel-General Ludwig Beck, and scribbled down the main points in his diary.

Hitler told those present that his aim was to maintain the "racial community" and enlarge it. Germany required *Lebensraum*, not in the country's former African colonies, which had been confiscated in 1918 (and which did not interest him), but in Europe, where new agricultural land would provide Germany with the self-sufficiency—or autarky—it craved.

He warned the generals that Germany was also painfully short of raw materials. It had to strike before potential enemies such as the Soviet Union could catch up. He predicted that the Russians would be ready to fight at

1

any moment between 1943 and 1945, which would allow Germany precious time to annex Czechoslovakia and Austria. The strike could come as early as 1938. By acquiring these two territories Germany's frontiers would be made that much more secure, and the manpower would provide him with twelve fresh divisions for the army.

Operations of this sort required minute planning. Sensing the opposition of his military chiefs, Hitler reassured them that there was no hurry. He predicted that the fragile bonds between Britain and France on the one hand and Italy on the other would collapse by the summer of 1938, leaving Mussolini resolutely in the German camp. He was convinced that Britain would recoil from fighting and that France would not participate either, as the country would be confined to its bed by yet another political crisis: During the waning years of the Third Republic, French governments came and went with indecent speed.

BLOMBERG AND FRITSCH were the first to throw up their hands in exasperation after the meeting. Neurath was also jittery. Much of what Hitler had said may have looked dangerously radical, but to nationalists and National Socialists, Austria and Czechoslovakia were the obvious targets. The treaties of Versailles and Saint Germain that followed the defeat of Germany and Austria-Hungary had accorded the precious right to self-determination only to the victors in the First World War, or the formerly oppressed peoples of their enemies. Austria had been shorn of all its territories and left in possession of only its German-speaking core. It was expressly forbidden to link up with Germany, because the creation of a superstate might have made Germany stronger than the Allies desired.

British politicians had also begun to question the wisdom and morality of the Versailles settlement and were increasingly conscious of these open sores. There was much discussion of the former German colonies and whether Hitler should be granted an African empire. In general the British were happier with the idea of concessions on the European mainland that did not threaten their empire. Many—particularly in the British Foreign Office—saw revision of the Austrian and Czech borders as inevitable and a German presence in Bohemia and Moravia as preferable to a Soviet one. It was unfortunate, perhaps, that the man who clamored loudest for such changes should be Adolf Hitler.

When Hitler became chancellor in 1933, Germany had been a modestly wealthy, partly modernized society. The Third Reich had taken steps to change that, but the diversion of so many of the country's resources into the arms program had left many other areas underfunded. The German economy was simply not strong enough for the tasks imposed on it by the Nazis. Troops slept in bivouacs while money was plowed into arms construction. The German railway network, together with its rolling stock, was falling apart. The finance minister, Graf Lutz Schwerin von Krosigk, was tearing his hair out over Germany's economic crisis, which he thought would last to 1940 at the very least. He told the propaganda minister and gauleiter of Berlin, Joseph Goebbels, about it, but Goebbels came out with a typically Nazi line: He did not believe a country could be killed by debt, only lack of weapons. Raw materials were vital to Nazi Germany's survival. Austria had the iron ore of the Erzberg, but Czechoslovakia had much more. Both countries could offer foreign currency, which was vital for purchasing arms and materials abroad.

On November 19, two weeks after the meeting with his service chiefs, Hitler received Lord Halifax at the Berghof, his opulent country house above Berchtesgaden in the Bavarian Alps. As lord president of the Council, Halifax was a member of the British cabinet and would shortly replace Anthony Eden as foreign secretary. Halifax let it be known that Britain was not opposed to a revision of the Versailles settlement regarding Austria, Czechoslovakia, and Danzig, provided it came about peacefully. Halifax clearly had the backing of the British government: In December, Prime Minister Neville Chamberlain told the German ambassador, Joachim von Ribbentrop, that he was prepared to discuss both Austrian and Czech issues.

When Halifax left, Hitler emerged in an ebullient mood and told his entourage that Halifax was "a clever politician who fully supported Germany's claims." He summoned the Austrian Legion, an SS unit composed of Austrian Nazis, and told them, "The hour approaches when your wishes will be fulfilled."

Hitler did not talk of his need to become absolute master in his own house when he addressed his service chiefs earlier that month, but this was not far from his mind. It would mean removing from power all those who were less than a hundred percent committed to National Socialism. Like a balloonist, he was going to divest himself of the lead weights that impeded his ascent.

Göring took over Germany's finances from Hjalmar Schacht at the beginning of December. Schacht had suggested Göring receive an economic role in the first place, but Göring was increasingly impatient and wanted to use more draconian methods to find money for his projects. Göring now had the job of making Germany self-sufficient while financing German rearmament. Schacht had not thought this autarky feasible. Those who voiced objections to Hitler's more radical plans were in the firing line. Foreign Minister Neurath was the next victim: He had been appointed by Chancellor Franz von Papen in 1932 and had only joined the NSDAP (Nazi Party) in 1937. He was to be replaced by Ribbentrop, Hitler's "Second Bismarck." Three ambassadors were to be jettisoned too: Ulrich von Hassell in Rome, Herbert von Dirksen in Tokyo, and Papen in Vienna.

It seems unlikely, however, that Hitler had a master plan for these changes and no grand strategy that was specific to 1938. He responded to each crisis as it came along, and it was invariably he who came out strongest.

CHAPTER ONE

JANUARY

As the silver candelabra had been placed on the table, a wonderful light lit up the red and golden wine in all its splendor that was majestically mirrored in the noble wood of ancient furniture and in the wings and clothes of the golden angel together with the balls on the Christmas tree. Every feast day comes and goes in our house as our own new, clear and silent celebration: and the magnificence and the serenity become ever greater with every earthly joy. . . .

The angels and silver baubles shine from within the dark baroque room: everything is still steeped in Christmas, and therefore from renewed festivity, a new year!

—JOCHEN KLEPPER,
JANUARY 1, 1938

In the first weeks of January 1938, much of Germany lay under a thick blanket of snow. The Nazi regime's secret police were equally ubiquitous. For those who had no reason to love the Third Reich, it was best to keep your head down and talk to no one. Communists, Socialists, and Jews had most to fear.

At the beginning of a year that would prove thoroughly disastrous for the European Jewish population, it was not the Germans but the Romanians who turned up the heat. A Fascist government led by Octavian Goga had come to power in Bucharest in December. On January 12 he revoked the citizenship of the country's three-quarters of a million Jews, causing large numbers to flee. Some of these surfaced in Austria ("a gift," mocked Goebbels), and there was a fear that they might join the other groups of foreign Jews in Germany.

While the Nazi leaders were delighted to find a new ally in the Balkan state, they were less than pleased to become a haven for its Jews. "The Jewish question has become a global problem once again," wrote Goebbels. The Nuremberg-based weekly *Der Stürmer* celebrated the precipitate departure of the Jews from Romania with a series of cartoons by Philipp Rupprecht (known as Fips). One showed Jews in France, Britain, and the United States weeping impotently over the fate of their Romanian brothers; another, an avalanche of Jews descending on France; and a third, a Jew arriving at an Austrian hotel to find it "fully occupied."

Der Stürmer was the unofficial organ for the state persecution of the Jews, and it also reported that the French foreign minister, Yvon Delbos, had been in Warsaw for talks before Christmas, discussing the possibility of dispatching Poland's three and a half million Jews to Madagascar. The editor, Julius Streicher, preened himself: He had been one of the first to suggest the French colony as a new home for the Jews. On January 21, *Der Stürmer* published a special issue calling for the death penalty for *Rassenschänder*, Jews who slept with Gentiles. Goebbels—who had slept with at least one Jew—heartily approved. The cover showed the fourteen-year-old starlet Deanna Durbin on the arms of elderly Hollywood Jews. The periodical contained a regular column in which all Gentiles who continued to have professional or personal dealings with Jews were named and shamed.

Victor Klemperer, a rabbi's son married to a Gentile, had been fired from his position as professor of Romance languages at Dresden University. He was reduced to writing a diary that recorded each new blow leveled at his race. Like many Jews, he was beginning to have second thoughts about wanting to be more German than the Germans and complained of the "tragedy of the Jew, misled by his desire to assimilate." Sometimes it seemed the state's bugbears were Catholic priests, at others Protestant pastors. In January 1938 it was Jews.

Hitler was fully in sympathy with the persecution of the Jews, but as 1937 turned into 1938, he was thinking more about territory and how he would ensure that he remained absolute master of the Third Reich. There had been difficult moments in the past, but time and again, circumstances had come to his rescue, and he had been able—as he would put it, with the instinct of a sleepwalker—to turn difficult situations to his advantage. One such circumstance, the Blomberg-Fritsch affair, began with the first social occasion of the Nazi New Year, although it was a while before Hitler realized how events could be shaped to his advantage. Indeed, this time he was so innocent of the plot going on around him that he was able to accompany Goebbels to see *Die Fledermaus* that evening. The Führer was in complete raptures at the Strauss operetta and wholly unaware that behind his back his underlings were about to provoke a two-week crisis and bring the state to a standstill.

Hermann Göring's position was emblematic of the peculiar structure of power within the Nazi state: Officially Hitler's successor, he was also a minister of state and president of the emasculated Reichstag. As commander of the air force, he answered to Minister of War Blomberg but at the same time was on an equal footing with Colonel-General von Fritsch, the head of the army.

At forty-four, the former air ace Göring was one of the oldest in the gang, the same age as his enemy Ribbentrop. Goebbels was forty and Heinrich Himmler only thirty-seven. Hitler himself was a mere forty-eight. Nazism retained its appeal to an unfulfilled element in German youth—a generation born around 1910 who had failed to find employment during the depressed years of the Weimar Republic.

At his suitably gigantic birthday party on January 12, Göring was feted in the way he loved best—no one dared to stint on the presents. Hitler had just returned from his Christmas break and gave his old friend a splendid hunting scene by the Austrian painter Hans Makart. The party was interrupted, however: Göring and Hitler were due at the town hall in the Tiergarten district of Berlin to be witnesses at the wedding of the aging Blomberg to one Eva Gruhn. As he left the festivities, Göring permitted himself a loud chuckle. For some time now, Göring had been looking for a means to extend the Party's influence over the army. Now he saw his chance.

A widower with five children, the noble Blomberg was marrying a much younger woman. Some months before, he had divested himself of his uniform, put on civilian dress, and gone to Oberhof in the Thuringian Forest for the sake of his health. Seeing him eating his dinner all by himself, the manager of his hotel had asked him if he would like company. That was when the twenty-five-year-old Eva Gruhn sat at his table. Later she informed Blomberg she was pregnant with his child; he liked Eva so much that he asked for her hand in marriage.

He even went so far as to confess his love to Goebbels, who promised to help him square matters with any of the Nazi leaders who might have objected to his marrying a woman from the *bas fonds*. Eva came from the unglamorous district of Neukölln in Berlin, where her mother had run a massage parlor. Mother Gruhn had twice been convicted of prostitution, and her daughter had followed in her footsteps. Eva had a police record that documented participation in nude orgies, prostitution, and selling pornographic pictures—of herself. She had only just been granted parole when she met Blomberg.

As early as October, Blomberg had cried on Göring's shoulder and told him of his intended's humble origins. He had spared Göring the criminal record, which he probably did not know himself. His own officers disapproved of the match. Blomberg had been a stickler for their marrying within their social milieu and was now breaking his own code. Nevertheless, Göring found the story "very moving" and assured him that Hitler's consent would be forthcoming, as the marriage would strike a blow against the old monarchist order. He took great pains to be helpful, going so far as to dispose of a younger rival for Eva's affections by packing him off to South America with a well-paid job. Blomberg finally told Hitler on December 22, the marriage went ahead with the Führer's blessing, and the happy couple departed for their honeymoon on the island of Capri.

There was a slight glitch a few days later, when the Blombergs were obliged to cut short their honeymoon and return to Berlin, on account of the unexpected death of Blomberg's mother. After her funeral, the honeymoon couple prepared to set off for Italy once again. Goebbels saw Blomberg in Berlin on January 17 and still thought him a "fine fellow." The storm broke, however, on January 21, when an anonymous caller, claiming to be a general, telephoned Army High Command demanding to speak to Colonel-General Fritsch. When he was refused, the caller shouted, "Tell the general that Field Marshal von Blomberg has married a whore!"

The chief of police, Graf Wolf Heinrich von Helldorf, knew the story already: A member of his vice squad had been with a prostitute in the course of his duties, and she had seen the new Frau von Blomberg together with Hitler and Göring in the newspapers, instantly recognizing her as an old friend. The policeman had looked up Eva Gruhn's record and brought the file to Helldorf. At the Gestapa—Gestapo headquarters in the Prinz Albrecht Palace in Berlin—someone showed Franz Josef Huber, later Gestapo chief in Vienna, a picture of a naked woman, telling him the woman was now Freifrau von Blomberg.

Helldorf went to see General Wilhelm Keitel—whose son Karl-Heinz was engaged to be married to Blomberg's daughter Dorle—and asked him to identify the new baroness from a police photograph. Keitel had little to tell the police chief. He had not been invited to the wedding and said that the only time he had set eyes on her was at the funeral of Blomberg's mother. Keitel had not been able to make out her features through her heavy veil.

In a style to which Germany was to become accustomed, Keitel passed the buck. He told Helldorf to approach Göring, for the cogent reason that Göring had been at the wedding and would have had a good look at her. Helldorf drove out to Göring's mansion at Karinhall near Berlin. Göring, a long-time rival of Blomberg's, could indeed identify the woman in the picture. He admitted having known of Blomberg's intention to marry her for a long time: Blomberg had in all appearances walked into a honey trap—possibly set up by his rival.

WHILE DOUBT may still hang over Göring's role in Blomberg's fate, there is no question that he was behind the removal of the monarchist, anti-Nazi Colonel-General von Fritsch. He was to be pushed out by trumped-up charges of infringing Article 175 of the Prussian Criminal Code dealing with illegal homosexual activity: He was reported to have frequented a Bavarian rent-boy called Sepp Weingärtner ("der Bayernseppl," or Bavarian Joe) in November 1933. A blackmailer called Otto Schmidt had allegedly spotted Fritsch having sex with Bayernseppl in a dark place near

Wannsee Station. Posing as a policeman, Schmidt had followed him back to town and confronted him on the Potsdamer Platz. According to Schmidt, Fritsch had taken fright, produced his military pass, and asked Schmidt to be discreet. Over the next few weeks Schmidt had been able to pump over 2,000 Reichs marks (RM) out of the unfortunate officer.

Taking full advantage of the Nazi desire to adhere as strictly as possible to the draconian Article 175, Schmidt earned a living by spying on and blackmailing homosexuals. Arrested in 1936, he had saved his hide by giving the police the details of his business. Among his "clients" he had named Walter Funk, later the minister of economics; the tennis ace and Wimbledon finalist Gottfried von Cramm; and a Graf von Wedel, who was police president in Potsdam. He had also named Colonel-General von Fritsch. Schmidt's interrogator was Josef Meisinger, the chief of a Gestapo unit called the Reichszentrale für die Bekämpfung der Homosexualität (the Reich's Central Office for the Repression of Homosexuality). Schmidt told Meisinger that he had met the general in Lichterfelde Station—home to the cadet school—whenever he wanted more money. Meisinger had showed Schmidt a picture of Fritsch: "*Det is' er*," Schmidt said in his Prussian idiom—"That's the man."

Meisinger had taken the story to Reinhard Heydrich, head of the Reichs Main Security office and Reichsführer SS Heinrich Himmler, who had drawn up a report, but Hitler had called it *Mist* (dung), refused to look at it, and ordered it to be destroyed. He was still keen to retain Fritsch; only his entourage wanted to eliminate him.

It is not clear who—Göring or Himmler—had been the prime mover in smearing Fritsch back in 1936. It was Heydrich who relocated the incriminating dossier—his involvement would point to Himmler. Göring, on the other hand, had been meditating his coup since the end of the previous year, before Eva von Blomberg's shady past had come to light. Himmler wanted Fritsch out because he opposed the integration of the SS into the army. Göring objected to him because he assumed that Fritsch would be given Blomberg's job—which Göring coveted. With Himmler's permission, Göring had Schmidt brought to his home from Papenburg internment camp at the end of 1937. Schmidt was shown a picture of Fritsch, whom he once again identified as the man he had seen with Bayernseppl.

After Blomberg's wedding, Hitler had returned to the Berghof and was absent from Berlin until January 24. The next day Göring re-presented the Fritsch dossier along with the one Helldorf had penned on Blomberg's new baroness. When the Blomberg file was produced, the petit bourgeois Hitler was irate: He had been tricked into witnessing the ceremony—nay, even kissed the hand of a woman of the streets. He was particularly appalled that the pornographic pictures in the police file had been taken by Eva's one-time lover, a Czech Jew.

Blomberg was summoned. Hitler wanted the marriage annulled, but the general immediately refused. As it was, Hitler would not allow him to continue as minister of war. He seems to have made little attempt to save himself, going happily into retirement. He even recommended Fritsch as his successor. Hitler was relieved when Blomberg accepted a generous golden handshake, leaving soon after for Italy, but he continued to seethe. There is a suggestion in some circles that his shattered look was a pose, that he was acting, but Goebbels called it "the worst crisis for the regime since the Röhm Affair. . . . The Führer looks like a corpse." It is unlikely that Goebbels would be misled by Hitler's performance.

Hitler summoned Keitel and asked him who should succeed Blomberg. Keitel said all the right things: Göring was the man for the job. Hitler, on the other hand, refused to consider Göring, who he thought had enough on his plate already; he believed Göring to be "too idle" to take on the extra work. Keitel then advanced the name of Fritsch. Hitler went to his desk and returned with the Fritsch file. Keitel claims that he responded by saying it could only be "a case of mistaken identity or slander." Hitler asked Keitel who should have Fritsch's job. Keitel replied, Gerd von Rundstedt. Hitler thought him too old. Keitel's next idea was Walther von Brauchitsch; Hitler parried him with Walter von Reichenau. This must have seemed like a means of resolving the problem, given the fact that Reichenau was a keen Nazi, but Keitel said he was "*Hans Dampf in allen Gassen*"—a busybody too interested in politics and too little applied to the business of the army. He was unpopular with the other generals. Brauchitsch would have to do.

THE BACHELOR Fritsch had already aroused suspicions among some members of Hitler's elite. He had just been on a long holiday in Egypt, where he hoped to cure his bronchitis; he had left soon after the meeting in the Chancellery, together with his second adjutant, a former champion point-to-pointer called Jochen von Both. Göring had Fritsch tailed, but no proof was forthcoming. Fritsch knew a defamatory report about him was making the rounds, but he mistakenly believed the contents of the dossier to be based on malicious rumors about some lunches he had offered an impecunious member of the Hitler Youth a few years before. Other sources mention *two* Youths, and Fritsch's teaching them history and rapping them with a ruler on their bare calves when they got their facts wrong. The running joke among the SS was that Fritsch was a calf fetishist.

To find out if there were any truth in it, Hitler gave the file to Hossbach, who instantly smelled a rat. Against Hitler's orders, he confronted Fritsch, who denied everything. Fritsch seemed aware that the scandal had been brewed by Göring and Himmler, who sought to rid Germany of a reactionary general like himself. Hossbach told Hitler that Fritsch denied the charge, painting him in such a sympathetic light that Hitler was still keen to make him war minister. Hitler had not yet abandoned Fritsch on January 26, when the general was asked to come in and see Hitler, Göring, and his accuser in the Chancellery library. Fritsch entered shouting, "I really want to look at this pig!" He was not supposed to know that Schmidt would be present, but Hossbach had told him, thereby incurring the eternal enmity of Göring, who was looking forward to his coup de théâtre.

Hitler told Fritsch that he had been accused of infringing Article 175. Schmidt promptly identified Fritsch, who vigorously denied the charges. He swore on his word of honor he had never set eyes on Schmidt before and that there was no truth in the allegations. He made the mistake, however, of mentioning the Hitler Youth. Hitler was instantly suspicious; he may have felt there was no smoke without fire. Hitler wrote off Fritsch and Hossbach with him, telling Keitel he never wanted to see the colonel again. The firing of Hossbach compounded Hitler's depression, and Goebbels reported that he was quite tearful the next day. Hitler was not the only lachrymose person around; Keitel's deputy, Alfred Jodl, reported that his boss was tearful as well: "You get the impression of being caught up in one of the German nation's fateful moments."

Positive identification by Otto Schmidt had naturally been sufficient for Göring to declare Fritsch a guilty man, but on further inspection, the Gestapo man Huber alighted on a discrepancy: Deductions from the bank account of one Captain von *Frisch* amounted exactly to the sum paid to the blackmailer Schmidt. He went straight to see his superior, Werner Best, who sent him to Heydrich. Heydrich went pale and took him to Himmler. Himmler thanked him, saying, "You did well." Only when Meisinger informed Huber that the file had been around for a couple of years and had been put away for later use did he realize he had stumbled across a conspiracy. The missing *t* and lesser rank of Captain von Frisch would not stand in the way of the plotters' desire to block Fritsch's progress.

The apparent strike against the officer corps was causing concern. At midday on Wednesday, January 26, Helldorf called a meeting to discuss the Fritsch-Blomberg crisis at the headquarters of the Abwehr, or military intelligence service, on the Tirpitzufer. It was attended by, among others, Admiral Wilhelm Canaris, the head of the Abwehr, and his two deputies— Colonel Hans Oster and Hans Pieckenbrock. Helldorf defended Fritsch, but in his opinion Blomberg was too compromised, and he was shocked that Blomberg could have stooped so low. The meeting marked the parting of the ways between the nationalist fellow travelers and the Nazis. The suspicion that the whole affair was no more than an attempt to weaken the Wehrmacht's esprit de corps provoked the burgeoning cell of grumblers to consider launching a putsch.

Yet the scandal would not go away. On the 27th Fritsch endured a four-hour interrogation by Best, again in the presence of Schmidt. Both Fritsch and Schmidt clung to their stories. Since Schmidt's appearance at the Chancellery, the Gestapo interviewed a number of young men who had served under Fritsch's command, including Gottfried von Cramm, who had just returned from America and was later imprisoned for another offense under Article 175. The Gestapo ignored Schmidt's various claims that were clearly factually incorrect, and Franz Gürtner, the minister of justice, who was equally biased against the general, said Fritsch had not proved his innocence and regarded the story of the Hitler Youth as incriminating. Blomberg had thrown fat on the fire before his departure by saying that Fritsch was "not a woman's man." Gürtner recommended the case go before a military court. The four-hour interview coincided with the ex-kaiser's birthday, and the discontent within the officer corps was clear from the number of pro-monarchist celebrations that took place in their messes.

Hitler was distraught: An embarrassing crisis was discrediting the military elite of the Third Reich. His prudish nature found it hard to come to terms with the vices apparently prevalent among upper-class Prussians. He now had three positions vacant—minister of war, head of the armed forces, and head of the army—and there was a queue of job hunters forming: Göring, General Graf Friedrich von der Schulenburg—a former chief of staff to the Crown Prince turned Nazi, Himmler, the Nazi general Reichenau, and Karl-Heinrich von Stülpnagel. Hitler's advisors dismissed the last as being too disloyal, and Stülpnagel proved them right when he was caught up in the July 20th plot to kill Hitler. He was executed.

It was Goebbels, who had risen from the Left of the Party and had fewer illusions about the upper classes than Hitler, who came up with the answer: Hitler should take on the first two roles himself. He had seen the possibilities for divesting the regime of a potentially disloyal element in the traditional officer corps. It suited no one's purposes to exonerate Fritsch, and the process of shaming and removing him went ahead. Goebbels was able to elbow out Göring, whom the army favored for the job of war minister. There had been far less planning and a good deal more pragmatism in the decision than has been generally assumed.

THE PERCEIVED need to protect Fritsch's honor generated an organized opposition among the officer corps that would seek to depose Hitler for years to come, until July 20, 1944. Helldorf was in a position to push the files across the desk to his deputy, Fritz-Dietlof Graf von der Schulenburg, the son of Graf Friedrich and a former Nazi who had lost faith after the Night of the Long Knives of June 30, 1934. Graf Rüdiger von der Goltz went into action as Fritsch's lawyer. On January 29 emissaries from the opposition set off across the Reich to talk to the leading generals: Oster went to Hanover, Gisevius to Munster and the former mayor of Leipzig, Carl Goerdeler to Dresden to speak to Generals Ulex, Kluge, and List. The message was that the twelve commanding generals needed to make common cause with Fritsch. Some members of the officer corps were out for blood. Oster had to cool the heels of his son Achim and the rest of the garrison in Stettin, who were on the verge of mutiny.

The upheaval caused by the removal of Blomberg and Fritsch left Hitler "sullen and touchy." He cancelled the speech he was due to make to celebrate the fifth anniversary of his coming to power on the 30th. He had never failed his devotees before, and he was not to do it again until 1943. Rumors ran rife across Germany. The party went ahead for all that, and Hitler appeared on the balcony of the Chancellery to acknowledge the march past his Leibstandarte (SS bodyguard). A crowd of 100,000 had gathered by candlelight on the Wilhelmsplatz. There were events to distract his followers, and national prizes were handed out to the architect Gerdy Troost, the surgeon Ferdinand Sauerbruch, and the Nazi ideologue Alfred Rosenberg. Six million young people were reported to have tuned in to a Hitler Youth Festival at the Broadcasting House in Berlin. For Fritsch it was a hard night: He spent it being interrogated by Heydrich.

On the last day of the month, Goebbels spent two hours alone with the Führer, who continued to rant about Blomberg and Fritsch. Rundstedt saw Hitler that same day and said he was in a "fearful state of excitement such as I had never seen him." Blomberg had abused his trust. Hitler was firmly convinced of Fritsch's guilt. The general had been "all but unmasked." Goebbels had his own suggestion for Fritsch's successor: Ludwig Beck, who "came directly from Schlieffen's school." Goebbels couldn't have known the general well—Beck was on the point of throwing in his lot with the opposition. Had it been Beck and not Brauchitsch who had been in charge of the army in September 1938, the year might have turned out very differently, but it appears that Beck didn't want the job.

That day, Hitler revealed to Goebbels that he intended to make a huge shake-up in his household in order to create a smokescreen. He planned to appoint Ribbentrop to the foreign office (he came to regret it later). Hitler was not enamored of his London ambassador—he thought him boring and vain—but he valued his servility. He wanted to surround himself with men like Keitel and Ribbentrop, whom he believed trustworthy. Goebbels was not impressed: "I consider Ribbentrop is a waste of space. I made no secret of this to the Führer."

The Blomberg-Fritsch affair was an excellent example of the Nazi specialty of dirty tricks and a temporary alliance between three ill-assorted

men: Göring, Himmler, and Heydrich, with walk-on roles by various secret policemen. Hitler and to a lesser degree Goebbels were the dupes. The
machinations of his underlings left Hitler's faith in national conservative
Germany badly shaken; as a result, he decided he did not need them as
much as he had previously believed. In spite of their efforts, it was not
Göring or Himmler but Adolf Hitler who came out on top.

CHAPTER TWO

FEBRUARY

Hitler finally came to a decision about who was to lead the army on February 3, when he asked Fritsch to submit his resignation. That same day, Hitler confirmed to Goebbels that Neurath's days were numbered as well. He was looking to deflect attention from the farce in his armed forces and pass off the drastic shake-up as a "rejuvenation." Schuschnigg was also in Hitler's sights. As Hitler put it, "he ought to be quaking in his boots."

On Friday, February 4, the German cabinet met, and Hitler announced that he was to abolish the title of minister of war and take over the leadership of the armed forces. The War Ministry's functions were to be assumed by the OKW, Oberkommando der Wehrmacht (Armed Forces High Command). This was to be administered by another pliant figure, Keitel—who was accorded ministerial rank—while Keitel's nominee, Walther von Brauchitsch, was moved in to lead the army.

Both Keitel and Brauchitsch were reputed "God-fearing," something that would have recommended them to senior officers, but despite the latter's traditional credentials, Brauchitsch promised to lead the army toward National Socialism. Hitler had personally examined him on a number of issues and found him politically sound. His reputation was not spotless: He was keen to divorce his wife and marry another woman from a humble background. Nevertheless Göring was able to sort things out again by offering the first wife enough money to buy her consent. Another advantage for Hitler was that Brauchitsch's paramour was "200 percent rabid Nazi."

The army were not to be spared from the shake-up. Inspired perhaps by the Soviet Union's Great Terror, which took place that year, and the purge of the Red Army, Hitler pushed twelve senior generals into retirement and transferred another forty-four to new roles, where they could no longer make trouble. One of the announcements made it clear that Himmler would now be allowed to create his own armed SS of 600,000 men, the ancestor of the formidable Waffen-SS.

Walter Funk became minister of finance. Göring had kept the ministerial seat warm for him, but Funk had far less power than his predecessor: Characteristically, Göring made off with the plums, saving them for his Four Year Plan. Göring was compensated with the title of field marshal, while Neurath was to be given a sinecure and Ribbentrop moved across the Wilhelmstrasse to take his place as foreign minister. He already had his own National Socialist "Ribbentrop Bureau" putting its feet in the more delicate ballet of diplomatic process. One of his pet projects would be a German-Japanese alliance. Nevertheless, as the French ambassador François-Poncet put it, Ribbentrop maintained "a prodigious ignorance of diplomatic matters."

Ribbentrop was beside himself with excitement at his appointment. He had been a singular failure in London, where he had been sent to seal an alliance and had come back empty-handed. He had spent all of December concocting a report in "miserable German" in which he advocated a tripartite alliance with Italy and Japan instead. His former Anglophilia turned to hatred under the influence of his sparkling-wine heiress wife, Annaliese. He was finally summoned to appear before the Führer in the Chancellery conservatory on February 2, after which he repaired to his expensive rented wing of the Kaiserhof Hotel, ordered a whisky, and called his wife.

As the Reichsaussenminister (generally contracted to RAM), Ribbentrop told his Austrian secretary, Reinhard Spitzy, "My good fellow, now we are going to pursue a proper German policy." As much as possible, policy was to be dictated by ideology, although the Nazi leadership still hoped to avoid alarming foreign governments, which explains the moderate changes at ambassadorial level. The ambassadors in Rome, Tokyo, and Vienna were informed of their dismissal by telephone that day.

There were some positive results from the shake-up in the Wilhelmstrasse. The ambassador to Rome, Ulrich von Hassell, was retired. His dislike for Hitler and his regime had been only too apparent, and the Italians had complained. Ciano in particular loathed his habit of quoting Dante—"I distrust foreigners who know Dante." The fairly neutral, old-school Dirksen in Tokyo was not dropped but shifted to London. His retention was due to his mother's having once been useful to Hitler in Berlin society.

Significant changes came at a lower level of the diplomatic corps that was little permeated by the Party. A leading anti-Nazi, Erich Kordt became the head of Ribbentrop's secretariat in the foreign office and was instrumental in having his brother Theo shifted from Athens to take over his old job of counsellor at the embassy in London. Finally, on April 2, Ernst von Weizsäcker was promoted to become permanent undersecretary of state. The opposition was now in position to alert foreign governments to Germany's intentions. Despite many threats, the Nazis were never able to bring the Wilhelmstrasse wholly under their control.

On February 4 an official wireless broadcast explained the changes that had taken place in Germany. The "strongest concentration of all political, military and economic forces" was to be placed in the "hands of the supreme leader." On the 5th the new structure of the Reich was the main theme in Germany's newspapers and the source of a great deal of gossip and conjecture. It was believed that there had been a plot against the government and an attempt on the Führer's life. Hitler told his closest retinue not to let the public know that the real reason for change had been the fallout over the Blomberg-Fritsch affair.

The writer Jochen Klepper read all about it when his Jewish stepdaughters handed him the morning newspaper: "This is completely unexpected. . . . It is a day so heavy with destiny that it can only be compared to 30 January 1933: it is much more significant than June 1934 [the Night of the Long Knives]. It is as if the last barrier is gone."

———

As 1937 came to a close, Hitler had become more and more obsessed with Austria. At Berchtesgaden, Hitler surrounded himself with the Austrian

Legionnaires, who were trained in sabotage by members of his own Praetorian Guard—the Leibstandarte Adolf Hitler. The Legion had paraded before Hitler at the Berghof, and he had told them that he would not give up the fight for a Nazi Austria: Austria was his home too. While his hand was often stayed by consideration for Italy, Göring was much more gung ho, as Austria offered some morsels that were particularly delicious in the form of raw materials and foreign exchange that he craved for his Four Year Plan, and when Austria had been digested, the western parts of Czechoslovakia would be surrounded on three sides. Göring stood to inherit property there. Schloss Mauterndorf was being kept warm for him by the widow of his Jewish stepfather. Two of Göring's sisters had married Austrian lawyers, and his anti-Nazi brother Albert lived in Vienna, where he had taken out Austrian citizenship and was employed in the film industry.

Since the beginning of the thirties, Austria had been governed by clerico-fascist Christian Socials who had wound up democracy and replaced the power of the people with seven corporations representing occupational groupings that were allowed to send their advisors to various federal councils. The party had been subsequently abolished and merged into the Fatherland Front. Apart from Italy's Duce, few people—least of all *bien-pensant* intellectuals—expressed any sympathy for Austria's repressive government, and yet the "Corporate State" was the last bastion to hold out against a merger with German National Socialism.

Chancellor Kurt von Schuschnigg had signed an agreement with Hitler in July 1936 that was meant to guarantee Austrian sovereignty despite Hitler's persistent attempts to destabilize the country. He had had to agree to allow Austrian National Socialists a small role in government, but he had hoped otherwise to govern his country in peace. Hitler had not kept his word, however, and the terrorist activity had continued. Most recently the Nazis had been afraid that Schuschnigg intended to restore the monarchy under Archduke Otto, eldest son of the last Emperor Charles. According to Goebbels, the Austrian monarchists were becoming increasingly impertinent. Hitler was beginning to fear that if he did not move quickly, they would get there first. In June 1937 the German General Staff had been asked to draw up plans for an "Operation Otto" to seize Austria.

Every day Hitler's men let off bombs around the country in a bid to make Austria ungovernable, and the Corporate State was visibly crumbling, partly as a result of Nazi harassment, partly from its own internal contradictions. Schuschnigg had assumed some of the apparel of the Duce and the Führer, but he did not conform to the image of the strongman; he was more like a cross between Neville Chamberlain and a Jesuit. As the Nazis sought every opportunity to destabilize the state, Vienna became the principal stage of history for the last time.

At the start of 1938, Schuschnigg's police had discovered an extensive Nazi plot against his government: plans to assassinate him and for an uprising in the spring. The papers were signed by Rudolf Hess. On January 25, the police raided the Nazi Committee of Seven and arrested the civil engineer Dr. Leopold Tavs, who was deputy to Hitler's gauleiter for Austria, Josef Leopold. Tavs had been boasting a little too loudly of his invulnerability and was arraigned for high treason. As the Germans did not want Hess's role made public, a great deal of pressure was brought to bear by Berlin to scrap the trial.

The German ambassador to Vienna, Franz von Papen, was also to be assassinated. The Nazis would make it look like the work of the Fatherland Front, killing two birds with one stone. Hitler had been wanting to get rid of Papen for some time, for like Neurath, Papen opposed the Anschluss that would merge Austria with Germany. The former chancellor had only narrowly escaped death on the Night of the Long Knives in 1934. The Nazis were goading Schuschnigg to use his army against them; then they would have a pretext to march in.

Schuschnigg had already dissolved his own Praetorians: the Heimwehr had been the equivalent of the SA. Their leader had been Mussolini's protégé, Prince Ernst Rüdiger von Starhemberg, "a man of winning appearance, very modest political gifts, immense ambition and little love of work." Mussolini, however, who had protected Austria at the time of Chancellor Engelbert Dollfuss's assassination in 1934 by moving his troops up to the Brenner, had decided that his bread was better buttered with Hitler and jilted Schuschnigg. He needed Hitler now that the British and the French were ganging up against him over the invasion of Abyssinia, and he wished to avoid the embarrassment of Hitler bringing up the 250,000 or so Germans who had been living under the Italian flag in South Tyrol since 1919 and who had been persecuted by his government for wishing to remain German. Besides, Schuschnigg himself had once told Mussolini that the majority of Austrians would be in favor of a German occupation and that if Italy sent troops, the Austrians would unite with the Germans to fight them. The Austrian chancellor was clearly on his own.

With the leadership of the army in order, Hitler turned his attention to Austria. Once he had amalgamated Austria into the Reich, Germany would be able to bring Hungary and Yugoslavia into economic subservience. He had been reluctant to reveal his plans, fearing that Italy would protest against a German merger with Austria, but the Duce's opposition seemed to have abated. The meeting with Prime Minister Chamberlain's envoy Lord Halifax assured Hitler that Britain would not stand in his way either. Halifax had intimated that the British government would be prepared to accept the reversion of Danzig and border alterations in Czechoslovakia, too, with time. The redoubtable anti-appeaser Sir Robert Vansittart had been removed as permanent undersecretary at the Foreign Office, and the foreign secretary Eden was also on his way out. He resigned in a huff on February 20 after a tiff caused by Chamberlain's meddling in foreign affairs. His departure came as a relief to Hitler, especially as he was replaced on the 26th by the same Lord Halifax who had given him so much encouragement at Berchtesgaden.

Göring was egging Hitler on to invade Austria for economic reasons. Göring's Four Year Plan was responsible for providing the funding and resources for German rearmament, and Germany was seriously short of steel. The commodity was so precious to the Nazis that Hitler was the sole arbiter as to who got what. On February 8, Göring complained to Hitler that the Four Year Plan would never be complete. He was looking around for a means of achieving autarky in the shortest possible time.

If Germany lacked steel, Austria would not make up the shortfall: Austria's production was just 4 percent of the Reich's, but the iron ore mines of the Erzberg had great potential. Perhaps an even greater incentive to conquest was the reserves in Austria's national bank. With 782 million RM in foreign exchange, Austria possessed twice as much cash as Germany for shopping abroad and purchasing raw materials needed for war. On February 10 Göring met his economic advisors. The German balance of payments was bleak, and there was talk of cuts to high-priority projects. Göring's gaze turned greedily toward the river Inn that separated Germany from Austria.

Papen had been encouraging Hitler to hold talks with his Austrian counterpart for some time. The Blomberg-Fritsch crisis had forced the Nazis to temporarily postpone the meeting, but following his dismissal Papen had visited Hitler on February 5, anxious to restore his status as Hitler's personal representative in Austria. Hitler had put his recall from Vienna on hold, depending on his ability to bring him Kurt Schuschnigg in person. On Saturday, February 12, Papen took Schuschnigg to see Hitler in Berchtesgaden.

Schuschnigg was anxious: He told the mayor of Vienna, Richard Schmitz, that if anything were to happen to him, Schmitz was to assume the chancellorship. He gave orders that the border be closed if he failed to return by 9 PM. As they made their way up to the Berghof, Schuschnigg, Schmidt, and Papen passed a unit of treacherous Austrian Legionnaires, positioned to humiliate Schuschnigg. When they arrived in the Führer's study, they found him in no mood for small talk. The Austrian chancellor tried extolling the beauty of the view from the Berghof, but Hitler brushed his comments aside.

Although the conversation was conducted behind closed doors, Hitler's rants could be heard from the floor below: "I, an Austrian by birth, have been sent by Providence to create the Greater German State! And you stand in my way! I will crush you!" He, Hitler, was the better Austrian; he, Hitler, had no Slavic blood—an allusion to the Austrian chancellor's Slovenian name. According to one report, Hitler threatened to invade Salzburg. He told Schuschnigg that no one would come to his defense.

He demanded that the distraught Austrian chancellor add to his cabinet the moderate Austrian Nazi lawyer—Schuschnigg's former comrade in arms—Arthur Seyss-Inquart. Schuschnigg was also to amnesty all Nazi terrorists in Austrian jails and concentration camps. Austrians would be free to join the Nazi Party. Hitler also demanded the dismissal of the Austrian general staff chief, Lieutenant Field Marshal Alfred Jansa, who possessed a viable plan for protecting the country against German aggression. For his part Schuschnigg pleaded only that two of his bugbears be removed from Austria, Tavs and Leopold.

Schuschnigg then had to endure lunch, ending with an *Apfelstrudl*—no tribute to the visiting Austrian but prepared to please the vegetarian Führer's irrepressible sweet tooth. During the meal Schuschnigg looked pale, while Hitler talked on general matters, avoiding politics. The Austrian was desperate for a cigarette, but Hitler delivered one of his monologues against smokers and smoking. He had to wait until the meal ended before he could light up, and then he was allowed only a single cigarette, negotiated for him by a compassionate but wholly unbriefed Ribbentrop, whose one contribution to the debate was to propose a currency and customs union between the two countries.

After lunch and throughout the afternoon, Hitler continued to dictate a settlement to him in a way that would become increasingly infamous. The settlement went much further than the demands made before lunch, calling for a partial removal of Austrian sovereignty. Schuschnigg was to hand over some of his independent foreign policy to Hitler, inasmuch as it touched on the matter of mutual German-Austrian interest; there was to be a lifting of all bans on National Socialist activity, which was declared "compatible with Austrian sovereignty"; Seyss-Inquart was to be named minister of the interior to ensure that National Socialism was allowed full liberty; Schuschnigg had to fire his press secretaries; Edmund Glaise-Horstenau was to be made minister of war, and there were to be regular exchanges between the two armies; finally, the Austrian economy was to be integrated into that of Germany and Dr. Hans Fischböck made minister of finance. This settlement was based on the so-called Keppler Protocol, named after Wilhelm Keppler, the Nazi "commissioner for Austria," who was also present that day. It encapsulated the slow, "evolutionary" Anschluss favored by Hitler at the time.

Schuschnigg conferred with his foreign minister, then informed Hitler that such decisions had no value under the Austrian constitution: Nothing could be done without the agreement of the president. Hitler shouted "Get me Keitel." According to one account, the general was buckling on his sword in the conservatory below, one of a trio of military men who had been brought in to physically intimidate Schuschnigg. When Keitel appeared, asking for orders, the Austrians feared they were about to be arrested. Hitler grinned and said, "There are no orders. I just wanted to have you here." Hitler later told his circle that he had asked Keitel how many divisions Germany had at the Austrian border, and what sort of resistance they were likely to encounter from the Austrians. According to Hitler, Keitel replied, "Not worth mentioning, my Führer."

Papen intervened on Schuschnigg's behalf and managed to make Hitler agree to only a partial implementation of the Protocol by the 18th, as the rest would require the president's consent. Hitler told Schuschnigg he had three days to put the agreement into effect and that it was to last five years: "That is a long time and in five years the world will look different, anyway." Hitler ceased his hectoring while hinting at darker plans: "In tanks, planes and motorised vehicles we are the leading power today. It would be completely irresponsible and unjustifiable merely from a historical point of view not to use a magnificent instrument like the German Wehrmacht."

Schuschnigg appeared prepared to cooperate. According to Papen, the inclusion of the Nazi wooden horse Seyss-Inquart in the cabinet was the only concession that he had not planned to make before arriving in Berchtesgaden. Other sources suggest that he had been negotiating with Seyss since Tavs's arrest. The Austrians left at 11 PM after signing the Protocol. On the way back to Salzburg, Papen was the only one to speak: "Now you have some idea, Herr Bundeskanzler, how difficult it is to deal with such an unstable person."

SCHUSCHNIGG RETURNED to Vienna at once. The next day he conferred with the president, Dr. Wilhelm Miklas, who reluctantly agreed to give in to the appointment of Seyss-Inquart as minister for security and the amnesty for the Nazis then languishing in custody. Despite reservations, and in the face of mounting pressure, the Austrian parliament approved the agreement. Austrian Nazis in uniform were free to roam the streets again.

Hitler's policy was always to push for a little more. With that in mind, he turned up the heat. General Keitel summoned the Abwehr chief, Wilhelm Canaris, and ordered him to step up the campaign of sabotage until Tuesday the 15th. Canaris, who was still deeply involved in the dirty tricks in Austria and in whipping up the ethnic Germans in the Sudetenland, was provided with the detailed plans for "Operation Otto." Hitler also made concessions and appointed Major Hubert Klausner as gauleiter to replace Leopold, who was perceived to have overstepped the mark. Despite reservations, the Austrian parliament approved the agreement.

The Italian foreign minister, Count Galeazzo Ciano, got wind of the talks. He had been pleased with the news of Ribbentrop's appointment as foreign minister because "he has made clear his hostility to the English, who have treated him badly." The Anschluss, on the other hand, he thought inevitable. In his opinion, "the only thing to do is delay it as long as possible." Mussolini thought much the same; he was irritated that Hitler was snatching Austria away, but thought the merger a fait accompli.

Nazi bureaucrats had already carried out the preliminary spadework for the assimilation of Austria. In 1937, SS Department II-112 had drawn up lists of the most important Jews outside of the Reich, with the aim of building a huge personnel index on Austria. Jews were specially selected, as Adolf Eichmann made clear: "We looked at Jewish civil servants and freemasons in every ideological corner. We sat like schoolboys on benches and copied the information onto the cards; then they were arranged alphabetically, letter by letter, and anything that was not urgent was put to one side. With this card-index the first wave of the SD [Sicherheitsdienst—the SS's own secret service] stormed into Austria." Vital information had been supplied by Keppler, who also had close contact with the Freundeskreis Heinrich Himmler, the captains of industry who courted the leader of the SS. Keppler was also in touch with the Dresdner Bank, which was keen to mop up the Austrian Mercur Bank in the event of an Anschluss.

The cards for Austrian Jews were completed in June 1937, and in September of that year the head of the department, Herbert Hagen, and his expert on Zionism, Adolf Eichmann, undertook a trip to the Middle East. The two men had already hatched the idea of creating a central bureau for Jewish emigration to speed up the process of evicting the Jews.

The aim of their trip was to reach Palestine, where they wanted to send the Jews, but the British were reluctant to let them in. On October 2, 1937, Eichmann and Hagen docked in Haifa and were given authority to land for only twenty-four hours. They hired a horse-drawn carriage and drove around for the allotted time, even going to the top of Mount Carmel to admire the view. On October 3, they landed in Egypt and made for Cairo, where they spent twelve days. There they met Arab leaders and a couple of Nazi agents who had traveled down from Palestine to talk to them. When the two Germans tried to obtain visas for a better look at Palestine, however, the British authorities thwarted them. The district commissioner for Galilee—L. Y. Andrews—and a policeman had recently been killed by Arab terrorists, and the ensuing unrest proved a useful pretext to keep them out.

HITLER GAVE a speech to the Reichstag on February 20, but Victor Klemperer in Dresden already had a pretty good idea what Hitler was going to say. He noted in his diary "that he has been his own minister of war since February 4, that he has dismissed Blomberg and Fritsch and that he was halfway toward annexing German-Austria." Hitler spoke for three hours that day, addressing the issues of the return of the colonies, the League of Nations, German-Polish friendship, Russo-German hatred, and the need to protect the Sudeten Germans in Czechoslovakia. The overture to Poland was significant. He needed them on his side if he was to get away with the plans expressed in the Hossbach memorandum. The shambles in the armed forces was to be covered up by aggressive foreign policy: "The German Reich is no longer willing to tolerate the suppression of ten million Germans across its borders. . . . I am glad to say, however, that the Austrian Chancellor has shown insight and satisfactory agreement has been reached with Austria."

In general it was a mild speech, expressing warm feelings toward Austria. Papen thought Schuschnigg would resign soon. In his journal Goebbels noted, however, that Papen also stood up for religion while he (Goebbels) had been busy closing religious newspapers. He was itching to strike harder. On February 24 he noted a "cheeky speech" made by the cardinal archbishop of Munich, Faulhaber, and mentioned that "our revenge will not be long in coming."

In the Austrian provinces, jubilant National Socialist demonstrations greeted Hitler's speech. Reading the newspaper, Jochen Klepper wrote, "Austria was being spoken of as if it were already ours." From that moment onward, the Austrian city of Graz, which had offered Hitler tremendous support from the outset, together with the rest of the province of Styria, effectively fell to the Nazis.

The British foreign secretary, Eden, resigned on the day of Hitler's speech. "This is good for us," noted Goebbels. He wasn't wrong: The British Foreign Office had already abandoned Austria. Appeasement was now official policy, it seemed, and the British government felt the need to buy Germany off. The ambassador, Henderson, brought the Wilhelmstrasse an offer to return Germany's African colonies with the exception of South West Africa, which was now owned by South Africa. Goebbels joked that they would offer Germany Portuguese colonies instead. Eventually Henderson reappeared with a suggestion they might like the Congo.

SCHUSCHNIGG HAD conferred a piece of Austria's sovereignty on the Nazis, but he was able to redeem himself before the Austrian people to some degree with his speech to the Diet on February 24—the anniversary of the Nazi Party's foundation, so a holy day in Germany. He declared "*Rotweissrot bis in den Tot*" ("Red-white-red until we are dead," a reference to the colors of the Austrian republic), and in his patriotic announcements in various Austrian cities thereafter, he whipped up a last-ditch enthusiasm for Austria's independence. The speech drove Hitler into a fury, but Schuschnigg had moved too late. To unite the country he needed to bring the Socialists and the trade unions back. Outlawed under the constitution of the Corporate State, they told him that they could not fight the country's enemies with their hands tied. Schuschnigg's resistance, however puny, forced the Nazis to abandon the evolutionary method: "In the end we are really going to have to use force," Goebbels wrote.

In Berlin, Goebbels noted that more and more legitimists were rallying to Otto. When the crunch came, however, there was no serious attempt by the Austrian Left or the Right to move against the Nazi menace, which might have been brought down by a general strike. Some read the signals correctly: On February 17 the temperamental Italian conductor Arturo Toscanini cabled the Austrian government to inform them he would not be conducting at Salzburg, or anywhere else in Austria. He had flirted with Mussolini, but enough was enough. The musical director of the Vienna Philharmonic, Bruno Walter, urged him to reconsider. On Sunday, February 27, Walter conducted the Vienna Philharmonic for the last time. The music-loving Chancellor Schuschnigg was in his box. He was now at the height of his popularity and received cheers wherever he went.

In Berlin, Goebbels was flexing his muscles in all his domains and playing cat and mouse with the conductor Wilhelm Furtwängler again. Goebbels had not foreseen that Austria would fall to Germany so quickly: "I will let him get up again, otherwise he'll leave for Vienna or Salzburg." As the Reich's cultural supremo, he was concerned about painting as well as music. The Degenerate Art exhibition that pilloried avant-garde German painting was opening in the partly ruinous Reichstag building in Berlin, and he was in close contact with the curator, the painter Adolf Ziegler. On Sunday the 27th he went along to have a look. There were new elements to the show, which had opened in Munich the year before. "What rubbish!" noted the former collector of progressive modern artists such as Emil Nolde and Ernst Barlach. Still, he did not feel that the message struck hard enough, and ordered that the paintings be rehung.

In the second week of February, Goebbels was angry that the courts still failed to grasp the fact that they were meant to act according to the wishes of the government. Some homosexual members of the Party had been arraigned in Stuttgart: "I hope there will be the most draconian sentences." Another case was refusing to go as planned. Pastor Martin Niemöller of the Confessing Church was in the dock for subversion. He had managed, however, to make use of the courtroom and freely air his criticisms of the regime. "Just wait until I get hold of that pig Niemöller. The lawyers are incompetent twits." Goebbels was particularly livid that the pastor had spoken for seven hours about his "heroic life." Goebbels succeeded in having the case heard in camera, and Niemöller was transferred from Moabit Prison in Berlin to Sachsenshausen on March 2, after being sentenced to seven months "fortress detention."

With Niemöller out of the way, the opposition lost one of its most important early leaders, but others arose to take his place. At the very end of the month Fritz-Dietlof von der Schulenburg returned from his skiing holiday in Bergen, and Helldorf put him in the picture over Fritsch. That very day, Monday the 28th, Helldorf informed General von Stülpnagel of the activities of the opposition to date. Fritsch's agony had not ceased: A few days later he was interrogated in a Wannsee villa. The theme was no longer only his purported homosexuality, but also his political reliability. Fritsch protested that these sessions were a disgrace to him *and* the army.

CHAPTER THREE

MARCH

On March 1—Shrove Tuesday—Hermann Göring received his new field marshal's baton from his Führer. The portly former air ace had failed in his bid to further expand his portfolio of offices. The carnage lay all around him in the form of the shattered careers of Blomberg and Fritsch. He had been fobbed off with a bauble. Klemperer noted bitterly, "They have no sense of how ridiculous they are."

Austria appeared ripe for the taking, but the Austrian Nazi Arthur Seyss-Inquart warned Berlin that Schuschnigg did not intend to cooperate. Hitler still had a nagging fear that Mussolini would come to Austria's aid, as Italy had done four years before, after the Nazis murdered Austrian chancellor Dollfuss. Meanwhile his underlings were as disunited as ever, with Goebbels increasingly critical of Himmler's methods. Berlin's gauleiter thought the new German police state bred "cowardice, fear and hypocrisy."

Goebbels was also annoyed by the continued proceedings against Fritsch, which he thought "no longer decent. There is hardly a shred of evidence. In any case, they should never have drawn the Führer into the business." Hitler had continued to agonize right up to the moment he dismissed his army chief. At the same time, Fritsch's defense lawyer, Rüdiger von der Goltz, at last learned that the evidence the Gestapo was using against Fritsch was actually from the Rittmeister von Frisch dossier. The following day Helldorf took that file to Hans Oster at the Abwehr. On Sunday, March 6, Fritz-Dietlof von der Schulenburg appeared at Goltz's house to warn the lawyer that he might be spied on by the Gestapo, who could be bugging his telephone.

The court of honor was to sit in judgment on Fritsch at the Preussenhaus or old House of Lords on the 10th. The judges were Göring, Raeder, and Brauchitsch. Goltz, who had been able to offer Fritsch some solace at the end of February, now possessed the proof that the case was as leaky as a sieve: "Colonel-General," said Goltz, "you may now celebrate your victory." The lawyer brought the general a bunch of red roses.

A few days earlier, Schulenburg paid a call on General Erwin von Witzleben to assess the possibility of an armed revolt. Witzleben had been ill in January; now he was fully open to representations of this sort. He told Schulenburg that Colonel Paul von Hase was prepared to march on Berlin with his regiment, and that Witzleben had already talked to him about this very subject. Witzleben was still smarting from the murders of the former Chancellor Schleicher and General von Bredow during the Night of the Long Knives. An old fashioned Prussian officer who wore his heart on his sleeve, he had sounded out several generals the previous year on the need to prevent Hitler from taking Germany to war. As he was fond of saying, "I know nothing about politics but I certainly don't need to in order to know what I have to do." He almost certainly made contact with Oster as well, who was able to put him in touch with Schulenburg and another younger member of the Opposition, Ulrich Wilhelm Graf von Schwerin-Schwanenfeld.

When the court of honor convened, Schmidt initially stuck to his story, but when Fritsch's lawyer proved the case of mistaken identity, Schmidt finally broke down. At last he admitted, "Yes, I was lying." Some of the leading Nazis begrudgingly admitted that the case against Fritsch was null and void. On April 1, Hitler even went so far as to send Fritsch a goodwill message congratulating him from recovering from an illness. Goebbels rightly called it "cold comfort" for the loss of his entire world.

Austria was falling apart. On March 5, two Nazis, Seyss-Inquart and Glaise-Horstenau were admitted to the Austrian cabinet. The *Deutsche*

Grüss, or raised-arm salute, was permitted in private circles. Yet even as Nazis took over his own government, Chancellor Schuschnigg had evidently decided that he could go no further down the road designated by Hitler at Berchtesgaden. He summoned his parliament and told them, "Austria can and will live. It will never voluntarily give up its national existence." Austria was German, Schuschnigg was convinced of that, but he was not prepared to become part of a National Socialist—or "Prussian"—dominated Germany. The mention of Prussia signaled that Schuschnigg was trying to manipulate his people: There was nothing Prussian about Hitler or his regime, but ever since the victories of Frederick the Great in the eighteenth century and Austrian defeat at Königgrätz in 1866, Austrians had loathed Prussians.

There was a demonstration in Schuschnigg's favor in Vienna, but Nazis ran up a swastika flag at Graz town hall. The Italian foreign minister, Ciano, heard that Seyss would soon become chancellor: "The Duce is now strongly critical." Otto von Habsburg implored Schuschnigg to appoint him instead. The writer and director Ernst Lothar went to see Schuschnigg on Sunday, March 6, in the little house he lived in at Upper Belvedere. Lothar voiced the fears of Austria's Jews in the light of Schuschnigg's appointing Nazis to his cabinet. The writer suggested that Schuschnigg should make the Jewish conductor Bruno Walter director of the National Opera. The chancellor agreed and asked Lothar to convince Walter. They then lapsed into a pleasant conversation about the conductor's interpretation of Bruckner.

When Lothar saw Schuschnigg again two days later on Tuesday the 8th, at the Ball of the Vaterländische Front, he and his ministers were dressed in the black uniforms of the Ostmärkische Sturmscharen (storm troopers of the Ostmark, or Austria). Lothar thought they looked like SS men and said so. The Party secretary, the poet Guido Zernatto, merely shrugged his shoulders. Schuschnigg's new policy had been to remove the attractions of Nazism by offering his people an imitative homegrown version. Schuschnigg had decided on a radical course of action, however: He would hold a plebiscite to determine the majority's decision on unification with Germany. In this he was possibly encouraged by the French, who wanted evidence that there was no support for a merger. He went to Innsbruck on March 9 for a meeting of the Fatherland Front and made the announcement from the balcony of the royal palace. The poll was to be held on March 13 "for a free and independent, German and Christian Austria."

Schuschnigg was getting brave, encouraged by the international response to his defiant speech of February 24. His decision to call for a vote came as a bolt from the blue for most. He had sounded out Mussolini on Monday the 7th, but the latter had given him no leave to hope. Mussolini was pleased to hear of Schuschnigg's resistance, but he was aware that Italy was in no position to fight Germany to maintain Austrian independence. Now there was a risk of losing everything. "*C'è un errore,*" the Duce said. Halifax thought much the same: He dubbed the effort "foolish and provocative."

Hitler was struck dumb by the news, and initially at a loss to know how to respond. He had sent Ribbentrop to London; now he would pretend that the RAM was seeking British agreement to the Anschluss. Goebbels was also caught unawares: For him, Schuschnigg was a nasty peasant who was trying to catch them out. Once he recovered, however, Hitler wanted to see Spitzy, Ribbentrop's secretary, and vent his fury about the plebiscite: "Listen to me. This Schoschnik [*sic*], he wants to betray me . . . and by the foulest tricks like public polls, the exclusion of younger voters, an embargo on propaganda from the opposition and so on. That is an outrage, and I shall not tolerate it." Hitler realized that it was just the provocation he was looking for: The Anschluss would be accelerated.

General Alfred Jodl noted in his diary that the plebiscite would bring in a strong majority for the monarchists who were backing Otto Habsburg. That would have added to Hitler's fear of a restoration—and others' as well. The Czechs were petrified of the idea of the return of the monarchy, and Otto's progress might have destabilized the entire region. The Austrian chancellor sent out feelers to European capitals to see if there was support for military action against Germany. Ciano thought it bad news: "The Nazis are rising against the Plebiscite. . . . Schuschnigg has made a fatal mistake. . . . The Plebiscite bomb is fated to explode in his hands." The subject was brought up in the French Chambre des Deputés, where there was a desire to take "positive" steps to preserve Austrian independence. In the end they did nothing, and the British Foreign Office was still resigned to what they perceived as Austria's inevitable fate.

Schuschnigg and his men threw all the energy of the Corporate State into the poll. They printed and distributed huge numbers of flyers, scattering some by aircraft in Austria's most remote and snowbound corners, where many voters would have been Nazis. Trucks trundled about, transmitting the message of Austrian independence by loudspeaker. Planes trailing banners carried the word *Ja* over the cities. A flyer showed Schuschnigg and the Austrian *Kruckenkreuz*, the Corporate State's own version of the swastika. A second displayed a group of three men flashing Austrian folk costumes and was again emblazoned with the *Kruckenkreuz*. Everywhere the German theme was pushed home: To be a good Austrian was to be a good German; to be German was to be free. Austrians were better Germans than the Nazis.

The Austrian government took steps to ensure that the vote would swing in their direction. They raised the age qualification to twenty-four, making it impossible for young Nazi thugs to register their views. The electoral roll was not up-to-date anyhow, and there was no possibility of revising it in so short a time. Voters simply had to produce identification to register. Moreover, the ballot slip was printed with the word *Ja*. Anyone who did not want to keep an independent Christian Austria had to cut out a piece of paper himself and inscribe the word *Nein*. "Devious and shabby" was how one contemporary described it. Göring later gleefully pointed out that there were plenty of opportunities to rig the ballot—it was not in any way fair.

ON THE 10TH of March, German Heroes' Remembrance Day, Goebbels arrived at the Chancellery in Berlin to find Hitler bent over maps of Austria. The leader of the Austrian Legion, Hermann Reschny, was worried that the Austrian army would fight if Schuschnigg told them to. Lothar went to Linz and noted that Schuschnigg's popularity was running high: A boy who shouted, "*Heil Hitler!*" was all but lynched. Schuschnigg returned to Vienna that day, and Hitler ordered his military chiefs to prepare for an invasion on the 12th.

The humiliated Ribbentrop was stuck in London with instructions from Hitler not to move. He was to represent the German government in the course of the crisis. Like many of his contemporaries, Chamberlain had a low opinion of Ribbentrop's intelligence. It was not just with Britain that

Ribbentrop was prone to gaffes. In his passion for signing a German-Japanese alliance, he had already destroyed a profitable Sino-German trading relationship. The RAM learned of the Anschluss from Chamberlain, Halifax, and Cadogan in the course of lunch at Downing Street, and followed its progress on the BBC. To add insult to injury, his predecessor Neurath was temporarily brought back to the Wilhelmstrasse to deal with the flak from abroad. Many other important members of the gang were missing too: Brauchitsch was on leave and Reichenau in Cairo. Keitel was asked to produce the Operation Otto file and Beck to move two army corps to the frontier. Hitler still wanted a pretext for invading; Göring, delighted to control foreign policy during Ribbentrop's absence, thought they should go in anyway.

Schuschnigg revealed his decision to hold a plebiscite to his government and ministers as late as he could. The headquarters of the government party, the Fatherland Front, also had a visit from Dr. Desider Friedmann of the Jewish congregation or IKG (Israelitische Kultusgemeinde); he brought a check for 500,000 schillings to help fund the plebiscite. The following day he brought the Front another for 300,000. It was a reflection of the degree of anxiety that was going through the community. As the writer Gina Kaus put it, they hoped to win, "but we were worried for all that." The Jews were conscious that if Austria fell, they would suffer a terrible fate.

ON MARCH 11, two days before the plebiscite was to be held, Hitler performed the first invasion by telephone in history. The lines opened at 5:30 AM, when the Austrian chief of police, Michael Skubl, rang Schuschnigg to tell him that the border had been closed at Salzburg. The pious Austrian chancellor's first reaction was to take himself off to Mass at the cathedral. When he returned to the Chancellery he discovered that German forces had been mobilized in Bavaria and that Seyss-Inquart had disappeared. As it transpired, the German mobilization had been chaotic: The General Staff possessed no proper plans. Later, many German units actually broke down on the road between Linz and Vienna. It was a godsend that the Austrians offered no resistance.

No one had had much sleep in Berlin. Goebbels had been scribbling propaganda for most of the night, preparing to drop 13 million leaflets on

Austria. Papen arrived from Vienna to find Neurath, Interior Minister Wilhelm Frick, Himmler, Brauchitsch, Keitel, and their retinue plotting. He was kept in the dark in an antechamber of the Chancellery while the others made decisions. Around midday Hitler sent word of the invasion to Mussolini through Prince Philip of Hesse, but Operation Otto would go ahead regardless of what the Duce said. He took the trouble to sugar the pill: His letter contained "a precise declaration about the recognition of the Brenner as the frontier of Italy."

Hitler was a furious bundle of nerves, unable to issue coherent orders, so it was Göring who actually stage-managed the Anschluss from the Chancellery switchboard. At 9:30 AM, he directed Seyss-Inquart and his fellow Nazi minister Glaise-Horstenau to the Austrian Chancellery in the Ballhausplatz. Göring issued an ultimatum at around 10 AM: He wanted the plebiscite postponed within the hour and another one announced, to be carried out under the system established by the Germans in the Saar.

When Schuschnigg made inquiries in Graz, he learned that local Nazis had issued a statement that the postponement had already taken place and that he had apparently resigned. When the chancellor asked if he could rely on the police to defend Vienna, he was told that since the amnesty, the Nazi officers who had been sacked had been reinstated, and their loyalty to the Austrian Republic was doubtful. Schuschnigg was sure that the army was reliable, but he was convinced that Austria should not go to war with Germany—there was to be no repeat of 1866. He decided to formally postpone the plebiscite at 2:45 PM. The scene in Vienna must have been rendered all the more absurd by the ubiquity of loudspeakers blaring out the national hymn "O Du mein Österreich." Within a few weeks most of his ministers and senior bureaucrats would be breaking stones in Dachau.

Seyss-Inquart called Göring to inform him of the decision. Communication was not helped by a faulty telephone connection between the two countries. As there was insufficient power to take the calls in Hitler's private apartments, Hitler and Göring had to wait for news at the Berlin Chancellery switchboard. Göring's prodigious girth meant there was scarcely room for anyone else in the small room. Hitler stood with one knee on a sofa nervously twisting the curtain cord with his hand until Seyss finally came on the line. In his excitement he managed to pull down the curtain. "Yes, he should act!" Hitler shouted.

At 5:30, Seyss returned to Schuschnigg with a notebook containing the Reichsmarschall's prescription: "The situation can only be saved if the Austrian Chancellor resigns immediately and if Dr Seyss-Inquart is appointed Chancellor within two hours. If these conditions are not fulfilled, German armies will move on Austria." In Berlin it was still not certain whether the army would go in. Other conditions in the ultimatum had to be carried out by 7:30, and Seyss grumbled he was being treated like a receptionist. German forces were already mustered at the border.

In Austria, public loudspeakers told men born in 1915 to report to the colors, amounting to a partial mobilization. Troops were positioned here and there, morale was good, but nothing more came of it. A unit moving up to the border from the Neusiedlersee was greeted with mild enthusiasm in places, and at others—like the small towns of Melk and Amstetten—by a population that had already gone over to Hitler. The general inspector of the Austrian army, Sigismund Schilhawsky, described military resistance as "pointless," since Austria could not hope for any immediate support from outside. By 6 PM the troops were sent back to their barracks.

Lothar experienced this firsthand: In Amstetten there was a Nazi parade, and the firemen's band played the Nazi "Horst Wessel-Lied" tune. At that moment the Austrian army arrived, making for the Austrian-German frontier. Lothar talked to the captain, who told him, "We left Vienna to avoid bloodshed. From tomorrow we will be no more than a unit in the German armed forces."

By the evening of the 11th Hitler had still not fully decided on his course. The idea was to make him federal president, and the rest could come gradually. Austrian State Secretary Theodor Hornborstl madly telephoned potential saviors. The Italians had already washed their hands of Austria. Halifax replied that he could offer nothing. No one was prepared to guarantee the state's security. In the circumstances Schuschnigg meekly did what was required of him and tendered his resignation. In his memoirs Schuschnigg allowed himself a reflection: "That day meant not only the end of Austrian independence, it also meant the end of international morals." It is a wonder it took him so long to realize the gravity of the situation.

WHILE THE Austrian chancellor slowly divested himself of his offices, Seyss-Inquart and Glaise-Horstenau sat in a corner of the Chancellery and received messengers with close cropped or shaven heads, "most of them with heavy sabre scars across their faces." The Nazis had moved in. One was Gauleiter Joseph Bürckel from the Saar, who was meant to take over Papen's job. Keppler had landed at Aspern in his private airplane. Hess came by train. The new brooms snatched telephones from the hands of loyal officials and slammed them down.

After tendering his resignation to the president, Schuschnigg returned to the Ballhausplatz to clear his desk. He felt the presence of the images on the wall: the death mask of Dollfuss, murdered in the office next door, and a portrait of the empress Maria Theresa. He rehearsed the golden moments of Austrian history, prompted by the same pictures of the great and good, and the hall that in 1814 and 1815 had witnessed the glory days of the Congress of Vienna. A retainer entered to tell him that the Germans were broadcasting spurious reports of a Communist uprising in Austria. The government was said to be helpless; there were hundreds of casualties. The announcement of his resignation was broadcast at around seven. President Miklas was still fierce in his reluctance to appoint Seyss-Inquart chancellor, but he gave in half an hour later. Schuschnigg's departure was the signal to the Nazi thugs to take over: The violence began as local bosses were ousted from their offices and the barracks of the Fatherland Front were taken over.

At the cabaret Simplicissmus in Vienna, the German comedian Fritz Grünbaum made his last appearance before he and his partner, Karl Farkas, were banned. The lights had already been switched off: "I can't see a thing, nothing at all. I must have stumbled onto the Nazi cultural stage." In the Jewish-owned Café Herrenhof, the German exile Walter Mehring was sitting with his agent when Seyss-Inquart and Glaise-Horstenau came in to confer. It was Seyss-Inquart's regular haunt or *Stammlokal.* The waiter told Mehring, "Seyss ordered only soup, now it's getting serious."

Schuschnigg made his last broadcast at a quarter past eight that evening. He had postponed the plebiscite because he had been determined to avoid bloodshed at all cost.

Writer Gina Kaus lived above the Jockey Club. She listened to the speech and went to the window and looked down onto the Lobkowitzplatz, where she saw a policeman put away his red-white-red armband and put on a swastika: evidence that the police played a crucial role in the death of Austria's First Republic. Her lover, Eduard Frischauer, was a baptized Jew whose uncle owned a Sunday newspaper. He told her, "We leave tomorrow."

HITLER WAS cheered by the news from Austria. Now that the army had been muzzled, he gave the order for his troops to march at 20:45. Austrian army units received orders to withdraw toward the east—they were not to open fire. At 10:30, Hitler received the information he had been waiting for: Mussolini gave him the go-ahead. Hitler was over the moon. He told Göring's friend Prince Philip that he would never forget Mussolini's gesture, and he never did.

Hitler's Austrian agent, Keppler, had already moved into his office. The initial arrests were going ahead, and Viennese Mayor Schmitz was the first to be taken into custody. He had refused to fly a swastika from the town hall and had armed the municipal militia. The Nazis also captured and consumed 166 brace of sausages they found in the Rathauskeller. Miklas finally summoned Seyss shortly before midnight. The president was now in no position to object, having been confined to his villa by SS man Otto Skorzeny, who was the discovery and protégé of the Austrian SS chief Ernst Kaltenbrunner. It was Skorzeny's first appearance as the Nazi Germany's chief daredevil. His career would include liberating Mussolini from Il Grand Sasso in 1943 and leading the storming of the Bendlerstrasse after the plot of July 20, 1944.

Seyss appointed a cabinet of conservative Nazis. Göring insisted on the inclusion of Dr. Franz Ulrich Hüber as minister of justice. (He was the husband of Göring's sister Paula.) As it was, Seyss's reign as an independent Austrian chancellor was short-lived. When the German military attaché, General Wolfgang Muff, rang Berlin at Seyss's request to inform Göring that everything had been carried out according to his wishes and he could now recall his forces, Göring told Muff that, on the contrary, he was to demand the assistance of German troops to reestablish law and order. Göring had been enjoying his sport. That evening he was the host at a winter ball at the Air Ministry in Berlin. He arrived fashionably late after his exertions on the telephone. He found an opportunity to talk to British Ambassador Sir Nevile Henderson, who delivered a predictable protest, and the Czech minister, Vojtech Mastny, who, despite Göring's anxieties, gave him the assurance he wanted: Czechoslovakia would not mobilize to save Austria.

When around midnight, Göring heard that Miklas had given in, he collected Goebbels from his table, and together they drove to Hitler at the Chancellery to listen to the first broadcast of the "Horst Wessel-Lied" from Vienna. Only one thing marred Göring's enjoyment of the evening: the news that Himmler was already on his way to Vienna. Göring called Seyss to tell him that he did not want the wire-tapping services to fall into the hands of his rival. He alone held the bugging monopoly for the Reich.

EXPATRIATES AND German Jews were also tuning into Austrian wireless to learn of the country's fate. Schuschnigg's broadcast had ended with the Austrian national anthem followed by some Austrian classical music. When listeners heard the "Horst Wessel-Lied," they realized Austrian freedom was dead. Naturally Goebbels thought otherwise: "The bells of freedom have struck for this land too." In Nuremberg, Julius Streicher's *Stürmer* exulted in the emergence of "Greater Germany" and the end of "Jewish rule."

In the luxurious Zu den drei Husaren, that evening's atmosphere was jubilant. A Mr. and Mrs. Friedrich Frankau of Montreal, Canada, signed the restaurant's golden book: "We are both very happy to have been in Vienna the very day Austria became a part of the greatest country in the world. God be forever with the Austrians." Over the next few weeks others would make their way to Vienna's best (and still Jewish-owned) restaurant. On the 15th Edmund Veesenmayer, who achieved fame later for his role in deporting Hungary's Jews to Auschwitz, praised the day when "our Führer's homeland returned to our great, ethnic-German Reich. After a hard struggle the finest day of my life and at the same time the day of commitment towards our Sudeten-German brothers." A table full of German railway officials decorated the restaurant's book with a swastika.

———

The next day, March 12, an excited Göring called his friend Prince Philip of Hesse in Rome. He wanted to make sure that Mussolini was happy.

Prince Philip told him that a swastika was already flying from the Austrian consulate—an indication that pro-Nazi elements had overpowered anyone loyal to the Austrian republic. The king of Italy (Philip's father-in-law) had informed him that Colonel Beck—the Polish foreign minister—had relayed the news that 25,000 Viennese Jews had asked for passports. "The view is here that it's best to open the frontiers for a while so that the whole scum gets out."

Göring made no secret of what he wanted in his reply: "All right, but not with any foreign currency. The Jews can go, but they will kindly leave behind their money, which they have only stolen."

The Anschluss not only scattered the political elite of the Corporate State; it struck terror into the hearts of the Jews. Up until 1938, Austria's Jews could be broadly divided into Zionists and assimilators. Once Hitler arrived, assimilation was to prove a dead letter, while, for Zionists, the dream of a Palestinian homeland was still a possibility. The assimilated Jews, on the other hand, realized that their Gentile manners availed them of nothing. The Nazis hated them even more than they despised the Zionists. Some Jewish Communists headed for the Soviet Union, joining those who had left for fear of imprisonment by the Corporate State in 1934. This was nevertheless risky, as there was every chance that they might end up in the gulag.

A. R. Penn, the British secretary of the Church Mission to the Jews, arrived in Vienna from Romania and Poland on March 11 to find the city in a state of overexcitement about Sunday's plebiscite. When he woke the next morning, Schuschnigg had resigned, and the SA had occupied the political vacuum. The air rang out with cries of "*Heil Hitler!*" At midday on March 12, Penn heard Hitler proclaim the Anschluss while he sat talking to Hugh Grimes, the philo-Semitic British embassy chaplain. Before he left, a Jewish friend took him up to the hills that overlook the city. She told him, "I feel as if I were looking at my beloved Vienna for the last time."

VIENNA WAS the largest Jewish city in the German-speaking world. As of March 11, 1938, there were 185,028 Jews in Austria, of whom 176,034 lived in Vienna—just under 10 percent of the city's population or 2.8 percent of Austrians. Vienna had a hefty Jewish infrastructure with ninety-four synagogues and 120 welfare organizations under the umbrella of the IKG, an organization dominated by Zionists since the twenties: Both the president, Friedmann, and the vice president, Dr. Josef Löwenherz, were Zionists. Another significant Jewish body was the 8,000-strong Bund Jüdischer Frontsoldaten, or Jewish Old Soldiers' League, founded in 1932 and led by Captain Siegfried Edler von Friedmann. In addition there were those who no longer admitted to Judaism, and many who were "racially" Jewish but had converted to Christianity or were simply agnostic or atheist.

Hitler's antisemitic policies were bound to find favor in Austria, as they had been developed there in the first place. Young Adolf had come up from the provincial city of Linz and was appalled by Vienna's Jews. The party behind the Corporate State—the Christlichsozialen or Christian Socials—had been founded by the same Mayor Karl Lueger who coined the phrase "I decide who's a Jew." He meant that in a few cases Jews could aspire to social acceptability.

When Austria became a republic in 1918, Vienna's Jewish population filled the social and political vacuum created by degradation of the imperial nobility. There was a large influx of so-called Ostjuden from Poland and Russia. To the Austrians, they appeared as strange apparitions with their beards and kaftans. Their lives had been wrecked by pogroms and war, and now they were heading west to seek their fortunes. They were greatly resented in Germany and Austria, not only by the Gentiles but by the assimilated Jews, who found them primitive and felt they held up a grubby mirror to their more refined selves.

In 1921 there was a three-day meeting arranged for antisemites in Vienna, and in 1923 between 50,000 and 100,000 marched around the Ringstrasse protesting against the Jewish "dictatorship." By the time the Corporate State arrived in 1934, some Jews were already able to see the writing on the wall. Stefan Zweig's house on the Kapuzinerberg near Salzburg was searched for weapons in 1934. The writer was so scandalized that he turned his back on Austria and went to live in England.

A year later, on September 16, 1935, Austria introduced racial law under the *Blutschutzgesetz* (law for the protection of blood). It was no longer permitted to enter the description *konfessionslos*, or nondenominational, on a birth certificate. Any Jews who had lost their religion without gaining another were obliged to list themselves as Jewish. The law was more in keeping with Catholic thinking than Nuremberg, but it was undoubtedly prompted by the latter.

Although the Corporate State was not officially antipathetic to Jews, its policies exhibited a cold persecution, squeezing Jewish citizens out of public life. There were now very few Jewish members of the National Council, as the legislative body was called. Contracts in Viennese hospitals were not renewed with Jewish doctors, publishing houses refused to print books by Jews, and newspapers were increasingly reluctant to employ Jewish journalists. The *Neue Freie Presse* was purged of Jewish staff by 1937. Film production companies did not employ Jewish actors and actresses, as they needed to be able to sell their films across the border in Germany, and Jewish sportsmen could not compete in events if there were Germans about. It was believed that Schuschnigg intended to reduce the percentage of Jews in the professions to reflect their share of the population.

Many of Vienna's assimilated Jews were virtually indistinguishable from the German elite: They read their Goethe, Schiller, and Nestroy and went to concerts to listen to Beethoven, Schubert, Brahms, and Franz Schmidt. Believing themselves to be good "Germans" (people spoke little of being Austrian at that time), they had no desire to leave, only to assimilate. The Ostjuden, lately come from the shtetls, were more likely to be attracted to the idea of Zionism and the establishment of a Jewish state, preferably in Palestine.

Baptism was a way around the various *numerus clausus* that limited Jewish entry into branches of public life. With the *Taufschein* or baptismal certificate, the Jewish *Taufjude* could become a judge, a professor, or a high-ranking civil servant with far greater ease. A measure of how many members of the Jewish elite were Christians is evident in the fact that a third of the Jews in Dachau were baptized, and not only for political reasons— many of them had a Christian grandparent or two. The British chaplain Grimes reported on the success of the Swedish pastor Tarrel at the beginning of 1937, who carried out thirty to forty conversions every year: "He [Tarrel] thinks there would be many more if it were not for the pressure exercised by the Jews themselves who will not employ Christian Jews." Tarrel had converted a hundred Jews in 1934, possibly because of the creation of the rigidly Catholic Corporate State.

After the Anschluss, it was calculated that 20 percent of potential refugees were non-Aryan Christians—ethnic Jews who had been baptized. The Quaker Emma Cadbury, who was based in Vienna, estimated their numbers at 60,000 Catholics and 10,000 Protestants, although the official figure was a comparatively lowly 24,000. The philosopher Karl Popper, for example, had been baptized a Protestant in infancy. Conversion was gaining popularity among Jews. The arrival of Hitler in power across the border in Germany seems to have provided a further spur: There were 42 baptisms in 1932 and 102 in 1933. In the first half of 1934 there were 152.

———

The birth pangs and infancy of the First Austrian Republic had been aggravated by chronic unemployment. Where Germany had been able to create jobs after the Nazis came to power, up to 300,000 chiefly young Viennese were out of work at the time of the Anschluss. They gravitated toward extremist organizations that purported to be able to solve the problem. One of the promises delivered by the Nazis was the 100 percent elimination of unemployment (it was one of the messages in Göring's speech at the Northwest Station on March 26). As one contemporary put it, "Hunger drove millions into the arms of the Nazis." The Jews were, as ever, considered to be the principal enemy; they were seen as idle and rich, feeding off human misery.

On March 11 the Hitlerites were already out and about in the largely Jewish Second District, shouting slogans and flailing fists hours before the German army had reached Vienna. Hitler Youth members between the ages of ten and sixteen were chanting against Schuschnigg, the Jews, and priests. Schuschnigg's resignation was the signal for the revolution to begin. Illegal Nazis donned swastika armbands or SA uniforms and took over key offices. Jews were immediately dismissed from their jobs or sent on extended leave. That same day Emma Cadbury wrote to Alice Nike in London: "The Jews here are very much worried and there has been an increase of antisemitic propaganda, but I hope this may quiet down."

The London *Morning Chronicle*'s reporter in Vienna, Eric Gedye, recorded disgusting scenes in which the Viennese showed the Jews the pent-up hatred seething within them:

It is the heartless, grinning, soberly dressed crowds on the Graben and the Kärntnerstrasse . . . fluffy Viennese blondes, fighting to get closer to the elevating spectacle of an ashen-faced Jewish surgeon on his hands and knees before half a dozen young hooligans with Swastika armlets and dog-whips that sticks in my mind. His delicate fingers, which must have made the swift and confident incisions that had saved the lives of many Viennese, held a scrubbing brush. A storm trooper was pouring some acid solution over the brush—and his fingers. Another sluiced the pavement from a bucket, taking care to drench the surgeon's striped trousers as he did so. And the Viennese—not uniformed Nazis or a raging mob, but the Viennese Little Man and his wife—just grinned approval at the glorious fun.

The Czechs prudently sealed their borders to prevent an influx of Jews; only those with the appropriate entry visas could pass. The Vienna-Prague train left Vienna at the usual time (11:15 AM), and it was due to reach Czech soil forty minutes later. It arrived in the capital with no Austrians on board. The numbers on board were progressively whittled down by a succession of brutal searches. The few who made it to the border at Breclav were crushed to learn that the Czechs would not let them in. The Czechs were not unhappy about the Anschluss: They were happier to see the Germans in Vienna than face a Habsburg restoration.

Those Jews who had fled on four wheels abandoned "a whole car park" of vehicles and hid in the woods closest to the frontier. The cabaret artist Jura Soyfer tried to cross the Swiss border on skis but was arrested and taken to Innsbruck. Other Jews boarded trains to Romania but were turned back at the border; even when they had Romanian papers, the authorities refused to take them back.

Naturally the wisest ones made for the borders as quickly as they could. That was particularly important for anyone on a Nazi blacklist. Malwine Dollfuss (widow of the murdered chancellor), two Habsburgs, and Guido Zernatto of the Vaterländischen Front were successful, as was the comedian Karl Farkas; but many found no way through. Brno, in Czechoslovakia, was often the goal. It contained a large German minority even in 1938, and many of Vienna's Jews had family in southern Moravia. Once in Czechoslovakia, they could catch the "flying Moses" from Prague, the aircraft that flew the children of Israel away from the Nazi peril.

Writers whose works had been burned on the Opernplatz in Berlin were best advised to go before the Germans took hold of the city. One of these was the German dramatist Carl Zuckmayer, who had been living near Salzburg for years but who happened to be in Vienna at the time of the Anschluss. He was in the theater all day and oblivious of political developments until he heard Schuschnigg's resignation broadcast that evening.

Zuckmayer had survived a dozen battles on the Western Front and the terrible upheavals of the postwar years; he had been on the streets at the time of the Hitler putsch in Munich and witnessed the Nazi takeover of power in Berlin, but nothing compared to those days in Vienna. "It was the witches' Sabbath of the plebs that laid all human values to rest." That night he was traveling in a taxi when the mob decided that he and his companion were Polish Jews and needed to be beaten up. Zuckmayer only escaped by shouting out something that sounded like "*Heil Hitler!*" in his best Reich German accent—like a sergeant major drilling his squad. When the skies blackened with German bombers making their way to the airport at Aspern, a new, equally sinister noise joined the screams of the tortured. After a while one got used to that too. All those new sounds merged into one: "The air was filled with the cacophony of Armageddon."

Zuckmayer's play *Bellmann* was shortly to open at the theater in the Josefstadt, directed by Ernst Lothar. In the middle of rehearsal on Sunday, two actors came to Lothar and declared they represented the theater's National Socialist cell: Zuckmayer's play could not be performed because the author was part Jewish. Lothar promptly resigned and went home to his flat on the Beethoven Platz, next to the Imperial Hotel, where Hitler was staying that night. Shortly afterwards, the police arrived to impound his passport. Lothar's wife, the actress Adrienne Gessner, lost her temper: "Go to Mr Gauleiter, or whatever title the idiot uses, the fellow who sent you . . . and tell him that I threw you out." Lothar apologized for his wife and gave the policemen his passport. He sensed that he would have considerable problems getting the papers back and promptly negotiated an exit visa from the local police for the vast sum of 25,000 schillings, then set out for his brother in Switzerland with his daughter in a new, chauffeur-driven car.

Everything went well until they approached the border at St. Anton in the Vorarlberg, where they were flagged down by the local gendarme. He had been told to look out for the car. He was perfectly polite and had even read Lothar's novels, but he had been told to inform the SA. Lothar waited upstairs in the police station while his daughter and the driver stayed by the car. The SA men rolled up soon after. They said the Lothars would have to undergo a strip search, grabbed the daughter, and prepared to tear off her blouse. Lothar was quick on the uptake: The SA too wanted to be bought off, in this instance with the car. The Nazis were in raptures over their booty. As soon as he had signed an affidavit to say that he had given it to them of his own free will, they drove the Lothars to the border in Feldkirch. The SA headed off in the car, leaving the theater director and his daughter at the station. Fortunately the border official was a fan and had been to several of Lothar's productions; he waved them off to freedom with a friendly *"Auf Wiederschaun in Österreich."*

AUSTRIAN OFFICIALS weren't all so friendly. Writer Gina Kaus's books had been burned in Berlin. She had an Italian passport by virtue of the fact her former husband had been born in Trieste. Together with her son, Peter, and her lover, Eduard Frischauer, she managed to board a train on Monday that was full to bursting. They were delayed five hours at the border. An outraged English skier related that she had been "gynaecologically investigated." When they reached the Swiss border, she felt like hugging the conductors.

As a rule only Jews or *Mischlinge* of mixed Jewish and Gentile blood made haste to leave. Exceptional was the Gentile writer Franz Theodor Csokor or the musicians Erich Kleiber and Ralph Benatzky. The Nazis wrongly thought the latter actually was a Jew. Those who went, or preferred to remain abroad, make an impressive list: musicians like Robert Stolz and Fritz Kreisler and the more heavyweight Arnold Schönberg, Hanns Eisler, Erich Wolfgang Korngold, and Egon Wellesz; conductors such as Bruno Walter and Joseph Krips; singers of the caliber of Lotte Lehmann, Maria Jeritza, Alfred Piccaver, and Richard Tauber; theatre and cinema artists like Max Reinhardt, Otto Preminger, Fritzi Massary, Elisabeth Bergner, Oskar Homolka, and Anton Wohlbrück (later Walbrook).

In Berlin, Goebbels was hatching plans to "de-Jew" Vienna and located a few collaborators in the process, such as the actor Attila Hörbiger, who was able to report on his wife Paula Wessely with her many Jewish friends. Vienna's music was all "Jews and Jew-lovers." A desire to set some traditional Aryan composers on the pedestals formerly occupied by Brahms and Bruckner led to Franz Schmidt's commission to write "Eine deutsche Auferstehung" (A German Resurrection) in 1938. Goebbels wanted the pro-Nazi Karl Böhm for the National Opera, while Hitler favored Hans Knappertsbusch.

Bruno Walter had had the good fortune to be in Holland for the Nazi triumph. He took out French citizenship, and the new powers in the land made off with the contents of his flat. Arnold Rosé, for fifty-seven years the leader of the Philharmonic, fled to London, where a new Rosé Quartet was founded. The portraits of Mahler and Walter and an engraving of Rosé disappeared from the historic wall of the offices of the Philharmonic. Mahler's bust was removed from the foyer at the Opera. The Gustav Mahlerstrasse became the Meistersingerstrasse. The wife and children of the poet and dramatist Hugo von Hoffmannsthal emigrated in March. The writer Hermann Broch spent months in prison before he was able to reach England. Robert Musil left in August, clutching the manuscript of *A Man Without Qualities*.

THE PLEBISCITE had been largely funded by Jewish money, something that made the Jews appear particularly culpable. The first acts of bestiality were carried out by the homegrown SA, although they were quickly joined by Himmler's men, who carried their own hit lists. Before Adolf Eichmann's arrival, the most important body in Vienna was Department II-112, SS-Oberabschnitt Donau. There were two days of "wild" persecution between March 11 and formal annexation on the 13th. Franz Rothenberg, president of the Creditanstalt bank, was hurled from a car at top speed but survived. Others were not so lucky. Isidor Pollack, managing director of the Pulverfabrik chemical works, died of the wounds he sustained from his beating. Later the Deutsche Bank would take over the Creditanstalt, and I. G. Farben would appropriate the Pulverfabrik.

Jews were made scapegoats for the last acts of the Corporate State and had to wash the pro-Schuschnigg graffiti off the walls and pavements. At the

Café Herrenhaus, the owner and his wife, together with seven customers, were forced to scrub the—presumably unsullied—walls. The chief rabbi, the Zionist Dr. Israel Taglich, was philosophical about cleaning the streets: "I am washing God's earth." They called themselves *Araber* (Arabs), because they were *a raber* (*reiber*) or scrubbers. This was not a Nazi invention; it was the Fatherland Front that had originally instituted this form of punishment and meted it out to illegal Nazis, when they were caught daubing slogans.

As in Zuckmayer's case (see below), it was still possible to impress some Nazis by flashing a medal for bravery. The writer Leo Perutz, for example, escaped a nasty scene on the 13th by pointing to his EK1, Iron Cross 1st Class. Later, even this would have no effect on the Viennese thugs. The huge amount of booty they accrued was taken to 36 Prinz Eugenstrasse, the headquarters of the SA group Donau-Wien, before being transferred to the Hotel Metropole, which had been seized from its Jewish owners and turned into Gestapo HQ.

The Prinz Eugenstrasse was the location of the Rothschilds' town palace, and their vast fortunes naturally concentrated the minds of the Nazi brigands. The young Dudley Forwood, equerry to the Duke of Windsor, knew the Rothschilds well and had the run of their country house. He was on vacation there on March 12, prior to leaving for Paris the next day. A footman brought him a message: The *gnädige Baronin* had called. He was not to show surprise if anything strange were to happen on the train. He found the station filled with troops. At Feldkirch the passengers were ordered off. Over the loudspeaker he heard: "*Alle Leute 'raus. Juden auf der linke Seite*" ("Everyone out. Jews on the left"). At that moment he saw the Rothschilds' English nanny coming toward him with the children. They pretended to be his. He remembered what the servant had told him and went along with the game. He got them out.

The mask had fallen, revealing the depths of antisemitism in Austrian society. In an officers' mess in Neudiedl am See, a subaltern suddenly refused to play billiards with another officer because he was a Jew. The latter walked out of the mess. No one attempted to hold him back. On March 14 the army was purged of Jews, and officers and men had to swear an oath of loyalty to Hitler. The Jewish general Erich von Sommer appeared on the street in full rig with medals. This time the SA showed respect and saluted him. It did not work twice.

It was not just violence. "Confiscations" were the order of the day—shops were emptied of their wares, garages of their cars. Rich Jews were incarcerated for months until they were convinced to hand their property over to the Gestapo. This was important if there were artworks and collections to steal under a dubious cloak of legality. Money disappeared into the pockets of Nazi thugs. The Zionist Leo Lauterbach expressed his astonishment at their ferocity: "Nobody who knew the average Viennese until that moment would believe that he could sink to such a level."

In the Twentieth District, a local thug called Josef Graf had taken it upon himself to visit the cafés, beat up Jewish customers, and make them drink from the spittoons. On the fourteenth he was leading a squad of Jews toward the Northwest Station hall to perform physical jerks. A group of SA men coming in the opposite direction decided he was going too far, and liberated the Jews. Graf had earlier forced a Gentile to carry a panel up and down the street after visiting a Jewish café. It read *"Arisches Schwein geht zum Judencafé rein"* ("Aryan pig goes into Jewish cafés"). The gymnastics were extended to Jewish children, who were assembled and forced to perform until they collapsed. The purpose behind this was to extort money from the parents, who could not bear to watch their offspring being abused in this way. Once the torturers had been paid off, more Viennese appeared and took over where the others had left off.

RICH JEWS were arrested and prepared for the first transport for Dachau. Since the police and the SA had drawn up their own lists, there was a certain rivalry over their prey. The brothers Schiffmann, department store owners, were seized in the Taborstrasse and their staff dismissed—likewise Gerngross and Herzmansky in the Mariahilferstrasse, the shoe magnate Krupnik, the carpet merchant Schein, the stocking manufacturer Schön with its eighty branches, the industrial baker Anker, the lightbulb producers Kremenzky and Pregan, the jeweler Scherr, the men's fashion merchant Katz, and the clothier Gerstel. The emptying of the Schiffmann stores lasted three whole days. Jews with valuable art collections, like various members of the Gerngross family, found their possessions put up for auction.

At least some of these people had made large donations to Schuschnigg's plebiscite funds. Gerstel's surname was unfortunate: It was the slang word for cash. As the local Nazis put it at the time, "*Darr Jud muss weg und sein Gerschtl bleibt da!*" ("The yid must get out, but he has to leave his dough behind"). The Nazis took over prominent businesses and arrested the owners, like the Kuffners, proprietors of the famous Ottakringer brewery. Of assets totaling 9 million marks, two and a half were confiscated at once, and when the Kuffners sold out, they gave a further 35 percent to the Nazis. Restaurants were obliged to hang up signs banning Jews.

One of those who tried to cross the Czech border on the 13th was Fritz Grünbaum, but the train was sent back and those on board plundered. The unlucky ones were also arrested, including Grünbaum, who was sent to the new prison in the Karajangasse, where he shared a mattress with Bruno Kreisky, later Austrian chancellor. Grünbaum died in Dachau after a bungled suicide attempt. His wife, Lilly, was murdered at Maly Trostinec. His huge art collection sold for a song, and the money went into the coffers of the Reich.

IN THE provinces the atmosphere was calmer. With the exception of Burgenland, there were few Jews. Graz had the reputation of being the most Nazi city in Austria. The Jewish legal clerk Helmut Bader observed on March 13 that all his judges had donned swastika armbands. He was summoned before the head of personnel and summarily dismissed. The physiologist Otto Loewi, who had won a Nobel prize for medicine in 1936, was arrested. The money he had been awarded was placed in a closed account.

A *razzia* mopped up Austria's Jewish journalists on the 17th, when Maximilian Reich was arrested. The Black Maria went on to pick up the others, and one of them evidently refused to come. Reich heard a shot. When the Gestapo men returned to the car, they told the driver, "The chap didn't want to come with us. Now he can stay at home." They laughed. Reich was taken to the Liesl, the police prison on the Elisabeth Promenade, where he found his friend the amateur boxer Willy Kurtz, the mayor, and numerous prominent Viennese.

The carnage continued unabated. On Tuesday, March 15, the critic and cultural historian Egon Friedell hurled himself from the fourth floor of his apartment block as the Nazis came to claim their game. He apparently told the Gestapo men to wait, went into his study, and shouted down to the people in the street to clear a space. It is possible they had only come in the tradition of good *Adabeis* to enjoy the spectacle of Friedell's arrest. He had refused to flee, feeling that he would cut an absurd figure as an exile. In one account, the Gestapo men had not come for Friedell at all but to visit a maid with whom one of them was dallying. Friedell had jumped to conclusions and then to his death.

The Gestapo arrived at 19 Berggasse, the home and surgery of Sigmund Freud, and proceeded to search the flat. His daughter, Anna, was taken away for interrogation a few days later. Freud was powerful enough to be able to take his family and most of his possessions into exile when he left in June. The building Freud lived and worked in for forty years was eventually turned into a *Sammelwohnung*—a Jewish collection point—from which Jews were deported to their deaths. Freud's four sisters were all murdered in the east.

ZUCKMAYER FINALLY left Vienna on the 15th. Wilhelm von Ketteler at the German embassy had told him that he would be safe, that the Austrian version of National Socialism would be gentle. Ketteler was almost certainly a decent man, and an opponent of National Socialism who had been involved in a plot to kill Hitler. He was murdered by the SS man Horst Böhme on Heydrich's orders and fished out of the Danube two weeks later.

Zuckmayer reckoned his chances of escape at fifty-fifty. Everything went smoothly until he reached Salzburg. He was even able to see his own bathing hut at Henndorf and thought he could hear his dogs barking. They stopped while a troop train passed. The Austrians lowered the windows and obsequiously shouted "*Heil Hitler!*" at the conquerors. The soldiers reminded the writer of himself in 1914. They looked embarrassed at this effusion and carried on eating their soup.

Salzburg station resembled an armed camp. The cigarette woman, who had provided for Zuckmayer's needs for years, was running after the soldiers, squawking ecstatically "*Daitsche Brieder*" ("German brothers") and sticking cigarettes in their pockets. It was a repellent vision that made it easier for him to accept the need to quit his adoptive land. There was no passport inspection until the train stopped in Innsbruck, some three hours from the Swiss frontier, at which point a fat man in plain clothes and a swastika armband, with a police badge in his lapel, came in accompanied by two brownshirts with revolvers in their belts.

All went well until he saw Zuckmayer's profession: writer. "Get off the train, and take your luggage." Zuckmayer wanted to know why.

"Our Führer does not like the press."

"I am not from the press."

Attempts to argue with the man availed him of nothing: Zuckmayer and other "delinquents" left the train and were taken to the police station, where they sat and waited. He was angry by the time his turn came to face the interrogators, and he barked at them in military German. He threw down his German passport and continued to perform his version of an offended member of the master race. He showed them a telegram from Alexander Korda, indicating the time he was due to be in London, and noted that they were unable to construe the English. The man who had taken him from the train insisted that Zuckmayer was a writer: "That is suspicious. . . . Our Führer does not like the press."

"But I am a screenwriter. . . . The Führer likes films."

The man at the desk agreed that Hitler was a film fan, and he admitted that he knew Zuckmayer's house and had swum in the lake there. "A lovely spot," he said. Zuckmayer agreed: "What more do you need from me?"

The official rose from his desk. "In times like this errors occur, but we try to do our job. Go quickly, but through the back door. Those people out there," he said, gesturing toward the line outside, "they won't escape so easily. They're all Yids."

Zuckmayer had not got far before he heard one of the brownshirts coming up behind him. A hand was placed on his shoulder. His body went cold. The Nazi drew a small book from his pocket. Zuckmayer recognized it as the novella he had published the previous year. It was called *Ein Sommer in Österreich* (A Summer in Austria). "I have just read this. . . . Would you sign it for me?" Zuckmayer did this with the fountain pen provided. The brownshirt was standing close and leaned over him: "There will be no more 'Summers in Austria.' . . . Good-bye, and make sure you don't come back. Take care at the border." With that he clicked his heals and disappeared.

Zuckmayer got on the next train. It was stuffed to the gills with people trying to leave. He was bathed in sweat and, as he opened a carriage door, unbuttoned his coat for the first time. There was a sudden silence. A man of Jewish appearance jumped up and offered him his seat. "But that is your seat; please sit down again," said Zuckmayer. The others moved up to create some room. Then Zuckmayer caught on: They were staring at his buttonhole. He had bought a swastika at a newsagent in Vienna. Only Party members wore swastikas in Germany, but in Austria they were on sale everywhere, and people put them on simply to tell the thugs they were not Jews. On March 11 they had cost thirty-five groschen, but the price had risen since. It was a simple device to ensure a modicum of peace, but he had done more: He had also put on his war medals, including his EK1. The combination of a Nazi and a war hero was not easy for the Jews in the carriage to decipher, but they offered him schnapps and told him of their fears at the approach of the border.

The closer they came to the frontier, the more the carriage panicked. There were constant patrols in the corridor. The doors were opened, and they were asked over and over again about how much money they had on them. They were allowed ten RM or twenty Austrian schillings, the precise sum Zuckmayer had brought with him. The playwright studied those around him: There was an Aryan soccer player with his Jewish fiancée, and a supposed general's son—the one who had offered him schnapps—who, just before the train reached the border, literally threw all his money out of the window. A Polish woman recognized Zuckmayer and wanted to ask him about forthcoming theatrical events.

Then the train arrived in Feldkirch, and Zuckmayer's hopes all but vanished when he saw the spotlights outside. He concentrated his mind on survival. "Everyone out with their suitcases. The train is to be evacuated."

The station was teeming with men in black and brown uniforms. There were tables onto which the contents of suitcases were being poured out and pored over, while cases were tested for false bottoms. Everything was examined with a fine-tooth comb. Some of the passengers were being strip-searched. Zuckmayer recalled that his case contained a number of autographs by fellow writers—most of them "degenerate." He feared the worst.

The official looked at his name for a long time, then tossed his head back as if he had been suddenly struck by lightning: "Zuckmayer? . . . *The* Zuckmayer."

"What do you mean by that?"

"I mean the notorious."

"I don't know if I am notorious, but there is certainly no other writer with my name."

"Come with me."

"I must stay with my luggage."

"You don't have to do that." And he laughed a mocking laugh as if to say: You won't need any luggage anymore where you are going. Zuckmayer was led away to a hut at the end of the platform. Another man was being taken away into custody. Behind the desk sat an SS man with steel-rimmed spectacles. "Carl Zuckmayer, ah ha!"

He examined his passport. It was valid for five years. Jews received theirs for six months. The SS man was vaguely aware that Zuckmayer was "racially" Jewish—his mother's family were converts—but the passport appeared to contradict this. He reached for a printed list but could not find Zuckmayer's name on it. "Funny. . . . I had heard something about you once, but I can't remember now what it was. So you are not a Jew at all."

He laughed, and Zuckmayer permitted himself a smile. He did not feel it was incumbent upon him to tell the official that his mother was born Goldschmidt. The Nazi read from the passport: "Catholic . . . *na ja.* We are going to deal with those priests too." He became chatty and looked as if he might be going to give him back his passport. They talked about his screenplays. The Nazi had seen his latest film. Then he asked Zuckmayer if he were a member of the Party. Zuckmayer said no. Then the tone changed: "German writer and not in the Party?" Nor was he a member of the Nazi writers' organization. Zuckmayer admitted that his works were actually banned in Germany, and then regretted it.

The SS man reacted queerly: He reached out his hand and shook Zuckmayer's. He said he was impressed by Zuckmayer's honesty—most of the people who came before him lied. He volunteered to smooth his way into the Party. The writer thanked him but said that would not be necessary. Zuckmayer took the opportunity to snatch his passport back and asked if he might have his luggage now.

The SS man offered to come with him, expressing the hope that there would be no difficulties occasioned by the search. Zuckmayer envisaged problems for all that: the manuscript, the autographs. He decided to open his coat again and pretend he was looking for something in his pocket. It did the trick: The Nazi wanted to know if he had been at the front, if he had held a commission. He stared at the EK1. "Then you must be a hero," he said, staring wide-eyed at him. Zuckmayer played down his heroism but told the SS man that medals could not be bought for small change on the streets all the same. He was alluding to the price he had paid for the swastika in his buttonhole.

The SS man was now eating out of his hands. Not only did he under-stand the reference to the "opportunists," he relished Zuckmayer's wit. He bellowed out to the SS and SA men around him: They were to honor a hero with a rousing cry of "*Heil Hitler!*" They did just that, "as if I were the Führer himself." Zuckmayer admitted to feeling like Captain von Köpenick from his own play. The SS man told his soldiers to take Zuck-mayer's cases on to the train. They had not even been examined. He coun-termanded the strip-search as well. He was the only person on his train to be exempted.

As the SS man took him to the station buffet to wait for the rest to pass or fail the examination, an acquaintance of Zuckmayer's wife came up to him and identified himself. His Jewish wife was on the other train waiting in the station. She had a broken leg. Zuckmayer now chanced his luck again. Omitting to tell the SS man she was a Jewess, he said she was not able to come to the interrogation: "If you testify for these people, then it is all right," the Nazi said. The couple were placed on the Swiss train.

There were agonizing moments before the train left. He sat in the buf-fet with the SS man, and they drank their way through Zuckmayer's last twenty schillings. The Nazi told him he wanted to prove himself in the field. Zuckmayer comforted him: There would be a new war soon. He did not hate the Nazi; he pitied him. He saw him as he had seen so many, lying ashen-faced in a pool of blood. Every now and then an SA man interrupted their drinking to report a big haul in marks or valuables. Dawn was break-ing when Zuckmayer's train finally began to move, and he was able to quit his sinister companion. Only when Swiss guards entered his carriage did he know for certain: He was not going to Dachau.

Not just the Jews but all the Corporate State's elite had been enemies of the Third Reich. Zuckmayer records that aristocrats were forced to scrub the streets because they, too, had stuck up for an independent Austria. Both the former vice chancellor and head of the Fatherland Front, Emil Fey, and the Minister of War, General Wilhelm Zehner, apparently "committed suicide." Fey allegedly killed his wife and son first. Their bodies were removed from his flat in sealed tubes and taken to the anatomical institute. His corpse was reported to contain twenty-three bullet holes.

Göring saved the foreign minister Guido Schmidt by sending his own aircraft to collect him. Schmidt was later appointed to the board of the Hermann Göring Works. Around 15 percent of the judges were dismissed; both the minister of justice, Robert Georg Winterstein, and the senior judge Alois Osio perished in the camps. Other victims of the new broom were monarchists. Otto von Habsburg was still perceived as a threat. They naturally had no time for the upstart Hitler. Many of them were arrested and dispatched to Dachau.

THERE WERE only tiny pockets of Jews outside Vienna: some 2,000 in Styria, in the Vorarlberg just 18. There was a significant community in Burgenland, however, where 3,632 Jews inhabited seven acknowledged, protected old communities: Eisenstadt, Matersburg, Kobersdorf, Lackenbach, Deutschkreuz, Frauenkirchen, and Kittsee. They amounted to a little more than 1 percent of the population in Austria's easternmost state, but they had lived there for several centuries, whereas many Austrian Jews had only quit the shtetls of the east a generation before.

Until 1921 the region had been a part of Hungary, and the older Jews were often in possession of Hungarian papers. The Nazis wanted to assert Burgenland's "Germanity" before all else, and the violence against the Burgenland Jews began as soon as Schuschnigg announced his resignation. It frequently took the form of rounding them up and driving them over the nearest frontier. The Czechs, Hungarians, and Yugoslavs responded by closing the crossings. The leader of the Frauenkirchen Jews, Ahron Ernst Weis, managed to escape on a tourist visa to Palestine, while his dentist brother committed suicide. Most of those expelled found refuge in Vienna. Lauterbach and Sir Wyndham Deedes visited three families from the dusty border town of Deutschkreuz who had been expelled "with a few trifles" by the local gendarmerie. In Rechnitz there were brutal murders. Whole villages were cleared. In one, three hundred were driven from their homes. An

American Quaker who witnessed the expulsions recorded: "We have never seen anything as bad as that in Germany." The sentiment was echoed at the monthly meeting of the British Board of Deputies: "The Situation in Austria is even worse than the situation in the German Reich. What took the Nazis five years to accomplish in the Reich has been done in five weeks in Austria."

The fate of the ancient Jewish community rapidly became a cause célèbre. On May 3, 1938, a Czech rabbi, Michael Dov Weissmandl, visited Lambeth Palace to drum up support for the Burgenländer. He had a letter of introduction from Isaiah Porritt, the senior Orthodox rabbi in Vienna, and Samuel Epp, the senior rabbi in Burgenland. They were seeking a safe haven for 3,000 Jews. Lang's secretary, Alan Don, wrote to Samuel Hoare at the Home Office to ask if a special favor might be granted in this instance.

The plight of the Burgenland Jews is the subject of Franz Werfel's short story "Die wahre Geschichte vom wiederhergestellten Kreuz" ("The True Story of the Remaking of the Cross") of 1942. Werfel conceived it as part of his unfinished novel *Cella*, which was set in northern Burgenland. The Catholic priest Ottokar Felix relates the martyrdom of the rabbi of Parndorf, Aladar Fürst, on the night of March 11 and his own role in seeking to protect the Jews in his village and accompany them into exile. Aladar Fürst did not exist, but the other events described in the story took place on April 20. The local SA, drunk with power—and wine—threw between twenty and thirty Jews out of their homes and took them to the Hungarian border at Mörbisch on the Neusiedlersee. There they spent four nights in no-man's-land, as the Hungarians were not prepared to accept them. They were eventually allowed to go to Vienna. Another event that was later dramatized was the expulsion of the Jews from Kittsee, which formed the basis of Friedrich Wolf's play *Das Schiff auf der Donau* (*The Boat on the Danube*). In Kittsee the Jews were forced across the border into Czechoslovakia, but as they had no papers, they were made to endure weeks on an island and later a boat before the Czechs would take them in.

In the state capital Eisenstadt, an exception was made for Alphons Barb, the director of the state museum. The commissioner for cultural issues in Austria asked for a stay of two or three months in his case, since the archaeologist had made an important contribution to knowledge of German pre-history in Burgenland through his excavation of gravesites, proving that the Germans got there before the Magyars. Barb had been making an unconscious contribution to *Ahnenerbe*, the research into Germanic roots that was replacing religion for Nazi extremists. He was allowed to continue to live in Vienna until 1939, when the British Museum organized his transfer to London.

———

Heinrich Himmler was the first Nazi VIP to arrive in Vienna. His two Ju-52 aircraft touched down in Aspern at 5 AM on March 12. On the way down from Berlin he slipped and almost fell out of the aircraft, and his intelligence chief claimed he saved his master's life. He was accompanied by the lofty figures of Reinhard Heydrich, Karl Wolff, and Kurt Daluege and a large team of SD and Gestapo men dressed in grey uniforms: This was to be the unveiling of the new Waffen-SS kit. They were met on the tarmac by Austrian police chief Skubl and a police guard of honor. The Germans then went about their task with proverbial efficiency, ridding their new province of the enemies of the Reich. A willing civil servant was able to provide Himmler with all the state's police records, including criminal records of the banned Left. Very few wriggled through the net.

Skubl's attentiveness did him no good. He was replaced by Kaltenbrunner, one of the few Austrian Nazis ever to achieve high rank in Berlin. Himmler set up his base in the Hotel Regina. The Gestapo were the first to take up residence in the Hotel Metropole. With the mayor, Schmitz, gone from the town hall, the huge square in front of the building was renamed the Adolf-Hitler-Platz two days before the arrival of its new dedicatee.

Himmler and Heydrich immediately unleashed a week of the "wildest manhunt," followed by wave upon wave of arrests. Between 50,000 and 76,000 people were arrested in March. These were classified as "damaging to the nation": intellectuals, public figures, and businessmen. Most of them were released after the plebiscite was carried out under Nazi scrutiny on April 10. Communists were also at risk. Even though the Communist Party had been banned by the Corporate State, and its members were locked up in the concentration camp at Wöllersdorf, there were still active cells, and the Nazis took over the job of hunting them down with renewed vigor. When Himmler went to look at some of his catch in person, he was rather surprised to see Louis von Rothschild, who had been arrested at Aspern airport. He did not look sufficiently like a Jew, with his bright blue eyes and uncowed manner. When Himmler asked if he knew who he was, Rothschild replied, citing Himmler's name and rank. The Reichsführer SS was so taken aback that he ordered that Rothschild's cell be made more comfortable. He was to get fresh furniture and a new lavatory seat and basin.

Himmler accompanied the chief of his economic administration, Oswald Pohl, as he traveled to Upper Austria to look at suitable quarries where they might establish concentration camps. Their eyes lighted on Mauthausen and Gusen. Between April and August various plots of land were bought and the site in Mauthausen rented from its owners, the city of Vienna. (Mauthausen stone was used to make Vienna's pavements.) On August 8 the first prisoners were transferred from Dachau. Mauthausen was to gain the reputation of being one of the grimmest camps of them all.

HITLER'S DESIRE to bind his old country to the land he had adopted had incurred fresh problems. With Austria, Germany had now acquired 200,000 or so more Jews, all of whom needed to be encouraged to get out. An example was to be made of certain Jews. One of these singled out in Linz was a Dr. Eduard Bloch, whose sign was smeared with the word *Jude*. In 1907 this same Bloch had treated the Führer's mother, Clara, who was dying of cancer. Hitler had expressed his gratitude in a letter he wrote to the physician at the time. The desecration of the sign came to Kaltenbrunner's attention, who sent two SS men to clean it up.

Department II-112, responsible to Himmler, was in charge of emigration. Eichmann was the department's expert on Zionist organizations. Ironically, the Nazis and the Zionists had shared aims: They both wanted the Jews to go, and both were keenest on choosing Palestine for their promised land. Eichmann promoted Zionism "with all means." The assimilated Jews, on the other hand, were the principal enemies of the National Socialists. As Eichmann's colleague Dieter Wisliceny put it, they were there to "crush the assimilatory organisations." Employing the Nazis' favorite method of divide and rule, the assimilated Jews and the Zionists

could be played off against one another; there was, after all, little love lost
between them.

HITLER HAD been making a slow progress toward Vienna. Leaving Göring
to manage the shop in Berlin, he flew to Munich with Keitel. Around noon
Hitler reached the Austrian border, where he stopped to confer with General Fedor von Bock and receive a report from his press chief Otto Dietrich.
He crossed into Austria at his birthplace, Braunau on the Inn, where he
was received by the mayor, and then drove on to his adopted hometown of
Linz. For the first time Hitler was revisiting the city he had once quit as a
"penniless vagabond." The reception accorded him by the Linzer was so ec-
static that he was moved to tears. Indeed, the Austrian response to the Anschluss surprised Nazis and non-Nazis alike. Most people had shared
Schuschnigg's optimistic view that a clear majority of Austrians were opposed to the merger. From Berlin, Klepper noted that the larger and most
active part of the Austrian population must have been in favor: "Otherwise
these scenes of brotherhood would not have been possible."

Beds were hastily prepared at the Hotel Weinzinger. It was not ideal:
There was just a small porter's lodge and one telephone. Ribbentrop, who
was angry and frustrated at being isolated in London, could not get
through to Spitzy until 7 AM on the 13th. He was told to stay put. Seyss
had traveled up from Vienna to await Hitler's arrival, and on March 13 he
gave a speech announcing the scrapping of Article 88 of the Treaty of Saint
Germain, the one that forbad the unification of Germany and Austria. In
Nuremberg, Fips of *Der Stürmer* celebrated the end of the "shameful"
treaties of Versailles and Saint Germain, while in another cartoon a Jew
was concerned to read that "Italy was not at all opposed."

The enthusiasm that Hitler observed in Linz caused him to have a
change of heart about maintaining Austria as a separate state. He chose to
"manage" the revolution instead. He had originally planned to create a National Socialist Austria, closely linked to Germany, but now he decided
that he was going to incorporate Austria as a self-governing province of
the Greater German Reich. The federal states were to be replaced by Nazi
territorial divisions or *Gaue*, under the control of a Party boss or gauleiter.
Seyss legitimized the constitutional changes, and Austria duly became a
province of the Reich on the 13th. Even the prime mover behind the An-

schluss, Hermann Göring, was amazed at the speed at which the changes were made. A new plebiscite, to be conducted under Nazi rules, was now ordained for April 10.

Seyss was to relinquish his post as chancellor of Austria under the new constitution and become *Reichstatthalter* or governor. Under him served a small group of ministers. Joseph Bürckel was brought in from the Saar-Palatinate as Reichs Commissioner for the Reunification to manage the new plebiscite, as he had done successfully before in the Saar.

Bürckel's appointment from outside was significant: Austrian Nazis were to play a paltry role in the new territory. Bürckel imported his own men, who were surreptitiously mocked as members of the Pfalzer-Postenjäger-Regiment or Palatinate Job Hunters' Regiment, while Austrians dubbed their drunken gauleiter Bierleiter Gaukel (Beerleader Mountebank). The man who would have been gauleiter, Josef Leopold, ended up as a lowly Party inspector in Munich before dying in the Russian campaign. Walter Riehl, who had founded the NSDAP in Austria after the First World War, was actually imprisoned on March 18 and only released on Hitler's orders. He was given no work by the new administration. Theodor Habicht, who had been the strongman in Austria before the Anschluss, was compensated with the town hall of Wittenberg in Saxony. The only exceptions to the marginalization of Austrians were Carinthians such as Gauleiter Hubert Klausner and Odilo Globocnik.

Hitler did not trust Austrians and preferred to have Germans from the Altreich (as it was now called) occupy almost all the important positions. He may have doubted their loyalty, but as it was, he used a rather more German justification: laziness. As he had said in his first speech in Linz, the Austrians needed to lose their fondness for cozy *Gemütlichkeit* and put their shoulders to the wheel. The cold-shouldering of homegrown Nazis led to considerable resentment in Austria, where the Nazis from the Altreich quickly transmogrified into Prussians—the traditional enemies, even though most were no such thing. Bürckel very rapidly became a more powerful figure in the land than the governor, Seyss, who was shunted on to Poland when the war started, then Holland in 1940.

As Hitler had hoped, there were no great international repercussions. The Duce was satisfied that Hitler would not create problems for him in South Tyrol. Britain declined to act to secure Austrian independence.

Chamberlain told the House of Commons on March 14 that Britain had no obligations toward Austria. The British confined themselves to a pious hope that the Germans would not take it out on their political and racial enemies. Two days later Lord Halifax told the Upper House that Austria's status had been bound to change in the long run. The French could not respond for the simple reason that their government had resigned. They were in no position to act on their own anyway. The U.S. Secretary of State, Cordell Hull, forbore from comment until the 19th, when he more or less recognized the Anschluss by saying that the Germans were now responsible for Austria's debts. On March 17, the spokesman for the Soviet regime, Maxim Litvinov, called for action against German aggression but had nothing specific to say about Austria. Only two countries protested: republican Spain, which was shortly to be eclipsed by Franco's forces, and Mexico.

ON MARCH 14, Hitler finally drove from Linz to Vienna via Amstetten. Vienna was seething with excitement over the prospect of Hitler's arrival. He was a day late, hindered by the unpreparedness of his army and his own desire to create a frenzy of anticipation. Even then, no one could explain the massive enthusiasm of the population. The city was filled with 40,000 Hitler Youth and Bund deutscher Mädel girls waiting to salute their leader. His cavalcade made for the Imperial Hotel on the Ring. Once upon a time he had earned a few Kreuzer digging snow in front of the hotel, and since that time he had always cherished a desire to stay there.

Hitler had left word that he was "too tired" to address the public, but after repeated requests from the crowd, he appeared on the balcony of the hotel to enormous acclaim. There was no denying the enthusiasm of the Viennese, although some maintained that they were less delighted to see the German army and turned away in silence. Others have pointed out that the crowds were swollen by hordes of provincial Nazis who had been bussed in to boost numbers. Quite a lot of those who came out to gawk were mere *Adabeis*, but that does not account for all of them by any means. Certainly appearances supported Göring's view that "apart from the Jews in Vienna and part of the black ravens, the Catholics, there is nobody against us."

One black raven, Cardinal Theodor Innitzer, paid Hitler his respects at the Imperial Hotel on the 15th (as did the new rector of Vienna University,

Fritz Knoll). He had been considering a fitting reaction to Anschluss. The Sudetenländer Innitzer had been a minister in the clerical government of Ignaz Seipel and was seen as one of the pillars of the Corporate State. When local Nazis demanded a gesture acknowledging the Anschluss, the cardinal ordered the bells rung in Vienna's churches. He prudently expressed his "delight at the old dream of German unity" and sent a telegram to Hitler on the road to that effect.

He was more than aware of the tough line the Nazis were taking toward the Church. On March 12 the Primas Germaniae, Cardinal Sigismond Waitz, archbishop of Salzburg, had been placed under house arrest, and the prince bishop of Graz and Sekau, Ferdinand Pawlikowski, was taken to prison by a jeering crowd. Elsewhere the abbot Ambros Minarz of Altenburg Abbey refused to fly a swastika flag, causing the SA to occupy the abbey on the 17th. The bishop of Linz, Johannes Maria Gföllner, had famously said it was impossible to be a National Socialist and a Catholic. He took no notice of Hitler's presence in his see. The Church was second only to the Jews in unpopularity, and the mood was so explosive that Innitzer must have felt a need to prevent it blowing up in his face. Everyone in the Church feared a new Kulturkampf. On March 13, the bishop had offered prayers of thanks for the bloodless transformation. Such behavior appeared to mar a good record. As rector of the university he had been sympathetic to poor Jewish students, when many of his fellow bishops had been openly antisemitic. Now he appeared to be cowering in the face of Austria's new masters.

Innitzer had taken advice from the Catholic former German chancellor, Papen, who was anxious that the relationship between Hitler and the cardinal should start on the correct footing. The Church had been hand-in-glove with the Corporate State, and the Nazis wanted to see its influence curtailed, but Papen believed that Austria would soon become ungovernable if the Church were not treated properly. To that end, Papen and Seyss convinced Hitler to see Innitzer.

Innitzer made his way to the Imperial at 9:15 AM, accompanied by two clerics, his secretary Joseph Weinbauer and Johann Jauner-Schrofenegg. There was an ugly crowd of Austrian Nazis outside, whistling and shouting *"Pfui"* and *"In den Kanal mit dem Kardinal"* ("Throw the cardinal in the canal"). Hitler made to kiss the cardinal's ring, but Innitzer raised the

chain on his chest and made the sign of the cross. Hitler reassured Innitzer that, provided the Church remained loyal, there would be no trouble. Innitzer suggested that loyalty was conditional on the maintenance
of the concordat guaranteeing the position of the Church. Hitler was
impressed by the behavior of the Austrian prelates, whom he compared
favorably to the Germans. The SS scattered the hostile crowd as Innitzer
left. Innitzer would later regret these actions, when he realized that the
Catholics had been duped. The Vatican was outraged by Innitzer's fif-
teen-minute audience. The pope condemned the cardinal for "breach of
loyalty and treason," although this was later rescinded. Austria's small
Evangelical Church had declared the Anschluss "blessed" the day before
the Catholics. Certain Evangelicals had been hoping that the Nazis
would launch a new Reformation and free Austria from the power of the
Catholic Church.

After the cardinal left, the devoted Ribbentrop had finally been given
leave to join his master for his moment of glory in Vienna. Around noon
on the 15th, Hitler addressed an audience of some 250,000 people on
the Heldenplatz. Goebbels thought it "a popular uprising in the truest
sense of the words," but to some extent he had connived at it by making
it a public holiday. Hitler returned to the Heldenplatz after lunch to lay
a wreath at the Tomb of the Unknown Warrior at the Burgtor. Austria's
army and police were paraded before him to swear their new allegiance.
On returning to the airport at Aspern, Ribbentrop got lost and ended up
in a farmyard.

Hitler flew to Munich. As the aircraft passed over the Austrian Alps, he
turned to Keitel and said, "Now that is all German again." After a quick
snack with Keitel at the airport, he repaired to his own apartment. The
next day, he returned to Berlin, where he was met by Göring, proudly
waving his baton. Goebbels had ordered that the factories and places of
business be closed at 1 PM so that the people could be on the streets to
welcome the conquering hero. It was to be a reception "such as the capital has never seen."

THE AUSTRIAN "revolution" and the violence directed against the Jews
had gone too far, even for the Nazis. On March 17 Heydrich threatened
Commissar Bürckel with disciplinary action for the rowdiness of the rank

and file. He would send a Gestapo unit to deal with Party members who had allowed others to act in a "completely undisciplined manner." At the time of the plebiscite in April there was a halfhearted attempt to blame the Communists, who had been dressing up in Nazi uniforms and robbing people. The next day Berlin reaffirmed its authority in Austria with a second regulation: Power was in the hands of the Reichsführer SS. Bürckel took the hint; he threatened to expel the plunderers from the Party. On April 29 he thundered in the Austrian edition of the Nazi *Völkische Beobachter*, "Germany is governed by the rule of law. That means that nothing happens that has no foundation in law. . . . There will be no organised pogroms, not even by Frau Hintenhuber against Sara Kohn in the third courtyard, one floor up next to the taps." Himmler too vented his fury on any Reichs German SS men found working for their own personal profit. They were to be arrested and ejected from the SS. Once again the Nazis were conscious of foreign opinion and the fragility of German exports.

On the 18th Hitler addressed the Reichstag to report on the union with Austria. He promptly dissolved the assembly before fresh elections on April 10. This time the poll was to give total power to the Führer: "Then we'll throw away the last democratic-parliamentary eggshells."

Hitler was closely monitoring events on the Baltic and wondering whether it might afford him the chance to right one of the wrongs perpetrated at Versailles—the peace treaty that concluded the First World War. A rumpus had broken out between the Poles and the Lithuanians. Memel, with its largely German-speaking population, had been awarded to Lithuania in 1919. Under the terms of the treaty, the Lithuanians were meant to allow the Poles to use the port, but they refused to honor their obligations and looked to Moscow to protect them. Faced with the threat of invasion by Poland, they backed down on the 19th, but Hitler now saw the time was ripe to gather the fruits of his good relations with Poland.

The policy of Beck, the Polish foreign minister, was dictated by the German-Polish rapprochement of 1934. The Poles coveted Memel too, but Beck wanted to hold both Germany and Russia at arm's length and maintain Danzig. He therefore needed to make concessions. For Hitler, the Teschen pocket in Sudetenland, with its largely Polish population, was a gobbet to dangle in front of the Poles to gain their support for the dismemberment of Czechoslovakia. In the meantime any German claims to the Corridor were played down—the price of cooperation from Warsaw.

On March 19, Goebbels found Hitler studying the map. "First comes Czecho. We are going to split it with the Hungarians and the Poles. And we are going to exploit the next opportunity should Warsaw come to blows with Kovno to pop Memel in the bag. Good, but not yet: we are a boa constrictor digesting its prey. Then the rest of the Baltic [and] a piece of Alsace-Lorraine. . . ."

In Vienna, the Austrian bishops were being subjected to all the bullying Bürckel could muster. They met on the 18th and were given a draft document urging all Austrians "as Germans to recognise the German Reich." Innitzer objected to an article in the text that had them agree to assimilate the Church's youth organizations. The document passed to and fro, until all six bishops gave in. Innitzer even added "and *Heil Hitler*" in his own hand at Bürckel's insistence. The message was doubtless put out to try to ease the situation and to create a modus vivendi: After four years of "clerical fascism" the clergy had a great many enemies. Austrian priests had already suffered physical violence. Bürckel passed as a man sympathetic to Catholics. Waitz wrote of his astonishment that the bishops had submitted, however, and the bishops were not proud of their pusillanimity. Only two published the text in their diocesan organs, and Gföllner had boycotted the session.

EICHMANN ARRIVED in Vienna on March 16 to take up the job of directing Department II-112. Two days later he took part in the *razzia* at the IKG building (the headquarters of the Jewish congregation) in the Seitenstettengasse, seizing documents relating to Jewish support for Schuschnigg. Friedmann, his two assistants, the architect Robert Stricker, Jakob Ehrlich, and the office director Löwenherz were arrested together with the president of the Zionist National Union, Oskar Grünbaum. Eichmann slapped Löwenherz, telling him that he had been to Palestine and that he had been born in the old Templar colony of Sarona. This was evidently a fantasy: Eichmann came from Solingen near Düsseldorf but had been brought up in Linz. Others taken into custody were the presidents of the Jewish Freemasonic lodges and sixteen high-ranking Jewish Masons.

The Duke of Windsor was supposed to have intervened in an attempt to save Louis von Rothschild and the ear specialist, Professor Heinrich von Neumann. The duke was told that Rothschild would be released when he had compensated the state for the losses that occurred with the collapse of the Creditanstalt bank, although Rothschild had resigned a year before the crash. There was a rumor too that Freud had been taken into custody, but that proved unfounded.

The university was purged on March 17, the same day that the formal machinery of the Corporate State was shut down. Out went the professors of physics (Leo Ehrenhaft), ethnology (Wilhelm Koppers), and Romance languages (Alfred Kurzbach). They also expelled Stefan Meyer and Karl Przibaum together with Ernst Zerner, the professor of organic chemistry and an old frontline soldier, and the chemist Fritz Feigl. Eichmann's men also mopped up the head of the Jewish old soldiers' league, Friedmann. The IKG was asked to raise a contribution of 500,000 RM, more than half what they had paid out to the former chancellor's fund-raisers.

The Gestapo operated from the *piano nobile* of the former Metropole. The secret policemen were mostly young, educated people, many of them lawyers with doctorates. Half of Prussia's 4,000-articled lawyers had been out of work in 1932, and the percentage of Austrian advocates who were idle in 1938 must have been similar. The Gestapo provided work of sorts. Othmar Trencker was head of the SD, and Dr. Viktor Siegl of Department II/E was appointed to the task of making sure the Jews left all their valuable possessions behind them. This was a serious position: The Gestapo had an office dealing with the location of hidden assets that stopped at nothing. They didn't wear kid gloves. The father of writer Erich Fried had his stomach kicked in by the Gestapo man Göttler from Düsseldorf because he wouldn't tell him where his money was concealed.

Eichmann was a relatively lowly Nazi then, a significant cog in a larger wheel. The formal machinery of terror was established with the Gestapo office, responsible to Himmler and Heydrich. The chief was the Bavarian Franz Josef Huber assisted by the jurist Humbert Pifrader. Huber was a favorite of Heydrich's and a personal friend of Heinrich "Gestapo" Müller, the big man in Berlin. He had run the Austrian branch of the Gestapo since 1934 and had probably been involved in the planning of the putsch against Dollfuss. He was also one of the three greatest enthusiasts for the extermination of the Jews, together with the future gauleiter, Baldur von Schirach and Huber's later assistant, Karl Ebner.

At the Gestapo's Department II/D Rux and Heger had responsibility for the imprisonment of Jews, while Department III dealt with illegal emigration. Eichmann took the portfolio of legal emigration, the interpretation of the Nuremberg Law, and the issue of passports and passes, helped by Emil Komers of the Emigration Office. The Vienna Gestapo grew to become the largest in the Reich, with 850 of the 2,000 men active in Austria. As many as a third of them were German, as Austrians were often dismissed as "soft and spineless." Every day between 450 and 500 people were examined in the Metropole.

The Gestapo could avail themselves of a network of between six hundred and eight hundred police spies. The Café Viktoria was often used to lure the unfortunate victims to their fates, as it was close to the Gestapo headquarters. The Gestapo's work was massively assisted by the Viennese propensity to denounce all and sundry. There was a mythical Viennese saint called Sancta Denunziata. After the war it was reckoned that a quarter of all investigations came from information provided by private persons. They even reported the assistant Gestapo chief for allowing his Russian maid to go out without the statutory "Easterner's Badge."

THE STARS of the Nazi scene now came to visit their new province and its capital, Vienna. Göring loved Austria and was popular there. After visiting the former home of his Jewish godfather, Epenstein, he arrived by boat from Linz and spoke in the decommissioned Northwest Station on the 26th. He claimed 300,000 Jews had caused the impoverishment of Vienna. In a radio broadcast he mentioned the increasing numbers of Jews who were taking their own lives. He said he could not put a policeman behind every Jew to stop them. If they were unhappy, they had only to go to Palestine. Everyone knew of a good Jew, but that would not solve the Jewish problem.

The real message behind Göring's speech was that he was expecting to be able to fund German arms production by making off with the coffers of the state and fleecing Vienna's Jews. On the other hand, he was keen to avoid anything that would disrupt trade, particularly the export trade, and left instructions with Bürckel to preserve it at all costs. Goring's Four Year

Plan was formally introduced on March 19. On March 23 Austria's economy was brought into line with that of the Altreich. The federal reserves would provide a brief respite for the German economy and allow the country to run its highest trade deficit since 1929. Jewish businesses were to be "Aryanized" without further ado. The Four Year Plan had been acquiring chunks of Germany's most important industrial concerns. Göring, it seemed, had only to ask, and a part of the empire was made over to him. In the case of Jewish factories, he was not content with a slice of the action: He wanted the whole lot.

There were three huge Jewish concerns that had eluded him to date: the empires of the Rothschild, Petschek, and Weinmann families. The acquisition of these was made all the more difficult for their international ramifications. Shortly before he left for Vienna, Göring had had a letter from Queen Mary of Great Britain asking him to intercede in favor of Louis Rothschild. Her appeal would fall on deaf ears: Göring was more interested in getting his hands on Rothschild's money than anyone. The Rothschilds owned businesses in Austria, France, and Czechoslovakia, and the assets were divided up among branches of the family in Vienna, Prague, and Paris. Sensing danger, the Rothschilds had transferred ownership of their Witkowitz steelworks to London in 1937, together with its Swedish subsidiary. The company was now British. Baron Louis was being held as a hostage in the Hotel Metropole until a means could be found of giving the company to Göring. Nevertheless, Göring would not even get close until German troops occupied rump Czechoslovakia a year later, and only then by paying around a third of the asking price of £10 million. The Rothschilds agreed to the deal chiefly to liberate Louis and also because the Czech works were now effectively imprisoned too. The deal was still not tied up when war broke out, leaving the Germans with no claim to the Swedish subsidiary and in illegal possession of the Czech works.

Keppler's time was taken up with the appropriation of Jewish big business. He had cut his teeth on the holdings of coal baron Ignaz Petschek. Old Ignaz had died in 1934, and the firm was in the hands of the founder's heirs. Several non-Jewish firms were interested but were only prepared to pay a percentage of the company's worth. In July Göring ordered the Aryanization of 200 million RM of Petschek property in Germany. The

Petschek empire owed some 30 million RM in taxes, which proved the lever for the appropriation of the whole business. When Germany walked into the Sudetenland, the Nazis grabbed the firm's headquarters in Aussig. The foreign minister of the rump Czech state, Frantisek Chvalkovsky, promised his help in tracking down the money. The business was eventually split between Göring and Flick.

In Austria, Keppler "Aryanized" the Hirtenberg weapons factory and the mammoth Bunzl & Biach paper concern. Göring's problem was that he had come two weeks too late to catch the smaller fry. Many valuable Jewish possessions had already disappeared into other people's pockets. The Viennese wanted the money for themselves and were even refusing to pay their debts to Jewish businesses, which led to a further shortfall in Göring's expectations. It was important that the state itself should receive the Jewish businesses at the lowest price and have the ability to sell them to respectable interested parties at a profit.

In the event, the new Vermögensverkehrsstelle (Office for the Traffic of Assets) was helpless in the face of the Viennese desire to plunder their Jews. When the Office sought to find out what had happened to the fortunes of their victims, it discovered that the money had disappeared during the "wild" time, and there was no hope of relocating it. From now on the Nazi authorities had to make sure that they got there first. This put Göring's plans on a collision course with Eichmann's, who wanted the Jews out as quickly as possible and was prepared to use the money from the rich to finance the departure of the poor. Göring desired that money for himself. The result was a push-me, pull-me situation whereby the Jews were being held back from emigration until they could be proved to have turned over their assets. Their passports were therefore impounded until they had paid their dues to the conquerors.

The Jews were feeling the heat from Austria's new masters. This is borne out by the figures: In January that year there had been 88 suicides, of whom 5 were Jews; in February 62 and 4 Jews; in March 213 of whom 79 Jews; in April 62 of the 138 suicides were Jews. Suicide among Viennese Gentiles was also a daily occurrence. An anti-Nazi Colonel Deloge had been offered the editorship of a pro-Nazi organ. He was found dead with a revolver in his hand and a note that read "I cannot serve the Godless." A senior judge called Meyer poisoned himself and his wife and four children.

Before he died he put up a sign in his window saying, "I cannot take responsibility for bringing up my family in the spirit of atheism and crime. God forgive me!"

Another package of measures introduced by Göring's ministry was meant to cure the unemployment problem in Austria. Jobs were to be created on the German model: New fast roads, dams, and motorways were to be built; the mines were to be developed; there was to be a reform of agriculture with improvements to the soil; new cooperative dairies were to be created; new housing was to be made available. This was meant to lure the old Socialists over to the Nazi side. Giving them work would make them the new brooms superior to the "Blacks" (or Corporate State-ists) they had replaced.

WITH AUSTRIA in the bag, and no blood spilled on the German side at least, Hitler proceeded to his next territorial objective mentioned to the service chiefs: Czechoslovakia. A creation of Versailles, Czechoslovakia had begun life in the rosy light of the idealistic conception of its founder, Tomás Masaryk. The Allies had bundled a number of incoherent peoples together. In Yugoslavia there was an overwhelming Slavic majority in all its constituent parts (even if they didn't necessarily get on with one another), but in Czechoslovakia the non-Slavic element was more than a third. For a while there was a small degree of accommodation, but matters changed after Masaryk's retirement in 1935, when Edvard Beneš took over as head of state. Beneš was opposed to any accommodation with Germany over its non-Slavic minorities.

The Czechs and the Slovaks were both Slavs, but they had no previous history of cooperation. Prague had been ruled from Vienna, while Bratislava (Pressburg) was a Hungarian city, ruled from Budapest. In practice the Czechs looked down on their rustic cousins to the east. The two minorities that rocked the boat the most were the Germans in the Czech lands and the Magyars who had been stranded in the Slovak provinces. There were three and a half million Germans in western Czechoslovakia, living mostly in northern Bohemia (the so-called Sudetenland) and southern Moravia. There was also a small but prominent minority in Prague and Brno (Brünn) and a number of islands deep in the Czech-speaking core, such as Iglau, south of Prague.

The Hungarians were mostly to be found in southern Slovakia, disgruntled at their estrangement from their motherland and at the fact that Versailles had awarded Pressburg—the coronation capital of Hungary—to Czechoslovakia, henceforth to be known by its Slovak name of Bratislava. Ragbag it might have been, but Czechoslovakia had acquired considerable strengths since 1919: The French had guaranteed its borders in 1925 and the Soviet Union ten years later—although the Soviets required the French to act first. The Czech flirtation with the Soviet Union, however, sealed its fate in the eyes of some Western conservatives, who would rather have seen the Germans occupy the country than Bolshevism establish an outpost in Central Europe. Even without the promised Soviet aid, however, Czechoslovakia also had a powerful army, an exemplary chain of border defenses (all of them in the German-speaking regions in the north and none facing Austria in the south), and a thriving arms industry.

Hitler intended to intervene on behalf of the German-speaking minority in the Sudetenland. Though Goebbels had been let in on his plans, most of Hitler's entourage did not learn of them until the end of May. Hitler had, however, already taken the trouble to square things with the Yugoslav minister Milan Stojadinovitsh on January 17. He did not want the Yugoslavs walking into Hungary if the latter came to his aid in Czechoslovakia. From Halifax he had learned that the British had already looked at the problem and decided—realistically enough—that military intervention on their part was practically meaningless. The most they could do was starve the Germans out with a naval blockade, which would require two to three years to take effect.

On March 28, Ribbentrop, Werner Lorenz (who was responsible for ethnic Germans), Hess, and an impressive bevy of diplomats met the Sudeten German leader Konrad Henlein, whom Germany had been subsidizing since 1935. This Czech "führer" was a gym teacher, scoffed at in SS circles for suspected homosexuality. Hitler had told Henlein to refuse all blandishments from Prague, for the Czechs were now becoming aware that what had previously been an annoying domestic matter had more serious implications. The Anschluss had also raised the Sudetenländers' hopes of becoming part of Greater Germany, and there had been Nazi demonstrations in some of the smaller, German-speaking towns. The Nazis hoped for post hoc verbal protests of the sort delivered after March 12. Then on March 29 Goebbels flew to Vienna. From the aircraft he could just make out a large chunk of Czechoslovakia. "Just wait!" he wrote.

PROTEST OVER the treatment of General Fritsch had given birth to a new opposition within the old German elite, which would put pressure on army command to eliminate Hitler. The two most important dissenters were Admiral Canaris in military intelligence and Ernst von Weizsäcker in the German foreign office. Although Canaris had little questioned Hitler's government at first, he became increasingly anti-Nazi with time. When he recruited the Austrian military intelligence man Erwin von Lahousen-Vivremont after the Anschluss, he warned him, "You may not, under any pretext, admit to this section . . . or take on your staff any member of the NSDAP, the Storm Troopers or the SS, or even an officer who sympathizes with the Party."

Canaris communicated with the chief of staff, Ludwig Beck, through Colonel Hans Oster, a Christian monarchist who had fallen foul of the army after a bedroom scandal. He was outspoken in his opposition to Hitler, whom he referred to as "the pig," and made no bones about the fact he needed to be slaughtered. It was Oster who had recruited Beck, probably as a direct result of the Fritsch affair. Many others rallied to the cause for similar reasons, even some who on the face of it seemed unlikely opponents to the regime, such as the Berlin police chief, Helldorf, a one-time antisemitic thug and playboy who now had access to all sorts of useful material from the police files.

Another of Oster's key contacts was Hans von Dohnányi, a departmental chief in the Abwehr. Dohnányi was part of the legal team defending Fritsch at his "court of honor." Dohnányi painstakingly assembled material on the crimes of the Nazi state, which he stored in an old filing cabinet in the corner of his office. Neither he nor Oster took much care to conceal their activities. Dohnányi was also instrumental in bringing in a host of like-minded contacts, starting with his own relatives by marriage, the Bonhoeffers.

Ernst von Weizsäcker was the permanent undersecretary of state at the Auswärtiges Amt, or German foreign office, in the Wilhelmstrasse in Berlin. His concern over Hitler's aggressive foreign policy led him to secure appointments for like-minded persons in German embassies and legations and to maintain contacts with Canaris. Two of his most trusted diplomatic sources were the Kordt brothers (see chapter 2). Ulrich von Hassell, the sacked ambassador to Rome, was another foreign policy expert. He was sponsored by the industrial magnate Gustav Krupp von Bohlen und Halbach's son-in-law, Thilo von Wilmowsky, and his position as advisor to a European economic think tank afforded the cover he needed to travel. Both Hassell and Beck were brought together by the venerable Mittwochsgesellschaft or Wednesday Society, together with other opponents to the regime such as the Prussian economics minister, Johannes Popitz, and the economist Jens Jessen.

That spring, the former mayor of Leipzig, Carl Goerdeler, went to London. Goerdeler had been suggested as a successor to Brüning as chancellor in the Weimar Republic and was a universally respected politician. He served the Third Reich as a commissar for price control and managed to tolerate the regime inasmuch as it furthered his own causes. He was not enamored of the Left and lived in profound fear of Soviet Russia. As a former deputy mayor of Königsberg, he wanted to see a revision of the Polish border drawn at Versailles and Danzig regain its place in the Reich. He had resigned from Leipzig town hall in 1937 at the removal of the statue of Mendelssohn and the failure to place a church at the center of a new housing estate. He was kept in funds by the Stuttgart industrialist Robert Bosch, which allowed him to carry out his work abroad. Goerdeler's "grand tour" started in June 1937, taking in various parts of Europe and the Americas. In March and April 1938 he was off again, this time traveling only to France and Britain. In August he went on another trip, this time to Switzerland and the Balkans.

His problem, however, was discretion—or lack of it. He was distinctly verbose and insisted on writing extensive reports, which were copied to hosts of people. While he was in London, he revealed the fact that he had had some assurance from Brauchitsch that the general would confront Hitler over his failure to rehabilitate Fritsch after the court of honor dismissed the case as a pack of lies. The loose talk proved too much for the fickle Brauchitsch, who ran to Hitler to clear his name of involvement with the frondeurs. The gaffe threatened to blow Goerdeler's cover too, as his mission was under the aegis of Canaris and Weizsäcker.

As it was, Goerdeler had made the trip with former Chancellor Brüning. Brüning had thought Chamberlain a nonstarter but was anxious to put Goerdeler together with Churchill, and a talk was arranged in Sussex on April 3 at the house of some English friends. At the last moment a suspicious telephone call scotched the meeting. It eventually transpired there was a Gestapo agent in the household. The lunch went ahead without Goerdeler. Brüning was able to fill Churchill in on recent events in Germany.

At the same time as Goerdeler emerged as the civilian leader of the opposition, Ludwig Beck moved into the position of military chief. Beck was opposed to Hitler's military "adventures," but he was probably less outraged by some of the border revisions that Hitler was to make. Few if any Germans believed that the Versailles settlement was just.

Beck's chosen weapon was the memorandum. These memos were dispatched to Brauchitsch and mocked by Hitler. In the first half of 1938, Beck must have believed that Hitler could be made to see the light. In one famous paper written at the time, he informed officers of the limits to their oath of obedience, when their consciences and responsibility would not allow them to carry out orders. Beck feared the growth of the paramilitary elements in the Third Reich and called for a new program "for the Führer, against war, free expression, and end of secret police practices, the return of law to the Reich, the halving of all levies, the end of palace building, the construction of homes for the people and Prussian cleanliness and simplicity."

Another who joined the ranks of the opposition was president of the Reichsbank Hjalmar Schacht, encouraged by his wounded vanity as his importance declined in the Third Reich. Schacht could see better than anyone that autarky was leading the German boat onto the rocks. The country was pathetically short of foreign currency, which merely encouraged the gangsterlike Göring to steal it from the enemies of the regime: the Jews. Schacht's impatience can't have been helped by the Anschluss, which had required him to rescue his sister and her non-Aryan husband, then ferry them to Holland together with their money.

Some of the opponents of the regime were monarchists, which did not go down well in Britain, where some felt they should have finished the First World War by hanging the kaiser. One was Ewald von Kleist-Schmenzin, a Pomeranian squire and a member of the right-wing DNVP.

He was connected to the plotters in the Abwehr through his brother-in-law, Ulrich von der Osten. In March he approached the British journalist Ian Colvin in the Casino Club in Berlin's Bendlerstrasse and revealed details of Hitler's aggressive program. The message from the opposition was always the same: that Hitler needed a firm approach that was the very reverse of the policy of appeasement pursued by the British government. Colvin took the message to Sir George Ogilvie-Forbes, the chargé d'affaires at the British embassy. By the time Kleist set out for London in August, his credentials had been properly screened on both sides of the North Sea.

HITLER HAD made it plain from the start: The Jews had to go. Göring had added that they should leave their *Gerstl* behind. There were a dozen or so methods of transferring money abroad, but in almost every case the sums involved were pitifully small. Any emigrant who had satisfied all the requirements could leave with 10 RM, or 20 schillings, or double that amount if going to a country with no common border with Germany. They could also bring 1,000 RM worth of goods. Personal belongings could also be removed, providing the emigrant had submitted a list for approval. Jewels generally had to be smuggled, as the state was particularly interested in impounding them.

One-way tickets could be paid for in Reichs marks. Traveling, for example, to South America would require a huge sum. Until 1938 there had been Altreu (Allgemeine Treuhandstelle für die Jüdische Auswanderung, the General Trust for Jewish Emigration), which had permitted Jews to transfer anything up to 50,000 RM to Palestine. This had been created to encourage trade between the two countries, much like the Ha'avara Agreement. The latter allowed for a complicated system of exchange whereby the emigrant paid his money into a closed account in RM and received it in sterling once he had landed in Palestine. It amounted to a favored trading status for Germany in the Mandate, an extraordinary situation in the circumstances and one that allowed German Jews numerous commodities from the old country.

Jews with foreign nationality could sell interests in a foreign company. Money that was not exported by one of these methods had to be paid into a closed account that could not be touched, which was later raided by the Ministry of Finance. Smuggling was a possibility, but German currency was virtually worthless on foreign exchanges. There were various schemes whereby the money could be given to a poor Jew and recouped from a rich friend or relative at the other end.

On March 26, the IKG in Vienna was dissolved, together with all the other organs of the Jewish congregation, greatly adding to the panic among the Jews "who were besieging the various foreign consulates in an effort to get out of the country."

The process was Ulyssean. The first paper required was the *Steuerunbedenklichkeitsbescheinigung* (certificate of fiscal harmlessness), proving that all taxes were paid. The process of obtaining it was as long and clumsy as the word itself. It involved visits to and payments to the *Bezirkshauptmannschaft*, the directorate of the applicant's district, where the *Kleiner Meldenachweis*—a certificate of domicile—was to be obtained. The next stop was the Magistratsabteilung, the district commissioner's department in the town hall; this was followed by the Accountancy Department or the central tax office and the tax office of the district where the applicant lived. If the forms had been filled in properly and the right sums paid, the applicant received his *Steuerunbedenklichkeitsbescheinigung* and could proceed to stage two.

That is, if he had enough money to pay for emigration tax or could raise it by selling off his goods. Jewish assets were technically worthless, and many people were reduced to borrowing money to finance their departure, when a few weeks before they had figured among the richest inhabitants of the city.

Stage two consisted of a visit to the Devisenstelle, where the Jew's assets were released and the department granted certificates of good conduct. The long lines outside both offices provided a means of making a little money for both the Nazis and unscrupulous Jews. The corruption did not abate. In December, Gertrude Löwenhek complained that she had spent six nights camping outside the British consulate in the Wallnerstrasse while Nazis with swastika armbands took 100 RM bribes to issue numbered passes.

Doing a little business on the side was not restricted to the men loitering around the consulates. Certain Jews styled themselves documentation experts: They stood outside offices and offered to obtain papers for individuals for a fee. "They knew every back door. It was the poor Jews who queued for hours outside the front doors." Those waiting in the lines were sitting ducks. They could be picked out and sent off to clean up a barracks by SA men or Hitler Youth boys. When they reached the front of the line, they were told the form was incorrectly filled in and that they had to do it all again.

Stage three was the passport itself from the emigration office. The applicant first went to the police station of his district, where he had to answer questions as to the nature of the passport: new, for all lands, a passe-partout, an extension of an existing document. Then the applicant went off to the emigration office in the Herrengasse and then to the Passamt in the Wehrgasse, where the appropriate visas had to be obtained.

The passport office in the Wehrgasse in the fifth district was one of the most feared stations of abuse and humiliation. One witness recounted, "How frightful this Wehrgasse was! A much too narrow room in an old Viennese house, a narrow suburban street, in which thousands pushed, shoved, sweated and cursed." On average people waited for a day and a half before receiving their papers.

The applicant still needed money. "The only foreign exchange he can obtain is that put at the disposal of the community by outside refugee organisations, which is completely reserved for the purpose. In return for his last Marks he obtains the necessary dollars or pounds: if he has none, he receives an advance from the community."

For many countries a certificate of moral probity was required as well as proof of residence. For the moral certificate two witnesses were necessary. Beginning on July 23 a new ordeal was established: The applicant had to provide a photograph with an exposed left ear and register his or her fingerprints. Once the *Ausreisebewilligung* was granted, the applicant had to promise never to darken Austria's doors again.

It would be hard to argue that there was no element of sadism in the long-drawn-out business of obtaining the relevant papers to leave, even if Eichmann could justify it by saying that it ensured that the Jews left their money behind. The crucial interrogations of would-be immigrants took place in the Palais Rothschild in the Prinz-Eugenstrasse. Lines gathered several hundred meters away on the Schwarzenberg Platz at nightfall in order to make sure of being seen the following day. There were two lines: one for "normal" Jews and the other for those who had been bought out of

Dachau and who were recognizable by their shaven heads. The *Dachauer* took precedence.

By the end of September Eichmann could boast that he had rid Austria of 50,000 Jews. It was much tougher for Austrians to find a safe haven than it had been for the Germans after 1933. Visas had been abolished for Germans and Austrians in 1927, but the Home Office in London changed the rules in response to the Anschluss, reinstating the restrictions. The new rules came into force on May 21. The British government did not want to see the country flooded with poor Central European Jews, and it knew that once they were in, it would prove difficult to send them back. There was even a suggestion that MI5 had warned the government that the whole thing was a Nazi plot to flood Britain with Jews and create a "Jewish problem" in the United Kingdom.

At first discretionary powers were left with the passport control officers, who were often more sympathetic to the cases before them than the government would have been. The argument behind this was that they had the ability to find out more about individual cases than an immigration officer at the ports—and by then it would be too late. It also shifted the onus of guilt from the Home Office to the Passport Control Office (PCO), which was nominally under the control of the Foreign Office.

Later the Home Office changed its mind—perhaps because too many Jews were being let in. The Passport Control Office had to forward all applications to the Home Office for its approval. The Home Office clearly did not trust the PCO. There were accusations of favoritism, and the consul-general in Vienna, St. Clair Gainer, admitted that all his officials seemed to have some "pet Jew" they wanted to see admitted. In December the Home Office finally proposed that all applications be made in Britain, providing that the persons in question give the right assurances that they could maintain themselves. The distrust might have been caused by the occasionally pragmatic approach of MI6 and the PCO.

ADOLF EICHMANN was the model Nazi civil servant, "a totally obedient receiver of orders." Hitler intimated the broad lines of policy; the Nazi satrap filled in the detail in such a way as to please his master. Austrian Jews were to be treated with a good deal more savagery than had been experienced in Germany up to then. Despite rough handling, however,

Eichmann had yet to advocate the "final solution." For the time being his policy was an economic solution: Jews would be fleeced first and then driven into exile.

Eichmann was creating the Viennese model for forcing Jews out, preferably to Palestine. His concern was how that could reasonably be funded. Rich Jews could get themselves out, but not the poor. The Ha'avara Agreement of August 1933 was defunct by the time of the Anschluss. Of the 170,000 Jews who left German lands between 1933 and 1939, 50,000 found their way to Palestine, taking their home comforts with them, including furniture, household equipment, paintings, and objets d'art.

At the beginning Eichmann wanted emigration to Palestine to be carried out according to the proper procedures. This was doomed to failure while Britain opposed Jewish emigration in large numbers. A Palestinian journalist called Mosche Krivoschein (code name Galili) had a plan to help Revisionist Jews get to Palestine. He had won over Dr. Kagan, the president of the Makkabi (Zionist sports clubs). Money would be found to get around the quotas imposed by the British. Galili had contacts with Greek shipowners who had formerly been involved in gunrunning during the Spanish Civil War. Now that it had become legal, there was no money to be made anymore, and they were looking for new business. They were prepared to transport Jews for a price, in small and not particularly seaworthy vessels.

Galili's organization Af-Al-Pi (Despite Everything) brought together the services of the Viennese lawyer Willi Perl and the industrialist Hans Perutz together with an "extremist" called Paul Haller. They operated transports in 1937 and 1938, but the last to leave was April 25, 1938. Perl went to see Eichmann to suggest ways of shipping Jews to Palestine illegally. He drew attention to the risks involved, for the British were liable to compensate for illegal entries by docking their number from the number of legal entry visas. Eichmann was scandalized by the suggestion; he did not wish to create "centers of crime." He was apparently so angry that he told Perl "I'll put you up against a wall and shoot you!" Perl replied, "We need your cooperation for a more important matter." With time Eichmann was convinced.

Perl did not abandon his project. After he was forced to give up his legal practice in the Stubenring, he dedicated himself to emigration. Together with Galili he went to Berlin to promote his ideas. It was a dangerous game, as he was incurring the wrath of numerous London-based Jewish organizations that were there to seek legal ways of increasing the number of people allowed into Palestine.

Another organization that grew up at the time was Mossad, or Mossad leAliyah Bet (the Institute for Immigration). As the Hebrew name implies, it was created to facilitate illegal entry into Palestine. In a report dated August 17, 1939, the Zionist Norman Bentwich, representing the Council for German Jewry, related an interview he had had with "Captain" Eichmann in Vienna. The British had formally ended Jewish emigration to Palestine, but Eichmann persisted: The Nazi authorities "systematically foster illegal transports to Palestine, and for this purpose do provide a certain amount of marks from the confiscated Jewish property."

Eichmann's plan was to drive out 7,000 to 8,000 Jews a month. That way he would have eliminated the Austrian Jews by the beginning of 1940. "They prefer a disorderly to a planned emigration, as a means of making trouble for Jews in other countries," Bentwich noted when he attended the meeting with Dr. Löwenherz from the IKG. Eichmann claimed to be acting on orders from the "highest quarters." He was prepared to allow that 20,000 to 25,000 Jews could remain in Austria. They were to be made up of old people "who could not be emigrated," "pensioners of the government or the municipality," and "very poor persons." Bentwich was told that Eichmann was retraining the Jews for their new lives. Most of it was for menial work, an intentional humiliation: "There is a class, for example, for bar-mixers, and several for butlers, which are attended by lawyers, doctors and industrialists. The possibility of domestic service in England has been a Godsend. Thousands of children and adults are learning English somehow."

The outside world was not necessarily ready for the brutal treatment of the Austrian Jewry. In Germany the persecution had cooled down after the boycott and the Nuremberg Laws, and during the Berlin Olympics of 1936 the obvious signs had been cleared away. The Aliens Committee of the British Board of Deputies had been more concerned with other Jew-baiting nations, such as Poland, Romania, and Russia. On March 23 the Aliens Committee held an emergency meeting. Austrian Jews seeking refuge in Britain had been turned back at the frontier. The Home Secretary was determined to "treat each case on its merits." Even those who managed to cross the border were—in theory at least—to register their presence in Britain with the German consul.

THE POPULAR board game "Juden raus!" sold nearly a million copies in Germany between 1936 and 1940. The aim was to bring as many Jews as you could to one of six *Sammelplätze* (collection points) and then it was "auf nach Palästina" (off to Palestine). You threw a die and, if you were in luck, landed on the shops of Kohn, Gorstein, or Stern. There were homely instructions for the children written on the board, such as *"Zeige Geschick im Würfelspiel / damit Du sammelst der Juden viel"* ("Throw the dice with all your skill / and with sundry Jews your baskets fill"). And finally *"Gelingt es Dir 6 Juden rauszujagen, / so bist Du Sieger ohne fragen!"* ("Should you manage to drive six Jews out / You'll be the winner, there is no doubt"). The board was covered with caricatures of Jews in the style of *Der Stürmer*.

But the British didn't want the Jews to go to Palestine, first choice for 90 percent of Austrian Jews. The Balfour Declaration had stipulated the creation of a Jewish homeland (as opposed to *the* Jewish homeland), but after 1935 the British had had a change of heart, partly based on the levels of street violence in Palestine. March 1937 had seen a spate of Zionist bombings of Arab cafés and buses. Official attitudes had also changed after the Italian attack on Ethiopia. Between 1936 and 1938 immigrant levels had fallen. For the time being immigration was limited to around 12,000 per annum. There were "strong Arab demands for the complete stoppage."

To obtain a permit to go to Palestine, Jews had to visit the British Passport Control Office. Many years later, Kenneth Benton, Thomas Kendrick's second-in-command at the PCO, described a typical day of dealing with Jewish hopefuls:

> They used to fill up the courtyard by about nine o'clock in the morning and I used to stand on the steps and give them a lecture on what chance they had of getting away. "Your only chance of getting to Palestine now is either if you've got relatives or a capitalist visa. But you might be able to get to Grenada. You might be able to get to Jamaica. India will only take you if you are a qualified dentist," and so on.

Then during the day they were coming in one after the other. I had a whole lot of women who were examiners working for me spread through the office. But the stories were so terrible: that they had been separated from their children; that they had seen loved ones go off in a Nazi convoy with the Gestapo and so on and it just went on all day and at the end of it it made one desperately unhappy that you could do nothing. The American vice-consul who was a pal of mine said: "I've got to the point where if any woman leaves my office not in tears, I feel I haven't done my job." It was a dreadful, dreadful time.

The British clung to their policy despite the crisis brought about by Nazi racial law. A British white paper published in May 1939 outlined the government's new policy: Palestine was to be a state with an Arab majority and a Jewish minority fixed at no more than 75,000 Jews settling before 1944, unless the Arabs consented to more. Meanwhile Secretary for the Colonies Malcolm Macdonald looked at the possibility of establishing a Jewish state in British Guiana. By the end of the year, however, the Foreign Office had decided that British Guiana was "climatically unsuitable." The new policy was as leaky as a colander: 51,186 managed to reach Palestine illegally between April 1, 1939, and March 31, 1945.

Lucian Meysels's case was typical of many Jews who realized they had to act fast:

On the evening of 11 March we knew we had to get out—*hic et nunc.* My father had been cultural editor of the *Neue Freie Presse*, a job for life, he thought. This had the advantage that he had not written a word on politics under his by-line for the past three years and at the same time had contact with several legations. We immediately started to get visas—a prerequisite for getting an exit visa. The first visa we got was Czechoslovakian, which we intended to make use of although my father never intended us to stay there: "fifty miles between us and Hitler is not enough."

A couple of weeks later, a friend of my father in the Wallnerstrasse told us to apply for a pilgrim-cum-tourist visa for Palestine *since that quota had not been used up by the spring of '38.* After all, who wanted to make a pilgrimage to the unruly Holy Land then. "Gesagt, getan" [Sooner said than done]: my father got us three visas for a deposit of £30 or £40 each, to be refunded "on our return." We could have gone direct, but my mother wanted to say goodbye to her brother before leaving Europe. We stayed in Bratislava for three weeks and took a train by a circuitous route via Hungary, Yugoslavia and Italy, after the travel agent where we had bought the rail tickets told us we would not need any transit visas. However, hardly had we been on the train, than we were bounced off by the Hungarian Frontier Police. Fortunately we had left a day earlier than required. . . . My father sent my mother . . . to the Hungarian Consulate to get transit visas. No sooner had she met the consul, than the man told her: "we don't give visas to Jews!" Whereupon she told him "I'm not Jewish," putting her baptismal certificate, which she had wisely taken with her, under his nose. Minutes later she had three visas. We caught the train the next morning and this time got through in time for the boat.

As a result of the Anschluss and the tightening up of passport controls, emigration became more difficult from the Altreich too. Long lines formed outside the offices of the Jewish Hilfsverein in Berlin, the Palestine Agency, and the British consulate in the Tiergartenstrasse. In a great many instances it was the passport control officer in Berlin, Frank Foley, or his counterpart in Frankfurt, Robert Smallbones, who found some means of issuing them with the precious papers. Many Viennese Jews went to Berlin themselves, where the atmosphere was calmer and there was as yet little or no violence directed toward them.

THE BRITISH were not the only people helping to save Jews. The Chinese consul-general Ho Fengshan is credited with issuing 4,000 visas to Jewish residents between 1938 and 1941. In the first three months of his posting he is supposed to have helped 1,200 Jews reach Shanghai. Ho was Christian and believed this was the natural thing to do. Once in Shanghai there was an infrastructure to help the Jews, but it was quickly stretched. Shanghai was open, but the immigrants needed transit visas. Iraq, for example, could not be crossed unless the Jew was in possession of a British or Palestinian passport. By June 1939 there were 9,500 Jews registered and another 1,500 unofficial migrants. It was thought the town would have 25,000 by the time the influx slackened off. Only 350 had found work.

If you bought a one-way steamship ticket, the right of abode was thrown in with it. A visa for Shanghai did not necessarily imply that the possessor was serious about going to China. In many cases it was simply a means to leaving German territory, and the ultimate objective would have been to enter Britain or the United States. It was a precious means to get out of a concentration camp after November 10.

Wolfgang von Weisl operated the New Zionist Organization from the rue de Bassano in Paris's affluent *seizième* quarter. He reported that there were already 24,000 applications lodged at the French consulate in Vienna by April 26. Some Jews got stuck in India, where there were 26,080 toward the end of the war, 10,000 in Bombay alone and 2,000 of them acknowledged refugees from Hitler. Desperate Jews set their sights on different countries that they thought might offer them a refuge. Unscrupulous persons set about selling bogus visas. Paraguay appeared to encourage immigration, but then it turned out that they wanted recruits for a war against Bolivia. Some countries responded by setting quotas. Australia was one of these, fixing the number of possible places at 500 in March. By the end of the month there were already in excess of 6,000 applicants. The first to arrive landed in October: twenty-two Austrians, three Germans, and two Czechs. Australia looked to be the only one of the dominions to respond to the plight of the Jews, but the government soon began to renege on their promises.

IN 1938 the Foreign Office in London thought there could be as many as a million baptized Jews on the Continent. No one was clear about what was in store for them. Bishop Bell of Chichester had responded to the potential threat by creating the Church of England Committee for Non-Aryan Christians in 1937. It was ready to provide travel expenses, grants, and tuition fees for non-Aryan Christians deemed to be at risk. The Committee was founded on the idea that there was no specific body looking after non-Aryan Christians other than the Quakers. The Jews had their own organizations, whereas the Christian "number was as great, if not greater, than that of Jewish victims."

It seems doubtful now that the number of non-Aryan Christians exceeded that of Jews, but assimilation had indeed led to a great many conversions, and as yet it was not clear how much risk the *Mischlinge* ran. Bishop Bell may have been sympathetic, but that was not true of all bishops.

The most pro-German of the prelates was Headlam of Gloucester, who thought the Jews "clever, malicious and untruthful, and they have excessive influence on the press of Europe."

The unsung hero of the British bishops was Basil Staunton Batty, bishop of Fulham, who was responsible for the British parishes in northern Europe. As early as March 12, 1933, he told Cosmo Gordon Lang, the archbishop of Canterbury, to put pressure on the Nazis over their treatment of the Jews and to oblige the German Protestant church to react: "I am asking for further information from those I can trust. . . . My object in writing is to suggest that if I can stir up the church in Germany to protest against any persecution on religious grounds . . . we might make some pronouncement in England which would show them we stood behind them in this matter." At the end of the month, Batty wrote to Lang again about the persecution of the Jews. "My own opinion is that a protest should be made by the Lutheran Church and that the Christian Church throughout the world should support it but I fear that the Lutheran Church will not take action through fear of Hitler."

He was right: The Lutheran Church in Germany was largely silent. As its foremost martyr, Dietrich Bonhoeffer, wrote at the time, "She was silent when she should have cried out because the blood of the innocent was crying aloud to heaven. She has failed to speak the right word in the right way and at the right time. She had not resisted to the uttermost the apostasy of faith, and she has brought upon herself the guilt of the godlessness of the masses."

Batty sat on the Foreign Committee of the Church of England, and two years later he took Headlam to task over the Confessing Church in Germany, the only Protestant organization that was resisting Hitler: "The Confessional Church deserves our sympathy. It is putting up a good fight for the essentials of the Christian faith." In Canterbury, the archbishop was also quick to condemn British policy. On March 22, 1938, he wrote to the home secretary, Samuel Hoare, to protest against the entry restrictions placed on Austrian Jews, pointing out the dramatic rise in Austrian suicides. Jews had been turned back at Croydon Airport. Both Hoare and Chamberlain were at pains to tell the Commons that indiscriminate immigration would cause difficulties at home and that they did not believe there were grounds "for an alteration of the laws."

Archbishop Lang had been measured in his approach to the An-schluss. On March 29 he told the British House of Lords he was aware that the Austrians had sought just such a merger after the Great War and thought that it had been inevitable. The statement was interpreted as approbation in Germany. On the other hand, he believed the manner in which it had been carried out was reprehensible, even if he was thankful that it had taken place without bloodshed. That last line caused him some considerable embarrassment, and he regretted it later; several peers were better informed than he was of the murderous nature of the German occupation.

Lang atoned for his error. On July 17 he was one of the church leaders to institute Sunday prayers for the Jews. The chief rabbi of Great Britain, J. H. Hertz, asked for Jews to assemble at five that same day, so that Jews and Christians could be united in prayer. The Jews said prayers for imprisoned Christians such as Pastor Niemöller, while the Christians prayed for the Jews. In the Anglican Church in Berlin a similar service was held. Bishop Batty was naturally behind the latter and reported on the service to Lang. By the end of the year, not only had Lang lost his reputation for sympathy for the Nazis, but *Der Stürmer* had made him the cover story for issue 52 for "standing up for Jewish assassins."

ACCORDING TO the Nuremberg Laws (enacted in Austria on May 20, 1938) baptized Jews were still Jews. The Quakers played a leading role in helping "non-Aryan Christians" to safety. Later a third of the places on the kindertransports were reserved for their nominees. The idea of bringing Jewish children to safety had been mooted by Richard Cary, secretary of the International Secretariat, as early as the summer of 1933. The British and American Quakers maintained an office for the German Emergency Committee in the Singerstrasse in Vienna, dealing mostly with Catholic converts. After November they were besieged by applicants: 11,000 applications were made for 15,000 people. The Quakers succeeded in getting as many as 4,500 out by the time war broke out in September 1939, including around 1,200 children. Of these 60 percent went to Britain, with somewhere between 200 and 300 going to America and about 150 to Australia, where the colonial government required £200 before granting a visa.

The Quakers succeeded by sheer doggedness, trying to bend the home secretary's ear in every instance or to find someone who would sponsor the Jew, so that he would not be a burden on the taxpayer. In May, the Quakers asked one of their number, Corder Catchpool, to go out to Austria to see what could be done. He wanted to talk to the "highest authorities. . . . It appears that efforts for relief are being made difficult, if not deliberately obstructed, and that little can be done until the position is cleared." Catchpool had been in touch with Sir Wyndham Deedes and Norman Bentwich. Sir Robert Vansittart put him on to Sir Ernest Holderness, who gave him an introduction to Thomas Kendrick at the PCO. The Quakers' brief was severely limited. As one official ("HNN"—possibly Alice Nike) wrote on August 27, "I can only help non-Aryans, Mischling [sic] and Confessionslos [sic]. . . . I never take up an entirely Jewish case unless, for instance, a married pair where one of the couple is Aryan."

The other bodies that dealt extensively with Jewish Christians were the Swedish Church and the so-called Aktion Gildemeester. Frank van Gheel-Gildemeester was a fifty-seven-year-old Dutch pastor's son, an idealistic charity worker who wanted to see the Jews settled in the Harrar Province of Ethiopia, where they would have been reunited with Falashas or Ethiopian Jews. He had been in and out of Vienna for years, working for charities and latterly as a prison visitor for Nazis imprisoned in Stein or at the Corporate State's concentration camp in Wöllersdorf. They included Anton Rintelen, the Austrian Nazis' chosen successor to Dollfuss. His charitable work had brought him into contact with leading Nazis, making him an ideal front man for a scheme that would benefit Vienna's Jews. By his own testimony, he had no interest in race or nationality. He was only interested in humanity.

His activities were not confined to Austria. Catchpool said Gildemeester had been responsible for the release of the pacifist Fritz Küster from Buchenwald. If this is true, he was playing a similar game to Catchpool himself, operating a humanitarian trade, seeking favors in return for looking after German nationalists imprisoned abroad—although Catchpool annoyed the Nazis so much they locked him up for a while.

Gildemeester's close links with the Nazis in general, and Göring and Eichmann in particular, led to his being distrusted then and ever since.

His organization smacked of a profitable business, hiding "under the cloak of charity." There is no evidence that Gildemeester profited from it, but there remains a slight whiff of sulphur about him. Somehow Rintelen's son-in-law, Erich Rajakowitsch, managed to work his way into the machinery of the Gildemeester Aktion. Rajakowitsch was an "ambitious Nazi," and his role was probably to make sure that Gildemeester remained in with those in power. Professor D. Cohen of the Dutch Committee for Special Jewish Affairs warned the British Board of Deputies not to trust him. The American Quaker Florence Barrow noted that Gildemeester worked "closely with the Gestapo," extorting rich Jews to give their money to the poor. She wondered "whether Mr Gildemeester was being 'used.'"

He was probably just naive. The Zionist Norman Bentwich called him a "well-meaning but eccentric Quaker." On his visits to Vienna he stayed in a simple room in the Dom Hotel in the Singerstrasse, close to their offices. He had been involved with the Friends during the First World War, when he had lived in Chicago, and it may well have been the American Friends' Service Committee that sent him to Vienna in 1918, when he worked for Herbert Hoover. One woman who worked for him after the Anschluss thought he had been in Vienna during the First World War and had helped bring undernourished children to Holland. Nothing is known about his activities in the twenties and early thirties, but he remained in touch with the Quakers and visited their offices in Berlin in 1938 with a view to cooperation.

Willi Perl was also suspicious of Gildemeester at first, but he came to the conclusion that he "was most likely genuine, otherwise we wouldn't help baptised Jews," who were anathema to Orthodox ones. He came to the conclusion he was "a Christian who was truly concerned for all humans."

The first test cases for what was to become the Gildemeester Aktion were the Kuffner brothers, Moritz and Stephan, owners, among other things, of the huge brewery in Ottakring. Moritz Kuffner was also a director of the Reitler private bank that was liquidated on March 17 by the lawyers Heinrich Gallop and Pollak. The Kuffners had been imprisoned after the Anschluss. Under the scheme, the Kuffners offered to pay out 10 percent of their total fortune to finance the emigration of poorer Jews. They had, of course, to discharge the other taxes too. That meant 25 percent emigration tax, and another 20 percent *Judenvermögensabgabe* (Jewish fortunes forfeit) and any unpaid arrears.

If they were lucky, they could escape with something under half of their money, but that was rarely the case. Once the Kuffners offered to pay over the required sums, they were released and allowed to emigrate. Gildemeester was brought in to be the front man in a scheme that would ultimately bring together between 120 and 180 rich Jews who would hand over similar sums to finance the emigration of poorer Jews. All but one of the rich Jewish families who participated left the Reich safely.

Few banks were interested in acting as trustees for this scheme. They feared that the Nazis would revoke the project and they would lose their money. On May 30, however, Krentschker & Company of Graz agreed to take on the business. They charged 3.5 percent for fortunes over 300,000 RM and 3 percent for anything below. The lawyers demanded another 1 to 1.5 percent. By the time the scheme was scrapped, Krentschker had turned over 25.7 million RM of Jewish assets. Others earned themselves small fortunes out of the misery of the Jews: An SS officer called Fritz Kraus made between 1.7 and 1.8 million RM.

The basis for the Action was the so-called Ha'avara Agreement, which had allowed German Jews to ship their money out to Palestine after 1933. The drawback with Ha'avara was that it only allowed the big fish, while the little ones remained caught in the net. The Gildemeester Aktion set out to let the big fish help the little ones. The elimination of the smaller fry though emigration was exactly what Eichmann had foreseen, and the Gildemeester organization can only have been good news as far as he was concerned. The advantage for the richer Jews who availed themselves of Gildemeester's organization was that it arranged everything for them: passports, visas, preparation for emigration, and so forth.

Another area where the Gildemeester charity could help was in releasing Jews from "protective custody" in a concentration camp. A man might be bought out of Dachau for sixty RM. Gildemeester also provided affidavits for emigration to the United States. Altogether they sold 24,500 questionnaires, and 8,378 Jews received grants amounting to 905,936 RM, not including the children who left on the kindertransports. Of the 2,675 non-Aryan Christians who left Vienna before October 21, all seemed to have been sponsored by Gildemeester's charity. All in all, about 30,000 Jews profited.

Gildemeester's more idealistic vision remained on the drawing board. He wanted to finance 13,000 plots of land in Harrar Province in Ethiopia. To this end he intended to create a Gildemeester Bank in the City of London. Mussolini, on the other hand, showed no interest in having Germany's rejected Jews in his new African Empire. When the Germans brought the subject up, he told them he would not part with so much as a square inch of territory, but thought a Jewish homeland might be established in Russia, Brazil, or the United States.

NOT EVERYONE by any means was sympathetic with the Jewish émigrés. "Some, a few," wrote *Times* correspondent Douglas Reed, "have had themselves baptised; but they remain Jews." He continued:

> In three Central European capitals that I know the baptism of Jews, since the annexation of Austria, has become an industry. The step is taken in all cynicism, as a business proposition, a means of getting into countries that have banned the admission of Jews, a device to tide over the years until the antisemitic wave subsides again. The Jews joke about it among themselves, and the Jews I know, who talk frankly with me because they know that I understand the racket, joke about it with me. One Jew, discussing it with me, told me of an acquaintance who, to his annoyance, found that he had to pass through a period of instruction in the faith he was about to acquire before he received the coveted baptismal certificate, and how he cut short the priest's explanation of the immaculate conception with the words "Schaun S', ich glaube Ihnen sämtliche Sachen" (Look here, I believe everything). This was thought very funny and sent a roar of laughter around the table. In one of the capitals I speak of, several hundred Jews were baptized as Church of England Christians in the summer of 1938, and by a trick they succeeded in pre-dating the baptismal certificates, so that the reason for the conversion should not be too apparent. The convert is usually re-converted to the Hebraic faith when the antisemitic period passes.
>
> These baptized Jews, who have no belief whatever in Christianity, join the community of "non-Aryan Christians" for whom your Church leaders constantly appeal.

Streicher's weekly, *Der Stürmer* ran a cartoon of Jews racing toward a baptismal font—"Only if the Jews might live more Jewish lives."

Reed and Streicher naturally overstate the case. Some Jews had been edging toward Christianity for some time. One example is the Viennese Jew Karl Josef Balner, who converted to Catholicism in May 1938 and was baptized by a priest in Erdberg called Franz Brenner. Balner chose to live the life of a "U-boat," i.e., in hiding like a submarine, rather than emigrate, and during the summer months he inhabited a tomb in the Jewish part of the Central Cemetery. In the winter he was hidden in a monastery by men working for Father Bichlmaier's Pauluswerk charity, which was responsible for Jewish Christians. Balner survived the war. Marriages were also a means of getting out. In 1938 there were advertisements in Prague newspapers offering the services of Christian grooms for Jewish brides. Such gallantry did not come free of charge.

At the end of March, Eichmann convened a meeting of the most important representatives of Zionist bodies who were still at liberty. He told them that he was going to solve the Jewish problem, but he needed obedience and cooperation. Alois Rothenberg was appointed his collaborator to head a twelve-member *Dachverband* (or committee) for Palestine.

MARCH HAD been a good month for Hitler: Everything was going swimmingly. Hitler's plebiscite campaign began with a speech in Königsberg on March 25. He was going to show the outside world that they were the true democrats. Much of his time was spent in Austria. On the 31st, a speech in Frankfurt filled with mystical deism was broadcast over the airwaves. Hitler continued to spice up his language with references to the All Highest: "I believe that it was also God's will that from here a boy was to be sent into the Reich, allowed to grow to manhood, and be raised to become the nation's Führer, that he might lead his homeland into the Reich. There is a divine will, and we are nothing but its tools." Hitler, the Messiah, spoke. Germans remember hearing this speech assembled in the halls of their schools.

This messianic and self-congratulatory tone was too much for the Austrians. The Socialist leader and former chancellor, Karl Renner, let it be known on April 3 that he would vote yes in the plebiscite. There is a suggestion that his decision was horse-trading, and that he wished to arrange the release of leading Socialists. On the other hand, the Austrian Socialists had been in favor of the merger after the First World War. The Anschluss would end the "stray wandering of the Austrian people." He was not alone to break ranks and join his fellow travelers: Ex-President Miklas and Prince Ernst Rüdiger Starhemberg both tested positive.

On April 3, he was in the faithful city of Graz in Styria, where on March 13 60,000 to 70,000 people had formed a parade to celebrate the Anschluss. Graz was close to the border with Yugoslavia, which had received large amounts of Lower Styria in the Versailles settlement. Styrians and Carinthians resented their Slavic neighbors. That very day the Austrian concentration camp at Wöllersdorf, which had been used for Nazis, mysteriously burst into flames. In Berlin, Goebbels gloated: "a shameful blot swept from the horizon."

CHAPTER FOUR

APRIL, MAY, JUNE

B y April, the rights enjoyed by Austria's Jews had reverted to what they were before 1867, when they were first accorded permission to settle in the Austro-Hungarian capital. In 1868 they had also been granted leave to renounce Judaism. This had now been revoked. With each new measure introduced in Vienna, Jews were pushed outside the boundaries of law. The Gestapo chief Huber had made it clear that "unpleasant" Jews and "above all Jews with criminal records" would be arrested and sent to Dachau. Jews older than fifty were not to be sent unless their cases were deemed serious, as they were unlikely to survive the regimen in the camp. The first transport left on March 31 and arrived on the first of the month. It was organized by a Major Herzog, working from a list thought to have been drawn up by a Dr. Hackl, an *Illegale*, an Austrian Nazi who had fled the Corporate State and worked for the Gestapo in Berlin. It contained 151 persons, the majority of them Gentiles who had loomed large in the Corporate State rather than Jews.

After a shower and shave in their prison on the Rossauer Lände, the 151 passengers were transferred to five Black Marias. At the West Station there was a cry of "Get out, you dogs!" Guards beat them viciously with rifle butts, forcing them into the compartments of the train. Some were counseled by a more compassionate policeman: "Take off your spectacles, look after your eyes."

The train left at around midnight. The brutality was relentless. One man ran onto a guard's bayonet to put an end to it. From Dachau Railway Station they were taken in cars to the camp. They arrived in the late morning and were received by the commandant oozing mockery and disdain, a foretaste of what some would endure for the next seven years. They were led to the showers again and issued striped uniforms. Their heads were shaved. When this was over, other compassionate prisoners appeared with little presents of sausage, jam, or butter—treasures extracted from their lockers. The Austrians proved a great attraction to the other prisoners, some of whom had been there since March 1933.

Austrians formed over half of the 18,695 men admitted to Dachau in 1938. They were kept apart from the others and dismissed by the guards as "Lazy, Jew-infested, priest-ridden coffeehouse scum." At one point in the spring of 1938, they were put to work building a perimeter road around the camp: "Amongst them were two ambassadors, three ministers, a state secretary, a senior judge, a state prosecutor, the mayor of Vienna, a general, a colonel and three majors, two university professors, some senior police officers, two prominent Viennese lawyers and a number of well-known journalists and authors." The extent of the Nazi purge was noticed by one Berliner in the camp, who acknowledged the impressive rank of Dachau's new intake, saying, "Looking at you one would almost be ashamed to be free."

There were several leaders of the Fatherland Front, such as the Corporate State's counterpart to Goebbels, Colonel Walter Adam, as well as Richard Alexander and Hans von Becker; other political grandees included propaganda man and later vice chancellor of the Second Republic, Fritz Bock; Eduard Ludwig, the minister for the press, responsible for dealing with foreign journalists; Dr. Viktor Matejka, who had run the cultural wing of the Christian trades union movement before converting to Communism in Dachau; Ludwig Draxler, the former minister of finance; the later chancellors Leopold Figl and Alfons Gorbach; the mayor of Vienna, Richard Schmitz; and the future governor of Lower Austria, Josef Reither. There was Johann Staud, who ran the Corporate State's trades unions (who died in Flossenbürg in 1939), and General Baron Karl Werkmann, the last secretary to the Emperor Charles. Baron Theodor Hornbostl was the permanent undersecretary at the Austrian foreign office who had tried to drum up support from abroad at the moment the Nazis were gathering at the frontier.

Several people were there because of their earlier role in the persecution and suppression of National Socialism: the later minister of justice, Josef Gerö, who as public prosecutor had imprisoned Nazis at Wöllersdorf; Dr. Robert Hecht was the secretary of state in the Ministry of Justice who had found the legal apparatus needed to end democracy and ban the Nazis. He was also a Jew and committed suicide in Dachau. Dr. Eduard Streitmann, who had been an anti-Nazi police commissioner, was sent to Dachau with his son. There was the head of security in Styria, Colonel Franz Zelburg; the police general Rudolf Manda; Dr. Alois Osio, who had been head of the high court and naturally handed down impressive sentences to Nazis; and Major Baron Emmanuel Stillfried, who had been the camp commandant at the Austrian concentration camp at Wöllersdorf.

There were also the Socialists Robert Danneberg and Major Alexander von Eifler, chief of staff of the Republican Schutzbund. The highest-ranking Socialist caught by the Nazis, Danneberg had tried to flee on the night train to Prague on March 11, but was one of the unlucky ones who were packed off back to Vienna. A Jew, he was killed in Auschwitz in 1942. The Socialist leaders Otto Bauer and Karl Seitz got away, but Bauer died in Paris in July. There was also the political informer Theodor Krisshaber and a Communist called Josef Händler who had been in and out of Wöllersdorf for four years and had little fear of Dachau. They joined General Archduke Josef Ferdinand of Habsburg-Lothringen and the two Hohenberg brothers, Max and Ernst, the children of the Archduke Francis Ferdinand, who had made no secret of their revulsion toward Hitler and who reached Dachau the day before.

There was a total of sixty full Jews among the 151 prisoners, including Friedmann, Ehrlich, and Stricker from the IKG; four members of the Schiffmann family, whose premises had been so rigorously plundered on March 11; and Willy Kurtz, who had been prominent in street combats between the Fatherland Front and the Nazis. The Nazis took particular pleasure in beating him now that he could not hit back. His size made him dangerously noticeable, as did his clothes: his trousers reached to his calves, while his tunic could only be buttoned at the top. He was finished off in Auschwitz in 1942.

Six of the eight Burstyn brothers were there, who owned a well-known bathhouse as well as the Viennese taxis; Dr. Wilhelm Blitz, a millionaire who was big in the Pan-German movement; Ludwig Klausner, who ran the Delka chain of shoe shops; the hatter Robert Korff; and the spice-merchant Johann Kotanyi (he hanged himself in the camp). Pictures of their "healthy" life in Dachau were shown in *Völkische Beobachter* to coincide with the opening of the Eternal Jew exhibition in August. What the "elite" thought of the inclusion of the Jews has not come down to us, but within the camp, we are assured, there was no antisemitism. Others dispute this and say the criminal "Greens" and the antisocial "Blacks" were as antisemitic as the SS.

The Socialist bookseller Josef Kende joined newspaper magnates such as Alexander Geller, Ernst Buchbinder, and Paul Kolisch; and journalists like Bruno Heilig, Markus Siegelberg, Bela Felsenburg, Ernst Colbert, Rudolf Kalmar, and Maximilian Reich. Raoul Auernheimer was the vice president of Austrian PEN, and a *Mischling*. Among the other Jews who had the honor of being among the first to go to Dachau was Franz Lehár's librettist Fritz Löhner-Beda, the author of the lyrics for much of Hitler's favorite music. In Buchenwald he wrote the camp song that the miserable prisoners had to sing during their travails. It was set to music by another unfortunate victim who arrived on a later transport: the violin virtuoso Hermann Leopoldi. Lehár could not intercede for him with Hitler, as he was protecting his own Jewish wife. Löhner-Beda was beaten to death in Auschwitz in 1942.

There was also one Nazi on that first transport: the Burgenland peasant Paul Hutfless. He had betrayed secrets to the Fatherland Front. Gestapo chief Huber's concern for elderly or infirm Jews was a sham. Bruno Heilig's book, *Men Crucified*, first published in 1941, makes it abundantly clear what they faced. Heilig was arrested on March 15 and had been locked up in four prisons before the day came to ship him to Dachau. His book is a chilling record of brutality. The newspaper magnate Kolisch weighed three hundred pounds when he came to Dachau and was the butt of much cruelty. By the time he reached Buchenwald his weight had halved. They also singled out the Hohenberg brothers, whose work involved emptying the latrines. Prince Ernst remained in the camp until 1943.

A FEW weeks after the first Austrian transport, the camp received a visit from Heinrich Himmler. He paid particular attention to the Austrians, whom he endeavored to humiliate. "You know that from now on you are in protective custody, that means I shall accord you my most special protection." He paused so that his retinue might voice their appreciation for his joke. He told the prisoners that they fell into four categories: professional criminals—they were the nicest; political prisoners—who were much more dangerous and would be given less protection; Jews—who belonged to the scum of humankind; the worst, however, were the Communists. To Stillfried of Wöllersdorf he said, "So you see what it is like!" Stillfried answered back, "Herr Reichsführer, I would truly love to say that we are treated here like your people were in Wöllersdorf!" The others expected a reprisal, but none was forthcoming. Stillfried survived.

At Wöllersdorf political prisoners had been detained without trial, but the Austrian camp was not to be compared with Dachau, unless you accepted Eric Gedye's quip: "There was one thing in common between Wöllersdorf and Dachau. The Nazis seemed thoroughly to enjoy both."

The work was literally backbreaking. Any answering back was rewarded with horsewhipping, kicks, and beatings. The Jews were separated from the Aryans and placed in their own block. Yet despite the grim existence led by the prisoners, there was a semblance of cultural life in Dachau. Sunday afternoons were free. Viktor Matejka put on a play written by Rudolf Kalmar strewn with oblique references to Hitler, which remained undetected by the guards. Grünbaum continued to perform with Paul Morgan and Hermann Leopoldi, and the Berliner dancer Kurt Fuss joined in. Jura Soyfer wrote a poem, the "Dachauerlied" (song of Dachau).

The rest of the time the prisoners were subjected not only to the whim of the guards but also to the commandant's vicious dog and chimpanzee. In the middle of the brutality, there were flashes of mercy on the part of the guards, although these were few and far between.

The transports to Dachau aroused international condemnation, particularly in Britain. This motivated State Secretary Weizsäcker at the Wilhelmstrasse to seek an interview with Heydrich on July 5, 1938. Heydrich admitted to having 3,900 Austrians in "protective custody." Weizsäcker sought to have all those released against whom no charges had been preferred. It transpired that most of the middle-class prisoners were indeed released before war broke out. Jews were let out if they could show that they had an entry visa for another country. The Communists were often left to rot in the camps until the end of the war.

Until the Jews arrived that April, Germany's concentration camps had been filled with Gentiles, chiefly political prisoners and habitual criminals. Certain inmates had caught the attention of Catchpool, particularly Fritz Küster of the Friedensgesellschaft (Peace Society); Hans Litten, a half-Jewish solicitor; the well-known social democrats Ernst Heilmann, Carlo Mierendorff and Kurt Schumacher; as well as the Communist Theodor Neubauer. Like Gildemeester, Catchpool had been cleverly working his way into the Nazi regime's good books by visiting German political prisoners in captivity in Lithuania and Czechoslovakia. There had been eighty in Lithuania, and there were still sixteen serving long sentences at the beginning of 1938. In February that year he estimated the German prison population to be between 110,000 and 120,000, "of these about a quarter are political cases, mostly undergoing long sentences." Of course this did not include those in concentration camps, who had been neither tried nor sentenced.

There was an expansion in the number of categories of prisoners eligible for "protective custody" in 1938. That was going to mean more concentration camps, like Mauthausen, and the enlargement of existing ones such as Buchenwald on the Ettersberg above Weimar, which had opened its gates in 1937. In the course of 1938, the population of Dachau tripled. Between April 21 and 30, the Gestapo rounded up around 2,000 "work-shy" (men deemed to be resistant to employment) and took them to camps. In the summer Heydrich turned his attention to the "antisocial." Each criminal department was to locate around two hundred gypsies, tramps, beggars, pimps, violent criminals, and Jews with criminal tendencies. The arrests started on June 13, with the police working their way through railway stations and dosshouses—twenty-five years earlier, they might have arrested their own Führer. The bag totaled over 10,000. They were taken to a new generation of camps: Flossenbürg, Mauthausen, and Neuengamme, located close to quarries. The SS needed labor for their own stone business.

The arrival of "work-shy" and antisocial elements altered the social structure, swamping the Communists and Socialists who had previously been the mainstay of Sachsenhausen. They wore black triangles, as opposed to green for criminals and red for political prisoners. Although some ascended to the level of the green aristocracy among the prisoners, others fell victim to the terrible physical strain imposed by the camps, perishing in the mud or crushed to death in the quarries.

———

The Jews—the assimilated Jews in particular—had nowhere to go. With the Anschluss, would-be Austrian immigrants to the United States were added into the tally from Germany, fixed at a little over 27,000 a year; Canada and Australia did not want their wide-open spaces polluted by Jews.

SINCE THE Olympics in 1936, Berlin Jews had enjoyed a holiday from persecution, but after the Anschluss the authorities began to get rough. As the son of an Austrian Jew, Gerhard Beck and his family were obliged to quit their spacious flat in Weissensee and move into the Scheunen-viertel, the nearest thing Berlin had to a ghetto. The only hope of escape now was to join the endless lines that radiated from the offices of the Jüdischer Hilfsverein and enquire into the possibilities of emigration. Beck's family soon came to the conclusion that escape was only possible if you were rich or a "Zionist zealot." Peter Fröhlich, who would later change his name and achieve fame as the cultural historian Peter Gay, was thrown out of his *Gymnasium* or grammar school in Berlin-Wilmersdorf. With a little flourish of Prussian decency, the boys were issued with proper leaving certificates, which recorded—fallaciously—that they had left to take up a profession. In July Fröhlich's father had been fired from his job. The family then set to work applying for visas. That meant paying calls on consulates to pick up forms, typing out applications, and applying for residence.

The harassed Jews were prey to rumors. At the beginning of the month a ripple of optimism went through the community. It appeared that Australia was going to open its gates to the Jews and issue 6,000 additional visas. The rumor created siege conditions outside the British consulate in Vienna. Eventually the Australian Prime Minister Lyon released a clarification that Jews would only be admitted under the normal constraints of emigration. Two weeks later Miss Stamper at the Passport Office was forced to issue a leaflet to explain the separate policies on emigration of the various British colonies and dominions—Cyprus, Palestine, and

Australia in particular. It warned against bogus organizations that claimed to be able to help and had "sprung up like mushrooms, enriching themselves from Jewish misery." At the consulate Gainer, Consul J. W. Taylor, and Kendrick (responsible for Palestine) all handled the Jews with understanding and sympathy in spite of the outrages going on outside their doors. On one occasion the SA forced the Jews in the lines to wash cars. The consul general issued a formal protest, after which they were allowed to line up in the "neutral" courtyard.

Despite the formal closure of the Swiss borders with Austria on March 12, 1938, 3,000 Austrian Jews had managed to make it across the border. *Der Stürmer* ran a particularly pungent caricature showing a "Kosher snack": Jews crammed into a Swiss sardine tin. Others crossed the border into Italy and obtained visas for Switzerland there until this loophole too was closed in August. Jews were still managing to cross the frontiers into Czechoslovakia, Hungary, Yugoslavia, France, Holland, Luxembourg, and Belgium, even if the only *legal* form of emigration was Eichmann's Zionist solution.

For Eichmann, Jews remaining in Europe formed *Greuelzentralen*, or centers of atrocity. He wanted an end to assimilation; Germany had no foreign political interests in Palestine, and he thought that the Jews should move there without delay. The quickest method was to obtain a tourist visa to Palestine and then sit it out. Zionist organizations could effect this in Palestine itself. The British government was under fire: Despite the rigidity of official policy, there was an elasticity provided by the consular officials, who took pity on individual cases. This meant that something under 80,000 central European Jews did find a refuge in the Mandate.

———

On the 10th of April a plebiscite was held throughout the Reich so that Germans on both sides of the river Inn would be able to voice their approbation for the Anschluss. Hitler concentrated his campaign on Austria in the days immediately before the poll. At the same time Cardinal Innitzer traveled to Rome for a private interview with the pope. The Supreme Pontiff was displeased with the head of the Austrian church. The secretary of state, Eugenio Pacelli—the future Pius XII—reprimanded Innitzer for the "unfavourable impression" he had made by signing the bishops' letter condoning the Anschluss. On April 6, *Osservatore Romano* published an explanation: The pope did not approve of anything that went against the laws of God, or the freedom and rights of the Catholic Church. A particular sticking point was the Nazi's assault on youth organizations. The Roman declaration had naturally angered Hitler. For the time being, however, he forbore from punishing the Austrian church until the results of the plebiscite had come in.

Hitler's campaign ended in Vienna on the 9th. He addressed hundreds of thousands of his faithful from the Rathaus. His language was steeped in piety, presumably as a sop to the Catholic Viennese. When he spoke to them a second time that day in the Northwest Station, Goebbels said it was "like Mass . . . at the end, it resembled a prayer." Even Goebbels enjoyed cult status. When Hitler appeared on the balcony of the Imperial, they called for him too: "*Lieber Führer, ach ich bitt', bring doch unseren Doktor mit*" ("Please our Führer, oh we pray / Let the doctor have his say!"). Hitler and his propaganda minister traveled back to Berlin on the train on the 10th. Over breakfast they discussed plans. "The Führer wants to drive the Jews completely out of Germany, to Madagascar or whatever . . . a people smitten by God. Prague has also written them off." From the Jews they progressed to the princes: "They are worthless and must never be allowed back." They were satisfied that the Hohenbergs were out of the way, but the Habsburgs were the worst. "Get rid of this rubbish." Hitler and Goebbels had also placed the dispossession of the Austrian nobility high up on their agenda.

The result of the poll on the 10th was a 99.08 percent *Ja* for the Führer. In Austria there were just 11,929 nos. Goebbels feigned joyful surprise: "Germany has conquered a whole country with the ballot-slip." The plebiscite did, however, reflect the Führer's popularity. It showed that Hitler was exceedingly successful in Germany at the time, and it marked the high watermark of his stature in the land of his birth. The vote had obviously been manipulated and the electorate cowed into saying *Ja*, as proven by the near unanimous assent from Dachau concentration camp. But Hitler's aims had struck a chord with national German aspirations, and for the time being it was bloodless. The plebiscite had been marginally fairer than that proposed by Schuschnigg: All Germans and Austrians over the age of twenty were eligible to vote, with the exception of Jews, criminals, and the many thousands of suspects in Hitler's jails and camps. In Vienna some 300,000 voters had been deducted from the roll in this way. Nevertheless, Hitler's appeal for the Austrians was not to last. The appropriation of so much of Austria's wealth by the Reich and by Reich Germans, escalating prices, the failure to appoint Austrian Nazis to high office, the brutal treatment of the Church and its priests, the dastardly suppression of the old elite, and a supercilious attitude the Austrians liked to associate with the dreaded "Piefke" or Prussian all contrived to make the honeymoon a short one.

The ballot was not exactly secret. A big circle contained the word *Ja*, a smaller one *Nein*, and the voter's name and address were printed on the back. Despite the pressure to conform, there were dissenters, like Friedrich Reck-Malleczewen: "I can now prove that the plebiscite to legitimise Hitler's takeover of Austria was falsified in the crudest possible way. Together with the other four adults of my house, I naturally voted 'No.' In addition, I know of at least twenty other reliable people in the town who did the same. Nevertheless, according to the official results, the town unanimously and without a single dissenting voice 'approved the actions of the Führer.'"

THE EAST Prussian writer Ernst Wiechert was arrested soon after the election and taken to a Gestapo prison to be interrogated. In the car leaving his home one of the secret policemen asked him if he had cast his vote. They knew that he had not. "Half an hour after the closing of the ballots they were careful to beat anyone who had written 'No' half dead." One of the very few who made his decision not to vote public was Bishop Sproll of Württemberg. It was not that he disapproved the merger; it was that he disliked the regime and did not wish to congratulate the Nazis. This led to a campaign against him by Gauleiter Murr that ended up with Sproll being banished from his diocese, after Nazi thugs wrecked his residence. Goebbels approved these "spontaneous" demonstrations: "The Bishop of Rottenburg did not vote. Now the people have erupted and are rioting in front of his palace. He is looking for protection, so now the state is good for something at least. He can protect himself. I shall not lift a finger." Sproll's eviction established a precedent that would later be used in the cases of Cardinal Innitzer in Vienna and Cardinal Faulhaber in Munich.

THE RAPE of Austria set its people at odds with their new masters. The "Prussian" Reck-Malleczewen was in Salzburg soon after the Anschluss and was able to witness the sort of scene that would put the Austrians off their new friends from the north: "These Berlin potato-faces fill the streets, together with their full-bosomed females. Thanks to the rate of exchange they are able to make off with everything for a song, including goods that are no longer available in Germany and the . . . shelves are empty. They are behaving like a horde of servants whose masters are away, who have found the keys to the wine cellars and are now having an orgy with their women." Some Germans mopped up the flood of Austrian Jewish property. One of these was Papen, who was destined for the embassy in Istanbul. He acquired the country place of the Eggers, industrialists in Styria. Ribbentrop absorbed Schloss Fuschl and added to his burgeoning collection. The former owner, von Remnitz, was murdered in Dachau.

On the same day as the poll, the new government in the "Ostmark" introduced the *Reichsfluchtsteuer*. It had actually been introduced in Germany on January 31, 1931, before Hitler came to power: Any person (not just Jews) leaving the country had to pay the tax if they had an income of 20,000 RM (30,000 Austrian schillings) in any year since 1931, or if they possessed a fortune of 50,000 RM (75,000 Austrian schillings) at the time of applying to leave. It is a measure of the success of the "Viennese model" that state income from the emigration tax more than quadrupled in 1938, from 81,354,000 RM to 342,621,000 RM. In 1939 it fell by a third to 216,189,000. Smuggling was rife, particularly of jewelry, which was small and potentially of great value.

On April 13, as Poland and Lithuania moved to the brink of war over Memel again, a law was passed requiring Austrian tradesmen to find Aryan owners for their businesses before October 10. The Nazis had coined a new verb to dignify this particular process of robbery: *arisieren*. Until their sale, Jewish businesses were to be placed in the hands of commissioners, who tended to be trusted Party members. These temporary owners often bled the businesses white before depositing a lifeless carcass on the market for sale. After the takeover of Jewish businesses, the only Jews left working were a very few doctors who could treat Jews only and a similar number of lawyers who were allowed to act as consultants to Jewish clients. About 1,500 Jews were retained in industry, where there was a shortage of labor.

Between 3,000 and 4,000 were being retrained, subject to the payment of certain taxes. Many elected to learn agriculture with a view to getting to Palestine. Artists and writers saw their publishers refuse to pay out royalties, even when those came in from abroad. Such was the case of Felix Salten, the author of *Bambi*, whose publishers were now able to absorb a huge income from his foreign sales. Another ripe plum was the royalty income of the film score composer Erich Wolfgang Korngold.

At first some thought they would be able to ride out the storm. The dentist Hugo Schneider felt that now that Jews could no longer go to Aryan dentists, his business would expand. Within three months, however, his hopes were shattered by the appearance of a man in SA uniform at his door. He announced that he was also a dentist, and half the practice now belonged to him.

There were 26,236 Jewish businesses in Austria—one for every 270 Austrians. This was a far greater concentration than in the old Reich, where the figure was one to every 1,693 Germans. The Aryan Austrians rushed to take over the firms. There were four times as many applications as there were businesses to acquire. Some Austrians, however, were still not keen on the legal route; parents encouraged their children to pilfer from defenseless Jews. Apartments were stolen under the noses of their owners by maids with the assistance of their lovers. The victims could not go to the police. The only way to protect themselves was to offer the maids presents on their departure. Some companies were robbed over and over again, as fleets of trucks took away the goods.

There was a particularly high concentration of Jews in certain professions. One in seven of Austria's pharmacies was Jewish owned, and in Vienna the figure was more than a third. The normal sale price for a business of this sort was two to two and a half times the yearly income. Now the official sales price was one tenth of the pre-1938 value. The 25 percent *Reichsfluchtsteuer* had to be subtracted from this. There was no recourse to the courts; if a Jew complained, he was put in prison.

Such measures did not benefit the Austrian economy. The dismissal of the Jewish textile workers, for example, caused a slump in the clothing industry, as there were no skilled workers to take their place. The interpretation of the law was draconian, especially in a city like Vienna, where many people had a dash of Jewish blood. The illegitimate children of Jews,

HAPPY FAMILIES

Hitler admires Edda Göring, a crown princess for the Third Reich.

Onkel Adolf with
Joseph, Magda,
and three younger
members of the
Goebbels clan.

PALACES

(*above*) The Führerbau in Munich, completed in 1938. It was to be the scene of the Munich Conference in September.

(*left*) The old Chancellery in Berlin was pulled down to accommodate Speer's magnificent new building, which opened its doors at the end of the year.

(*below*) Hitler's flat on the second floor of the Prinzregentenplatz in Munich. It is now a police station.

ANSCHLUSS

(*top*) In Salzburg the Wehrmacht is received with enthusiasm.

(*above*) Not everyone was so happy: Jews queue for visas outside the Polish consulate in Vienna.

(*left*) In the former Austrian capital the shops were rapidly "Aryanized."

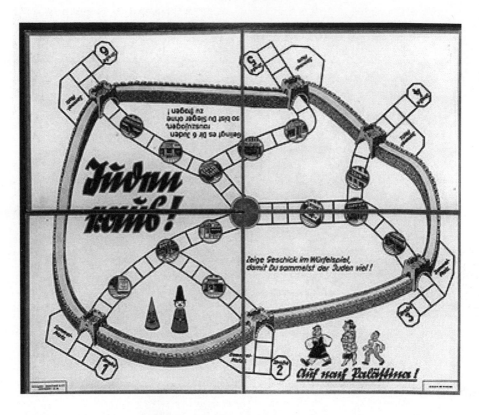

Juden Raus ("Jews Out") was a popular board game. To win, the player had to round up six Jews from their shops and send them to Palestine.

THE ANGLICAN CHURCH AND
THE VIENNESE JEWS

(*top left*) Basil Staunton Batty, Bishop of Fulham, was responsible for the Anglican parishes of northern Europe. He secretly encouraged priests to help Jews.

(*top right*) The Reverend Hugh Grimes, chaplain in Vienna.

(*above*) The British Embassy chapel in Vienna, where 1,825 Jews converted to Anglicanism in the summer of 1938.

HOMMES FATALS

(*above left*) Herschel Grynszpan, whose attack on the diplomat Ernst vom Rath on November 7 formed the pretext for the pogrom of November 9—10.

(*above right*) On the left, Blomberg, Minister of War, whose marriage to a former prostitute provoked a national crisis in January. On the right, Fritsch. The army leader was the victim of trumped-up charges of homosexuality.

(*right*) Max Schmeling, German prizefighter who failed to clinch the world heavyweight title that year.

KINDERTRANSPORTE

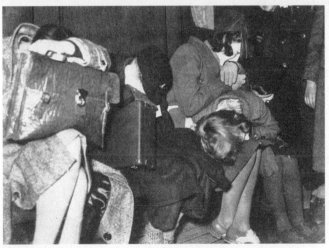

(top) Members of *Jugendaliya* (Jewish teenagers) leaving the Anhalt Station in Berlin.

(*above*) Jewish children prepare for a new life, leaving their parents behind.

(*left*) The half-Jewish dramatist Carl Zuckmayer escaped by the skin of his teeth in March.

CONCENTRATION CAMPS

(*above*) Goethe's oak at Buchenwald —a photograph taken by a French inmate in 1944. The tree was a source of solace for the prisoners.

(*left*) Political prisoners in Dachau. In 1938 Austria's governing elite were despatched to the camp.

even *Mischlinge* who had only one Jewish grandparent but who could produce no baptismal certificate, forfeited their rights. If one of these had 25 percent of the company, or even held a seat on the board, the company was defined as Jewish.

As the authorities removed the Jews from the food chain, the Viennese began to feel the loss. The central market in the Naschmarkt emptied out. The corn trade was 80 percent Jewish, as well as 31 percent of the leading wine companies. At the time of the harvest that year, a cooperative had to be created to take the place of the old trade. The Hungarians complained that their firms were being closed down too and made a diplomatic protest. When foreign trade began to suffer, Göring started to worry. On October 29, he told the Viennese authorities to slow down.

———

Hitler turned forty-nine on Wednesday, April 20. His birthday was marked by the usual military parades and a laudation from Göring as well as a special gift from Goebbels—a collection of recordings of his speeches on Austria. Two weeks before, Hitler Youth leader Baldur von Schirach had decreed the Führer's birthplace, Braunau, to be a place of pilgrimage for young Germans.

Since the death of Paul Ludwig Troost, Albert Speer had become the Führer's favorite architect. As a present for Hitler's birthday he was able to bring the plans for the first part of Berlin's intended great axis, four miles long and flanked by four hundred street lamps. It was to house the principal ministries and part of a crossing of streets that would stretch thirty miles to the east and west and twenty-five to the north and south. Some of the designs—the great dome and the triumphal arch—had been sycophantically worked out from drawings supplied by the Führer himself. For technical reasons, Hitler was of two minds about Berlin as a capital. The city was built on sand, and there was a high water table, requiring the new Chancellery to be constructed on a concrete raft. Hitler had previously wanted to shift the capital to Lake Muritz. On the 24th his ministers had the chance to look over Speer's building, which was already impressively grandiose.

On the evening of Hitler's birthday there was a command performance of *Die Meistersinger* conducted by Wilhelm Furtwängler. The Third Reich also celebrated by issuing a warrant for the arrest of Archduke Otto von Habsburg for high treason, while *Der Stürmer* revealed that the first Habsburg had actually been a Jew.

After the festivities, Hitler asked Keitel to adapt the plans for Operation Green, a preemptive strike against Czechoslovakia. Keitel was given the brief to study the Czech system of fortifications. The original blueprint had been drawn up to deal with the eventuality of a Soviet attack on Germany, using their Czech ally as a springboard. Hitler told Keitel there was to be a big opening in the east. The attack had to succeed in four days— the time the French needed to mobilize and come to their ally's aid.

The German foreign office had been sponsoring ethnic German resistance within Czechoslovakia for the past four years. Now with Ribbentrop in power in the Wilhelmstrasse, there was an even greater desire to see the Czechs embarrassed by the complaints of the Sudetenländer. On this subject, Göring was not the prime mover; he was one of the last to be won round to a Czech adventure. After all, he had given the ambassador, Mastny, his word that Germany would not attack. He pointed out that the defensive West Wall was not ready. It would be the answer to the French Maginot Line, designed to keep the French out if they chose that moment to honor their commitments to the Little Entente. Nevertheless, Hitler convinced him. On April 23 Göring was secretly named Hitler's successor.

In Karlsbad on April 24, the Sudeten leader Henlein outlined his new eight-point program. The Karlsbad Program called for autonomy for the German regions and German-speaking regiments in the Czech Army. On April 28 Goebbels noted with interest that Prague was looking for security from London and Paris, and that Chamberlain did not appear keen. The British put pressure on Czech President Beneš to accommodate the Sudetenländer, even as it became clear that by honoring Henlein's requests, he would have destroyed his own state.

———

In the days leading up to Passover, on April 23 to 26, the spotlight fell on Berlin's Jews. Their movement was to be curtailed: They were to have one swimming pool and a few restaurants and cinemas but otherwise, Goebbels wrote, "access forbidden. We are going to take away Berlin's character as a Jewish paradise. . . . The Führer wants to drive them out gradually. He is going to negotiate with the Poles and the Romanians. The best place for them would be Madagascar." Göring too was turning on the heat in his fight against Jewish capital. "It won't be long before we floor them," he wrote.

On the weekend of April 25 and 26, prominent Jews were subjected to unspeakable acts of public degradation in the Prater, a park in Vienna. Kaltenbrunner had made attempts to rein in the SA but with little success. Near the Reichsbrücke over the Danube, Jews were forced to spit in one another's faces. One who refused died in a concentration camp soon after. In the Taborstrasse in the heavily Jewish Second District, orthodox Jewesses were obliged to remove their wigs and form a parade for the amusement of the Nazi thugs. Jews were strapped into the giant Ferris wheel and spun around at top speed. Jews were forced to run around with their hands up. Others were stripped and beaten by SA men. They had their beards shaved off and were obliged to lick human excrement. The sixty-six-year-old chief rabbi of Vienna was beaten up. On the 26th and 27th twenty-eight Jews committed suicide, including five members of the same family. The Jewish General Sommer appeared on the street in uniform and was made to wash the pavement. In the Aryan Johann-Strauss Café, opposite Gestapo HQ on the Morzinplatz, Jewish regulars were protected by the owner. When the SA came to make the customers clean the streets, the proprietor replied "over my dead body." The café acted as a welfare center.

The violence was followed by a new edict from the Ministry of the Interior: Jews and Jewish women married to Aryans had to reveal their fortunes of 5,000 RM or above by June 30, whether in the Reich or abroad. In Austria the fortunes of a quarter of the Jews accounted for a sum of 2 billion marks. At the same time, the ministry decreed that its approval was required for all transfers of businesses from Jews to Aryans. The British consul-general Gainer noted bitterly, "It would almost seem as if the manner of their going, whether by the process of emigration to other countries, or by starvation in their own, was of little consequence to those in authority."

The Zionist Leo Lauterbach wrote to the British Central Bureau for the Settlement of German Jews on April 27. Since the closing of the IKG, the process of emigration had come to a standstill. He had observed in Vienna that the authorities were "bent upon an early evacuation of Austria by the Jews," but this couldn't happen without the reopening of Jewish emigration organizations. According to Lauterbach the message had gone home and was voiced in the lines outside the British consulate. He was concerned that the maximum number should reach Palestine and that there were funds to help them.

Lauterbach arrived in Vienna with the Christian Zionist Brigadier-General Sir Wyndham Deedes on April 18. Deedes was representing the Council for German Jewry and came with promises of financial support for those wishing to travel to Palestine. The two left again on the 21st and proceeded to Berlin, where they stayed from April 22 to 24. Sir Wyndham was equipped with letters of introduction to the appropriate bodies—the Auswärtiges Amt or Foreign Office in Berlin and its Viennese branch. The message Deedes transmitted to German official bodies was that it was important to reopen the offices of the Jewish congregation as quickly as possible so that organized emigration could proceed. They wanted the Jewish leaders to be released from Dachau to this end. The financial costs could not be entirely borne by foreign institutions, and it was therefore necessary that the IKG raise money to fund emigration. The wild seizure of Jewish property would not help in the long run.

Deedes and Lauterbach met Gainer, Taylor, and Passport Control Officer Kendrick, as well as the American chargé d'affaires, John Wiley. Deedes paid similar calls in Berlin, as well as visiting officers of the German army, Quakers, and "non-Jewish non-Aryans." In Vienna they were fobbed off with minor officials from the foreign office and the emigration office. Attempts to see the governor, Seyss-Inquart, or members of the Gestapo came to nothing. They were able to visit the mayor, Hermann Neubacher, who expressed the desire to see emigration proceed in an orderly and humane manner. In Berlin they had a sympathetic meeting with Freiherr von Marschall at the Auswärtiges Amt, but he admitted to being powerless. He directed them to Himmler, who was not available. They saw some Gestapo officials, including Dr. Leo Lange, who was on his way to see Eichmann. He informed them that the problem of the Austrian Jews was being dealt with in Vienna. They did not receive the impression that the policy had been fully decided. Their meetings hardly inspired them with hope.

According to the system in force at that time, visas were only issued on a temporary basis. There was also the problem of finding transit visas. Switzerland and France were generally willing to grant these. Italy needed proof of baptism, which led at least one Jewish family to visit Hugh Grimes at the Anglican chaplaincy. Lorli Rudov née Perger, then age ten, remembered him "totally unruffled . . . surrounded by a crowd of Jewish people. . . . He was taking an enormous risk in offering help." Like many other Jewish families, theory was stymied by practice: The Pergers needed to sell their house and pay the *Reichsfluchtsteuer*. By the time they had done so, the Italian window had closed.

For many, business connections proved useful. That way money could be transferred without taxation by Nazi authorities. Connections could also yield employment once the refugee entered Britain. Women could generally enter the country by agreeing to go into domestic service. A note in the files at Friends' House asks whether the dentist Dr. Edith Mahler is "capable of doing housework." "We are trying to get her a permit, but have failed once." The equivalent for men was to enter full-time education. A remarkable number of Central European Jews, for example, applied to enter the Royal Agricultural College in Cirencester—one can only imagine because its entrance requirements were relatively undemanding. Zionist organizations also set much store by farming, and there was even a small cooperation with the Gestapo in Austria, which ran a farm where non-Aryans trained Jews. Many went because it was seen as a means of leaving the country early. The baptismal certificate *might* work, but it was no guarantee; an Anglican conversion was of more interest for someone hoping to go to Britain or the Dominions.

The facts don't always bear this out, however. The British Empire let in a smattering of Jews: Southern Rhodesia was taking 50 a month by May 1939; Kenya admitted about 650 but demanded a valid reentry visa to Germany as a precondition of acceptance, something the Germans were not prepared to consider; Mauritius took 1,250, Cyprus 744, Jamaica 500, British Guiana 130, Hong Kong 42, Malta 18, British Honduras 12, Ceylon 6, and Aden, North Borneo, and Grenada 5 apiece; Fiji, Tanganyika, Barbados, Leeward Islands, and Uganda 2 each; and Sierra Leone 1. St. Helena allowed a solitary dentist. The Dominions were all different: Australia admitted 10,000 "in spite of the government's best efforts"; South

Africa took virtually none after passing the Aliens' Act of 1937; New Zealand took 1,100, including Karl Popper, who mentions a helpful man at the New Zealand High Commission in London.

Many are now skeptical of the use of such conversions. One of these was the writer George Clare, who escaped from Vienna via Berlin and ended up in Ireland before joining the British Army. The problem he, like so many others, encountered was how to get to his chosen destination while lacking the necessary transit visas. For some, the English Channel was an insurmountable obstacle: "You would have got on the back of a crocodile if it was crossing the Channel."

As April blossomed into May, Salzburg enjoyed a copycat performance of the 1933 book burning in Berlin. Special attention was given to the writings of Austrian Jews: Stefan Zweig, Arthur Schnitzler, Emil Ludwig, and Franz Werfel. In the first week of May, Jews were banished from the cattle and meat markets, which had been a prominent area of activity in the past. Later that month Jews were excluded from the press and the arts. The First of May was the National Labor Day. Even though it was grey and wet, the flag-waving, marching columns and Arcadians on the village green went ahead as planned, combining tradition and the Party. The highlight was a gathering of 150,000 girls and boys at the Olympia Stadium in Berlin. At the Staatsoper on Unter den Linden, Goebbels awarded the cultural prizes for the year. Leni Riefenstahl was honored for her *Olympia* film. Later there were speeches in the Lustgarten nearby: Hitler, Ley, and Goebbels. For those who had toadied to the Germans, an "Austria Medal" was to be struck for services to the Anschluss.

HITLER MADE his first visit to Rome on May 2. He was treated to a state visit in return for the favor granted to Mussolini in Berlin the year before. The Duce declared a public holiday. It was a huge jamboree with three special trains filled with five hundred officials worthy to accompany the Führer, together with their wives. The wags called it "The Invasion of Italy."

The diplomats were all got up in their "admiral's uniform," a costume dreamed up by Frau von Ribbentrop and the Nazi theatre designer Benno von Arendt, replacing the morning dress used in the past. Spitzy had to model the new outfit, which came in various prototypes ranging from one of Lützow's riflemen from the Wars of Liberation to a Prussian musketeer or a hotel porter. The final version caused Göring to needle Ribbentrop, saying, "You look just like the porter in the Rio-Rita-Bar." When the diplomats finally emerged from their offices into the Wilhelmstrasse, a Berlin ragamuffin exclaimed, "Oy! Look at that! A lot of admirals!" As it was, the party traveled with a bewildering array of costumes ordained by the head of protocol and were forever being instructed to change their clothes. Germany's leading clotheshorse, Göring, remained behind in Berlin as acting head of state.

The Italians accorded the uncouth brownshirts an operatic reception. A special station had been constructed in Rome, where the Nazis were greeted by the governor, Prince Colonna. Carriages drawn by four horses conveyed the party to their lodgings. Hitler traveled with the king, as he was a guest at the Quirinal. Goebbels observed that the Italian sovereign was "stiff."

There were baskets of fruit and bottles of grappa in every room at the Grand. Goebbels reveled in the glory that was Rome, and regretted that Germany had nothing to match it. It would be up to the Nazis to provide durable monuments of this sort. And there were pretty women wherever he looked—although Ciano thought they only had eyes for Hitler. The only thing that marred their pleasure at being in the city was eternal rain.

Hitler was also in raptures over all he saw, although he thought the monarch and his wife were looking down on him. The king was indeed perturbed by his houseguest, who allegedly called for a woman at 1 AM because he needed to have his bed turned down (and this had to done by a woman). The king also gained the impression Hitler was injecting himself with stimulants and narcotics, which was possibly true. Even Mussolini told Ciano he was convinced the Führer had been wearing rouge to hide his pallor.

Hitler found compensations. He was able to admire the beauties of Florence and Naples. At a banquet at the Palazzo Venezia, he put the Italians' minds at rest by stressing that he had no desire to reclaim the quarter of a million Germans stranded in South Tyrol, whom the Italians had persecuted at least as aggressively as the Czech majority had ridden roughshod over the aspirations of the German minority in the Sudetenland. He understood the strength of the Duce's opposition to any border changes. Only recently Mussolini had decided to send the German Tyroleans off to fight in the front line in Abyssinia, presumably in the hope they would not return. Hitler's abandonment of the German minority south of the Brenner was the price he was willing to pay for freedom of movement in Austria and Czechoslovakia.

Intelligent Germans in his party did not fail to notice this development. The poor Tyroleans appeared like Banquo's ghost to watch Hitler's cortege pass. Goebbels looked out of the train window and felt pain in his heart. Hess agreed. According to Paul Schmidt, they showed no enthusiasm: Scarcely a single handkerchief was waved, and there were no Fascist salutes. There was no sympathy for them among Mussolini's blackshirts. Some Nazis who had been agitating for South Tyrol were arrested before the cortege set off.

Taking advantage of the mutual good feelings, Ribbentrop was anxious to foist a treaty on Mussolini that would assure mutual assistance in the event of attack on either state. In his vision, the pact would bring Germany, Italy, and Japan together against Britain. The treaty was sprung on Ciano as they watched the fireworks over the Bay of Naples from the battleship *Cavour*. In their new uniforms the diplomats looked very much the part at the naval display. The Italian Fascists wanted to hang on to the Anglo Italian Agreement they had signed the previous month, and Ciano knew how to face Ribbentrop's crassness with diplomatic persiflage: He suggested that the solidarity between the two countries was so great that they hardly need put it in writing.

Ribbentrop refused to be fobbed off, and a heated argument broke out between the two men. Ciano thought such a pact would endanger his chances of having Chamberlain recognize Italy's new Mediterranean empire. Mussolini was not opposed to a treaty, but he was distinctly unimpressed by Germany's new foreign minister. He told his son-in-law Ciano, who didn't like Ribbentrop either, that this man who talked nonstop about making war was to be given a wide berth: "He belongs to a category of Germans who are a disaster to their country." Even leading Nazis were pulling their hair out over Ribbentrop's idiocy. On May 4 Goebbels, Hess, and Himmler had a discussion about the foreign minister's "megalomania." Hess agreed with Goebbels that Ribbentrop needed to be reigned in soon.

After the naval display there was a performance of *Aida* at the Teatro San Carlo. The German Head of Protocol, Vicco von Bülow-Schwante, had badly slipped up and sent the Führer along bare-headed and dressed in tails to review the guard of honor, while the king was in full dress uniform. Hitler had felt like some "despicable democratic leader." Goebbels felt they were treated like shoeshine boys. Bülow-Schwante was summarily dismissed.

Hitler expressed his anger at the court ceremonial in a letter to Winifred Wagner, the daughter-in-law of the composer Richard. His gaffes caused chortling among his own men as well as the Italians. The humiliations suffered by Hitler in Italy had the effect of hardening his resolve to resist any attempt to restore the monarchy and move against the nobility. Ciano was sympathetic and relayed Ribbentrop's line that the one good thing the Social Democrats had done in Germany was to "liquidate the monarchy for ever." As the nobility was still prominent in the army and the diplomatic service, Hitler planned to purge both. Naturally Goebbels egged him on: "The nobility is international; it sees the nations only in terms of its own possessions. It should be banished."

One point of agreement struck between the two dictators was a greater coordination in internal affairs. In particular, Italy would finally adopt racial antisemitism. Over the next month Italian newspapers published articles by well-known professors showing that the Italians were racially "Nordic" and that the Jews were a peril. Many academics had to quit their posts, and senior army and naval officers were dismissed; Jews were banned from the professions. Mussolini had to find a new dentist.

One important Roman refused to attend the festivities, however. In Paris Wolfgang von Weisl voiced his admiration for the Supreme Pontiff, Pius XI, to the British Board of Deputies, citing "[the] *Osservatore Romano*, the mouthpiece of the Holy See, who [*sic*] ignored the presence of Kaiser Adolf in the eternal Rome. This policy of the Pope is not only dignified but also clever." But nevertheless, the pope had no power to apply the brakes to Hitler's forward momentum.

———

In Vienna, Eichmann was tightening his grip. On May 7, it was announced that Austrian civil servants would be required to furnish baptismal certificates going back to their grandparents. On the 20th the
Viennese were warned that the Nuremberg Laws would take effect on June
28. *Der Stürmer* celebrated the purification of blood in a brace of cartoons,
which showed the appropriation of Moritz Kohn's dress shop by a proper
Aryan Fritz Schulz. The transition was not as easy as that.

All over the Reich, Jewish businesses were proving hard to sell. They
were expensive, and they had run out of buyers. The German economy
was suffering from Nazi mismanagement—there was not a lot of money
about. The easiest method was to allow the firm to be bought out by a
conglomerate. Buyers would then dictate prices. That meant that they sold
at between two-thirds and three-quarters of their market price. Some Jews
were tempted to hang on and hope that the situation improved, often with
disastrous results.

The Jewish-owned papers in Vienna were now shut down. These included *Die Stimme, Die Neue Welt, Die Wahrheit, Der Jude, Jüdische Front,*
and *Der Legitimist.* They were to be replaced by just one—the *Zionistische
Rundschau*—edited by Emil Reich. Twenty-five issues appeared between
May 20 and November 4, 1938, bringing welcome morale to a humiliated and despairing people. Eichmann was able to write to his old comrade
Herbert Hagen on May 8. He was on top of the work and looking forward to the first issue of the Zionist *Rundschau*, which he had the "boring"
job of censoring. It was to be *his* paper. He was also getting on with the
business of forcing Jews into emigration; he had told the Jews that 20,000
indigent members of their community had to go before May 1939. The
physical pressure was to be exerted by the SD, while the gauleiter was to
deal with the economic issues.

The institutions of the Jewish congregation had been re-created as
Lauterbach had requested, but from now on they were ruled by Eichmann
with a rod of iron. In agreement with his Berlin boss, Dr. Six, Eichmann
had authorized the relaunch of the IKG, the Zionist National Union, and
the orthodox organization Agudas Jisroel. The IKG was reopened on May
2 and the Palestine Office the day after. After a hiatus of six weeks, Eichmann's desire to see the Jews go to Palestine could begin. In theory at least,
this would be a legal form of emigration. His first task was to see that

20,000 poor Jews would leave in the following year. The IKG was instructed to create a Central Emigration Office to deal with all other countries. For Palestine there was the Zionist National Union. Eichmann's aim was to create a self-funding expulsion. To the end of his days he insisted that what he was doing was not personal: "I was no Jew-hater. I have never been an antisemite; I have never made any bones about that."

On May 11 Monty Waldman of the American Jewish Committee in New York got wind of a bit of horse-trading at the British Passport Control Office in Vienna.

I learn from a reliable but indirect source that 300 young Jews will leave in the next few days secretly Vienna in order to travel *without passports* by sea to Palestine. . . . Representatives of these Jews have approached the authorities in Berlin and got their consent for leaving the country and even for the export of the money necessary for the travelling expenses (some 700 Schillings per head). I am informed that the *British Consulate of Vienna* is aware of the illegal activity, but instead of hindering them the Consulate has so far rather been *helpful*, though of course not one of the Jews will get a regular visa.

If the attempt of those Jews should succeed another transport will follow immediately. I may add the leader of this adventurous enterprise is known to have already succeeded three times in bringing secret transports of young Jews from Austria to Palestine. The importance of those news would not consist in the fact of 300 Jews leaving a town of 160,000 but the silent encouragement of the Nazis as well as the British Consulate which should be obliged to hinder them.

On May 16, Weisl reported tensions: "Practically every European country [has] hastened to close its doors to Jews from Austria . . . especially *France*." He pointed out that the French were considering new legislation that would affect up to 250,000 foreign Jews who were planning to enter the country. The premier, Edouard Daladier, had already threatened to expel 10,000 Jews, including 2,000 Austrians.

A note of Schadenfreude creeps into the correspondence between Weisl and Waldman in a document written at this time: "The Nuremberg Aryan Laws have been introduced formally in Austria, not withstanding grave apprehensions due to the fact that practically the whole of the Viennese bourgeoisie and a good part of the Austrian aristocracy too, has Jewish blood. Exclusion from auctions means Jews can't sell property at a reasonable price. He has to give away whatever he owns, for a song—for the Horst Wessel Song." Weisl gloated: "Most of the victims being converted or even half-Jews. The sacrament of baptism did not save them."

The sacrament was not recognized anyhow. The Jews and the Nazis had that in common: As far as they were concerned, Christian converts were still Jews. Only the Christian churches had the power to change that, when there was a will. On May 18, Catchpool wrote to Alice Nike after a meeting with Sir Alan Holderness of the Aliens Department of the Home Office. There had been no deviation from official policy as far as the bureaucrat was concerned, and faked references by Jews were causing problems. "The greatest difficulty of all, however, is that advice given in Vienna is not a guarantee that the individual who has received it will be allowed to enter this country. The last word is always the immigrant officer at the port of landing."

On May 20 Keitel finally sent Hitler an outline of Operation Green for the invasion of Czechoslovakia. The slowness might have been a reflection of the German Military High Command's lukewarm feelings about it. After his success in Austria, Hitler was keener than ever to lay his hands on the western parts of Czechoslovakia. He wanted to achieve his mission in his own lifetime. The new foreign minister Ribbentrop lusted to prove himself and would be his accomplice.

If possible, Hitler was going to wait for "provocation" rather than risk naked aggression. This meant exploiting "increasing diplomatic controversies and tension linked with military preparations so as to shift the war guilt onto the enemy" or by waiting for a "serious incident which will subject Germany to unbearable provocation" and "affording the moral justification for military measures."

Hitler was well aware that the Versailles settlement had given him two potential allies in the rape of Czechoslovakia. Hungary wanted to redeem the Magyars of Slovakia, while the Poles felt that they also had a right to Teschen in the north. Hitler realized that France would be unlikely to rescue Czechoslovakia if they were going to unleash a European war in the process. The only danger, felt Hitler, was from the Soviet Union.

The pot came to the boil that very weekend of May 19–20. The contents of Keitel's plan were possibly leaked, although this was probably no more than a device used to make the Czechs tense. German troops were reported to be on the move near the Czech border. Local elections loomed, and a worried President Beneš ordered a partial mobilization. Two Germans were killed by Czech police and a hundred hurt during a demonstration in Eger. The British ambassador at Berlin, Sir Nevile Henderson, sent his military attachés to report on the situation, and he demanded assurances from Keitel, thereby further infuriating the already bitterly Anglophobic Ribbentrop.

Goebbels agreed with Ribbentrop for once, gladdened by the way the Czechs seemed to be hastening their own downfall. Ribbentrop made unseemly threats against the Czech people during a stormy meeting with Henderson and convinced him that Germany would fight. Henderson responded by telling his staff to start packing. The British and the French took the opportunity to warn Germany of the consequences of invading Czechoslovakia, and the French and the Russians promised immediate military assistance. Halifax was relieved to be communicating with Ribbentrop's undersecretary of state, Weizsäcker, whom he warned of the consequences of precipitate action, which might put an end to European civilization.

Hitler was forced to back down, putting him in a foul mood. Ribbentrop's impotent rage continued. He ran to his master at the Berghof; Hitler was yet more hardened in his desire to do away with the Czech state. Germans felt certain that they were on the verge of war. On May 23 the Czech ambassador in Berlin was informed that Germany had no designs on Czechoslovakia. On the 25th Chamberlain made it clear to the Commons that on the basis of the report from the military attaché, Colonel Mason-Macfarlane, there was no cause for alarm.

In the aftermath of the crisis Hitler spent a week sulking at the Berghof before returning to Berlin on May 28 and summoning a conference of the service chiefs in the Chancellery. Göring was still dragging his feet; his Research Bureau had tapped various reports that indicated that the French would not let this one pass. On the table was a map of the offending

Czechoslovakia, and they were to hear how it was to be eliminated. "I am utterly determined that Czechoslovakia shall disappear from the map of Europe," Hitler told them. On the 30th he voiced his intention to smash the Czechs in the immediate future. Keitel's plans needed to be effected by October 1.

The Sudeten Party leader Henlein was still charged with the role of refusing any offer that might alleviate the position of the German minority. The German government was not to be officially implicated. Hitler wanted the boil to get bigger so that he could lance it by the Nuremberg Rally in September. The British were losing sympathy with the Czechs and sent the former president of the Board of Trade, Lord Runciman, to investigate. Beneš was urged to make concessions to the Sudetenländer on the basis of Henlein's Karlsbad Program.

At this time Hitler was also watching the Russians, who were, with the French, guarantors of the Czech state. He asked the Romanians to refuse permission for them to cross their frontiers to intervene and was pleased to hear from his ambassador in Warsaw that the Poles had no intention of accommodating the Soviet Union either. The Polish foreign minister, Colonel Beck, still had his eyes on Teschen. Hitler hoped that the British and the French would be reluctant to act in concert with the Soviet Union. He was unimpressed by the Hungarians dithering about committing themselves: "He who wants to sit at the table must at least help in the kitchen."

Hitler's plans alarmed his chief of staff, General Beck, who feared an "adventure" of this sort would lead to war with the Western powers. The military planners saw that any attack on Czechoslovakia would entail the heavy risk that Germany would be dragged once again into world war. It was a view largely shared by Göring, who was now losing favor as a foreign policy advisor. Beck wrote a series of memoranda beginning on May 5, in which he tried to bring in Brauchitsch over to his way of thinking. The memoranda were intended for Hitler too, but Brauchitsch did not even dare show him the more contentious parts. Hitler already believed the general staff were sabotaging his plans.

Beck's reaction to the service chiefs' meeting of the 28th was to pen two more memos on May 29 and June 3. He was little concerned about legitimacy; he was worried that Germany would ultimately lose a war against the British and the French and was aware that the United States was prepared to back them. Göring shared his doubts but continued producing weapons at a rate that had set off an arms race with the Western powers. It was obvious to French and British intelligence that Germany saw them as potential enemies in a future conflict caused by German aggression toward Czechoslovakia. Göring had ordered 7,000 Ju 88s, medium-range bombers capable of hitting targets in France and Britain. He had turned over half the workforce of the aeronautics industry to their manufacture, but progress was still slow. Germany also had an alarmingly low supply of explosives, with production at only half the total for 1918. On July 12 a New Military Economic Production Plan was launched, which placed the German economy on a war footing.

Göring was in a quandary. On the one hand, he wanted to prevent a war against France and Britain that Germany was likely to lose in the long run; on the other, he hoped to get his hands on Czech goods that would be a considerable boon to the Four Year Plan. There was an added incentive in the massive Skoda arms firm, which was producing some of the most technically advanced weaponry in Europe, including the famous "bren" gun beloved of the British army. In the summer of that year all he could say was "ways will be found," as it became increasingly clear that Germany was on the brink of economic collapse. Even the timing of Operation Green reflected this: The deadline allowed for the bringing in of the harvest, as food stocks were low too.108 When the West allowed Germany to make off with the Sudetenland without a fight later that year, Göring was over the moon. It was all he wanted, and they would achieve it without the war that he did not believe Germany could win.

Hitler rightly perceived that the British were unlikely to produce the only winning card they had and enlist the support of the Soviet Union. They detested the Soviets even more than Nazi Germany, but together with France, the Soviet Union was a guarantor of Czechoslovakia's independence. On June 13 the top army commanders had their own meeting at Barth in Pomerania. For the first time they were informed of Hitler's designs on Czechoslovakia. Hitler arrived late. He assuaged his generals by telling them the Fritsch business had been a mistake, that the general was innocent. Goebbels thought this would be a humiliation for Himmler— the gauleiter of Berlin evidently did not know of Göring's involvement.

No one objected to Hitler's wider plans, agreeing they were not as unfeasible as some had suggested. Beck was absent from the meeting.

No one seemed to be able to talk sense into Hitler. The minister of finance, the former Rhodes scholar Lutz Schwerin von Krosigk, asked for an audience with Hitler to alert him to the disastrous state of the economy. He had to content himself with writing the Führer a memo. In the second quarter of the year the stock market went down 13 percent. Beck's lamentations also went increasingly unheeded. On July 16 he made his famous call for the senior officers to resign en masse: "Extraordinary times require extraordinary measures." On July 29 he produced a formula for Brauchitsch: "The Commander in Chief of the Army, together with the most senior commanding generals, regret that they cannot assume responsibility for the conduct of a war of this nature without carrying a share of the guilt for it in the face of the people and of history. Should the Führer, therefore, insist on the prosecution of this war, they hereby resign from their posts."

Brauchitsch kept the memo back and only had it read out at a meeting of the generals on August 4. While many agreed that Germany could not win a war against the Western powers, no one heeded his call. The Nazi Reichenau suggested that such ideas would have a negative effect on Hitler, while another general thought that political decisions should be left to politicians. Gerd von Rundstedt drew attention to the February crisis and thought a challenge to Hitler inopportune. Erich von Manstein thought Beck should stop worrying about politics and get on with his job. Beck went out into the wilderness on his own. Nor was Brauchitsch thanked for his work. When he passed on Beck's memorandum through a third party, Hitler summoned him to the Berghof and subjected him to a tongue whipping in his study that was so loud that its contents were heard by those assembled on the terrace outside. He would not accept political advice from others; he alone knew what to do.

———

On the 24th, the second Dachau transport set off from Vienna. This time there were 120 on board, of whom 50 were Jews. There were further arrests from May 25 to 27. Intellectuals, doctors, engineers, and lawyers were told to report to the Rossauer Lände or the Karajangasse and bring nothing with them. A week later a purely Jewish cargo of 500 set off, followed by another on June 2. Ninety percent of Vienna's jewelers left on these transports, including Moritz Österreicher, whose family had served the emperors as court jewelers for generations. Those who had been in the camp since April 1 were curious about the newcomers. Bruno Heilig noted the arrival of Grünbaum, the actor Paul Morgan, and Hermann Leopoldi. The Viennese hangman Lang came too, together with his assistant; Lang had killed Nazis, notably after the murder of Dollfuss. He hanged himself on the first night. In another account he was tortured to death before the eyes of the other prisoners. The assistant refused to end his life, so they ended it for him.

Dachau was getting seriously overcrowded. The summer's new arrivals sought support from the hardened men who had been there since April. "Comrades around me were discussing the chances of release," wrote Bruno Heilig.

> These men were in a terrible state of mind, which I could well understand. A political prisoner accepts his punishment as one of the vicissitudes which one always risks in politics—and anyone involved in the fight against Nazism had to be prepared for concentration camp—but these men had never thought of things in that light. They had simply gone about their own affairs, paid their taxes, played cards in cafes, slept with their wives and confined their political activity to reading the newspapers. And now they had suddenly become participants in a political struggle. Utterly disconcerted, they faced their fate without understanding, and the only defence they had was their hope of speedy liberation.

Himmler had been inspecting the camps and told Goebbels, "There is only rabble. They need to be exterminated, in the interest and well-being of the nation." Naturally suicides in Austria rose that month; there were 143 in May and 144 in June. In November many of the Jews in Dachau were transferred to Buchenwald above Weimar. The purpose of these shipments from Dachau to Buchenwald was to put pressure on Vienna's Jewish colony to emigrate as soon as possible.

ON MAY 28, Schuschnigg, who had been under house arrest, was finally taken into Gestapo custody at the Hotel Metropole. He was brought to a large room on the fifth floor with "two heavily barred windows of opaque glass." He was told he could smoke, for the time being. Any food he ordered was at his own expense. The hotel still seemed to function, and the food was brought up from the kitchens by waiters. Sentries had orders to shoot him if he made trouble. He was denied books and newspapers. He was deprived of sleep; his light was left on, and in the middle of the night there was an inspection of his belongings. Fortunately four years of service in the First World War had steeled his nerves.

With his one towel he dusted his room and cleaned the windows, and then he was forced to go next door and do the same for the sentries. He emptied their buckets and basins and cleaned the lavatory after they had made a mess of it—again with his own towel. Then the charwoman came to do the job all over again. One guard, known as the Stinker, used to amuse himself by aiming his gun at him. It appeared that these performances were revenge for the way that Nazis had been treated at Wöllersdorf and in the Corporate State's prisons. With time the guards relented and became reasonably friendly. They told him that he was to be tried for calling the French and arming the Communists. But if he was in deep water, that was nothing to what was going to happen to "the Jew" Louis Rothschild, who was occupying another room on that floor.

———

Central Europe was thawing out and swallows announced the summer. For Greater Germany's Jews, however, there was little or no relief from their dark lodgings. In Vienna they were now banned from public parks and gardens. The only area still open to them was the Jewish part of the Central Cemetery in Simmering. From his Swiss exile, Franz Werfel penned a little poem.

> *Volksgarten, Stadt-und Rathaus Park,*
> *Ihr Frühling war noch nie so stark.*
> *Den Juden Wiens ist er verboten.*
> *Ihr einziges Grün wächst bei den Toten.*
> *Zur Stunde, da die Stadt erblasst*
> *Von sonntäglicher Mittagslast,*
> *Drückt es sich scheu in Strassenbahnen.*

Hinaus zu halbervergessenen Ahnen.
Der Totenstadt von Simmering
Sind Christ und Jud das gleiche Ding,
Verschieden nur durch Zins und Kosten.

City, People's and Town Hall Park
Your spring was never quite so dark.
The Jews are banished and now it's said
Their one splash of green lies among the dead.
The moment when the city slumps
Under the weight of Sunday lunch,
They shyly join the queues for trams
To pay respects to half-forgotten grans.
The Valhalla of Simmering, that is
Where Gentile and Jew share privileges
Distinguished only by rent and charges.

On June 1, Hitler officially launched the Kraft-durch-Freude car—the prototype for the Volkswagen Beetle that he had had a hand in designing—by opening the new factory at Helmstedt. Every German was to own a car at a price of 990 RM, a subscription of just 5 RM a week. At the end of the war, a lot of ordinary Germans had paid out to receive their Beetles, but to date no one had received a car.

Some Jews had headed for the big cities of the "old Reich," where they believed they would be safer, particularly Berlin—a notion especially galling to Goebbels. The gauleiter believed he had a firm ally in Helldorf, who had begun rounding up Jews at the end of May. By June 1 he had bagged three hundred of them before taking temporary leave of the city. In his absence, an outraged Goebbels discovered that Schulenburg had taken it upon himself to let all but six go, retaining only those who were suspected of criminal activity. "You little bureaucrat!" Goebbels harangued him on the telephone, he was so angry that Schulenburg had to hold the receiver well away from his ear. "I was livid. I have never made such a fuss. Helldorf is to return at once and I will give him such a bollocking. You can't do anything with all these jurists in Police Headquarters."

On June 10, Goebbels lectured the Berlin police on why the Jews had to go. He did not want them spoiling his fun a second time by releasing them. Helldorf still had the reputation of being a committed Nazi and an intimate friend of Goebbels, but he was playing a double game. At the time of the Fritsch crisis he had joined the opposition. He later lied to Goebbels, claiming that he had purged the police, when he had done no such thing, as Schulenburg remained at his desk.

Other "old" Reich cities began to get tough too. The first synagogue was destroyed in Munich on June 9. Hitler had decided that it was a blot on the landscape when he had visited the new Deutsches Künstlerhaus— the House of German Artists—a few days before. The congregation was given a few hours to empty the building. In Nuremberg, the gauleiter Julius Streicher was anxious to destroy his synagogue. He ran a picture of it on the front page of *Der Stürmer* in July, calling synagogues "dens of thieves" and "Nuremberg's disgrace." The "eyesore" came down on August 10.

The Reich was jubilant on June 2: its first lady, Emmy Göring, gave birth to a baby girl. The child was named Edda. The actress was forty-five, and her husband had been shot in the groin during the Beer-Hall Putsch, so there was talk of immaculate conception. In Nuremberg, Streicher put it about that Emmy Göring had been artificially inseminated. There were naturally rumors that the Duce was the father, as Emmy had been in Italy with her husband nine months before. Adolf Hitler sent several hundred roses to the mother. When Göring came to pick up his wife and child from the sanatorium ten days later, the streets were black with cheering crowds. They went directly to show the baby to the Führer, who volunteered to be her godfather. He shared that office with Göring's old comrade in arms, Pilli Körner. Tributes came in from all over the world, including telegrams from Lords Halifax and Londonderry. Later that month a family gathering in Berlin to celebrate the birth mustered two hundred Görings.

Little Edda had come two weeks late for Mothers' Day, a festival held on the second Sunday in May. That year the state had decided to honor motherhood, granting crosses of gold, silver, or bronze to women "rich in children." Candidates were selected by Nazi block or cell leaders. The children had to be legitimate and have Aryan fathers. Childlessness was declared grounds for divorce. There had to be no history of mental illness, no dependence on alcohol, and no known antisocial traits. The crosses were to be worn on important occasions, but mothers were also provided with miniscule replicas for everyday use.

Germany's model for motherhood was surely Magda Goebbels, who had a fifth child while her husband was away in Rome in May and was to go on to produce a sixth and last in 1940. That daughter was described as the "reconciliation child," as it was produced after Hitler had forcibly patched up their marriage. For the time being the actress Emmy Göring would have to play the role. For the next few months Germans could purchase postcards of Emmy with little Edda.

Officially, no countries admitted Jews anymore. A cartoon by Fips showed a Jew marching past Polish, Swiss, and Dutch doors marked "Jews no longer welcome." In practice there were still loopholes. Wolfgang Weisl told Waldman that he had run into an illegal immigrant from Austria in Paris. The man had told him that the smuggling of Jews across the border from Germany's best-known exit point, Aachen, to Eupen in Belgium was "quasi-legal." Jews with papers were often given a last kick in the backside to help them into their new world of freedom. For those who had none, smugglers charged them anything between twenty-five and five hundred RM. The migrants assembled now in groups of twenty to thirty, where formerly the groups were smaller—five to six.

German border guards were very superficial in their examinations, and curiously, Weisl was told, they never removed jewels. People who wanted to avoid the German frontier posts, however, could do so by paying that little bit extra to the smugglers. Weisl's informer had marched forty-five kilometers on foot. Once they reached Eupen across the border, they could take a bus or taxi to Liège and then the train to Brussels. If they were caught by the Belgian police, they would be handed back to the Germans at Aachen, where the Jewish Kultusgemeinde looked after them until they found a chance to try again. Two thousand Jews had been able to cross in this way since the Anschluss. "Most of the Jews had no passport," reported Weisl. He was bitter about events in Vienna: "Not one Christian . . . has interfered in favor of his Jewish friends." Jews had been forced to urinate on the Torah. This was less than the truth, but Weisl could be forgiven for believing it.

On June 13, the American consul-general, John Wiley, expressed some of his frustrations in a report to the State Department. There had been a "new wave" of Jew-baiting, as Jews were told they had between two and eight weeks to leave or else face Dachau. He had also learned of the illicit transports: "The authorities are encouraging clandestine emigration. I have received what I believe to be a conservative estimate from an authoritative source that over 1,000 have been obliged to cross the frontier at night into Belgium. A few days ago 350 were sent in sealed cars to Greece whence they will be shipped to Palestine without visas or permits of entry. It was explained to me that the competent British authorities are unofficially in the picture and not raising obstacles."

Wiley had other complaints. One of these involved the treatment of *Mischlinge*. A distinguished composer had been refused admission to a Jewish hospital because he was not a Jew, yet he could not be treated by an Aryan hospital because as far as they were concerned he was defined as a Jew. Another bugbear was Gildemeester, whom he found highly suspicious: "I am not in the position to cast any additional light on the nature of Mr. Gildemeester's activities in Austria." He had had a letter from Gildemeester objecting to the Americans describing him as a German agent, and that this was jeopardizing his work. He cited a list of Quakers as his friends. In his reply Wiley suggested the Dutchman write in German or French, as his English was not doing him any favors.

Further repressive measures were introduced on June 14, which were to lead the way for the compulsory transfer of all Jewish business to German hands. Branches of a business were Jewish if the branch was managed by a Jew. Moreover the measure was backdated to January 1, 1938, so that any shifting of positions after the Anschluss would be null and void. That same day, Frick proposed compulsory Aryanization of businesses. A year before, Hitler had declared that the removal of Jewish doctors was even more important than the firing of Jewish civil servants, because people regarded physicians as models. The Führer had been slow to enact his will, because the removal of Jews from medicine would have depleted the service by some 4,000 souls in the Altreich alone, some 8 percent of the whole. In Austria it was much worse: nearly half of Austria's 7,000 doctors were Jews. Hitler nonetheless went ahead and signed the decree on July 25.

On the 17th, Jews were banned from practicing dentistry. In response, the Viennese dentists Hugo and Bella Schneider, together with their eleven-year-old son, Hans, decided to risk flight. They took a train to the Czech border and bribed a border guard to let them cross. They forfeited "what had been a secure middle class existence" and became "refugees without resources, status or prospects." They went to live in Karvina on the Polish border, where Hugo had come from and where his brothers still lived. After the Munich Agreement it was ceded to the Poles, and they became illegal immigrants in Poland.

The Schneiders' prospects were little better than those they had left behind. In the autumn, however, they found a place for Hans at a Quaker school in the Netherlands that had been established for German and Austrian refugees. Hans had to go to Warsaw to get a visa from the Dutch consul. Then he had to fly first to Prague and then to Amsterdam. The aircraft was cancelled due to bad weather, which meant that Hans and his father had to hang around Warsaw without papers for ten days. Hans recalled what his father did: "He asked the first reliable looking man he saw in the street for help, who sent us to a member of the German embassy in whose apartment I then stayed. Equally amazing, the man who sent us there turned out to be a Polish policeman in the very department charged with deporting illegal aliens. I presume there was an anti-Nazi underground in both organisations. . . . I was told to say that I was a relative from Vienna if anyone asked."

Hans made it to safety in the Netherlands, but his parents were denounced in Karvina. The local police turned a blind eye while they disappeared into the Polish interior. They stayed with distant relatives while they waited for a British or American visa. In April 1939, Hugo Schneider became one of forty dentists allowed to enter Britain, traveling from Poland by boat. Hans rejoined them in August.

Thwarted by his failure to rid his city of Jews, Goebbels was now being badgered by another group of pests: "A large number of pastors have signed a petition for Niemöller. Wastepaper basket!" More pleasant work took the form of the Vienna Theatre Festival; "Vienna needs to become a fun city once again." He flew in on June 12, visiting the Cobenzl in the Vienna Woods with its magnificent views. The festival opened with a performance of *Rosenkavalier* conducted by Böhm. That night Goebbels soothed the ruffled feathers of the Austrian comedian Hans Moser in a suburban wine tavern in Grinzing. There were violins, and Moser sang *Heurige* songs. It was "indescribably romantic." Dawn had arrived before Goebbels made it back to his hotel.

He stayed to see the performance of *Hamlet*, starring Gründgens and Marianne Hoppe. The "genius Shakespeare" was clearly an honorary German: "How paltry others appear beside him." On June 18 Goebbels was back at the festival with Magda and the following day drove up to the Kahlenberg, which overlooks Vienna from the west. The festival closed with a performance of *Lohengrin*, given by the Berlin opera ensemble and directed by Tietjen.

On June 14, while Goebbels was busy persecuting Jews in Berlin, things began to accelerate in Vienna's Anglican Church. The incumbent Grimes initially decided to take matters in his own hands in a quiet way by marrying Jews in the Anglican rite, thereby conferring baptism at the same time. Grimes had been chaplain in Vienna since November 1934, and in October 1935 he had paid a visit to Germany following the issue of the Nuremberg Laws and had written to Bishop Bell: "I may say that I myself am pro-Jew and have always been so." He believed that Britain and the United States should tell the Germans to stop persecuting the Jews: "Obviously such declarations need to be conveyed to the government as wisely as possible, otherwise they will only strengthen the wild men on the left [of the Party] in their cry for the extermination of the Jews who are plotting against the Reich."

That Grimes may have suggested baptism as a way out is implied by the next document in the file at Lambeth Palace, which examines the use of baptism for humanitarian ends. It advises against it, as under the new German law everything was based on race: "Baptism alters nothing." Grimes knew better. He was aware that he could not guarantee success, but he could offer a glimmer of hope. There were the countries that accepted baptized Jews, at least in cases of transit, and there were the officials who were prepared to accept a baptismal certificate, even if it meant turning a blind eye to the physical appearance of the person trying to pass the frontier. The Germans were anxious to be rid of the Jews, after all. The only thing that held them back was the "dough."

Once Grimes had begun the process, word got around to the assimilated Jews, and they began to form a line outside the chaplaincy. Grimes baptized 8 Jews on June 14; 12 on the 19th; 16 on the 26th. He reached a massive 103 on July 10, beating that on July 27 with a mighty 129. The greatest number of baptisms he managed in a day was 229 on July 25. After that he went on leave. The probable destination of the applicants was Britain, its colonies and dominions, or the United States. Only in certain cases would Palestine be the final goal; there were other ways of getting to Palestine that did not require this sort of compromise.

The entries in the register provide evidence of the sort of Jews who were prepared to go through a "political" baptism for the sake of acquiring papers of transit. Most of the applicants were from Vienna itself, although there are Burgenländer among the entries—driven to Vienna by the move to "purify" Austria's easternmost province. A few Germans figure in the books, but they are mostly married to Austrians. The rest come from the former lands of the Austro-Hungarian Monarchy—Viennese residents rather than fugitives. Many of them were hoping to go to Australia, but the contradictory polices of the Australian government proved a frustration. Some might have believed that baptism in the Anglican rite could have helped.

WEISL HAD more news on June 15: 300 Revisionists had been allowed to leave Vienna "with the silent encouragement of both the Nazi authorities and the British Consulate in Vienna." In fact a total of 480 had left on June 9. This flatly contradicted British policy in Palestine, as it was Kendrick's duty to interpret it, and yet it is improbable that he allowed the Jews to leave without seeking advice from Whitehall first: "The British Consulate in Vienna seems to be aware of that illegal transport." Wrote Weisl, "The secretary of the emigration department, a Miss Stamper, is told to have advised would-be emigrants not to wait for a certificate but to leave with that illegal transport. Incredible as that story seems to be I have heard it from different quarters, and I would be glad to be able to believe that not all of humanity has been lost even in consular offices."

Weisl was at a loss to understand the Janus features of Nazism, which could encourage emigration on the one hand while arresting young Jews and putting them to forced labor. The policy seemed contradictory: On the one hand, Jews were being told to go; on the other hand, it could take weeks to obtain the necessary papers. What he failed to appreciate was that the Third Reich not only wanted to be rid of the Jews but needed slaves if they were to succeed. Young German men were bound for the army.

EICHMANN'S WORK in Vienna pleased his masters. He was getting results, whereas in Germany the pace of emigration had been slow. George Clare remembered the particular kindness of the Berliners toward the Jews after his family's experience in their native Vienna. Neither Hitler, nor his Berlin gauleiter was happy about this. Hitler had even managed to connect the Jews with another of his bugbears: the nobility. Nobles, he said, married Jews. On June 16 the police mounted a *razzia*; "the persecutions were carried out exactly to the Viennese model." On June 18, the gauleiter reported "lots of arrests. . . . We are going to make Berlin free of Jews." There was outrage in the foreign press.

The fact that so many Jews were emigrating to the capital of the Reich formed one theme for Goebbels's summer solstice speech that year. An audience of 120,000 gathered in the Olympia Stadium. The last movement of Beethoven's Ninth was played followed by fireworks. He reported that no fewer than 3,000 Jews had settled in Berlin in the past few months. Together with Helldorf he made plans to step up the persecution and later came up with the idea of creating a proper ghetto in a largely Jewish district of Berlin, to be funded by the richer Jews.

After the speech, Helldorf relayed the instructions to the Party. They were to daub slogans on Jewish shops. This upset Walter Funk, the minister of finance, who said it was illegal. When the *razzia* took place, various unwanted elements joined in the looting, including gypsies. Goebbels had them taken to a concentration camp but defended his fondness for "spontaneous demonstrations": "For the rest this sort of popular justice has certainly done some good once more. The Jews are terrified and they will certainly think twice before they see Berlin as their el dorado." He was to use these methods again on a grander scale in November.

On June 22 the German prizefighter Max Schmeling lost his bid to regain his title. He had beaten the black man Joe Louis in 1936, which had resulted in rioting in Harlem. This time Louis cracked two of Schmeling's vertebrae two minutes into the fight, and when he screamed with pain, the German broadcasting authorities turned off the live link. Later Goebbels decided that the film of the fight would not be shown in Germany. Schmeling arrived back on a stretcher. Goebbels sent flowers to his wife, the Czech actress Anny Ondra. He had a weakness for Czech starlets.

The defeat was a return to the embarrassing theme that had haunted the Berlin Olympics, when German sprinters had proved no match for Americans. Not only was German defeat keenly felt in Nazi circles, but the Americans too saw it as an ideological victory. In the run up to the fight, Jewish lobbies had tried to prevent the match from taking place. The fastidious Reck-Malleczewen naturally objected to being told that Germany had been subjected to national defeat.

There was another anti-Jewish *razzia* on June 28 in Berlin. The Jewish hostess Bella Fromm, who was protected by her contacts in various embassies and legations, went out with a friend to survey the damage. Jews were being roughed up by SA men who had daubed various Jewish-owned shops in the Kurfürstendamm with slogans and cartoons. In the poorer Jewish areas, shops had been looted or trashed. Even pint-sized Hitler Youth boys had joined in the sport. The mob had also attacked the Israel department store, which was owned by the eponymous family who had joint German-British nationality.

The next day the municipality had to send people out to remove the graffiti. After Funk, it was Göring who tried to queer Goebbels's pitch, but even if the action had been a failure this time, the latter would accept no criticism. "For the rest, the fight against the Jews will go on, legally. . . . They have to get out!" On the 29th Jews had to lay off their Jewish employees within two weeks. On the pretext of ascertaining the wealth of Vienna's remaining Jews, searches for gold, silver, and jewels were carried out between June 29 and July 3. Confiscations yielded 600,000 RM.

CHAPTER FIVE

JULY

With the warmer weather, Hitler was spending much of his time at the Berghof. The Chancellery was in chaos; he had commissioned Speer to tear down the building and construct something worthy of the Führer of the German Reich in its place. A fire broke out at the site, causing fears that the Führer would not be able to move in on August 1 as desired. As it was, he did not have a chance to show it off to the press before the New Year.

In Vienna one of the Nazi authorities' most valuable weapons blew up in their faces, when Hitler's Austrian Legion mutinied. In other areas, however, the expropriation of the Jews was going to plan: Louis Rothschild remained under arrest, and all Rothschild property was placed under the control of a commissioner. Governor Bürckel gloated: "This is a revolution. The Jews may be glad that it is not of the French or Russian pattern." The next day he returned to the theme. Vienna was "overfilled with Jews, who have obtained an overwhelming preponderance in industry and trade, the theatre and other branches of culture and in every branch of public life, a certain amount of time is necessary to clear them out, as we intend to do. . . . I seize hold of the big offenders and lock them up." Bürckel warned the world's press that the Jews would not be allowed to hang on to more than around 4 or 5 percent of their property after they had paid the *Reichsfluchtsteuer* and other taxes.

Despite his bluff pronouncements to Helldorf and the rest, Goebbels claimed that he was not happy with the *physical* maltreatment of the Jews—at least for the time being. On July 4 he heard that some Jews had been picked on in Sachsenhausen, which was part of his fiefdom as gauleiter of Berlin. He sent word to stop it. On the 7th he dispatched Helldorf to investigate these obscenities: "I don't want this." Helldorf appeared to be doing his bidding, but a few days later Himmler—who had the means to find out—warned Goebbels of the police chief's questionable loyalty. On July 11 Goebbels took the opportunity to dress Helldorf down. "He looked very small" when the gauleiter had finished with him.

The following day, July 5, Goebbels had a long chat with Ribbentrop in the Kaiserhof Hotel. Ribbentrop and Goebbels spoke about the imminent strike against the Czechs, better relations with Britain (Germany would honor Austria's debts), and the Berlin-Rome Axis (they needed to forget about South Tyrol for the time being). The German foreign minister also had cold feet about the savage treatment of the Jews. "I promised him I would be a little gentler," Goebbels confided to his diary. "The principle, however, remains unchanged and Berlin must be cleaned up. For the rest we want to launch a great propaganda campaign about the Jewish problem all over the world, soon."

Himmler had no such reservations. Speaking to the boys of the NAP-OLA schools (National Political Educational Institutes), Himmler outlined the ideological fuel that was generating the SS:

> We as a nation of seventy-five million are, despite our great numbers, a minority in the world. We have very, very many against us, as you yourselves as National Socialists know very well. All capital, the whole of Jewry, the whole of freemasonry, all the democrats and philistines of the world, all the Bolsheviks of the world, all the Jesuits of the world, and not least, all the peoples who regret not having completely killed us off in 1918, and who make only one vow: if we once get Germany in our hands again it won't be another 1918, it will be the end.

Der Stürmer was naturally in agreement with Goebbels. The worry was that powerful American Jews might spoil their plans. In issue 30, the car-

toonist Fips showed Jews defiling the Stars and Stripes. Another pair of
cartoons presented a Jewish emigrant:

When I asked the wanderer
Where are you going to?
He said I'm off to exile
Because I am a Jew.

The flanking cartoon, however, showed the same Jew returned to Germany. He was laughing: Armed with a non-German passport he was now
a foreigner and enjoyed protection from foreign powers. Germany needed
to know its enemy. That July, Munich hosted a meeting of the Academic
Society for Research into Jewry.

In July, *Stürmer* dedicated a special issue to Austria's Jews. It mocked
the lawyers Hecht and Winterstein, who were already in Dachau, and
cited the fact that 85 percent of Vienna's advocates were Jews, followed
by 80 percent of cobblers and newspaper proprietors, 75 percent of
bankers, 73.6 percent of the wine trade, 73.3 percent of the rag trade, 70
percent of dentists, and 70 percent of cinema proprietors. Of course
none of this was true anymore.

There was more bad news for the Austrians. The regalia of the Holy
Roman Empire were going to be moved to Nuremberg, in addition, increasing numbers of foreigners had cancelled their visits to the Salzburg
Festival. In Vienna it was announced that the city was already one-third
"Aryanized," but the disadvantage of removing Jews from public life was
plain in the hospitals, where there were already 147 positions vacant. Jews
were now being cleared out of their more luxurious homes in Sievering
and Hietzing, on the Ringstrasse and the less salubrious Taborstrasse.

On the 6th of July it was reported that there had been eight hundred
Jewish suicide attempts over the past few days. They followed the final
order removing Jews from their posts. Jews also had to leave flats with
windows onto the streets and move into the courtyards, which were always of lesser value. "Jews are hardly ever seen in the streets of the city, except in queues at the special passport offices." Gentiles could also justify
not paying their rent if there were a Jew in the building. The British press
reported that Viennese businesses had to place a card in the windows

saying that the premises were for sale to an Aryan buyer. Streicher's special Viennese issue of *Der Stürmer* pointed out—inter alia—that Jews still owned or controlled many Viennese papers. The official *Wiener Zeitung* published long lists every day of Jewish businesses going into liquidation. The *Reichspost* was culled in the second week of July; the *Neue Freie Presse* and the *Wiener Journal* remained.

ON JULY 5 Weisl recorded that, contrary to pessimistic reports in the Jewish press, 381 illegal immigrants had arrived in Palestine. They were described as "Revisionists," including nearly a hundred Agudist sports club members. "I learn that the Austrian authorities are ready to allow a new transport to leave Austria in July, under the same conditions, i.e. granting permits to £15 for transport fees per head of emigrant at the price of 12 RM per pound." It transpired that the British would be prepared to turn a blind eye to 1,000 illegal migrants and that Eichmann had been brought around too.

The coup had been brought off by Willi Perl and his associates. Perl gathered around him the richer Jews who were ready to pay the costs of young Jews who wanted to go to Palestine because they were unable to get their money out. On July 9 the young Jews left for Greece via Yugoslavia, thanks to a Greek consul they'd convinced with a few banknotes. They were going to Palestine theoretically to attend a sports camp. The Yugoslavs had even granted transit visas. Eichmann voiced his pleasure at seeing the back of them; quoting the line of the Revisionist Vladimir Jabotinsky, he told them, "You need a Jewish state on both sides of the Jordan." At the South Station they sang the Zionist hymn "Hatikwah" in triumph.

On July 25 Mosche Schapira wrote to Eliahu Dobkin to tell him that Kendrick had been asked to give an account of illegal emigration to Palestine by the British Foreign Office. Kendrick had not been satisfied by the answer Schapira had sent him from Jerusalem "but required positive steps to be taken against the Revisionists," else there would be disadvantages for legal emigrants. He showed understanding in a difficult situation, but "the law was the law." As it was, British policy was more liberal than it might have appeared. Rich Jews were the most welcome in Palestine, but there were quotas for artisans and workers too. In 1937 214 Austrian Jews went to Palestine, representing 28.1 percent of legal immigrants. In 1938, that figure rose to 2,964, or 40.5 percent of legal immigrants. Given that PCO officials could not handle more than twenty-five applications a day, it shows that Kendrick's office was working flat out to process the applications. Austrians and Germans were always preferred to Poles.

If one of Kendrick's staff were more sympathetic to the activities of the Perl Bureau, it must have meant Miss Stamper. She suffered a breakdown later, possibly brought on by stress. Mary Ormerod lodged a complaint against Miss Stamper, claiming she had been rude to applicants, told them that there were quite enough Jews in Britain, made antisemitic remarks, and torn up a visa application in front of the petitioner. She resigned soon after but justified her conduct, saying she had gone out of her way to help Jews, which was undeniably true. A report at the time describes the Passport Office staff as being "so overwrought that they will burst into tears at the slightest provocation." The consul general complained a few days later: "We should need a staff of forty people and a building the size of the Albert Hall."

The Passport Office in Vienna had already been reinforced with extra staff from Sofia and Copenhagen; so that it could now handle between 150 and 175 applications a day. There were sometimes 600 waiting, all the while preyed upon by black marketeers trading in tickets. The mood was desperate. Some pregnant women tried to go into labor in the line, thereby having their babies on British territory; ushers were manhandled and occasionally struck by petitioners; and disappointed Jews hurled accusations at the officials. Kenneth Benton, Kendrick's number two, admitted that the one and only time in his life when he had been reduced to tears was that summer. "It gets under your skin you see. In the end it just builds up."

Kendrick, however, remained adamant that there were to be no more exceptions to the strict policy, and he put pressure on the Yugoslav government to that effect. Transit visas for crossing Yugoslavia were annulled, together with the entry visas for Greece. At the end of July the Greeks officially closed their borders to Jews. The visas were already in the hands of the agent, who kept quiet about it and tried to get the Jews to the Adriatic anyhow, without success. The Revisionists were stopped before they could reach the boat at Fiume. Some 850 despairing Jews went back to Vienna.

Later that month the Royal Navy intercepted the *Attrato* with 100 Austrians on board. It was on its seventh journey to Palestine.

Kendrick's forcing of the hands of both Yugoslavs and Greeks was a setback, closing two important escape routes simultaneously. At the Anglican Church in Vienna Grimes was just off on leave. His verger, Fred Richter, was without question bringing candidates for baptism from among the assimilated Jews of the city. They would have hoped to use one or the other land route to escape from Austria. Richter was also Kendrick's office manager. It begs the question how much Kendrick knew about Grimes's activities.

Perl was still hiring Greek boats, and on September 20, 130 of the original party left Fiume on the *Draga* for Palestine. Now that Italy, Yugoslavia, and Greece had closed their borders to the Jews, the only possible way out was down the Danube. No visas were required for the river steamers, but on the other hand Romania would not let them leave from their ports without entry visas. The Liberian consul in Vienna, however, was prepared to issue 1,000 visas for 10,000 RM on condition that none of the Jews turned up in Liberia. Perl not only had the use of the *Draga* but had two other ships, the *Gheppo* and the *Ely*. On the Danube route he was using the cruisers *Melk* and *Minerva*. On October 31, 1,100 people left Vienna on the two ships, successfully making it to Palestine.

THE DESPAIR of the Jews struck many visitors to Vienna. Mosche Schapira of the Zionist organization Hechaluz Hamisrachi in Palestine reported on their terrible despondency at the beginning of July: "I try to console them and give them courage, but this is all in vain if we cannot offer them real consolation in the form of certificates [visas]." On July 9 the Quaker Ethel Houghton in Vienna wrote to Alice Nike in London: "The situation here has become infinitely more acute. . . . Practically all Jews were dismissed from their employment on 1 July, without notice and given no compensation. . . . All Jews are being given notice to leave their houses if they are living in municipal blocks of flats, and also those living in the better districts of Vienna are shortly to be moved out." She added with a certain naiveté, "There is a rumour that even those entitled to pensions will not get them. . . . The time has come when relief in some form is becoming an absolute necessity." It appears that food parcels were suggested.

The gauleiter Globocnik made a speech on the 16th in which he asked disingenuously, "Why are the borders closed to poor Jews?" "No, comrades . . . we will solve the Jewish problem, and will not be dictated to by anybody else as to how." In London, the *Times* published a letter on July 19, signed by—among many—the archbishop of York and George Bell, the bishop of Chichester. It related that there had been 7,000 Jewish suicides since the Anschluss. This is almost certainly a wild exaggeration. It called on Britain and the United States to act against this "degrading reproach against our humanity." Bell made his maiden speech in the House of Lords on the 27th. He used the occasion to attack Nazi antisemitism. He chided Germans who had lowered themselves to "dishonour and cowardice." He reported that even ministers of state in Vienna who had said openly that the place for the Jews was the Danube or in one of the city's cemeteries.

———

The Evian Conference ran from July 6 to 15. Its purpose was to find homes for Europe's oppressed Jews. President Roosevelt's appeal of March 25 had set the ball in motion. He created a Presidential Advisory Committee on Political Refugees, while Secretary of State Cordell Hull invited the British, French, Belgians, Dutch, Danes, and Swedes, together with twenty Latin American countries. At first it seemed that America, Australia, and South America could absorb a large number of them. In March the American consul in Vienna had issued 25,000 forms, but this proved another false hope: The Jews had first to find backers in the United States, and the quota permitted from Austria was low—just 1,413. Later that small tally was subsumed into a figure of 27,130 for the whole Reich; this was better than Ireland (17,853) but less than half the quota for Great Britain (65,721), where no one was being forced to emigrate.

The League of Nations high commissioner for refugees, Sir Neill Malcolm, created difficulties too. He felt the Americans should not have convened the conference if they were unprepared to improve their quotas, and he refused to accept that the League was responsible for Germany's Jews. The Viennese-born Dr. Henry I. Wachtel offered assistance to Jews, sending out copies of the New York telephone book and telling them to try their luck by contacting American Jews to secure affidavits.

The delegates arrived on the 5th, and Roosevelt's emissary to the Holy See, Myron C. Taylor, had dinner that night with Lord Winterton and Sir Charles Palairet, the former British ambassador to Vienna. Although the meeting was called at Germany's behest, the delegates were there to discuss the fates not just of German and Austrian Jews but also of Jews from Poland, Romania, and Hungary, countries that had also introduced racial laws and were anxious to see the backs of their Jewish populations. The conference had been called to deal with a pan-European problem and was in response to the Romanians, who on April 13 had proposed an annual export equivalent to the number of Jews born every year. They also pointed out that "Jewish problems" were not confined to Germany. Jewish exiles were already causing internal problems in many countries. The big three closed ranks. The Americans did not want to change their quotas. There were 40,000 German exiles in France, and both France and Britain expressed their reluctance to take in any more. At Evian Lord Winterton excused the British record by pointing out that the Mandate had already absorbed 300,000 Jews, including 40,000 Germans.

Countries such as Britain were interested in creaming off the best immigrants. The United Kingdom only desired physicians with a worldwide reputation or younger ones with two years of practical experience. On the other hand Britain was open to Jews wanting to enter full-time higher education, although the money to pay for the courses had to be found first. Those taking medical degrees were not allowed to practice. Other countries had more specific demands. In Central America they were against doctors and intellectuals; in Peru they wanted no lawyers. The Argentinians said they had done enough. San Domingo offered to take 100,000 Jews. A Belgian Catholic group agreed to help on condition that they submitted to baptism. Canada was not interested unless they brought riches with them; Denmark and Holland were fine for transit, but the Belgians required a visa—otherwise they would be sent back. China was still possible. Cuba wanted $500 dollars a head.

The idea of a homeland in Madagascar was raised again in the French press. Later Taylor looked into British suggestions. Their first choice of British Guiana was "not ideal," as it would only accommodate 5,000 at the most. Northern Rhodesia could house four hundred to five hundred families. The Jews in Palestine believed that the British should have re-moved all restrictions on emigration and that they could have fitted in 80,000 to 100,000 new arrivals every year. On the other hand, peace be-tween the Jews and the Arabs was the first priority. The British agreed on a compromise limiting emigration to Palestine to 75,000 Jews spread over five years.

One of the greatest disappointments of the conference was the stance of the British Dominions, countries with huge unpopulated expanses that showed great reluctance to allow significant numbers of Jews to settle. Kenya seemed particularly open to Jewish settlement. Northern Ireland was looking for industrious artisans.

As one Australian said at Evian, "We have no real racial problem [and] we are not desirous of importing one." The Australians would not even allow Jews to land.

At the end of the conference the delegates had made provision for the intergovernmental committee to be opened in London "to continue and develop the work of the Evian meeting." This was a British idea. A direc-tor would be appointed whose job was to improve the "conditions of exo-dus and to approach governments and countries of refuge." In short: Nothing much had happened.

The British government went back to sleep and left it to Sir Wyndham Deedes and Bentwich to put pressure on the Dominions to accept more immigrants. Lord Winterton agreed to chair the new committee, and the American George Rublee became the director. Writing to his friend and collaborator Wilfred Israel at the end of the month, Catchpool called Evian "a catastrophic setback."

Der Stürmer exulted. Fips drew a picture of a Jew in black tie being pelted with eggs and fruit: The Jewish "distortion" on Lake Geneva had come to nothing. The Jew was mocked for his cries of "Oy vey!" Not all doors had closed, however. Writing on August 27, an official at Friends' House in London said, "I'm afraid we were too hopeful about the results of the conference. We frequently suggest Bolivia to people who have friends in London, who are prepared to help them to a small extent, be-cause we understand that a visa can be obtained from this end if a passport can be sent here. . . . For an enterprising foreigner with some sort of tech-nical training, prospects are good."

Bolivia was considered "the Rolls Royce of emigrations." Entry cost £36 or £50 if traveling from Brazil. On the other hand the fee was waived if the immigrant had a job to go to. There were further complications from the point of view of transit to the landlocked state: Brazil was closed to non-baptized Jews, and in theory even Christian Jews had to have been baptized as infants (Grimes's backdated certificates might have helped here). Argentina admitted Jews only if invited by a relative. It had nonetheless been clear before the conference that South America was a rather more promising destination than the north; after the meeting, however, they created difficulties. The conference closed more doors than it opened. To some extent the Americans were to blame for this: They were worried that a large influx of German immigrants would upset their trading arrangements in Latin America, especially if something like the Ha'avara scheme were introduced.

Some Austrian Jews had also been allowed to attend the conference. Arthur Kuffler was there from the Gildemeester Aktion, together with the ear specialist Heinrich von Neumann, who had a brief to sell the Jews to anyone who would buy them. There was also Berthold Storfer, who was negotiating with the American Jewish charities HICEM and JOINT. They were offering similar ideas to Gildemeester: a waiver on property rights and a lump-sum payment into Nazi coffers. Nothing came of their projects, or indeed Evian.

Italy's racial policy was falling into line with Germany's. On July 13 a manifesto was published against the Jews, provoking the pope to speak out against Fascist ideas on race. "That is wonderful!" noted Goebbels, "but how cheeky these priests are." The pope did not desist and condemned racialism once again at the end of the month.

With Italy closing its doors, the easiest path to safety for an Austrian Jew was still a quick dash across the green or lightly patrolled border at Bratislava. Sometimes the Gestapo simply pushed the Jews across, as in the case of some eight hundred reported by the *Jewish Telegraphic Agency* to be in Brno on August 10. From Brno there was a chance of getting on a Danube steamer. The first refugees to arrive in Greece were recorded in July. Here they waited until they could find someone to bribe to take them across the Mediterranean. It could be a long wait and risky too. In April 1939 the British fired on the *Aghios Nicolaos*, killing one Jew and wounding others. The ship sailed back to Athens. There were eighty-three former Austrians on board.

The Dutch and Belgians were showing their teeth, evicting Jews without transit papers, even when they had visas for another country. As the Jews had generally used up their money getting as far as they had, they had to reimburse the authorities for their repatriation. Sometimes the Gestapo or customs officers connived at pushing them over the border in these circumstances, but only if they could prove they had paid all their taxes. Some even helped by changing their papers for them. In Aachen there was a Gestapo man called Nägele who charged 100 to 200 RM to take Jews over the border. This sort of behavior further incensed the Swiss police chief Rothmund to insist that Germany print the visas in the passports. The Italians now affirmed that they would take no more Jews with Portuguese visas, as the Portuguese had told them they were worthless without permission from the Portuguese minister of the interior. The Italians made it clear that these hopefuls could not stay in Italy either.

While Austrians began to grumble about Nazi rule, Berlin chose its moment to move against the Church. Cardinal Innitzer had ceased his cooperation with the authorities; the Nazis, for their part, decided there was no need to observe the Austrian concordat by which the Church's role had been guaranteed under the Corporate State. The doubtful morality of a few monks in the past was used for propaganda purposes in justification.

On June 2, Schuschnigg, in Gestapo custody at the Hotel Metropole, had been equally astonished and delighted to learn that he got married—by proxy. His brother had stood in for him. A package arrived containing a wedding ring. His pleasure was interrupted by the shouts of his tormenter informing him that he should have hanged Innitzer rather than Planetta, the man who killed his predecessor, Dollfuss. The cardinal had failed to placate the Nazis. Schuschnigg cried out rather pathetically, "But Innitzer never killed anybody."

The temptation to move against the clergy must have been strong. The Nazis were jealous of the wealth of the Austrian Church. In the diocese of St. Pölten alone, the bishop and eleven abbeys owned 35,439 hectares of land (some of it in Romania), and there were over a hundred well-endowed abbeys and convents. Their first move was to secularize education on July 19 and move state schools into the vacant spaces. On July 24 Hitler's secretary Lammers informed Bürckel that there was no concordat operating in Austria, and he could do what he liked. On the 27th, the Nazi authorities began to take over the Cistercian abbey of Lilienfeld and majestic Melk on the Danube. With time they would fill up with soldiers, POWs, and injured soldiers. A NAPOLA was established in the great Benedictine abbey of Göttweig.

<hr />

After vacationing on his yacht, Göring returned to work on July 8th and was informed of the latest intelligence vis-à-vis the Western powers. Britain was opposed to war, and he did not think the French would fight on their own. Chamberlain was still making noises in the House about finding a solution to the Sudeten question. America was unpredictable. The Jews were dismissed as troublemakers. The airplane manufacturers Claude Dornier, Ernst Heinkel, and Willi Messerschmidt were told that the war with Czechoslovakia would begin with a provocation, but the world would see all too clearly that the Germans were to blame. The compensation was in the form of markets: Germany would control them, and the industrialists would be richer than ever.

The next day he entertained the Italian chief of staff, Alberto Pariani, and repeated his claim that no one would go to the aid of the Czechs. General Pariani disagreed and warned Göring that he needed to slay the enemy with one blow. On July 11, Göring held a conference on securing manpower for the air industry. The problem was acute in Germany and would result in the drafting of millions of slave laborers to leave the Germans free to fight. That day he conferred with a building contractor to find out if the new autobahns might be used as emergency runways. He discussed airraid shelters and underground factories. He was back at the grindstone.

As early as June 16, Hitler had reiterated his intention of grasping Prague but was isolated within his own entourage. He had support from Goebbels—who worshipped his master—the bellicose Ribbentrop, and to a more limited degree Himmler, but Göring was reluctant to commit Germany to war. He was behind the dispatch of Hitler's former commanding officer and present adjutant, Captain Fritz Wiedemann, to London on July

18. Wiedemann was a succession of things, including a prizefighter and a roué. Göring wanted to avail himself of the services of Wiedemann's lover, the remarkable Princess Stephanie zu Hohenlohe-Schillingfürst, a forty-seven-year-old Viennese Jewess who had charmed her way into Hitler's intimate circle and who lived in London's Dorchester Hotel.

Princess Stephanie was well-known to Halifax and was able to introduce Wiedemann to the British foreign secretary. She was summoned to Karinhall to prepare the way for a visit by Göring or a possible state visit from Hitler. Hitler smiled on the plan, but Ribbentrop was naturally not to hear of it. Göring told Princess Stephanie that "it was no bluff, Hitler was going to declare war soon." Halifax was worried about receiving Göring, who was rather too large to bring over discreetly. He met Wiedemann at his residence in Eaton Square on July 18, with a nod and a wink from the prime minister. Wiedemann told him that Hitler would "solve" the Sudeten problem by violence if Britain failed to mediate.

As he flew home, Wiedemann saw an article in the *Daily Herald* that alluded to his secret mission. The author was another Viennese Jew, Willi Frischauer, whose brother, Eddie, would eventually marry Stephanie's half-sister Gina Kaus. The article hit the Wilhelmstrasse like a sixteen-inch shell, making Ribbentrop predictably furious. It excited almost as much fury in Prague, with the minister in London, Jan Masaryk, penning an angry letter to Halifax claiming there was no decency in the world and that he was being manipulated by a "Jewess." Wiedemann went to the Berghof to face the music. Hitler was walking with Unity Mitford when he arrived. Göring's London visit had already been ruled out. Ribbentrop forced Wiedemann to write out a pledge never to meddle in foreign affairs again. He was eventually banished to San Francisco, where he was appointed consul general. Princess Stephanie survived the storm for the time being. She was awarded the country seat of theater director Max Reinhardt, Schloss Leopoldskron near Salzburg, where she entertained lavishly.

———

The Munich-based festival of German Art opened on July 8. This year there was a reception for the artists favored by the regime and a chance to see the Third Reich's latest monument: the Führerbau, which would come into its own at the Conference in September. Karl Krauss conducted a performance of *Lohengrin* at the Staatsoper the next day, when the Führer in person graced the Reichs Conference on the Arts, at which the painter Adolf Ziegler presented his report on the artistic health of the nation. The solemn opening of the Great Art Exhibition occurred on the 10th, providing Hitler with the chance to make another speech. Despite early rain outside, a procession of floats, historic costumes, and animals thronged the streets for the "Day of German Art." Goebbels found the costumes effective and admired the pretty women.

The year before Hitler had issued guidelines to German artists: They were not to use any color other than those perceived by the human eye— a reference to the willful pigmentation of Expressionists and Fauves. Goebbels must have winced. Not so long ago he had to take down his Noldes because the Führer had voiced his displeasure at seeing them on his walls. In 1938, Hitler took aim at Jews, Dadaists, and Cubists. The exhibition was revolutionary that year for containing a brace of industrial scenes among the Germanic landscapes, Nordic nudes, and scenes of brave SA men toiling for national glory. There were the usual works by Ziegler, displaying the full-frontal German womanhood, which had led to his being dubbed the Master of German Pubic Hair, and sculptures by Josef Thorak, known as "Professor Thorax" as a result of his obsession with the body-builder physique.

Hitler lent huge support to the exhibition, buying no fewer than 202 works for his own use or for the various Party buildings at a cost of over half a million RM. It transpired that the modern works went mostly into storage, as Hitler preferred old German masters for his various homes. Goebbels prudently followed suit, but there was no danger of him buying any Noldes anymore: They were exhibited at the Degenerate Art show.

Munich was the capital of "German" art. The House of German Art played host every winter to an exhibition of architecture and arts and crafts as well. It had been designed by Hitler's former favorite architect Troost and officially opened the year before. The Munichois were quick to dub the building "Athens Railway Shed" or the "White Pudding Station." Troost had committed suicide in 1934, but his widow, Gerdy, remained a member of Hitler's circle. Despite the rigid limits Hitler had imposed on the German artist's imagination, there were rich pickings for painters and other artists in the Third Reich. In 1938 alone there were 170 competitions with prizes totaling 150 million RM. The sculptor Arno Breker earned nearly 100,000 RM that year.

After the art show, it was time for music. Following on the success of the "degenerate art" exhibition the previous year, there was a "degenerate music" show in Düsseldorf. Jewish composers were pilloried along with those who founded their rhythms on jazz or adhered to the twelve-tone scale. The exhibition was mounted by Severus Ziegler, the manager of the Weimar Theatre and brother of Adolf, who had put on the degenerate art show. The Ziegler brothers had the full support of Goebbels. In May 1938 the Nazis tried to make a little money out of their *salon des refusés* and had created the Commission for the Evaluation of Confiscated Works of Degenerate Art to sell them to foreign buyers or exchanged "for good masters": "We are hoping in this way to make a little money from this manure." What failed to sell was burned in March 1939.

Richard Strauss was not considered degenerate, but Hitler did not care for his work. On July 24, his new opera *Der Friedenstag* was premiered as part of the festival. It was possibly the last international cultural gathering in Germany before Allied soldiers arrived in 1945. *Der Friedenstag* was one of two one-act operas Strauss staged that year. Set during the Thirty Years War, it ended with a paean to peace—not exactly what Hitler had in mind. Even worse, the original idea had been Stefan Zweig's, who was not only a Jew but a pacifist. Hitler did not attend.

Goebbels was at the height of his popularity. In Innsbruck he was showered with flowers. On the 17th, Goebbels proceeded to his alma mater, Heidelberg, for the theater festival. A performance of *Faust* was staged in the castle courtyard, with Werner Krauss as Mephisto, Werner Hinz as Faust, and Maria Wimmer as Gretchen. Goebbels went on to Linz, where he dutifully took the trip to Leonding to visit his master's childhood home and the cemetery where his mother and father were buried: "Eery feeling that the parents of such a great historical genius rest here. I stayed standing by their graves for a long time." In the village he met people who had been at school with Hitler—he had always been a natural leader.

The Salzburg Festival had gone ahead, but without the famous director Max Reinhardt or the conductors Bruno Walter and Toscanini. Furtwängler, however, had come to the rescue and agreed to conduct four performances of *Die Meistersinger*—surely the most frequently aired opera of the

Third Reich. Goebbels thought the Festival Theater "dreadful . . . proper Viennese kitsch. . . . It should be pulled down." The conductor merited praise, but the rest of the performance was awful. Meanwhile, Hitler's favorite composer, Lehár, was still having a hard time. He had lost his librettist to Buchenwald and was having problems keeping the police off his Jewish wife.

The Führer may have preferred operetta, but as far as his public persona was concerned, Wagner captured the German soul. On the 23rd, Hitler and Goebbels met up at the Bayreuth Festival. The Führer was accompanied by a squad of his Leibstandarte, as he felt that his proximity to the Czech frontier merited particular attention to his security. As it was, 1,500 Sudeten Germans had crossed the border to cheer on their *real* Führer—Henlein was merely his stooge.

Hitler was jubilant and loquacious with Goebbels between visits to the opera house on the Green Hill. It was decided that Wagner was wrong for Salzburg and that it should focus on Mozart. The talks between the two men were by no means restricted to musical matters. Wiedemann was in London buying time. The generals in Berlin were "shitting themselves" because Hitler was going to lead them to war. He told Goebbels he approved of his campaign against the Jews. In ten years he would have got rid of them. The princes were also giving him trouble, particularly Weimar and Dessau. The fruit of the discussion was a wave of arrests on July 30 as the Gestapo mopped up well-known monarchists.

The program that year contained guidelines on how Wagner's music was to be interpreted by National Socialists. *Lohengrin* taught Germans to be hard, while Hans Sachs in *Die Meistersinger* made it clear that they were to honor all things German. *The Ring* was naturally about the seriousness of the racial problem, while *Parsifal* was not about Christianity at all, rather "the struggle towards a life made divine." Emil Preetorius had designed some radical sets for the production of *Tristan und Isolde*, which both Goebbels and the Führer disliked. Max Lorenz was a "fat and ursine" Tristan, even if he sang magnificently. Goebbels thought the sets for *Parsifal* awful, and the sacred spear toppled over during the performance.

Hitler, on the other hand, was always happy in Bayreuth; indeed, he was one of the few Nazi bigwigs who actually enjoyed the music. Goebbels thought it useful propaganda; the others endured it, as did the proletarian rank and file. Hitler was lodged in the splendor of Siegfried and Winifred Wagner's home, and for the performances he sat in King Ludwig's royal box. On Wagner's birthday that year, he initiated the Richard Wagner Research Center under Otto Strobel, with the intention of purging any unwelcome Jews from the story of Wagner's life and banishing the suggestion that Wagner's father, Ludwig Geyer, might have been a Jew.

Furtwängler was being difficult about Nuremberg, as he thought it might harm his image abroad. Goebbels had no patience with his circumspection and vowed to put pressure on him. Hitler would have been able to hear the more pedestrian Franz von Hoesslin conducting *Parsifal* again in 1938. Not only was Hoesslin a quarter Jewish, he was married to the singer Erna Liebenthal, who was completely so. Rudolf Hess's cabinet chief, Martin Bormann, was trying to have Hoesslin removed from the list of artists allowed to perform at Bayreuth, but Winifred was able to invoke Hitler's protective aegis. It was Hitler who insisted that the festival go ahead every year, as opposed to every second one.

At a small gathering in the new Führerbau, the Czech situation was discussed with suitable outrage. According to one source Hitler merely laughed and admitted quite shamelessly that it was he, and not the Czechs, who was "the instigator of the violence." He also boasted of the impregnability of the West Wall, which he was building so that Germans could sleep soundly. Hitler had to miss Siegfried, as he and Goebbels traveled to Breslau to see the Gymnastics Festival on the 30th, taking Unity Mitford with them. She had suffered for her love of Hitler. In June she was allegedly insulted and stripped by the Czechs. She had earned herself the name of Unity "Mitfahrt" (the Hitchhiker) as a result of her travels with the Führer.

In Breslau Hitler and Goebbels endured a four-hour parade performed by 150,000 gymnasts, but the real purpose of the visit were talks with Henlein, who was instructed to step up the Czech agitation. Goebbels found Henlein ebullient. There was no chance of negotiation: "The hatred between the Czechs and the Germans was insuperable." "What are we going to do with six million Czechs when we have finally got the country? It is a difficult, almost insoluble question." They flew back in Bayreuth via Nuremberg the next day to see *Götterdämmerung* with Lorenz and Ludwig Hofmann playing Hagen. A reception that night celebrated the fact that

Winifred's son Wieland had joined the Party. It was a dull evening, despite a number of animal games, with the soprano Germaine Lubin doing an imitation of the duck. Hitler indulged in one of his interminable monologues that lasted until six o'clock in the morning.

The 25th was party time in Austria. It was the fourth anniversary of the assassination of Engelbert Dollfuss. The thirteen Nazi thugs who had left him to bleed to death in his study on the Ballhausplatz had been executed but were now to be elected to the Valhalla of Nazi martyrs. By July 28 a third of Jewish property in Vienna had been transferred to Aryan hands. Göring's Office of the Four Year Plan had located 2.29 billion RM in the hands of just 50,000 Jews, the vast majority of whom lived in Vienna. Forty percent of Jews fitted into the lowest income group, those possessing between 5,000 and 20,000 RM. There were still 102 Jewish millionaires. The report also signaled that 16,000 had already left the city. In Vienna they had been cleared out of their villas in plush Hietzing and moved into "Judenhäuser" in the Leopoldstadt. Their former homes were to be had for a pittance. Dressed in borrowed robes, horny-handed Nazis and their toadies moved into the refined elegance of the former elite. Dachau's Jews were also on the move. That month the bulk of them were transferred to Buchenwald to help expand the camp.

WITH DACHAU bursting at the seams, Buchenwald was expanding to take more and more prisoners. Ernst Wiechert had been in Gestapo custody in Halle for weeks before he, too, was taken to Buchenwald. The train journey to Weimar was torture in itself. Then there were cars to take them to the camp. "The doors slammed shut and the motors started up, and then they set off towards the Ettersberg, the same hill from which Goethe and Charlotte von Stein had looked out over the Thuringian Forest and where now, wrapped in electrified fences, the camp now awaited them."

Wiechert was a Gentile. Jews had been sent to Buchenwald since the roundups in Berlin and other large cities in May and June. Reich was one of those transferred from Dachau later that summer. He noted that Dachau was a kindergarten beside Buchenwald, where brutality and sadism were coupled with a degree of corruption he had yet to experience. One favorite method of creating space in the camp was to toss the prisoners' caps into the no-man's-land next to the wire. Prisoners were forbidden to approach the fences. When guards ordered them to fetch their caps, the machine guns opened up from the towers. He estimated that 117 prisoners had been killed in this way since the camp opened.

Compared to the Bavarian camp, Reich's new home was filthy and the huts only half built. The food was even more paltry, and as a Jew Reich would have only received half as much bread as the Gentiles, and nothing whatsoever on Sunday. Prisoners were expected to work for thirteen hours a day in grueling summer heat, without a drop of water. The only liquid provided was half a cup of warm broth at lunch. In July alone, 103 prisoners died. A homosexual guard wandered around the buildings at night, hoping to find the prisoners indulging in illegal sex—presumably with a view to punishing them. It was quite prevalent, with the older, richer prisoners buying favors from the younger men. Very few of those who indulged in homosexual sex in the camps had been originally incarcerated under Article 175.

The smell of corruption in Buchenwald went all the way down to the capos—privileged prisoners who acted as assistants to the camp guards. In the beginning these had been members of the Communist and Social Democratic parties, who had been locked up after the Reichstag fire. In 1938, the "reds" were replaced by "greens"—criminals. They brought all their know-how to bear, and soon anything could be obtained in the camp for those with money: food, alcohol, cigarettes. Money was pumped from the prisoners on all occasions. When the SS had something to celebrate, a "contribution" was raised from the prisoners. The inadvertent killing of Commandant Rödl's pet wolf cost the inmates 8,000 RM. News of the corruption in the camp got out when production began to drop off. An investigation revealed large sums of money hidden in the capos' lockers. The "greens" were then replaced by "reds." Conditions improved very briefly, but life was still so bad that it was wise to develop a thick skin to deal with it. Wiechert was told, "You must hear and see nothing. You have to get through everything like a stone. . . . Anyone who feels pity here falls apart." One way he found of dealing with the camp was to make for Goethe's oak. Wiechert was suffering for having defied Goebbels, who described the distinguished novelist as a "piece of dirt." On August 3, the minister wrote, "After three months in a concentration camp I shall win him over to my cause."

One cruelly tortured inmate was a Pastor Schneider, who could be heard occasionally from the punishment block shouting, "Jews, fear this devil not! Your God will deliver you." His speech turned to screams when the guards rushed round to deal with him. He spent a year in the bunker before yielding up his spirit. Many became religious in the camps. Maximilian Reich learned later of an extraordinary phenomenon that occurred at Buchenwald at the Jewish New Year. A young Viennese rabbi had led prayers for an hour, undisturbed by the guards. Hundreds of Christians had come out of their huts to join the Jews in their orisons. There was a clear, star-lit night sky. "Jews and Christians, united in their great misery, were praying to the one immortal, the God of all men."

CHAPTER SIX

AUGUST

Goebbels had been using the garden pavilions at his houses in Lanke on the Schwanenwerder peninsula near Berlin to entertain "Babkova"—the Czech actress Lida Baarova, who lived around the corner in Schwanenwerder with the actor Gustav Fröhlich. Despite calling the summer "The loveliest holidays of my life!" Goebbels does not allude directly in his journal to the affair, but there are hints at problems within the Goebbels ménage. At the beginning of August he decided it was time to tell Magda. Rather than asking for a divorce or a separation, Goebbels proposed retaining both wife and mistress. At first Magda does not seem to have been too put out: "It is so good to possess a person who is so totally dedicated to you," he wrote. On the 3rd he had an "important discussion" with Magda. "She is of great importance to me. I am happy that it is now out on the table." Clearly there were arguments for all that. On the 9th he recorded unity with Magda: "Let us hope it lasts."

For two weekends Lida Baarova lived in the house at Schwanenwerder. Magda tried to make both him and his lover see reason, but she also asked her husband's second-in-command at the Ministry of Propaganda, Karl Hanke, to compile a dossier on Goebbels's infidelities. When she learned how numerous they were, she had him banned from the house. Magda poured her heart out to Emmy Göring. Hermann Göring naturally knew all about the affair from the "Brown Sheets" his manservant Robert brought him with his morning coffee. He called Hitler and told him that Magda desired to see him urgently; she wanted a divorce.

On August 15, Hitler returned to Berlin. The Goebbelses, husband and wife, were summoned in turns. Magda informed the Führer that she wanted no more to do with her husband. Goebbels went to see Hitler next. Hitler told him that he was a public figure and could not give in to private scandal. He had a choice between dropping Lida or forfeiting his career. This was a *Führerbefehl*—an order from the all-highest. He was not allowed to see the actress again. Goebbels's conversation with Hitler shook him to the marrow: "The Führer is like a father to me. I am so grateful to him. At this difficult time I need something like this. I am taking very difficult decisions, but they are final."

Hitler was not only sentimentally attached to Goebbels's wife; he had a horror of scandals, as he had demonstrated at the time of the Blomberg-Fritsch Crisis. He also had his time cut out with his Czech project. It transpired that Goebbels's various conquests had been found work through the Ministry of Propaganda. When Hitler discovered this, he was even angrier with Goebbels. In the end ambition got the better of him. Goebbels rang Lida Baarova: "A very long and very sad telephone conversation. And now a new life begins. My youth is at an end."

The actress, who was genuinely smitten with Goebbels, was summoned by Police President Helldorf and informed that she was forbidden to see her lover for at least six months. She reacted so hysterically that Helldorf was obliged to call Hitler for guidance. She insisted on speaking to Goebbels. He called her later that day. He was, he said, at the house of "his friend" Hermann Göring. Hitler had only allowed him to call if there were a witness in the room.

Magda would be slow to forgive him. Goebbels was wasting away, refusing to eat. "Humiliation. . . . She is so hard and horrible." "I have never seen her like this."

———

The Nazis continued to heap repressive measure upon repressive measure against the Jews. On August 1 Austrian Jews were forbidden from keeping servants, as the Nuremberg Laws were fully enforced for the first time. The measure was rescinded by Globocnik on the 3rd, however, after complaints from the servants themselves, who had lost their jobs as a result. There was a spate of divorces after the Laws were applied: Non-Jewish spouses dropped their wives and husbands to save themselves.

Jewish doctors were banned from practicing altogether on the 8th. In Vienna they represented 52 percent of the whole pool of physicians. The next day Viennese Jews were obliged to leave Aryan apartments, and the streets were clogged with removals vans. As many Jews no longer possessed the means to pay off arrears of rent, their furniture was detained by their landlords. In Italy Mussolini also introduced new drastic measures against foreign Jews. On the 6th a *numerus clausus* came into force. The price of support for Germany over Czechoslovakia had been increasing the pressure on the Germans in South Tyrol, where the place names were Italianized.

In keeping with other Nazi propaganda shows, the Ewige Jude (eternal Jew) traveling exhibition opened in the empty hall of the Northwest Station in Vienna on the 3rd in the course of a nationwide tour. It was inaugurated by Reichsstatthalter Seyss-Inquart and Gauleiter Globocnik. The whole front of the building was covered by a poster of a "Kaftan Jew," which could be clearly seen from the heavily Jewish Taborstrasse in the Second District. The aim of the exhibition was to demonstrate how German life had been weakened by Jewish influence.

The cruel mockery of the Jews was not limited to Germany; there was an international dimension too. In London, the *Daily Telegraph* reported that it exhibited "repulsive caricatures of Jewish individuals of all nations." The worst Jewish films were pilloried together with various prominent British Jews. The Rothschilds had a room to themselves. There was space given to the Goldschmidts, Charlie Chaplin, and Richard Tauber, the half-Jewish, Viennese-born tenor. The show had been put on first in Munich, but new elements had been specially designed for Vienna by the two local antisemitic businessmen—Dr. Robert Körber, author of a literary spin-off *Rassesieg in Wien* (Racial Victory in Vienna), which came out the following year, and one Gustav Zettl.

Ten thousand people are reported to have visited it on its first day, and 350,000 saw it before it was taken down at the end of September. By

September the number of visitors had declined to around 2,000 daily. The organizers nonetheless asked Bürckel if they could keep it open, particularly as it was the start of the new school year. From the capital of the Ostmark, the exhibition took off on its travels again. The Quaker Robert Yarnall saw it on his visit to Germany that winter. It was "the same as in Vienna—a terrible display of demagoguery—one felt like taking a shower bath after coming out, in order to wash away the impressions. [There was] just enough truth in it to make it take hold of the people." The London *Times* claimed the exhibition was the inspiration behind attacks on Jews in the city's cafés and could only add to their despair.

On August 17, the Party forced Jews to adopt the middle names of Israel (for men) and Sarah (for women). From then on, Jews would no longer be able to use Gentile names, and Gentiles had to forgo the use of Jewish ones. The list of names was drawn up by Counsellor Globke in the Ministry of the Interior. There were certain exceptions, such as Peter, Julius, Elisabeth, Marie, or Charlotte, as they had been wholly assimilated; Julius was Streicher's name; others, like Joseph and Jakob, were not mentioned. Joseph was Goebbels's Christian name and that of the Reichskommissar for Austria, Bürckel. Old Testament names were nonetheless discouraged, and it was deemed that Sepp was better than Josef, Jutta preferable to Judith, and Jochen less questionable than Joachim.

Three days later, the various Jewish organizations became the Central Office for Jewish Emigration in the old Rothschild palace in the Prinz-Eugen Strasse. The aim was to expedite the business at an even greater speed. The jumpy Swiss responded by once again closing their border. The Swiss action occasioned a limp British protest. The next day the British press reported that 30,000 now had permission to leave Austria but had no visas to enter another country. This was celebrated in a Fips cartoon, which showed a Jew sitting in a wastepaper basket, where he offered comparison to the contents. Another showed a Jew being grabbed by a Brobdingnagian hand at the frontier: They could leave, but not without observing the formalities. On August 12, the pope had spoken out in favor of tolerance for Jews and "colored people." The following day Vienna thrilled to the news of the trial of a Dr. Kurt Popper, who had tried to reach the Czech border with his wife and mother on the night of March 11 and had nearly run over a gendarme on the Prague Road. It had been discovered that he was also concealing assets in a Zurich bank account. He was sent to prison for two months.

———

Hitler was aware of dissent within his army, but he was determined not to let it stand in his way. His dissatisfaction with his army may have contributed to the decision, made that August, to allow Himmler to upgrade the armed force within the SS organization. The "Waffen-SS" or "SS in arms" were to be modern, political soldiers and under the ultimate control of Hitler himself. Their aim was to eliminate the ideological enemies of the Reich: Jews, freemasons, Marxists, and the Church. The army was to have no access to their command structure.

On August 9, Goebbels found Hitler poring over a map once again, dividing Czechoslovakia up into Nazi *Gaue*. Hitler quarreled with Brauchitsch, who was in broad agreement with Beck over Germany's readiness to engage in a major European war. Brauchitsch could have had little doubt by now of Hitler's expansionist dreams. Talking to him about the Balkans later that month, Hitler said, "We don't want these people, we want their land." The next day, he summoned a conference at the Berghof from which most of the senior generals were excluded. The younger men gave Hitler little solace. It appeared that some of them also sided with Beck and thought that Germany could not fight a long war yet. Hitler cursed his generals, young and old.

Artillery exercises on the old Prussian ranges at Juterbog five days after the Berghof meeting were taken as another opportunity to show the reluctant senior generals that Hitler was right about the feasibility of invading Czechoslovakia and they were wrong. Beck thought Brauchitsch might have seized the moment to drive home the army's point of view, but he lacked the courage. Nevertheless, Beck honored his threat and resigned on the 18th. For reasons of state, Hitler required Beck to keep his resignation a secret until October 31. The opposition could gain nothing from the éclat. At the Foreign Office, Weizsäcker and the Kordt brothers thought Beck had played his last card too soon. The Bavarian general Franz Halder took his place from September 1.

Hitler encountered resistance from another Bavarian general, Wilhelm Adam, who made no secret of his misgivings about the possibility of bringing France and Britain into a war over Czechoslovakia. Adam rode the storm for a while, even after an explosive meeting at the West Wall, which he was in charge of building as regional military commander. Hitler told him he was doing it all wrong and assaulted him with a barrage of statistics about the rival strengths of various European armies, some of which were correct (but only some). Adam pointed out that if Germany was so well prepared, and the Western Allies so little of a threat, there was little point in building the wall in the first place. Meanwhile ordinary Germans became increasingly aware that war was in the offing, as more and more people were being dispatched to help build the wall. Adam was stripped of his command in November.

Göring was increasingly worried about Hitler's bellicose policy, and it was rumored that fatherhood had rendered the Luftwaffe chief dovelike. On the 18th he was given the job of pacifying the gauleiters who had gotten wind of Hitler's plans, although his heart cannot have been in it. Even Goebbels was for a short war. The German people would not stand for more than that: "We must aim for surprise victories." Göring spent five hours alone with Hitler at the Berghof on the last day of the month. The upshot was a message sent in a roundabout way to the U.S. State Department, transmitted via Göring's chief economic advisor, Helmut Wohltat, and Edgar Mowrer of the *Chicago Daily News*: A highly placed gentleman in Berlin wished to know that if Germany were to lose another war, would Britain and America combine to prevent France from imposing an even more draconian peace? It was Göring's first peace feeler; there would be more in 1939.

THE CZECH Crisis was now causing international concern. In some circles in Britain the mood was shifting from appeasement to confrontation. In the Foreign Office, Sir Robert Vansittart felt that the moment had come to strike. On August 7 he wrote a memorandum calling for an emergency cabinet meeting to discuss Czechoslovakia. The intelligence he was receiving from Germany showed that an invasion was imminent. To prevent the mistakes committed by the British government in the weeks prior to the First World War, the prime minister needed to make a crystal-clear statement of intent—otherwise Europe would plunge into war. His plea fell on deaf ears. In early August, Vansittart sent an emissary to the resister Goerdeler, who reported back that Hitler was mad and his successes had made him believe he was God. The only man with any influence on him was Himmler. Meanwhile Germany was heading for bankruptcy, as they could no longer afford their rearmament program.

Trouble was brewing elsewhere. Catchpool had been in the former German town of Memel in Lithuania and visited the German political prisoners in the jails. Germany had been hoping to take Memel back when the bad relations between the Warsaw and Kovno governments degenerated into war. Catchpool sent Vansittart a report, claiming that there had been an improvement in the position, but he thought that the German Memelländer might well want more: "Probably Anschluss," excited by the "tireless propaganda of the Nazi Party, which here as elsewhere is determined to prevent the consolidation of any position won by a foreign country at Germany's expense as a result of the war."

Both before and after war broke out in September 1939, the British government was visited by a number of unaccredited German emissaries: men and women generally representing the German opposition, but who left the British government in a state of perplexity as to what they actually wanted. Possibly the confusion resulted from a lack of desire to learn or listen. One of these was Ewald von Kleist-Schmenzin, who had made no bones about his feelings about Hitler and who had seen the insides of the Führer's prisons. His usefulness to the opposition was severely limited, as he was closely watched as soon as he left his Pomeranian estate. Already in May Canaris and Oster had made Kleist aware of the situation: Hitler was extremely vulnerable if he wanted to make war on the Czechs. A few hours later Kleist relayed this to the journalist Ian Colvin. Colvin needed to tell the British that they had to stand firm and not waver when it came to German demands.

At the beginning of August Kleist reported Beck's message back to Colvin: "Through yielding to Hitler . . . the British government will lose its two main allies here, the German General Staff and the German people. If you can bring me positive proof from London that the British will make war if we invade Czechoslovakia I will make an end of this regime." Kleist wanted to know what the proof was. "An open pledge to assist Czechoslovakia in the event of war."

On August 16, Ambassador Henderson let Whitehall know that Kleist was coming to London. Detailed plans were drawn up, and Kleist arrived the next day armed with a false passport obtained for him by Canaris. In London Kleist met Halifax's friend Lord Lloyd, chairman of the British Council, and explained that Britain needed to take a firm stand and the opposition would remove Hitler. Kleist told him that all the German generals were opposed to the invasion. Lloyd took the story to Halifax, and Kleist then had a meeting with Vansittart.

Once again Vansittart missed the point. Kleist was in favor of a territorial link between Pomerania and East Prussia. This was not currently a Nazi cause, but it had always been a German national one, ever since the land between the two provinces was taken away at Versailles to give the Poles a path to the sea. Kleist had no truck with Hitler's claims to the Sudetenland, however, and thought that Prussia and Austria had nothing in common. Hitler was "Revenge for Königgrätz." Hitler was not asking for the Corridor, and that would take the wind out of his sails. Deny him Sudetenland, but make the much more popular move of altering the Polish frontier. Goerdeler had burned his boats with Vansittart by supporting the cause of the Sudeten Germans who wanted to be part of the Reich. The Corridor was a cause close to Kleist's heart; he was a Pomeranian landowner after all.

Kleist's next appointment was with Winston Churchill. Kleist told Churchill the generals needed encouragement, but once again Kleist insisted on the Corridor. Churchill thought the idea of the restoration of prewar German borders inopportune but nonetheless wrote Kleist a letter of support to show his German friends; it went to Berlin in the diplomatic bag. Kleist passed it on to Canaris, and the German foreign office edited it for internal use. It spoke of the inevitability of war, a war in which Germany would be "utterly and terribly defeated."

Chamberlain obstinately maintained that there was no opposition to Hitler in Germany. In a handwritten note to Halifax about Kleist, he made his now infamous disparaging remark that compared the anti-Nazis with the Jacobites at the court of Louis XIV: "We must discount a good deal of what he said" and duly reported to Canaris. Two days later Sir Nevile Henderson was summoned back to London for a meeting. He conferred with Chamberlain, Halifax, Sir Horace Wilson, and Vansittart. It was now that Henderson suggested direct talks between Chamberlain and Hitler. It was decided that Germany should be admonished, but Chamberlain was for a "softly, softly" approach, the one he would demonstrate at Berchtesgaden, Bad Godesberg, and Munich.

The opposition was increasingly worried. On the 27th, the Sudeten leader Karl Hermann Frank told the General Staff officer Helmuth Groscurth what he had probably gleaned from Henlein, that Hitler was bent on war and that Hitler had heaped insult on Beneš, saying that he wanted to catch him alive and hang him in person. Hitler boasted that Britain would stay neutral. Meanwhile the younger of the two Kordt brothers, Erich, had been working on the French journalist Pierre Maillaud in an attempt to influence French policy, and in Moscow he was in contact with Hans von Herwarth, the private secretary of Ambassador Werner von der Schulenburg. Herwarth was leaking information to the diplomatic community in the Soviet capital. Wilhelmstrasse officials like Kordt, Albrecht von Kessel, and Edward von Selzam did their level best to influence foreign diplomats, but their efforts were dismissed by Sir Nevile Henderson—and probably many others—as "a lot of treason." Many believed siding with this strange array of upper-class emissaries, many of whom were asking for large-scale territorial adjustments, was considered risky. Hitler was the bulwark against Bolshevism, and the removal of the bulwark might mean civil war and a victory by the Left.

German military intelligence, the Abwehr, had penetrated the British secret service and broken some of its ciphers. Ian Colvin, the *News Chronicle*'s reporter in Berlin, heard it from Fabian von Schlabrendorff. One of Schlabrendorff's friends had suggested working with British intelligence to bring down Hitler. Canaris thought it unwise:

> I must warn you against the British Secret Service . . . for several reasons. Should you work for them it will probably be brought to my notice, as I think I have penetrated it here and there. They will want to send messages about you in cipher and from time to time we can break a cipher. Your names would appear in files and registers. That is bad, too. It would be difficult to overlook such activities in the long run. It has also been my experience that the Secret Service will requite you badly—if it is a matter of money, let me tell you, they do not reward services well, and if they

have the least suspicion, they will not hesitate to betray you to me or to my colleagues of the Reich Security Service.

On August 17 Thomas Kendrick, head of Vienna Station MI6, was arrested. A small diplomatic crisis ensued. The British ambassador in Berlin, Henderson, told the Foreign Office in London that since Kendrick was a passport control officer and not a diplomat, he possessed no immunity from arrest.

It appears that Kendrick had been betrayed by Siegfried or "Fred" Richter, Kendrick's office manager who had doubled up as the verger in the Anglican Church since 1924. Richter was born in Vienna but hailed from Rechnitz in Burgenland, which was Hungarian at the time. His father was a Jewish horse trader, but his mother, Anna Schwach, may have been Catholic. He had gone to Britain as a stable lad in 1900 and met his Irish wife, Maud Dollery, there before returning to Vienna in 1912. He managed stables for the Schlesingers—rich Jews—and later for Graf Reventlow in Berlin.

The British nationality he had acquired by marriage had not prevented him from serving as a soldier-servant in the Imperial army in the Great War. He later possessed an Austrian passport as well, although the outgoing British ambassador, Selby, issued him with another British one in March 1938. Richter had had a checkered career since the war; he had been an interpreter and had an unsuccessful knitwear business. Soon after the Anschluss, Richter was formally engaged as a "marshal" in the British Passport Office working for Kendrick. He had been casually employed by Kendrick for some time, running errands for the legation and the consulate.

He earned 290 RM from both jobs, giving his wife 7 RM daily for the housekeeping. At the time of his arrest he owed the German state 600 RM in tax arrears. Introduction fees greatly supplemented his income. The Gestapo estimated that he was earning anything up to 100 RM a day, probably by bringing in Jews for baptism. He may have had agents working for him too, such as Edmund Pollitzer. There was a considerable amount of money burning holes in the pockets of his various suits. Once, in a tram, he pressed a wad of cash on his sister-in-law, telling her that he did not wish to be caught with so much on him.

During the Abyssinian War, Kendrick had asked Richter if he knew of anyone who could go to Italy to report on the Italian navy. Richter knew of a Korvettenkapitän von Gatterer from his time in the Reparations Commission. Gatterer refused but suggested the secretary of the Navy League, Rudolf Koren. Koren went to Italy to spy for Kendrick, with Richter acting as intermediary. Richter tried to introduce other potential agents to Kendrick, but he was not interested until Richter met Karl Tucek in May 1937, an ex-foreman with Böhm, an engineering firm specializing in compressed air and other machines. After being laid off he had turned inventor, fashioning a machine that he believed would be of interest to a foreign firm. Richter saw possibilities and asked for an introduction fee. He was even more interested when he learned that Tucek had been in the Austrian navy and that he was terribly short of money. He told Tucek he could find him some if he would go to Italy and "have a look around."

In his testimony at Richter's trial Tucek said he realized immediately that he was being asked to spy on the Italians and refused. Richter then suggested Germany. Tucek again refused. Richter found him a job, but he was still short of money. In January 1938 he said he was ready to take up Richter's suggestion. Richter then went to Kendrick and described Tucek as a Communist of great potential and a former naval engineer. Kendrick became interested when he saw some of Tucek's drawings. When Richter told Tucek that he was going to meet the head of the British secret service, he provided him with his service record and wanted him to tell Kendrick that he had a friend working in the Schicau Yard in Elbing who could employ him (Tucek) as a mechanic.

Once Kendrick had clearance from London, he arranged to meet Tucek in his flat. He said he would buy his patent for 1,000 schillings if he would do a job for him. Kendrick then produced a questionnaire to be completed in Elbing. The answers required concerned U-boat production and the possible power and speeds of the submarines. Richter told Tucek he had to learn the questions and return the document to him.

Tucek returned from Elbing on March 20. Some big changes had taken place in Austria in his absence. Two days later Richter and Tucek met in the Mondl pub in the Favoritenstrasse. Richter wanted Tucek to deliver the questionnaire to the British consulate the following morning. Tucek countered that he was now a German citizen and that on German soil he could neither make the drawings nor hand over the material. He would only do that on neutral soil. He wanted to see an MI6 man in Switzerland. He had precise information about submarine production in Elbing, Königsberg, and Danzig and where the submarines were built, in what number, and their speeds. He proved obdurate, adding that "he could give no details to a non-expert" and that he needed to talk to an expert in Switzerland.

Tucek took to dropping into the consulate, as he was anxious to go to Switzerland. He told Richter that he had the chance of getting a job in Wilhelmshaven and wanted to know if this was of interest to British intelligence. Richter relayed this to Kendrick and on April 4 was able to inform Tucek that he was about to get word from England, from a firm that was interested in his invention. It would instruct him to visit an address in Switzerland.

Finally Kendrick received a telegram. Tucek was to travel to the Berner Hof in Interlaken, where a British agent would be waiting for him. He was to have 600 schillings in expenses and hand over the information to an Englishman called Mr. Brandon (actually Captain Albert Brandon, MI6 officer in Geneva). Richter issued him with a third-class return ticket to Zurich. He had to buy his own to Interlaken because it was not to be clear what his ultimate destination was. Richter gave Tucek postal vouchers to the value of 150 Swiss francs. He was told that Brandon would give him more in Interlaken.

Tucek's meeting with Brandon took place in Interlaken on May 28. Tucek was as good as his word and told him everything he had learned in Elbing, Königsberg, and Danzig. Tucek could answer all Brandon's prepared questions on the spot. Brandon therefore gave him 150 Swiss francs and asked him what sort of expenses he might need for Wilhelmshaven for four to eight weeks. Tucek named a figure of 400 RM. Brandon thought there would be no problem obtaining such a sum.

Tucek returned to Vienna on May 29 and reported to the consulate on the 31st. There he told Richter that he was happy with the way things had gone in Switzerland. Kendrick gave Richter 600 RM to hand over to Tucek together with the message that the man in Switzerland was fully satisfied with the information provided. Tucek supposed that the real mission was to find out about the ships with tonnages in excess of 35,000. Kendrick said that 440 RM was for expenses, the rest for him, and there would be a bonus as soon as he had taken the new information to Switzerland after his return from Interlaken. Tucek found a job in Wilhelmshaven and left on June 12. Kendrick sent word that he would receive 600 RM monthly now, as an employee of the Secret Intelligence Service (SIS).

Tucek told Richter of the things he had seen in Wilhelmshaven. He had a pass that allowed him access to the dockyards. He was working in the submarine and torpedo boatyards as a technician. He said he wanted to see Brandon again in Switzerland, but Richter said he would need more information first, which meant going back to Wilhelmshaven. He was given another 800 RM in travel expenses and instructions, which he was to conceal immediately. They asked him to find out more about the battleship *Scharnhorst*. Tucek had to provide details of its capacity, speed, and its fuel consumption at different speeds. He also needed to bring back similar information about the *Tirpitz*, which was under construction. British intelligence wanted to know how it was laid out; horsepower, speed, and fuel capacity; strength and armor, both below and above deck; and the construction of the keel. Richter and Tucek met for the last time on July 17, just before Tucek left for Wilhelmshaven. It appears Tucek was a double agent working for the Sicherheitsdienst (SD). Once he had mustered enough evidence to destroy Vienna station, he filed his report.

Richter might have had an inkling that things would not turn out well, and in August he made arrangements to leave for England. He was arrested on the 13th on the Elisabethpromenade, together with Maud and his daughter Gretl. He had just locked up at the British consulate and had on him an envelope containing 1,000 RM. It was marked "Capt. Kendrick, Brit. Passport Office." This was initially thought to be composed of Jewish bribes.

On August 18, Reuters announced Kendrick's arrest by the Gestapo. He had been going on leave to join his daughter in the company of his South African wife and been stopped at Freilassung near Salzburg on the 17th, after skirting close to Wehrmacht maneuvers. Kendrick had been taken by train from Salzburg to Vienna and then to Gestapo HQ at the Hotel Metropole. He was interned in one of the attic bedrooms next to

Louis Rothschild and Schuschnigg. No reason had been given so far for Kendrick's arrest. On August 22 it was revealed that Kendrick was accused of espionage and had confessed.

The grouse shooting at Garrowby was interrupted to inform the foreign secretary, Halifax. Kendrick had been running the MI6 office for thirteen years. It is to be assumed that both Henderson and Halifax were aware of his real role. Henderson believed that Richter's arrest had started the ball rolling and that "Kendrick's attempted departure on leave immediately after it will certainly be interpreted as a guilty conscience." He was interrogated for three days on end in eight-hour relays. The Foreign Office noted that these were "practices usually observed in Moscow."

Kendrick was released at midday on the 20th and went straight to his flat in Hietzing, to find his wife and members of the British consulate. He had orders from Berlin to quit the German Reich within twenty-four hours. He left for Budapest after lunch, as he had no visa to enter any other country, and landed at Croydon Airport on Monday the 22nd. The following day the *Daily Telegraph* ran a picture of his triumphant return. The German authorities maintained that he had only been released because they placed such importance on good relations between the two countries. It appeared that Ribbentrop was angry because he had been kept in the dark by the SD. The spirit of Munich was already in the air. The Anglophobe Ribbentrop wanted to show off the panache that would earn him the title of "the second Bismarck."

After Kendrick's departure, the entire Vienna MI6 station had to be evacuated. His second-in-command, Kenneth Benton, and his wife, Peggie, were given twenty-four hours to leave and hotfooted it to Riga while the Gestapo sealed their flat. Mary Holmes and Betty Hodgson, the two MI6 secretaries, left in his wake. Eric Gedye, the *Morning Chronicle*'s correspondent in Vienna, a thorn in the side of the Nazis and another suspected agent, was asked to leave. On August 22 he went to Prague, where his wife had established a *Daily Telegraph* bureau. The vice consul, Walker, elected not to return to Vienna after his leave; he had been there for nine years. In Berlin, Frank Foley and his entire staff were recalled. It was the biggest disaster to befall the British secret service before the Venlo Incident of the Phony War. As Foreign Secretary Halifax put it in a letter to Anthony Eden: "It is altogether a most unfortunate case, and as I expect you know the Consulate General in Vienna have been put at a great disadvantage by the Kendrick Affair and its ramifications."

————

On August 3 the baptisms of Jews started up again at the Anglican church. A temporary incumbent, the Reverend Fred Collard, took over from Hugh Grimes. Collard was an unusual priest: sixty-eight years old, he was a decorated former stretcher-bearer who had risen through the ranks in the medical corps. He was promoted to major on his retirement from the army on the Rhine in 1924 and stayed on in Cologne after demobilization. He had been instrumental in convincing the mayor—Konrad Adenauer—to award the Rathaus chapel to the Anglicans. From 1935 he was attached as a curate to the church of Saint Anne and Saint Agnes in the City of London—Batty's church. Possibly Batty ordained him in 1936, and even if he did not, the bishop certainly knew all about him and would have been behind his appointment in Cologne.

On the same day they let Kendrick go, the Gestapo burst into the apartment of the chaplain to the British consulate (Grimes) at Lustig Preangasse 10. They discovered a large number of Jews receiving instruction into the Anglican rite in what was billed as a temporary chapel; the church across the road was being redecorated. The Gestapo drove the crowd away and led off Grimes's locum tenens, Collard, as well as the forty-six-year-old Pollitzer and an unnamed woman.

Collard was taken to the Metropole and interrogated at length until the Gestapo agent told him, "You can go now." He was badly shaken and asked for a police escort, as he feared for his life. The Gestapo preferred no charges, but they had ransacked the apartment, impounding the baptismal register for a while and confiscating all the money that had been collected from the Jews by Richter and Pollitzer. The latter was demanding an introduction fee of fifty RM a head.

Candidates for baptism were obliged to learn the catechism and the Lord's Prayer by heart. In return they received an—often backdated—baptismal certificate and the Book of Common Prayer. There was no attempt to convert them properly, and, controversially, there was no immersion in water. Neither Grimes nor Collard ever imagined they would become Anglicans. By the time the loophole closed in September that year, more than 1,800 Jews had become members of the Church of England in this way.

One likely path taken by Grimes and Collard's freshly baked Christians ran through Yugoslavia. Weisl recorded on August 29 that no anti-Jewish legislation had been introduced there yet and that there were a "few hundred refugees in Yugoslavia." That the Gestapo were also perfectly well aware of what was going on in the Anglican chaplaincy is clear from a report from Bovensiepen, the Gestapo chief in Eisenstadt, dated August 11: "In recent days the emigration has proceeded very slowly from here because Yugoslavia, Czechoslovakia and various other countries have either stopped transit or entry to their territories. They [the Jews] will try anything in order to receive an entry visa to a foreign country. A number of Jews have taken the decision to have themselves baptised according to the Anglican rite in order to obtain permission to cross Yugoslavia and enter Greece."

In Vienna Collard was also working overtime after the Gestapo gave him back his register. Huge numbers of hopefuls lined the Lustig Preangasse. Latterly he had started baptizing only every second day, because he needed to drill the candidates in their catechism. He was receiving more and more Hungarian Jews, possibly because they could no longer enter their own country without Christian credentials. Collard—and Grimes before him—baptized many babies, but they also converted several people in their eighties.

The British Union of Fascists member George Lane-Fox Pitt-Rivers witnessed the scene and rang alarm bells for those of his fellow countrymen who were not overly fond of Jews:

> Approaches to the British consulate in Vienna were blocked with thousands of Jews clamouring for British visas. A large quota were besieging the British Chaplaincy, applying for baptismal certificates in order to qualify for the special benefits and assistance in registering for employment in England under the schemes of the "Churches' Committee for Non-Aryan Christians" and other associated bodies. By the unflagging and persevering efforts of the temporary English chaplain, the permanent English chaplain being on leave, hundreds of Viennese Jews were weekly being baptised at the improvised font in the "Office Chapel" at the English chaplain's residence, which is situated opposite the English church.

The church unfortunately, was not then available owing to it being closed for the annual cleaning and redecorations. Through the courtesy of the temporary English chaplain I received personal assurance that the good work of "conversion" was proceeding with the utmost possible despatch. I gladly undertook to testify to the work of this hard-pressed representative of the Church of England, who, without other clerical assistance, succeeded in converting, preparing for baptism, and baptising so many hundreds of Jewish candidates for entry into the Anglican community, of whom not one in a hundred can speak a word of English. Qualifications for baptism were strictly laid down and complied with. Only those were accepted who were furnished with a) a British visa; b) an Ausweis or release from the Jüdischer Kultur Bund [sic], or Jewish congregation; and c) the German police permit to leave the country— and not return. Of course, in addition, converts paid the moderate baptismal fees.

I am informed it takes four days between application and baptism, during that time candidates are entitled to four hours of instruction in the tenets of the faith and in the Catechism. This, it must be admitted, is not too long a period for those who cannot speak a word of English. I am informed, also, that it is through the Anglican door of baptismal waters that alien Jews can most rapidly prepare for "assimilation and absorption" in their new English homeland, flowing with milk—canned in Switzerland and imported under arrangements of the Milk Marketing Board, and honey—imported from Russia under arrangements of the Board of Trade.

Comments like these caused concern in Canterbury, and Bishop Batty was called to account. Lang had already expressed concern about Batty's desire to send Grimes back to Vienna. They were worried that Grimes might be required to give evidence against Richter. Batty must have lost heart. On September 15, as war loomed, he recalled Collard to Cologne. Six weeks later he made a pastoral visit to Vienna. Little or nothing is known about what he did there, but the conversions ceased.

Grimes and Collard were not alone in their work: 1,702 Jews converted to Catholicism between March and September that year, joining around 8,000 Jewish Christians in Vienna. Father Bichlmaier reported to Cardinal Innitzer on non-Aryan Christians. His Pauluswerk charity was dissolved in August, and Bichlmaier was later deported to the east. In October 1938 two priests and a verger were arrested for falsifying baptismal certificates. Another was taken into custody in February 1939. He admitted to fifty counts. The Swedish church concentrated on Evangelical children of Jewish origin. The Swedish pastor D. Göte Hedenquist also admitted to baptizing thirty Jews.

In the Seegasse was the Swedish Mission to Israel at number 16, which had been seeking Jewish converts since 1920. After 1938, the mission was turned over to helping the Jews with emigration and housing, as well as providing food and a refuge at lunchtime. In his autobiography Hedenquist claimed to have helped over 3,000 Jews and Jewish Christians to escape. Younger members of the mission were permanently in Eichmann's HQ obtaining the necessary papers.

It was now clear that the British consulate had been a nest of spies. An official called Richter "a first class menace." Sir Geoffrey Mander tabled one of his usual irate questions in the House, and his fellow MP "Red Ellen" Wilkinson made cross noises until she received a visit from MI5 to warn her that it was not in the public interest to proceed. When the storm broke, Grimes contacted the Foreign Office, which was responsible for his appointment (he was officially chaplain to the ambassador who was no longer an ambassador, since Austria had been subsumed into Germany). The Foreign Office advised him not to return.

On August 25 he went to see Gladwyn Jebb in Whitehall. He was asked about the various people involved in the scandal. Kendrick, said Grimes, was a Catholic. He had not had many dealings with him, although he admitted to asking for nine or ten passports—a clear allusion to a relief channel for members of the embassy staff. When Grimes was asked about Richter, "he registered no surprise and no great dismay. . . . [Richter was] a slippery character, and though very useful had always been treated by him with considerable reserve." Grimes possibly objected to Richter's habit of feathering his nest.

———

With the German opposition hoping for a British declaration of war, its members were spurred into activity to make sure that Hitler could not wriggle free. He needed to be deposed, if not assassinated. Beck remained at the helm; in Berlin at police headquarters Helldorf and Schulenburg were primed. Hans Oster ran between Halder at the General Staff and Weizsäcker in the Wilhelmstrasse. Schacht too was playing his part. The Chancellery was to be stormed by troops commanded by General Witzleben. Erich Kordt had access to the building and was to make sure that the doors to Hitler's study were kept open. The older men were anxious that Hitler should stand trial, but the younger ones were keener on the Nazi formula: He should be shot trying to escape. It was important to make sure that Himmler's SS were disarmed immediately. Naturally the Gestapo needed to be taken out and the radio station occupied at the same time.

In London a meeting had been arranged between the diplomat Theo Kordt and Chamberlain's advisor Sir Horace Wilson on August 23. It took place in Thomas Conwell-Evans's flat in Cornwall Gardens. Sir Horace was told of the mood of the German opposition, and a report was drafted for the German foreign office in code. Sir Horace issued an assurance that Kordt's message would be given to the prime minister, but there was no promise of support. Theo Kordt was already doctoring all his reports from London to make the British appear more bent on war than was the case. Hitler's information on whether the British would act had been supplied by Ribbentrop, who was more bellicose than his master. He insisted that the British would not move a muscle, and he wasn't wrong.

Weizsäcker and Erich Kordt decided to send another message to the British government, to evince the declaration their plan required. This time it was transmitted by the Kordts' cousin Susy Simonis. The message provided exact details of Hitler's plans to go to war and his refusal to believe that the British and French would stand in his way. Susy Simonis committed the whole text to memory and took it to Theo Kordt in London on September 5. Kordt then wrote it down and conveyed it to Sir Horace Wilson in his office in Downing Street. Sir Horace promised to transmit the message to the foreign secretary and told Cadogan of the visit. A secret meeting between Theo Kordt and Halifax was arranged at Downing Street for September 7. He entered Number 10 by the garden. Once within, Kordt made it clear to Halifax that he had come as a representative of the opposition and proceeded to repeat the need for a clear and unequivocal statement of intent on Britain's part. He then described what would happen if this were to happen: Hitler would be eliminated. Halifax promised to inform the prime minister, but nothing ensued. Ciano summed the position up on August 29, when he said, "The English [*sic*] will do anything to avoid a conflict."

Weizsäcker sent for his friend, the Swiss high commissioner in Danzig, Carl Burckhardt, and implored him to get in touch with the British. The only way forward, he said, was to send someone who could shout back at Hitler: "None of these all-too-polite Englishmen of the old school. If Chamberlain comes, these louts will triumph and proclaim that some Englishman has taken his cue and come to heel. . . . They should send an energetic military man who, if necessary can shout and hit the table with a riding crop; a marshal with many decorations and scars, a man without too much consideration." Realizing the urgency of the situation, Burckhardt went hotfoot to Berne, where he roused the British minister from his bed. He was able to tell him of Beck's resignation and its cause. He followed this up by calling R. A. Butler, minister of state in the Foreign Office, and once again he presented Weizsäcker's views. In Geneva he consulted colleagues at the League of Nations about who was a suitable strong man to send to Hitler. The name suggested by Weizsäcker was General Ironside, a tough and powerfully built soldier who possessed the rare advantage of speaking fluent German. In the event, however, it would not be Ironside but Chamberlain who bearded Hitler in his lair, and compromise took the place of tough talk.

CHAPTER SEVEN

SEPTEMBER

In September, Chamberlain went north to declare war on the grouse, while Ambassador Henderson returned to Berlin and entertained Weizsäcker at dinner on the 2nd. Hitler was in his mountain aerie dreaming of Prague. It had been the ambassador's idea that Chamberlain should meet Hitler face to face; that way, he thought, the bellicose Ribbentrop could be shouldered out of harm's way. Henderson appears to have informed the German of Chamberlain's ostensibly top-secret plans, because the British premier didn't tell his "Inner Cabinet" until the 8th and the main British cabinet did not learn of the idea of the visit to Hitler until the 14th.

Weizsäcker clearly thought the personal audience a terrible idea, while Chamberlain for his part seemed reluctant to see the gravity of the situation. The British had never had any serious intention of fighting for Czechoslovakia. This message either failed to get through or was not seriously entertained by the Germans in the opposition so bent on ridding their country of Hitler. Beck was out of the picture, but continuity was to some extent assured by the new chief of staff, Halder, who agreed to depose Hitler on September 2.

At an emergency meeting of the British cabinet on August 30, it had been decided to make Beneš accept Henlein's Karlsbad Program and accord virtual autonomy to the Germans. Responding to British pressure, Beneš tried making concessions: He was prepared to take in four Sudeten German ministers, declare three German autonomous districts, and make sure that a third of all civil servants were ethnic Germans from now on. His more reasoned tone received British backing, but Hitler instructed Henlein to stay firm and make no concessions.

On the 3rd Keitel and Brauchitsch arrived at the Berghof to run over the plans for the invasion of Czechoslovakia. The army was to be ready at the border on September 28. Two days later, Beneš tried to spike Hitler's strategy by asking Henlein up to the Hradschin on the 5th and requesting that he write down his demands in full so that he might grant them. He promptly did this on the 7th, thereby removing the casus belli. All Henlein could do was point to the ill treatment of some ethnic Germans in Moravia and seek fresh instructions from Germany. Meanwhile his second-in-command, Karl Frank, was instructed to increase the number of such incidents.

It was said that the Czechs were prepared to give Henlein a ministry to shut him up. The ministry he wanted was the Interior. The story gave rise to inevitable witticisms. It is said that the premier, Hodza, had suggested that Henlein instead receive the portfolio for the colonies. At this Henlein countered, "That's impossible—Czechoslovakia has no colonies." "What of it?" replied Hodza. "Has not Italy a Minister of Finance and Germany a Minister of Justice?"

———

On the evening of September 4th, the chief warmongers—Hitler, Goebbels, and Ribbentrop—flew to Nuremberg for the annual party rally. Goebbels was looking forward to a week of putting pressure on the Czechs. That same day France called up its military reserves, and the Hungarians quietly introduced conscription. War was becoming inevitable.

The rally opened on the 6th with Hess delivering what Goebbels called "a good sermon." The Tribune of Honor at the opening ceremony exhibited evidence that Hitler continued to exert a powerful erotic pull on the women of the world. At one end was Stephanie zu Hohenlohe and at the other Lord and Lady Redesdale, the parents of Unity Mitford. Princess Stephanie was wearing her gold Party badge. The rally kicked off with the

"Cultural Conference," and Hitler made a portentous speech about art, as was his wont. It contained an unusually tolerant line about freemasons: Hitler said that "only a man lacking in national respect" would allow them to get in the way of his enjoying Mozart's *Magic Flute*.

Once the cultural overture was out of the way, the Nazi leaders descended into their habitual rabble-rousing tirades and malicious squabbles. Rosenberg launched an attack on the pope's pretensions to power. He would have had support from Goebbels; a new Kulturkampf against the Church was never far from the gauleiter's mind. Goebbels was thrilled that he had succeeded in eliminating the exemption from military service previously enjoyed by theological students. Now they had to serve in the front line as stretcher-bearers.

Backbiting was not confined to the leaders: Their aim was to eliminate the ideological enemies of the Reich: Jews, freemasons, Marxists, and the Church. Unity took the trouble to warn Hitler that his friend Stephanie was 100 percent Jewish. She was also advising Hitler that Britain would not fight, thereby supporting Ribbentrop. The brief reconciliation between Hitler's two biggest hawks, Goebbels and Ribbentrop, had ended. Goebbels now thought the foreign minister a "vain, stupid prima donna." As usual, Hitler appeared to take no notice of the discord among his underlings. He was planning a positive cacophony of saber rattling for the last day of the rally, September 12. The British ambassador, Henderson, was present, eating the local *Bratwürste* and disparaging the Czechs to his SS minder. Officially, he was meant to push the idea of holding a plebiscite in the disputed areas, which would hand the initiative to the Czechs. An article in the *Times* had advocated the cession of the Sudetenland to Germany. The leading Nazis believed this had been placed by the cabinet. Henderson thought Hitler had been led astray by evil people in his entourage, and if the British were to say what a good boy he was, he would behave better. His view was not shared by Halifax, who was now of the opinion that Hitler was mad.

But Hitler was impervious to any form of pressure to desist—be it from his diplomats; his own intelligence service, which brought him news of the Duce's unhappiness; or the army. Goebbels's admiration for his master knew no bounds: "He faces danger with the surefootedness of a sleepwalker." "The Führer says and does what he knows to be right, and never lets himself be intimidated." "Now the most important things are nerves." Goebbels was utterly convinced that the Western powers would stay out of any conflict. Despite his outward resolve, Hitler was less certain.

The 7th was cold and wet. Goebbels noted, "Things are ripening more and more into a crisis." The British, Dutch, and Belgian armies called up their reserves. The British offer of autonomy for the Sudetenland was now insufficient: "We have to have Prague," he gloated, for news of a couple of German deaths in Mährisch Östrau would permit a new, deafening chorus of Nazi outrage.

At a reception that evening for the diplomatic corps in Nuremberg, the doyen, the outgoing French ambassador, André François-Poncet (whom Spitzy called an "all-licensed fool"), made a speech in which he said, "The best of laurels are those gathered without reducing any mother to tears." All eyes turned to Hitler. In Berlin there was frenzied activity in resistance circles, where the plan was to seize Hitler and put him on trial before the People's Court or lock him up in a lunatic asylum. On September 9, following the usual son et lumière, Hitler held an all-night conference in Nuremberg attended by Halder, Brauchitsch, and Keitel. He was contemptuous of the army's plans and demanded there be an immediate uprising in the Sudetenland.

ON THE 9TH, refreshed from his shooting, Chamberlain met his Inner Cabinet. He rejected Halifax's proposal of sending a final warning to Germany and revealed his desire to go to Hitler directly, though he nonetheless set about mobilizing the fleet. He also issued a warning to Hitler on the 10th, that France would be duty bound to honor its obligations to the Czechs and Great Britain could not stand aside from any general conflict. Henderson had qualms about delivering this ultimatum, and it remained in his baggage. He had difficulty meeting Hitler anyway and had been frightened that any tough talk—or even a toughly worded note—might upset the German leader. He didn't even attempt to speak to Ribbentrop, thereby causing exasperation in some quarters. The message the Germans received was that Britain would agree to the cession of the German areas but would not permit a strike against Prague. "That would be disappointing, as it is only the half-measure," wrote Goebbels, who showed that he was well-aware of Chamberlain's message despite Henderson's refusal to deliver it.

ITALY

(above) Hitler's "Roman Holiday" in May: The Nazi leaders assemble with Mussolini on the steps of the monument to Victor Emmanuel II.

(left) Hitler felt certain Italians were looking down on him. After an incident at the opera in Naples, he sacked his chief of protocol.

DER STÜRMER

(*above*) *Der Stürmer*. Germans read cases containing copies of the magazine that was the unofficial organ of Nazi antisemitism.

(*left*) "Jewish Advertising Revenue: The so-called pressure of public opinion is the weight of Jewish sacks of gold."

ANTISEMITIC PROPAGANDA

Antisemitic propaganda cartoons from *Der Stürmer*. (*above*) Aryan woman defiled by Jewish gold. (*below*) Corrupt Jewish businessmen received into heaven.

LIVING IT UP IN VIENNA

(*above*) Hitler and Dr. Goebbels appear before the crowds in Steyr, Upper Austria, where the Führer had spent an unhappy year as a boy.

(*right*) Vienna's best restaurant, Zu den Drei Husaren, was Aryanized and placed in the hands of Otto Horcher, the restaurant tsar of the Third Reich.

NAZI ART

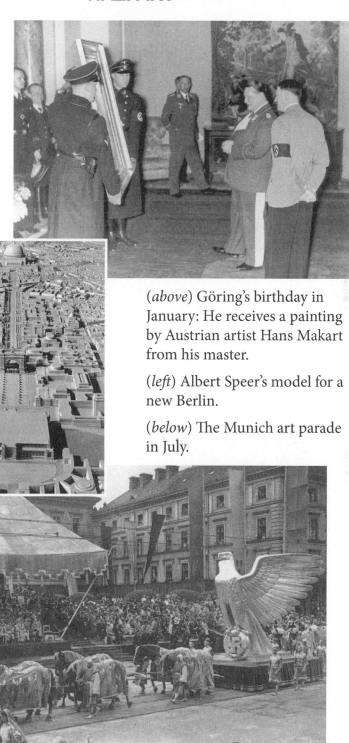

(*above*) Göring's birthday in January: He receives a painting by Austrian artist Hans Makart from his master.

(*left*) Albert Speer's model for a new Berlin.

(*below*) The Munich art parade in July.

KRISTALLNACHT

(*left*) A wrecked synagogue after Goebbels's pogrom of November 9–10.

(*below*) Jewish men from Baden-Baden are led off to a concentration camp.

(*bottom*) Jewish women are singled out for humiliation.

CONFERENCES

The Evian Conference in July failed utterly in its attempt to find a refuge for Germany's Jews.

In September the Munich Conference sealed Czechoslovakia's fate.

THE RAPE OF CZECHOSLOVAKIA

(*above*) Hitler visits his new domain, the Sudetenland.

(*left*) Ethnic Germans prepare to celebrate their return to the Reich.

(*below*) Poles and Hungarians were rewarded with a share of the spoils—here Hungarian troops enter Slovakia.

Canaris was also concerned about Hitler. He told the General Staff officer Groscurth, "He is already onto the next step; thinking about Romania, Ukraine etc." On the 12th Henderson signed as many as 150 autographs in the rally's diplomatic stand, now fragrant from the presence of so many Austrian girls in dirndls. Goebbels noticed them too: "I greet a hundred delicious Austrian girls, who can hardly contain their excitement." Goebbels adorned the cards with his signature, and Henderson was happy to hand them out to Sudeten Germans too.

Hitler's final speech went for Beneš's throat. "The Germans in Czechoslovakia are neither defenceless nor are they deserted," he bellowed. It had an "indescribable" effect on its audience. Hitler's liaison with the Wilhelmstrasse, Walther Hewel, said that Chamberlain himself had been alarmed by the tone of Hitler's speech at the rally. Göring too delivered a particularly stirring piece of invective and then took to his bed, leaving Hitler in the company of Ribbentrop, who wanted only war and as soon as possible. When four of his most senior ambassadors clubbed together to tell him this was a mistake, he banished them from Nuremberg and sent them on leave for the rest of the month. The effect of the rally was immediate: Hitler's and Göring's oratory inspired civil disobedience in the ethnic Bohemian German towns of Eger and Karlsbad. Czech and Jewish property was attacked. The Czechs responded by firing on the crowds and declaring martial law. In Prague the people went to work carrying gas masks. Henlein fled to Bavaria to organize a Freikorps to fight in his native land. It was at that moment that French resolve collapsed; their cabinet vote was split, with six calling for war and four against. Their leader, Daladier, asked Chamberlain to see Hitler and try to make the best deal he could that would forestall the need for France to honor its obligations to the Little Entente.

In reality Chamberlain's mission had already been prepared by Göring and Henderson on September 8—the rally and ensuing chaos had nothing to do with it. The Luftwaffe chief had invited Henderson up to his home at nearby Veldenstein, where the suggestion was aired that the Sudeten question be settled by direct talks. Göring dropped hints about a hunting party at Rominten at the end of the month, saying that he hoped that the Czechs were not going to disrupt it—meaning that peace could be maintained. He even promised Halifax the four best stags in Germany if Britain were to disclaim any interest in Czechoslovakia. Henderson filed a report and had it taken to London on a private plane. On September 13, Chamberlain proposed flying to Germany for a meeting.

As there was no doubt about Hitler's plans to invade, Halder conveyed the message to General Witzleben on the 13th. The opposition had to act fast. While the two men were talking, news came in that Henderson had told Ribbentrop of Chamberlain's intention to visit Hitler at the Berghof. Chamberlain's note was passed to Schmidt to translate: "Having regard to the increasingly critical situation, I propose to visit you immediately in order to make an attempt to find a peaceful solution. I could come to you by air and am ready to leave tomorrow. Please inform me of the earliest time you can receive me, and tell me the place of the meeting. I should be grateful for a very early reply. Neville Chamberlain."

The carpet had been pulled out from under the feet of the plotters. They could not proceed while Hitler was talking peace. Ribbentrop had been right all along: The British and the French would not fight. The interpreter Schmidt set off for Munich. He was fully aware of the plot. Weizsäcker's final piece of advice was: "Keep your mind quite clear. . . . Tomorrow at Berchtesgaden it will be a matter of war and peace."

———

"Peace-envoy Chamberlain" (as the Germans called him) flew together with Sir Horace Wilson and Sir William Strang on the 15th to Munich, where he was met by Ribbentrop and Schmidt. They traveled to Berchtesgaden on Hitler's train. It took the British prime minister seven hours to reach him. Not only had he just taken his first airplane, but there had been turbulence on the flight. Dressed in Nazi uniform, Hitler received him on the steps of his home. In reply to Hitler's "German greeting" Chamberlain waved his hat, as the inevitable umbrella hung from his left arm. After tea the two men went to Hitler's study, accompanied only by Hitler's interpreter, Schmidt. By divesting themselves of advisors, they were able to rid themselves of Ribbentrop.

The Poles had thrown a potential spanner into the works of Hitler's careful plans. The Sejm had been dissolved, and new elections in November threatened to bring in Germany's enemies. The German-Polish cooperation that had been Josef Beck's policy was hanging in the balance, as the Poles were expected to lend a hand in carving up Czechoslovakia by snatching the Teschen pocket in Czech Silesia. Many Poles thought Beck's policy brought Poland too close to Germany, and they feared finding the country on the same side as Germany in a war. Leading Nazis also believed the British were being cunning by off-loading increasing amounts of the guilt onto Germany should war break out. Hitler was more open to suggestion than he might have appeared.

The Berghof discussions lasted three hours. Outside the rain pelted down, and the wind howled. Chamberlain wanted to know if Hitler would be satisfied by the cession of the Sudeten areas. Hitler mentioned the Hungarians and Polish claims to Czech territory, but he was not interested in anything else. He exclaimed that he was ready to risk world war to settle the matter. Chamberlain rejoindered, "If that is so, why did you let me come to Berchtesgaden? Under the circumstances it is best for me to return at once. Anything else now seems pointless." At this Hitler conceded that if Chamberlain were to accept the principle of self-determination, then there could be room for talk. He promised not to attack the Czechs before they met again, unless, that is, the Czechs did something particularly atrocious. Chamberlain told Hitler he needed to consult his colleagues. He spent the night in the Grand Hotel Berchtesgadenerhof before traveling back to London with the news. He took with him the impression that Hitler was a man who would stick to his word—not that he had that word. He had not brought an interpreter and had left without a copy of the minutes, because Ribbentrop had churlishly denied him one—an act of private revenge.

At dinner on the 15th, Eva Braun's friends mocked the old-fashioned Englishman who had seemed so wedded to his umbrella. Hitler was pleased that "the old man took an aeroplane for the first time in his life in order to come and see me." Hitler had made a halfhearted offer to go to London but had expressed the fear that he would be heckled by Jews. Chamberlain had to some extent got the measure of Hitler too: He told the cabinet that he was "the commonest little dog he had ever seen."

After the Berchtesgaden talks Schmidt informed Erich Kordt of the conversations between the two men. Kordt took the record to Oster to show that Hitler had not abandoned his war plans. He wanted the terms imposed on the Czechs to be so humiliating that they would refuse to accept;

then he could strike. The opposition was now fired up again and waiting for Hitler's return to Berlin.

Chamberlain's visit had been a small success. His great achievement, if it might be expressed that way, was to get Beneš to accept detaching the Sudeten areas from Czechoslovakia and hand them over to Germany. This obliged Hitler to drop his plans to swallow up the rest of Bohemia and Moravia—for the time being. Goebbels consoled himself that even if their spoils were limited to the Sudeten areas, they would still have put themselves in a better position strategically to take Prague the next time around. The Czechs vented their frustration in what they believed to be privacy. Masaryk got wind of the talks on the 14th and referred to Chamberlain's right-hand man Sir Horace Wilson as "the Sow."

Hitler summoned Goebbels and a small staff to the Berghof. He was going to need his propaganda machine (Goebbels was the original "spin doctor"). Alarmed both by recent Czech violence toward ethnic Germans and by German scaremongering, streams of refugees were seeking shelter in Silesia. Goebbels had foreign journalists sent into their camps to witness their despair. Ward Price was brought up to Berchtesgaden to interview Hitler. They were very happy with the results. In the meantime Hitler and his little pressman distracted themselves by watching popular films and reading the minutes of Beneš's conversations with Jan Masaryk in London. They would have been amused to hear the British envoy Runciman dismissed as "the Lord who wrote the mad book," and Goebbels in particular would have liked the references to the "fat Field Marshal"—Göring.

Beneš, they concluded, was the problem. He was "dangerous, mendacious, sly and scheming." They were not wide of the mark: Beneš and his ministers were desperately trying to find friends abroad who would balk at negotiations and press for war. The former Foreign Secretary Eden was one of these. The Germans were later able to show the British that the Czechs were conniving at the overthrow of the cabinet. On September 19 they had a meeting with the Labor Party leader Clement Attlee. Churchill had been sounded out and had apparently expressed his hope that they "would not put up with it." On the afternoon of the 22nd there was an optimistic report that Chamberlain's cabinet was on the point of resigning. The Czechs also hoped for a change of government in France and referred to the foreign minister Georges-Etienne Bonnet as "the Swine." When the Poles offered to find a solution to the Danzig problem, Hitler was triumphant. In ten years he would have managed to reverse not only the punitive clauses of the Treaty of Versailles but also those of the Treaty of Münster, which closed the Thirty Years War.

Cadogan was detailed to tell Beneš to cede the Sudetenland on the 18th. The Soviet Union was exerting pressure on Germany by massing troops at the Russian border (it had no common border with Czechoslovakia), but Hitler was still undeterred and continued his military preparations. The state the Allies created at Versailles was falling apart. Encouraged by Henlein, the Slovak People's Party demanded autonomy for their half of the country. This was granted after the debacle at Munich. On the 19th, London and Paris agreed to waive the plebiscite but at the same time refused to grant concessions to Poland and Hungary. Hitler was furious with Horthy for dragging his heels. The Polish ambassador Józef Lipski was conjured up and told to make a gesture. Goebbels thought they had it in the bag, and the Führer "a genius." Urged on by Göring, the Poles and Hungarians began to wake up on September 21. The Poles demanded a plebiscite in Teschen, and on the 22nd the Hungarians finally made a similar appeal for the Magyar areas of Slovakia.

In Berlin the opposition was gritting its teeth. Something of Germany's desperate economic problems became clear from a meeting between Ulrich von Hassell and Schacht on the day of Chamberlain's talks with Hitler. Schacht was bitter about the Führer and referred to him as a "swindler." He did not think that the talks with Chamberlain would do anything to prevent war. Schacht made it clear that Hitler needed more than just the border areas if he were to stave off economic disaster: All his secret funds and all Austria's stolen reserves had been used up. He thought Germany was already in the red. When Hassell cautiously alluded to Schacht's own responsibility in this, Schacht denied it. Even as a cabinet minister he was informed of nothing. He did not know how they could get out of the mess unless they started printing money, and when that happened, he would resign.

On the same day the Sudeten Freikorps seized the towns of Eger and Asch. More and more Sudeten Germans were crossing the border into Germany to avoid the conflict they imagined would break out any day now. A camp was built for them in Hirschberg in the Riesengebirge.

Klemperer saw members of the Freikorps in Dresden on the 20th, poised to strike. He had no doubt as to the outcome: The Reich would win in the long run, either by force or bluff. Nor did Hitler have any doubts for the time being.

The raiding party that was to attack the Chancellery had been supplied with weapons by the Abwehr and lodged in safe houses and apartments all over Berlin. The chief fear was that the putsch would be thwarted by the SS. In Munich, General Hoepner's armored division was ready to move against the SS, should there be an attempt to intervene. The opposition had reason to believe that Hitler's end was approaching. When Schulenburg saw streams of military vehicles heading toward Berlin from Mecklenburg on the 17th, he said, "Look, in a few days these troops will liberate us from the nightmare of Hitler." On September 22 he hurriedly dispatched his growing family to the country estate of a friend to get them out of the way in the event of an uprising.

AT TEN minutes to 9 on the night of the 20th, Masaryk reported to Beneš that "the Old Man will soon be on his travels again." At 11 PM on September 21, Hitler, Goebbels, and Ribbentrop flew from Bavaria to Bad Godesberg near Bonn on the Rhine to meet Chamberlain. Hitler told the others that he wanted the Poles and Hungarians to attack so that he could push all the way to Prague. He was going to grant autonomy to Slovakia, but not to Bohemia or Moravia. The generals plied him with memos, but he refused to be shaken from his path. A few hours later, Chamberlain took to the skies for the third time in his life. Hitler lodged at one of his favorite haunts, the Hotel Dreesen, which had been refurbished for the occasion, and Chamberlain was put up with his party in the Hotel Petersberg on the other side of the river. The British prime minister had been able to win over the French, and after refusing at first, the Czechs had also given in. There was to be no plebiscite; a commission would settle the areas of mixed population and decree where transfers of population were to take place. Czechoslovakia's current alliances would be dissolved. Instead Britain would form part of an international body to guarantee Czech independence and neutrality.

Chamberlain had been receiving reassurances from Henderson, who had been speaking to a Göring anxious to minimize the risk of war. Sadly it was not Göring who was tugging at Hitler's sleeve now, but the war-hungry Ribbentrop. Göring had been lured away by the stags of Rominten, taking his old Richthofen Squadron cronies and Tsar Boris of Bulgaria with him, and was devoting himself to ridding the forests of East Prussia of horned beasts.

Chamberlain was having no such luck. After the preliminaries, he was taken to a map, on which the Germans had carved out a very large slice of the Czech cake for themselves. Then, to his astonishment and dismay, Hitler said it was too late anyway. Events of the past few days had made his offer unacceptable.

He again mentioned the Poles and the Hungarians and the grievances of the Sudetenländer; he said the matter needed to be settled by October 1. The Czechs had to withdraw from the areas he had marked on a map, and allow these to be occupied by German armies. The immediate German occupation of the Sudetenland was the essential condition. It may have been that Hitler had received word that Beneš had no more intention of honoring his word than the Führer had, although this was vigorously denied by Masaryk on the 28th. Göring's Research Bureau had intercepted some revealing conversations between Masaryk, Mastny, and Osusky—the Czech ambassador in Paris—spiced up with rude references to members of the British and French governments. Göring had presented the file to Henderson with obvious delight. They were calculated to make the Czech case even less sympathetic. After three hours of discussion Hitler took his guest out on the terrace: "Oh, Mr Prime Minister, I am so sorry: I had looked forward to showing you this beautiful view of the Rhine . . . but now it is hidden by the mist."

Both parties withdrew to their hotels. All night a motorboat plied the Rhine, taking messages from one to the other. Chamberlain had failed to understand that Hitler intended to destroy the Czech state and that he was simply using the German minority as a pretext. Hitler for his part had realized that he could safely ask for more, as Chamberlain was bound to concede. When Hitler refused to budge the following morning, Chamberlain sent word that there was nothing more for him to do, and he would return to London. Hitler entrusted his reply to Schmidt. It was in German, and his interpreter was to read it to Chamberlain, translating it as he went along. It took about an hour; then Schmidt, fortified with "the right stuff," fled through the lines of journalists back to the ferry and the Rhine.

There was a final discussion between the heads of state at 10:30 PM on the 23rd. The British prime minister insisted that Sudeten Germans control the evacuation of the Czechs, rather than German troops. The Nazis thought this was another of Beneš's tricks. In response Hitler insisted that the Czechs start to vacate the border areas on the 26th and complete them in forty-eight hours. Chamberlain threw up his arms in outrage, while Henderson, who liked to toss in a word or two of German, called it "*Ein Diktat*" (a reference to the hated "dictated peace" of Versailles). At this moment of deadlock, the door opened, and an official brought Hitler a note. He read it and asked Schmidt to translate it for the British. It was Beneš's order to mobilize. There was some question as to whether the Czechs had intended to wreck the talks by summoning their men to the colors; alternatively it might have been an Anglo-French ploy to force Hitler to compromise.

Hitler made his final "concession": He took a pencil and changed the date for the Czech withdrawal to October 1, the date set down long before for the attack on Czechoslovakia. Chamberlain brightened, and Hitler told him that most notorious lie: that this would be the last territorial demand he would make in Europe. Chamberlain was to relay this pledge to the House of Commons. Before Chamberlain returned to Britain, Hitler's official photographer, the drunkard Hoffmann, was able to snap the two leaders standing beside the "palm of peace" in the hotel lobby.

Halifax thought things had gone far enough. To Chamberlain's dismay, the British cabinet, which met on Sunday, September 25, refused to accept Hitler's demands and pledged support to France should it wish to launch military action. By all reports, however, the French were woefully unprepared for war. On behalf of the Czechs, Jan Masaryk handed over a memorandum rejecting the Bad Godesberg proposals. Daladier and Bonnet arrived in London to see Chamberlain and Halifax. As Goebbels had noted, Beneš was tougher than Schuschnigg, and he thought the Czech ambassador to London superior to Dirksen—who was "shitting himself."

Britain began to lumber toward war. The French got tough, manned the Maginot Line, and mobilized 500,000 men; the Russians voiced their readiness to move too. Hitler was convinced that Beneš would brazen it out, and he was worried about the Poles and whether they would give him the backing he craved. As it was, they made a small move and partially mobilized their armies, while the Italians called up three years of reserves. Hitler's other ally, Hungary, did nothing whatsoever, much to his fury. Göring had been sent on a special mission to Horthy but returned empty-handed.

Chamberlain had another card to play. He sent his closest advisor, Sir Horace Wilson, to Berlin with a letter asking Hitler to negotiate with the Czech government directly, with the British present as a third party. He was also to warn Hitler that France would honor her commitments to the Czechs, and Britain hers to France. When Hitler heard from Wilson that the Czechs had rejected his demands, he became overexcited, jumped out of his seat, and began to shout: "The Germans are being treated like niggers; one would not dare treat even the Turks like that." Hitler stopped short of biting the carpet. He told Goebbels he was pleased with his performance—the tantrums were a sham.

Jochen Klepper was in Krummhübel, a resort near the Czech border in the Riesengebirge. He gave a firsthand account; he could hear shooting in the distance. A Czech frontier post had been attacked with grenades. "Now we have arrived at the last consequence of the 'Peace' of Versailles. Eight million Czechs against three million Sudeten Germans; seventy-five million Germans against eight million Czechs! Twenty years ago the seed of all this was planted."

———

Goebbels may have been thinking wishfully when he described the mood of "his" Berliners that autumn: "half war mania and half determination." It was his idea that Hitler should address them at the Sportpalast on the 26th. Despite the apparent enthusiasm of the Berlin crowd, Goebbels was not taking any chances. The "audience should represent the people only," which meant he was going to rig it. On the night, the Führer reiterated his mendacious claim that this venture was his last territorial demand. He found easy meat in the Allied principle of self-determination: The Czech state was a lie, there was no Czechoslovakia, there were just Czechs and Slovaks, and the Slovaks did not like the Czechs. A catalogue of lies and exaggerations followed. The decision lay with Beneš: peace or war. Either he gave the Czech Germans their freedom, or the Germans would snatch it for them. "Now let Herr Beneš make his choice." Groscurth called it "a horrible, undignified rant."

War seemed unavoidable. In Washington, President Roosevelt was alarmed enough to make an appeal for peace and to tell Chamberlain to negotiate to the last moment. The threat was keenly felt in the concentration camps too. In Dachau they realized that if the conflict broke out, it would be curtains for them. They were perfectly aware that any lip service to international opinion or law would be jettisoned at that point. They noted the disappearance of their guards with trepidation. The younger SS men were sent to the Czech border and were replaced by older men of a more kindly disposition than the usual eighteen-year-old sadists. The bubble burst when Chamberlain flew to Munich at the end of the month; the young men returned and resumed their brutal ways.

ON THE morning of the 27th, Sir Horace Wilson found Hitler obdurate. Not even the mention of Britain's need to support France's mobilization had any effect. Hitler claimed to be wholly indifferent as to whether there was a European war: "So—next week we'll all find ourselves at war with each other." After Wilson left, Hitler assembled yet more elements of the Wehrmacht to go into action on the 30th. The gambler Hitler had been more impressed with British moves than he appeared, however, and he was prepared to lend an ear to the doves who made up the majority of his entourage. Once again the only other warmonger was Ribbentrop. Another intimate member of Hitler's circle who had increasing reservations about war was Goebbels, but he was still keeping his head down because of the fallout from his affair with Lida Baarova.

That day Hassell lunched with a number of conservative Germans at the Continental in Berlin. One of those present was Popitz, the acting minister of finance. Popitz told him that speeches like that which the Führer had just delivered at the Sportspalast gave him physical nausea. There were also fears that Hitler's next move would be to proceed against the "upper stratum"—as he called it. Before lunch Hassell had had a meeting with Emil Georg von Strauss, president of the Deutsche Bank. He was "one of the first business leaders to go over to Hitler. He is now filled with the greatest anxiety and disgust." It seemed certain that Hitler would go to war.

The German army was on the point of mutiny. There were desperate worries about the weakness of Germany's western defenses. France could bring sixty-five divisions to bear against a dozen German at the most. Meanwhile the Czechs had called a million men to arms. The German people were not enthusiastic. In some cities open criticism was heard in public places. When an armed division rumbled through the streets of Berlin for an hour and a half on the evening of September 27, the Berliners observed them with "frigid silence." At the Foreign Office Spitzy told Kordt, "Look at the people's faces, filled with pale horror at the prospect of war." At the beginning Hitler stood on his balcony to watch the parade, but when he saw how things were going, he went inside and hid behind a curtain. He had hoped that it would concentrate the minds of the foreign journalists and diplomats in the capital. He was amazed and infuriated by the apathy of the Berliners, which struck the journalists far more than the show of firepower on the roads. Goebbels either failed to notice, or he was taken in by his own propaganda; he observed, "Everywhere the most profound impression was made."

The hawks paid no heed to the reservations expressed by the military men nonetheless. Himmler—who hoped to be able to replace the army by his own Waffen-SS—"complained about the generals. The Führer added his sharpest verdict on the old, senile army leaders. They should be laid off as soon as possible." Not all of Himmler's men agreed with Himmler, or Goebbels's optimistic view of the Berliners. SS-Gruppenführer Lorenz told Ribbentrop, "If the Berliners knew how much you have been beating the drum for war, I'd have to position the entire Leibstandarte along the Wilhelmstrasse to protect you." The last thing the people wanted was war. There was a bad harvest, which was compounded by an outbreak of foot-and-mouth disease. For the first time since Hitler came to power it was clear that the Germans were ready for change.

That same day Chamberlain made his never-forgotten speech on the wireless about a "faraway country," reiterating his reluctance to fight. Czechoslovakia, it was clear, was not worth the bones of a British grenadier. The broadcast was not seen in the bad light it enjoys today, when it is perceived as an admission of indifference to the fate of Czechoslovakia. Groscurth thought, in contrast to Hitler, the British prime minister had been "calm and dignified." Later, Admiral Raeder brought Hitler the news that the Royal Navy had been mobilized. The planned declaration of war against the Czechs was hurriedly retracted. Hitler fired off a

letter to Chamberlain, leaving it up to him to make the Czech government see reason.

As THE gloom of impending war hung like a pall over the capitals of Western and Central Europe, the French were first to attempt to lance the boil.
François-Poncet arrived in the Chancellery at 11 AM. He found tables set
for lunch for commanders designated to invade Czechoslovakia. He
brought Hitler an offer that would allow partial occupation by the 1st and
complete evacuation of the areas in question by the 10th: "Why should
you take the risk when your essential demands can be met without war?"

Hitler was visibly moved by what the Frenchman said, but a little more
pressure was required to make him desist. The British had decided to bring
in Mussolini, who was as alarmed as anyone at the prospect of a European
war. Hitler had kept the Duce in the dark; the proposed meeting between
the two dictators at the Brenner had not taken place. Mussolini saw Chamberlain's policy as the "liquidation of English prestige," but both he and
his son-in-law Ciano were convinced there would be war. Chamberlain
also offered to fly for a fifth time, this time to Berlin.

At 10 AM, the British ambassador in Rome, Lord Perth, showed Ciano
a telegram from Chamberlain. With four hours to go before the German
armies went into Bohemia, Italian mediation was the last chance to save
Europe. Mussolini dispatched his ambassador, the highly experienced, anti-
Nazi Bernardo Attolico, who arrived on the heels of François-Poncet. Attolico was also a friend and confidant of Weizsäcker's. The Italian asked
for a twenty-four-hour stay of execution. Hitler was not impressed by the
sight of the Italian diplomat, who arrived flushed and breathless, and told
Linge, "He's shitting himself! If we took his advice we'd never see the end
of this business," but he listened for all that.

Göring and Neurath were also working on Hitler, while the finance minister Schwerin von Krosigk submitted his views in writing. Hitler dismissed
Göring's qualms, calling him an old woman. Schwerin von Krosigk's line
echoed that of Schacht: Germany did not have enough money to go to
war. The country was already "done for." Next Henderson arrived, bringing Chamberlain's reply to his letter. The prime minister wanted an international conference. Hitler said he would talk it over with Mussolini.
Attolico had a message from the Duce that he supported Chamberlain's

plan. In his "dazzling hatred" for Britain, Ribbentrop was alone in egging Hitler on. Göring took the RAM to one side and angrily berated him as a "criminal fool." Göring said he knew the meaning of war and that it was not to be undertaken lightly. If it were to break out, Ribbentrop should sit beside him in the first bomber. There was never any love lost between the two. It was a Mad Hatter's Tea Party, only to be compared to that which followed the abortive July 20th plot in 1944.

Hitler, who had been wandering around the Chancellery ranting, agreed to Chamberlain's suggestion shortly before noon. The Italian leader had managed to use his powers of persuasion to sugar the pill. It temporarily dampened Hitler's ambitions. "We'll carry on fortifying ourselves for a future opportunity," wrote Goebbels. Hitler decided that the conference should take place in Munich. Only the French and the British would be invited; the Soviet Union and Czechoslovakia would learn of the decisions later. Neither were great powers in Hitler's eyes. The information was carried back to London, where Chamberlain was addressing a House of Commons expecting to hear a declaration of war. The news was greeted with "indescribable enthusiasm."

The opposition was still hoping to strike on the 29th and eagerly awaited confirmation that their coup could move forward. On the morning of the 28th Kordt gave Oster the text of Chamberlain's letter to Hitler. It was circulated to Witzleben and Halder. They interpreted it to mean that Hitler was bent on war. Halder went to Brauchitsch, who was finally convinced to act. Kordt wanted it to happen at once, not waiting even one day. It was then that the opposition learned of the Italian demarche, which would preserve Hitler at the expense of Czechoslovakia. "Colombo" (so-called because he had been German consul in Ceylon) Brücklmeier, who was on duty in the Chancellery, took the news to Kordt. Hitler postponed mobilization for twenty-four hours.

On September 28 European war still seemed unavoidable. Hitler met Mussolini off his train on the platform at Kufstein on the old Austrian border, and they traveled together to Munich. Hitler thought he was briefing the Italian leader, but Mussolini was keener to calm Hitler down and prevent him from dragging Europe into war, all the time reassuring him that if the conference did break down, Italy would be behind him. Mussolini was of two minds. Half of him thought there was a chance of eliminating France and Britain forever. On the way to Munich, Hitler told him of his long-term plans: he needed to knock out Czechoslovakia to leave his hands free to fight Britain and France. They needed to go to war soon, while they were "young and full of vigour." Mussolini was to be the focus of the conference, largely because, unlike Hitler, he could speak the languages of the other attendees. Ciano accompanied his father-in-law.

Chamberlain was met by Ribbentrop and Bavarian State Councillor Christian Weber at the airport in Oberwiesenfeld. The RAM was still shouting for war, behaving "like a petulant child" and deliberately trying to wreck the conference. He was particularly furious at the presence of his predecessor, Neurath. Chamberlain was lodged in the Hotel Regina on the Maximiliansplatz in Munich, together with the Czech "observers" Mastny and Masaryk, who were present to receive whatever scraps were handed down from the top table. The French delegation stopped at the Vier Jahreszeiten. Outside, in the streets of Munich, people were on tenterhooks, hoping that peace would be preserved. Even Winifred Wagner thought that was what her "Wolf" really wanted.

The talks began at 12:30 PM in Hitler's study in the Führerbau. The seating had been managed so that Hitler had his back to the window and his face in shadow. Chamberlain was on his left. Daladier and Mussolini sat together on a sofa. The basis for the Munich Agreement was the document drawn up by Neurath and Weizsäcker, together with Göring, which stemmed from the British note. It had then been given to Attolico to send to Rome. Mussolini had passed it off as his, to mislead Ribbentrop.

There was little opposition to Hitler's diktat. A General Staff map was brought in, and the conference effectively took the form of a border commission. The international treaties that guaranteed the Czech state were torn up. There was occasional rearguard action from Daladier, on the advice of Alexis Léger, the head of the Quai d'Orsay, who expressed concern for the future existence of Czechoslovakia. Hitler seemed to take this well and later expressed his liking of the French premier, who impressed the Germans much more than the frigid, vulpine Chamberlain. The draft was signed at around 2:30 AM on the morning of September 30. The Poles and Hungarians had to lodge their claims to territory within three months.

Hitler could still march in on the first of the month; he appeared so pleased with the result that he ordered the guest book to be brought over from the Brown House so that the leaders could enter their signatures.

The agreement gave Hitler pretty well everything he had craved at Bad Godesberg, and the German armies went in on October 1 as planned. The new borders were drawn on strategic rather than ethnic lines, thereby leaving a quarter of a million Germans in Czechoslovakia and bringing 800,000 Czechs into the Reich. The Czech version of the Maginot Line was absorbed into German territory. Czechs who did not wish to remain in the new German Zone (these included ethnic Germans for whom Nazi rule would have been unpalatable, and some 30,000 Jews) were to leave before October 10, with only the clothes they were wearing; everything else was to be left behind. The Germans would pay no compensation. Chamberlain's attempts to win some sort of deal for the Czechs had caused the only disagreement between him and Hitler at the conference. In the end he had not even been able to save a few head of Czech cattle.

On November 20, an "international commission" allotted 11,000 square miles to the Germans. These contained 66 percent of Czech coal, 80 percent of lignite, 70 percent of iron and steel, and the same amount of the nation's electric power, as well as 40 percent of its timber. Göring rubbed his thighs in glee, and a humiliated Beneš went into bitter exile. On October 10 the Czechs conceded that the Teschen pocket belonged to the Poles, and on November 2 Ribbentrop and Ciano redrew the Czech-Hungarian border. Czechoslovakia was now defenseless against Germany's next blow, which would not be long in coming.

Hitler could be said to have won the day hands down, but he was still cross. He cared little for the Sudeteners—he wanted Prague. He was especially angry when Chamberlain was cheered by the Munich crowd as he traveled in an open-topped car after his visit to his "modest apartment" on the Prinzregentenplatz. Without informing Daladier, Chamberlain had gone to seek further assurance of Hitler's peaceable intentions. The Anglo-German agreement was to create machinery for constant maintenance of peaceful relations. Hitler seemed sullen and distracted. Schmidt (who was present once again) believed he appended his signature to Chamberlain's document only to placate the Englishman. That night the Munichois celebrated with double measures of beer. Even *Der Stürmer* congratulated

Chamberlain on standing up to the (Jewish) mob and working for peace. Hitler did not join them; he thought the British prime minister had spoiled his triumphal entry into Prague.

Chamberlain must have felt relieved, but he went home and told the relevant bodies to rearm, quickly. He had bought some time, and he was right about one thing: Hitler wanted war, and that had only been delayed. There had never been any intention of going to Czechoslovakia's aid anyhow. On March 18, shortly after the Anschluss, Vansittart's successor at the Foreign Office, Sir Alexander Cadogan, had written in his diary, "Foreign Policy Committee unanimous that Czechoslovakia is not worth the bones of a single Grenadier. And they're quite right too!"

Among the leading Nazis, Göring was also in the doghouse for spoiling Hitler's fun. Ribbentrop now moved into the ascendant, and the corpulent former air ace would never have Hitler's ear again when it came to foreign policy. Hitler may have been obliged to shelve his plans to absorb Bohemia and Moravia, but only until the next opportunity arose.

In Berlin, Klepper's mind was put at rest that war had been avoided. There was, however, no mention of the fate of the Czechs. He noted that the feeling of happiness was universal; even voices on the telephone sounded different. Everyone was "exhausted and happy"; Hitler's "magic was shattered." In the church in Berlin-Mariendorf that Sunday, people cried as they sang the "Leuthen Chorale"—*Nun danket alle Gott!*

Goebbels retired to bed "as happy as a child." Germany's prestige "had grown monstrously, now we are really a world power and that means arm! Arm! Arm!" The "old woman" Göring was naturally as pleased as punch at his success. He had got the resources he wanted, and he had managed to avert a conflict. "He fought bravely for the sake of peace." He woke Emmy at the conclusion of the conference and told her "We've pulled it off"; "It's peace." He was over the moon at all that he had acquired for his Four Year Plan. Taking Ciano to the station the next morning, he told the Italian, "Now, there's going to be rearmament the likes of which the world has never seen."

Far away in China, the German Rhodes scholar, Adam von Trott zu Solz, who was later to perish for his part in the July 20th plot, wrote to his friend Shiela Grant Duff on October 1. He felt the one advantage of what had taken place was that it had been a European decision and not merely a Germano-Czech one, "but I agree with you in your present apprehensions."

He wrote again on the 6th.

I confess that I failed to realise the intrinsic turning point which came about with the Anschluss and which opened up a path for a coercive settlement of the Central European problem—which I had never considered possible with the power, prestige and commitments of the Western Democracies in that area. Though I did realise there was in England a large body of opinion that favoured a negotiated settlement of the Sudeten question in Germany's favour, I believed that France and Russia would remain intransigent on the matter and that your country would back [them] up.

The opposition would have to shelve their plans too. There was a furious reaction against Canaris and Kleist-Schmenzin and all those who had implied that Britain would fight. For generals like Gerd von Rundstedt, who had been initiated into the plot by his friend Kleist, the whole thing now felt like a hoax. "Brauchitsch would hear no more talk of a revolt, the servile Keitel had been kept out of the picture from the start; Halder who had been found slumped at his desk by Hitler's adjutant, Gerhard Engel, had despondently told General von Witzleben, the most eager of the rebels, that he could not be answerable for military action against Hitler if Mr Chamberlain found a peaceable solution to the Czechoslovak dispute. Kleist went back to his estates in Pomerania, utterly disillusioned." There was not to be another coordinated attempt to remove the Führer until July 20, 1944.

On September 7, Italy closed another door: Jews were now to be defined racially and not religiously. Up until then, Italy had still been on the escape route for many baptized Jews. Foreign Jews who had settled in Italy after 1919 would now be expelled. The measure affected as many as 40,000 people, including an estimated 6,000 Austrian and German Jews. There were around 70,000 Jews living in Italy, defined as full Jews with two Jewish parents. From September 3 they were evicted from Italian schools and universities. In Rome, Pius XI quietly made his views clear to a group of Belgian pilgrims on the 6th, after delivering a reading about Abraham "our father, our ancestor." He said, "Antisemitism is not compatible with the sublime thought and reality which are expressed in this text. It is not possible for Christians to participate in antisemitism. Spiritually, we are Semites."

Collard performed his last nineteen baptisms on September 15, before returning to Cologne. Following his departure there were developments in Britain. Appeasement was in the air. An initiative from Sir Wyndham Deedes led to the creation of a Christian Council to assist Jews from Germany and Austria. The new body joined the others in Bloomsbury House, which had campaigned for non-Aryan Christians, children, and students, as well as the Quakers' own operation. It would put pressure on the Dominions to accept the Jews. Collard's departure came at a time when the first large-scale releases were being made from Dachau. Some were not so lucky. Bruno Heilig was transferred to Buchenwald on the 22nd. If anything, the camp was even grimmer, although one of the capos turned out to be a relatively sympathetic Prussian Junker, whose grandmother was a Jew.

The Jews showed little sympathy for the plight of the Czechs. President Beneš created the problem for himself by his attempts to prevent a Habsburg restoration in 1934 and 1935. "Better Hitler than Habsburg," he is supposed to have said. Weisl predicted that 6 million Jewish lives would now be lost between the Rhine and the Dnjester.

Nazi methods in Austria were not always crowned with success. In Mistelbach near the Czech border, the Jews were refusing to sell out. The Gestapo suggested they should be pushed across the frontier, as their closeness to Czechoslovakia caused a danger of Communist infiltration! The huge taxes levied on Jews leaving the country were also a disincentive. Eichmann was up against Göring. The latter wanted to fill the coffers of the state at the expense of the Jews, while Eichmann sought the fastest emigration possible. The number of Jews marooned in a hostile Central Europe was causing alarm in Jewish circles. There were 20,000 in the Sudetenland, which would soon be prey to Hitler's racial policies; a further 385,000 were in rump Czechoslovakia, which was about to pass racial laws of its own; there were 410,000 in Hungary, which had already promulgated racial laws, and 78,000 in Yugoslavia, where the government had decreed measures against the Jews. Romania had 800,000, with 50,000 Christian converts. Poland had another 3.2 million. If you included 170,000 in Austria and 350,000 remaining in Germany, that made a European total of 4.1 million, not including Russia. Latvia was now the sole European country that remained open to Jews.

In the autumn of 1938 there were an estimated 200 Austrian Jews stranded in Yugoslavia. At the beginning of October, however, the Yugoslav government finally ruled that they intended to expel all foreign Jews in three months. The Dutch, too, were showing frustration at the number of illegal immigrants, and on September 20 the *Jewish Telegraphic Agency* reported that 44 Austrian Jews had been sent home from Rotterdam. The British were flexing their muscles again over Palestine. Cyprus, with its proximity to the Mandate territory, was an obvious magnet. The numbers of Jews landing was causing concern, with 30 to 40 fresh refugees arriving every week. On September 21 it was reported that an 800-man transport from Vienna had been sent back. Weisl had promises of £1,000 to grease palms, but he needed twice that. In the wake of Evian he noted that Nicaragua was prepared to take in 3,000 Jews, but they had to hand over $100 on landing.

The news from Vienna was not all doom and gloom. There was a small sprinkling of that frivolity for which the city is famous. While the leaders of the Western world met to assign Hitler the German-speaking parts of Czechoslovakia, a court convened in the former Austrian capital to decide who possessed the right to sell the "original" Sachertorte: Sacher's Hotel or the café Demel. The court ruled in Sacher's favor; the cake labeled the "original" had to come from their kitchens.

CHAPTER EIGHT

OCTOBER

The German army officially took control of the Czech borderlands on October 1. The Poles wasted no time, occupying Teschen and Freistadt the following day. In Germany's new *Gaue* the Jews were now at great risk. There were 27,000 Jews and non-Aryan Christians in the Sudetenland. In the summer there had been antisemitic riots in Eger, Asch, and Karlsbad, and Jewish shops had been ransacked. Famous spas like Carlsbad and Marienbad had been immensely popular with rich Jews. *Der Stürmer* reckoned that 80 percent of Carlsbad's customers were Jewish, noting maliciously that although Jews had lost the choice to regain their health at Carlsbad, they could keep fit by running. The doctors who treated them were also likely to be Jews. There were other powerful Jewish clans in the region; the hop merchants of Saaz, for example, were largely Jewish. The message was clear, and thousands fled.

Although the Munich Agreement had laid down a provision for citizens to "opt" for Germany or Czechoslovakia, the Czechs refused protection to Jews who feared for their safety under the Nazis and forcibly returned as many as they could find to the German occupied areas. Many eluded them. By May 1939, only a tenth of that number remained in the new German *Gaue*. It was not only the Jews the Czechs were reluctant to accept; there

201

were thousands of ethnic German Social Democrats too. The Nazis said they had no right to opt for Czechoslovakia. There were also 5,000 to 6,000 Germans who had taken refuge in Prague and other parts of Czechoslovakia after Hitler's assumption of power. There was discrimination against Sudeten Jews, who were denied access to the funds they had been able to bring out, and the others who had crossed the demarcation lines penniless. The British donated £10 million to help alleviate the situation. This failed to prevent the Czechs from putting pressure on a quarter of a million Jews in the country to emigrate. Sopade, the organization of German Socialists in exile, also decided it was prudent to run. They set up their new home in Paris.

The new Czech government under President Emil Hàcha sought a rapprochement with Germany and aligned its policies accordingly. The French were to end their alliance with the country—which had done the Czechs little good—and the Czechs themselves decided to abandon their flirtation with the Soviet Union. German-style restrictions on the movement and employment of Jews were also introduced. On October 11, Mastny assured Göring that the Czechs would "seriously tackle the Jewish problem." To some extent the attitude of the new Czech "Second Republic" was dictated by weakness. Stripped of its fortifications, it now had no means of holding the Germans back. As it was, the settlement had been clumsy: 478,589 ethnic Germans remained in rump Czechoslovakia, while 676,478 Czechs were now living in Germany. Those half million Germans were hardly popular, either. Hitler was still straining at the leash. As he told Goebbels on the evening of the 2nd, it was his unshakable decision to smash Czecho. "And he will make it happen too: this dead, amorphous, artificial state must go."

Helmuth Groscurth accompanied Admiral Canaris on his tour of inspection of the new German *Gaue*. Canaris was anxious to avoid the Gestapo, who had made as many as two hundred arrests by the 3rd of the month. He did not wish to be seen shaking either Himmler or Heydrich's hands. In the regular army there was resentment against the SS too. General Bock complained about Heydrich, but Groscurth noted that they confined themselves to grumbling: "No general dares show this criminal the door." Groscurth nonetheless noted the excitement of the Sudetenländer: "There is a marked contrast with Austria. The people there were more or less drunk, here, however, you note a real liberation and a sigh of relief from people who have been freed of a heavy load."

HITLER WENT on a tour of the Czech defenses on the 3rd and 4th. SS bands played his favorite "Badenweiler March." He recognized Canaris and stopped his car to greet him. In his cavalcade of thirty-odd cars there were just three Wehrmacht men. The rest were SS or Sudetenländer. The RAM was with him, in the grey diplomatic uniform with "lots of gold." Groscurth discovered a boorish Reichenau knocking back *Sekt*, infatuated with Hitler. He repeated some of his hero's remarks on Chamberlain and Daladier. The latter he called a "master baker." Groscurth remarked that this was a case of the pot calling the kettle black. General Rundstedt had a different view: "Canaris, how long do we have to put up with this foolish performance?"

Groscurth was sent on a second tour of duty, this time on Henlein's staff. Contrary to the rumors of his homosexuality running riot in the SS, the Sudeten leader revealed himself as a family man with a fondness for burgundy. He had set up his HQ in a deserted Jewish villa. While Groscurth explored the new *Gaue*, he noted the misery of the 40,000 or so Czech coal miners around Dux and Brux, who had now become German citizens. In a fish factory he was greeted with shouts of "*Heil Hitler!*" by the 500 chiefly women staff but was told a few days before they would have cried "*Heil Moskau!*"

Hitler observed that the Czech fortresses were built in the same style as France's Maginot Line. He then turned them over to the Wehrmacht for gunnery practice. He was still sulking about Prague. Armed with his experiences of the Czech defenses, he toured his own West Wall before returning to Munich on October 14. He saw the new Czech foreign minister Chvalkovsky and uttered furious threats about how quickly he could crush them were they ever to transgress. On October 21 Hitler issued plans to take the port of Memel.

The Slovaks declared themselves an autonomous region on the 7th, just as Göring took off for a tour of the new German *Gaue* centered on the town of Reichenberg, where Henlein had established his headquarters. Göring was convinced that the rest of Bohemia and Moravia would fall like ripe fruit into German hands. There were drawbacks for the Nazis:

Eventually Germany would acquire all those Czech Jews who had failed to flee, just as they had gained a further 200,000 Jews in Austria. These disadvantages would become all the greater when Germany invaded Poland a year later. It was *relatively* easy to find homes for lawyers and doctors of the sophisticated assimilated Jews of Vienna and Prague, with contacts abroad who could issue them with guarantees, but there would be few if any takers for the shtetl Jews. As Germany absorbed more and more land to the east, the likelihood of a "radical" solution to the "Jewish problem" became all the greater.

Yet more doors were closing. On October 1, Argentina threatened to revoke six hundred visas it had granted to Jews from the Reich. This would also affect those traveling through Argentina to the landlocked South American states. George Rublee, who had been left with the unenviable task of implementing the decisions taken at Evian, quickly made them reconsider. On October 5 the Swiss police president, Dr. Rothmund, finally succeeded in putting pressure on the German authorities to stamp Jewish passports with a large red J, better to identify would-be Jewish immigrants and turn them back at the frontier. Otherwise they would interpret the passport as invalid. This was the final stage of a long process of trying to make Jewish passports distinct from those of Gentiles. The Swiss authorities had clearly had enough: 7,000 Jews had settled in the country since 1933; 2,000 of them had arrived illegally from Austria. The Polish government adopted the same policy the very next day.

On the 6th a letter went out from the SS man Peworezky to the SD in Vienna. An operation was planned in the suburb of Wieden for the 10th that would encourage as many Jews as possible to hurry up and leave. The first to be evicted were Czech Jews. Any Jews who did not possess the requisite papers would simply be pushed over the frontier into rump Czechoslovakia. If they were penniless, they were to be given forty RM. It was to be dressed up to look like a "spontaneous demonstration" as the Party was not meant to be behind it. Force would combat resistance. Jews were cleared from houses in the prosperous areas of Ottakring, Hernals, Währing, and Döbling and boarded on trains. No passports were required. The next day Jews in the suburbs of Mauer, Atzgersdorf, Liesing, Percholdsdorf, and Mödling were accorded the same treatment. They had to hand over their keys.

On the 7th the Nazis celebrated their victory in the Sudetenland by intimidating Jews in the plush Viennese suburb of Döbling, threatening them with "Dachau or worse." The *Times* actually reported that Jews were being released from Dachau and alluded to the interest in baptism among the assimilated Jews of the city: "It is reliably reported that besides Mr Frederick Richter, the verger of the Anglican Church in Vienna (who is a British subject of Austrian birth), eighteen sextons, registrars, and other officials of various Roman Catholic churches in Vienna have been arrested during the past three months on charges of forging or falsification of baptismal certificates for Jews." The Nazis were also closing the Catholic associations, bringing them into line with their own and taking away their flags and banners. Religious instruction in schools was being discontinued, and the schools themselves were closed while the regime helped itself to the treasures of Austria's monasteries. Hundreds of priests had been packed off to Dachau. Religious symbols and holidays came under fire too. The Nazis had enjoyed some success in luring Austrians away from the Church, but for many, the Anschluss was not looking as attractive to pious Austrians or south Germans as it had done in March. It was high time for Cardinal Innitzer to make a stand.

On October 7 he addressed some 6,000 to 8,000 young Catholics in the cathedral with what Goebbels called a "cheeky homily": "My beloved Catholic youth of Vienna, we will affirm our faith from now on and in these times, with yet more strength and resolution. . . . Christ is our Führer and king! Guard your belief and stand firm! For only belief can bring happiness!"

The homily resulted in a demonstration of support outside the archbishop's palace: "*Lieber Bischof, sei so nett: zeige Dich am Fensterbrett*" ("Dear Bishop, if you will, show your face at the windowsill"). The youths also cried "Innitzer command, we will obey!"—mocking the Nazi formula "*Führer befehl! Wir folgen!*" ("Führer command! We will obey!")—and "Christ is our Führer!" A crowd of two hundred Hitler Youths tried unsuccessfully to disperse them and were scattered in their turn. Some of the demonstrators were arrested. The storming of the archbishop's palace the next day poured cold water on any remaining enthusiasm for Hitler there might have been among the Austrian clergy. Around fifty members of the Hitler Youth aged fourteen to twenty-five spent forty minutes breaking and burning everything they could, including 1,245 windowpanes. What they did not break they stole. They also defenestrated Father Johann Krawarik, breaking his thigh bone.

Goebbels did not want the foreign press to make too much of the story, and played it down. However, as much as Goebbels might have hoped to conceal the new persecution of the Church in Austria, Bürckel answered Innitzer in his speech on the Heldenplatz in Vienna on the 13th. He denounced the Church, and the crowd carried banners with the legend "String up the priests!" At 10 PM that same day a mob of twenty or thirty people attacked the Cistercians in Lilienfeld, breaking 487 panes of glass while they claimed to be searching for weapons. One of the men told the monks, "You have Innitzer to thank for this." On October 17 all religious schools were closed, including Austria's oldest academy—the monastic *Gymnasium* in Kremsmünster. In rural Württemberg there was still confusion as to the level of participation in business life allowed to the Jews. Since February it had been unclear as to whether the Jews were allowed to trade in local markets. As far as farmers were concerned, as long as they came to market, they were happy to carry on doing business with them. A formal prohibition was only issued in October.

———

Hitler's anger over Munich had not abated. At the opening of the Westmark Gau's new theater, Hitler made what Hassell called an "incomprehensibly rude" speech in Saarbrücken on the 9th. He attacked Duff Cooper—who had resigned from the cabinet over Munich—Eden, and Churchill as warmongers and expressed his resentment at Munich and foreign interference in the question of the German Jews. He accused his British critics of behaving like "governesses" and reveled in their problems in Palestine. The speech was concluded with a performance of *The Flying Dutchman*.

Outside Germany it was thought that the speech was a signal he would soon be on the march again. Goebbels had been present and found the reaction to the speech in the foreign press hard to understand: "It wasn't at all aggressive and most of it was given off the cuff." He reported that his master had arrived "tired and weary" and full of his impressions of the Sudetenland. Hitler told his minister that having seen the Czech bunkers, he now realized that they would have cost much blood, and he believed he had done the right thing, "and we will swallow this Czecho one day. We have to free the road to the Balkans."

The one consolation for Hitler was the new theater, a representative Nazi-style building designed by Paul Baumgarten, and he promptly decided that Baumgarten should draw up the designs for the theater in his city of Linz. Hitler retired to Bad Godesberg, where he met up with the RAM on the 12th. The German Foreign Office was to issue a statement that that the country had no further territorial demands in Bohemia and Moravia.

He traveled from there to the Berghof. Goebbels was still in the dog-house, and Hitler was arbitrating between him and Magda. On the 23rd he was summoned to his master, where the couple's heads were knocked together. Goebbels resigned himself to his fate like a chastened cur: "I submit and arrange my personal wellbeing and happiness in the interests of the state and the people." It was the Führer who "remade the marriage" and ordered the photographs to be taken for the press of the happy reconciliation rather than his humiliated propaganda chief. A picture on the front page of the *Berliner Illustrierte Zeitung* showed the three of them together. Only Hitler was smiling.

When he wasn't too cross with Goebbels, he spoke to him about future plans. "In the distant future he sees a really difficult fight ahead, probably with England [*sic*]." At a birthday party Hitler told guests that all Germans were behind him. "Only the ten thousand in the upper stratum have any doubts." The French ambassador, François-Poncet, went to Berchtes-gaden to say farewell to Hitler on the 17th. The French had been alarmed by the Saarbrücken speech and were now seeking a Franco-German decla-ration that would tie Hitler's hands. There must have been a worry in the Quai d'Orsay that Hitler would snatch Alsace-Lorraine. From the German side, it was thought that the moment might be ripe to split the French from the British. Saarbrücken had been rude about the latter; the French had been let off the hook. François-Poncet was very impressed by the set-ting and the amazing piece of engineering that was the so-called Eagle's Nest—Hitler's tea room 1,900 meters up, which put the Frenchman in mind of knights of the Holy Grail at Monsalvat. François-Poncet was struck by what a baffling person Hitler was. Goebbels held the diplomat in high esteem and regretted his going to Rome.

Hitler returned to Austria on October 20, slipping back across the old border into his new Moravian territories, where Groscurth listened to a speech he described as "dangerous" made to a small circle of acolytes. "It was peppered with attacks on the English [*sic*], French, and above all the Hungarians, whom he characterised as cowards and wet rags." He did imitations of the Hungarian minister and heaped praise on the Poles and Yugoslavs. The Polish were "a great people," Ambassador Lipski "a statesman and towering intellect." Stojadinovitsch was also "acclaimed." Hitler was back on form.

———

Maximilian Reich was released from Dachau on October 12 after six months and more of servitude. His wife in Vienna had learned that six was standard for Jewish journalists with exit papers. As a Gentile reminded him before he left, there was no such hope for the many Communists; they were there until the bitter end. A guard showed him the way to Weimar and respectfully called him *Sie*. He had time to kill at the station but was not prepared to be seduced into the buffet by well-wishers who recognized him as a former inmate. One man enquired whether he had money; another called him *Kumpel* (mate, buddy) and wondered whether he needed help. He realized that it was true what they said in the camp: There were human beings out there. He arrived at the East Station in Vienna. The family had been alerted by telegram, but his wife failed to recognize her husband. He was wearing a worn-out suit that had been lent to him; his head had been shaved and he had lost his moustache; he was also emaciated. The second time she entered the station she spotted him. She had a shirt and a suit in a case for him to change into; they had to buy a hat in the Mariahilferstrasse on the way home. At least some of his dignity had been restored.

ON OCTOBER 14 there was a significant meeting chaired by Reichsmarschall Göring at the Air Ministry in Berlin, in the course of which the minister intimated that Hitler had big plans—almost certainly war. The economy was in a parlous state. Foreign currency reserves had been used up, and work performance had dwindled; he (Göring) was now going to produce some radical solutions. Once again it was Henry VIII's technique he was suggesting: Rob the richest part of the community. In good King Harry's time it had been the Church, but Göring was going to get the money from the Jews by "eliminating them from the German economy." The next day all Jewish passports were rescinded in the Altreich. This meant that they had to apply anew. It was a further measure to prevent their money from leaving the country, and it provided an opportunity for the police to make a little money on the side.

There were also changes in the administration of the Ostmark. Vienna was to be reduced to a purely administrative entity. New areas to the south were made part of a "Greater Vienna," a city of 2 million souls. A minor pogrom also took place on October 14. The windows of seven synagogues were broken. The next day seven more were profaned in the then-Jewish Second District. On the 16th a synagogue was torched in the Tempelgasse. On the 17th two prayer houses were destroyed in the Second District. The destruction continued until the 19th.

Later that year, the IKG in Vienna produced figures for emigration up until October 15. Of the 165,000 members before March 11, 40,000 or so had already left. The largest number (2,000) had reached the United States, followed by Palestine (1,384) and Britain (1,321); 681 had gone to Switzerland and 480 to Czechoslovakia. A total of 444 had reached Argentina, 155 Australia, 136 Greece, 88 Cyprus (these last two were stage posts for Palestine), 47 Bolivia, and 9 Canada. On October 22 the *Times* reported that there were 5,000 illegal Jewish immigrants in Belgium without visible means of support. The Belgian government had decided to intern 1,400 rather than expelling them. The British were having considerable problems with Palestine at the time, with the Arabs rioting and striking against the increasing numbers of Jews. Not only were many of Germany and Austria's Jews knocking on the door, but measures against them introduced by the Second Republic in Czechoslovakia meant that Czech Jews were also looking for asylum.

It wasn't only the Jews who were suffering as outlaws. Germany was now doing away with most vestiges of the rule of law. On the same October 22 Hitler spoke to proclaim that "Every means adopted for carrying out the will of the Leader is considered legal, even though it may conflict with existing statutes and precedents." In June that year all security police—the Gestapo and the Kripo (criminal police)—were enrolled in the SS and therefore became subservient to the Party through the SD. It was a process that reached its inevitable end when the police were taken away from the Ministry of the Interior and placed under the control of the SS. There were now no legal controls on the police, and divergent political opinion was ipso facto a crime.

Meanwhile, other parts of Central Europe were playing games with their Jewish citizens. Responding to the pressure exerted by its neighbors, Germany made moves to expel all its Ostjuden—generally Russian Jews who had settled as a result of the pogroms and the Russian Revolution. At the beginning of 1938 they were given weeks to get out or face imprisonment and the confiscation of their belongings. The next move was against the Romanian Jews. After the Germans moved into Austria and the Sudetenland, it was the moment to oust Czech and Slovak Jews. Camps were established for them in no-man's-land, as their countries of origin were very reluctant to take them back.

———

Mutual antipathy to Jews led to the end of the state of "benevolent neutrality" that existed between Germany and Poland. There were around 3.1 million Jews in Poland—just under 10 percent of the population. Their movements were restricted, and antisemitism was endemic. Earlier that year Ciano had defined the relationship between the two countries that managed to coexist despite the fact that Poland had been re-created out of the rib of Prussia: "The Polish Corridor is accepted for an indefinite period by Germany, which actually desires to see the power of Poland increased as a means of strengthening the anti-Bolshevik barrier."

The sticking point was the large number of Polish Jews living in Germany and smaller groups in Austria. Despite Polish citizenship, the Poles refused to readmit them, nor did they want to return, as many of them had fled to Germany in the first place to escape pogroms and persecution in Poland or the Ukraine. In 1936, the Poles had produced plans to make all Jews emigrate, and on March 31, 1938, they rescinded the citizenship of all Polish Jews who had lived abroad for more than five years. Nearly 40 percent of these expatriate Polish Jews had been born in Germany.

Such policies found favor in Poland, where successive governments had been trying to steal a march on the National Democratic or Endek Party, with its antisemitic policies and calls for ghettoes and boycotts of Jewish businesses. There was a certain rapport between Göring and Jozef Beck, the Polish foreign minister. Beck had served in the German cavalry in the First World War and liked the Germans, disliking both the French and the Russians. His policy was anti-Bolshevik, intending to maintain an equal distance between Soviet Russia and Nazi Germany. The timing of the Polish move was clumsy, however, as Göring was still trying to woo the Poles into approving an alliance directed against Russia, where Germany later intended to create its empire, and was dangling the Ukraine at Poland as compensation for border changes in the west.

Poland's acquisition of the Teschen pocket with its quarter of a million Poles and the railway knot at Oderberg made the Germans more popular in Poland too. Indeed, there had been cries of "Long live Hitler!" in Warsaw after the Polish incursion. Ribbentrop stormed in, holding talks with the Polish ambassador, Lipski, and on the 24th the latter was invited to Berchtesgaden. In return for a railway line or motorway to link Germany with its estranged province of East Prussia and possibly some border changes around Posen-Poznan, Germany was prepared to create a free port for Poland somewhere near Danzig. There would also be a sweetener of a nonaggression treaty lasting twenty-five years guaranteeing the present frontiers. Danzig itself would naturally return to Germany under the same arrangements.

While such treaties were not worth the paper they were printed on, it is an indication that the Germans were not seeking radical border changes in Poland for the time being, but Ribbentrop was unable to convince them to take up the offer. Under his tenure at the Wilhemstrasse, the Poles went from being friends to being enemies. They took no interest in the offer, which betrayed a certain degree of pragmatism on the part of the Germans, as any revision of the Polish-German border was bound to be popular with the German people and the Wehrmacht. Göring might have proved a better emissary. As far as Memel was concerned, things were coming to a head with mass protests against Lithuanian rule.

Meanwhile, the *official* foreign minister of the Third Reich, Ribbentrop, was in Rome at Hitler's behest, trying once again to make the Italians sign a tripartite military pact with Germany and Japan. The Japanese alliance was meant to deter America from coming to the aid of Britain and France, his enemies in the west. He told Mussolini Germany would be ready for war with Britain and France at the beginning of 1939. Neither Mussolini nor Ciano appreciated the visit. Mussolini told Ciano, "You only have to look at his head to see that he has a very small brain." Ciano, for his part, thought Ribbentrop "vain, lightweight, loquacious. . . . He has fixed in his head the idea of war, he wants war, his war." Whether or not Mussolini and Ciano despised Ribbentrop, they signed on November 6.

GERMAN-POLISH relations were declining ever further. On the 6th the Polish government had announced that October 30 was the last date for the renewal of passports for Polish Jews. On October 24 Ribbentrop demanded the return of the city of Danzig and free access to East Prussia through the Polish Corridor. On the 27th and the 28th, the Gestapo working with the German Foreign Office made the decision to expel the Ostjuden. Some 17,000 Polish Jews were pushed over the border into Poland. A memo from Best dated the 29th justified the policy, saying that the Polish government was foisting 70,000 Jews on Germany. Those selected for expulsion came from Germany, Austria, and the Sudetenland. The Gestapo entered schools in Berlin and dragged Jewish children away from their lessons. One of those expelled at the time was the later literary critic Marcel Reich-Ranicki, who had just finished school in Berlin. On the morning of the 28th, he was awakened by a policeman bringing him a document telling him to leave Germany within a fortnight. When Reich-Ranicki objected that he had two weeks, the policeman said, "No, come along at once."

He was allowed to take five marks and a briefcase. He put in a Balzac novella and a handkerchief. Everything else had to be left behind. Reich-Ranicki had no idea why he was receiving this treatment, and felt someone must have borne false witness. It became clearer at the police station: "Here I immediately found myself among ten or perhaps twenty fellow victims. They were Jews, all of them older than me. . . . They were speaking perfect German and not a word of Polish. They had either been born in Germany, or had come to Germany as small children and attended school there. But like me they all, as I soon discovered, had Polish passports." Only men were expelled from Berlin, although other cities had sent the women away too. When it was dark later that afternoon, they were transferred to a siding at the Schlesischer Bahnhof, where a train was waiting. Everything was done quietly and mostly by night. No one was supposed to see. At the frontier they had to form up in columns. There were shouts and shots fired. Then they were driven into a Polish train, where the doors were sealed from the outside. It was packed, and many of the women were wearing nightgowns under their coats—they had not been given time to dress.

The German plan was to get rid of the Jews before they finally ceased to be Poles and became their responsibility. As the Poles were not willing to take them back, around 8,000 of them sat in gypsy camps in no-man's-land from November 1938 until August 1939, while Polish Christians and Jews administered aid. Of the 4,000 who arrived in Gdynia by ship from Danzig, only 1,500 were allowed to land. The rest had to remain on board. In revenge the Poles expelled Germans from the onetime German areas of Poznan and Pommerelen. Later the expulsions were limited to German Jews.

The German expulsions, and the brutal way they were carried out, provided the Gestapo with what was for them valuable experience in rapid deportation. The Polish Jews were allowed to take the very minimum with them and often had to put up with nights of imprisonment before they were taken to the border. At the beginning of November Fips wallowed in the Jews' despair in *Der Stürmer*: "Three simple questions for Hebrews— What can I do against the Nazis? How do I get my money out of the country? Where oh where can I—a proper Talmud Jew—settle in peace?"

The tug of war over the Jews had been a bad omen for future relations between the two countries. When Canaris met Weizsäcker on December 12, the diplomat thought war with Poland unavoidable, despite Ribbentrop's best efforts to maintain the strongest ties with the Poles, while pursuing his war against the West.

CHAPTER NINE

NOVEMBER

More frontiers were being redrawn. On November 2 the German and Italian foreign ministers met in Vienna to arbitrate between the Czechs and the Hungarians over the Slovakian border. Ciano ran into Göring in the Imperial. He was wearing a flashy grey suit, a ruby tiepin, and more large rubies on his fingers. In his buttonhole was a large Nazi eagle with diamonds. The Italian found "a slight suggestion of Al Capone."

Ribbentrop surprised Ciano by being pro-Czech, which Ciano found inconsistent with the attitude toward the country Ribbentrop had helped cripple just a month before. Ciano thought Hàcha should give Ribbentrop a medal. Largely as a result of Ciano's superior preparation, the Hungarians recouped 12,000 square kilometers of territory but failed to regain their city of Pressburg (Bratislava). It spelled more bad news for the Jews, as the newly autonomous Slovak government also wanted to see the back of them. Klepper quoted a distressing report from Pressburg: "Without interruption, entire goods trains filled with Jews are rolling through Pressburg and into the area ceded to Hungary." The number of Jews was estimated at between 3,000 and 4,000, but it was thought the number from all over Slovakia was far higher. They had all been ejected from Czechoslovakia without a penny "in compensation for the damage that Jews had wrought in Slovakia."

There was a lull in the impending storm on November 4, when Göring's daughter, Edda, was christened by Reich Bishop Müller. She received some fine presents: a Cranach from Milch and another from the city of Cologne. The Luftwaffe subscribed to build a miniature copy of Frederick the Great's palace at Sanssouci in an orchard at Carinhall, where she might play with her dolls. There was shock and horror when it was discovered that Edda Göring's nanny was not a Party member. Emmy confessed that she wasn't one either. Hitler put the matter right at Christmas by sending her a gold party badge and investing her with the number of a member who had conveniently expired. Göring's star was in the ascendant again. Goebbels wrote, "He goes his own way, and does not allow himself to be waylaid by the hyper-radicals in the Party." The propaganda minister was still down in the dumps. Despite Hitler's ukase at Berchtesgaden, he was finding Magda hard to take. He went to the theater with her on October 26. Three days later it was his birthday—the saddest of his life. It was not helped by a telegram from Hitler that was "short and frosty." He needed to find a way back into his master's favor.

Hitler was also enjoying Berlin's cultural life. He went to see Werner Egk's new opera based on the tale of Peer Gynt. Critics found a good deal of the degenerate composer Kurt Weil in the music, but either Hitler didn't notice or he didn't care. He invited Egk to his box and gave him a commission worth 10,000 RM, and *Peer Gynt* became standard repertory for the opera houses of the Third Reich. It was almost certainly superior to some of the new music composed that year, such as Cesar Bresgen and Heinrich Spitha's three-movement cantata *SA Lives For Ever*, which was based on the "Horst Wessel-Lied."

IT WAS now Goebbels's turn to grab the limelight. Two of the Polish Jews expelled from Germany were Sendel and Ryfka Grynszpan. They had been herded into a barracks in the town of Zbaszyn with five hundred others. Twenty Jews died as a result of their rough treatment on the first day alone. Their seventeen-year-old son, Herschel, was living illegally in Paris helping his uncle Abraham, a tailor. Here he received word of their situation on November 3. After an argument with his uncle on the 6th, he left his apartment and spent the night in the Hôtel de Suez. He had been told that his request to remain in France had been declined. The next day he purchased a revolver for 245 francs and loaded it at Tout va bien, a homosexual bar. He went to the German embassy, where he told reception he had a document to give to a "secretary." A Frau Mathes showed him the door to the office of Secretary to the Legation Ernst vom Rath, while an embassy servant called Nagorka asked if he could have the document to take to vom Rath.

Grynszpan insisted on seeing vom Rath in person. Hearing Grynszpan's name, vom Rath ordered him shown in. Nagorka heard screams. Grynszpan had fired five bullets, two of which inflicted serious wounds. He was later arrested by the French police. Vom Rath was operated on at once, and surgeons removed his pancreas. Hitler sent his personal surgeon, Karl Brandt, assisted by Georg Magnus. There was hope for awhile, but his injuries turned out to be too grave. Grynszpan admitted killing Rath to avenge his family.

This official version still raises many questions, especially since the historical evidence was falsified in 1942 and a story inserted that Grynszpan had originally intended to kill the ambassador, Graf Welczek. The Nazis caught Grynszpan after the fall of France and put him in Sachsenhausen concentration camp while they concocted a show trial for treason (he was not a German and thus could not have committed a crime against a state that was not his own). In the suppressed version, he was said to have confessed to having had a passionate affaire with Rath and that he had been able to afford his lifestyle—the hotel, the revolver—from the money he earned as a homosexual prostitute. Rath was a prominent homosexual who frequented louche bars such as Le Boeuf sur le toit and was known in their circles as "Madame Ambassadeur" or "Notre Dame de Paris." He had just returned from the German consulate in Calcutta with a dose of anal gonorrhea. One of the men who claimed to have been aware of the relationship was André Gide. Grynszpan is supposed to have shot vom Rath because he had failed to secure papers for him allowing him to remain in France—hence the "document." The revelation of the relationship led to the indefinite postponement of the trial.

Was it a Nazi plot intended to be used as a pretext to launch a pogrom against the Jews? It was one of the Nazis' standard tricks to seize upon an attack on a German diplomat abroad as a pretext for some action within the Reich. Heydrich had planned to sacrifice Papen in Vienna and Eisenlöhr in

Prague in just this way. On the other hand, not all putative assassinations of Germans by Jews were Nazi fakes. In 1936, Wilhelm Gustloff was gunned down by David Frankfurter in Davos, and no one has suggested that he was an unwitting Nazi agent.

Grynszpan's ultimate fate is uncertain. He was officially declared dead in 1960, but some people believe that he survived the war and was living in Paris in the sixties working as a car mechanic.

There were reports that the hue and cry over vom Rath's attempted assassination extended as far as the non-Czech areas of Czechoslovakia. All the German newspapers had to cover the story. The *Völkischer Beobachter* was supposed to voice the attitudes of right-thinking Germans:

> It is clear that the German people will draw their own conclusions from this new deed. It is an impossible situation, that within our borders hundreds and thousands rule over whole streets of shops, occupy places of pleasure and as "foreign" householders pocket the money paid to them by German tenants, while the racial comrades abroad call for war against Germany and gun down German public servants. . . . These shots fired in Paris will not just mean the beginning of a new attitude to the Jewish question, we hope that they will be a signal for those foreigners who up to now have failed to understand the only person who stands in the way of a closer cooperation between peoples is the international Jew.

On the 8th the first outrages took place against the Jews, notably in Hessen. Two synagogues were set on fire and Jewish shops attacked in Vienna. That same day Himmler gave one of his pithiest definitions of the nature of political and ideological antisemitism. He noted with appreciation that increasing numbers of people were opposed to the Jews:

> We must be clear that in the next ten years we face unprecedented conflicts of a critical nature. It is not only the battle of the nations . . . it is the ideological battle against all Jews, freemasons, Marxists and the churches of the world. These forces, behind which I assume to be the Jews . . . are clear that if Germany and Italy are not destroyed, it will be them that are eliminated. That is elementary. In Germany the Jew cannot hold out. It is a matter of time. We will drive them more and more by

unrivalled ruthlessness. Italy is going the same way and Poland does not want its Jews. . . . The other states, Sweden, Norway, Denmark, Holland and Belgium, are not naturally antisemitic today but they will go that way with time. We are sending our best propagandists in there. The moment Jewish emigrants to Switzerland and Holland etcetera begin to go about their usual business, patriotic antisemitism will suddenly begin. . . .

You mark my words, in the decisive battle to come, if we are defeated we will be given no quarter, they will be allowed to starve to death or butchered. That will be the fate of every man, whether he be an enthusiastic supporter or not, it will be enough that German is his mother tongue.

Himmler fairly accurately predicted the first weeks of the Allied occupation in 1945.

Himmler's ideology was inspired by the need to preserve his *Volk*. It was a dispassionate view. People needed to be kind and decent, but when it came to preserving a race, there was to be no pity. Himmler would kill a hundred people in a town, and he would expect his men to do so without qualms.

REICHSKRISTALLNACHT or the Night of the Broken Glass, the pogrom that occurred on the night of November 9–10, was almost entirely the brainchild of Joseph Goebbels. Having been out of favor for the past four months, this magnificent opportunity to worm his way back into his master's affections dawned slowly on the gauleiter of Berlin. His diary does not allude to the expulsion of the Polish Jews, and it was only in his entry for the 8th that he finally records the wounding of vom Rath together with sporadic outbreaks of violence against the Jews. It was then that the penny dropped: This was the chance to expand the largely unsuccessful program he had conceived for Berlin to cover the whole Reich. "Now we want to be blunt. In Hessen big antisemitic projects. The synagogues are going to be burned down. If we could only let rip with the fury of the people once and for all!"

Goebbels needed to bend Hitler's ear first. That evening was the annual reenactment of the 1923 putsch that began on November 8 in the Bürgerbräukeller in Munich. Hitler returned to the theme of attacking his British enemies, Churchill, Eden, and Duff Cooper. After the speech, the leading Nazis went to the Führerbau, where Bormann addressed them on the plans for celebrating Hitler's fiftieth birthday on April 20, 1939. They proceeded to the Café Heck, where Goebbels and Hitler sat until 3 AM. He may have had a chance to talk over his plans, but nothing is recorded in the diary.

The main action occurred after the celebrations for the fifteenth anniversary, which began with a traditional march to the Feldherrnhalle on the 9th. There was the usual backbiting among Hitler's men. Lutze poured his scorn for the SS into Goebbels's ear. His SA was to do the spadework later. Göring took his place among the marchers on what was a grey November day, but at 7:30 that evening he boarded a train and returned to Berlin. Goebbels had by now begun to take a keen interest in vom Rath's deteriorating condition. In Kassel in Hessen the "spontaneous demonstrations" continued as well as in Dessau in Anhalt; some Jews were attacked by a hostile crowd outside the French tourist office in Berlin.

Hitler was talking war in his Munich apartment when vom Rath expired at 4:30 that afternoon but registered very little interest. Two minutes' silence was observed when the wireless announced the diplomat's death—instructions that must have been issued by the minister for propaganda. Goebbels seized his moment. "Now the dish is cooked," he wrote in his diary. "I go to the Party reception in the Old Town Hall. A huge crowd. I brief the Führer on the matter. He decides to let the demonstrations go on. The Jews should feel the wrath of the people once and for all. That is right. I immediately hand out fitting instructions to the Party and the police." And later: "The Führer has ordered that 25–30,000 Jews should be arrested at once."

Goebbels informed the Party leaders that they must not appear involved in the pogrom. It was to be the "demonstration" that they had been unable to enact at the time of Gustloff's death because his assassination occurred shortly before the Olympic Games. At 10 Goebbels called for hate and revenge. It has been suggested that Reichskristallnacht was a test of Hitler's ability as an actor and that he passed the audition with flying colors. He successfully kept his own role a secret, even going so far as to voice his condemnation of the excesses. Hitler was sensitive to the effect that association with the actions might have on his international image. German goods had been boycotted since March 1933, and that meant an ever-worsening balance of payments. Goebbels had been told to postpone his campaign against the Jews in Berlin until after the Rome trip in early May. Again in mid-June, the special mini-pogrom organized by Goebbels in Berlin was called off because Hitler was worried about opinion abroad.

As was often the case, Hitler was candid with his friend Winifred Wagner. He confirmed to her that getting the Jews to emigrate had been the point of Kristallnacht, and that justified the extreme violence. When her children asked him about it, he changed his tune and blamed it all on Goebbels. In September Hitler insisted that the laws passed removing Jewish lawyers from practice should be kept quiet until the storm over the Sudetenland had passed. Goebbels was a more than willing mouthpiece for his master, and he was anxious to accelerate the persecution of the Jews with the usual objective: to encourage them to go more speedily.

GOEBBELS'S POGROM caught everyone off guard. Neither Wolff nor Heydrich, SS leaders, had been informed. At midnight Heydrich was drinking in the Nobel Hotel in the Maximilianstrasse when Heinrich "Gestapo" Müller called to tell him that in Berlin Jewish businesses were being destroyed by roving gangs. Heydrich decided to call on Himmler, who was in Hitler's apartment in the Prinzregentenstrasse preparing to swear in a detachment of SS officers at the Feldherrnhalle. Wolff was to take Himmler there after the session with Hitler. They discovered Himmler had not been told either. When Hitler heard what was going on, he appeared beside himself with rage: "Unbelievable . . . I completely disapprove." Wolff believed to the end of his life that Hitler had not ordered the pogrom.

Hitler turned to Himmler and told him: "Find out immediately who issued the orders. I don't want my SS involved in any of these actions under any circumstances."

The times the orders were issued also give a further idea of how pluralistic the command structure of the Third Reich was. The Party (Goebbels) was told to move at 10:30 PM; the SA (Lutze) at 11; the police (Himmler) at midnight, and the SS at 1:30 AM. The SS were told they were to wear mufti. Himmler made no bones of his disapproval: "The order comes from the Reichs propaganda leadership, and I suppose that Goebbels in his empty-headedness and in his hunger for power—something that struck me long ago—has launched this campaign in what is—when it comes to foreign relations—a most difficult time."

Heydrich's instructions to the police and SD that night make curious reading. It was to be a well-mannered pogrom. German lives and property were not to be endangered, and where a synagogue abutted onto an Aryan property, it was to be left unmolested; there was to be no looting—any pilfering would be answered with arrest; care was to be taken to make sure no damage was caused to non-Jewish commercial properties; foreigners were to be left in peace—even foreign Jews. Heydrich also gave instructions that historical documents found in the synagogues were to be preserved and handed over to the SD. On the other hand, in keeping with Hitler's wishes, Heydrich ordered his men to arrest male Jews, especially wealthy ones, and to hold them in police cells prior to transferring them to concentration camps. They were only to arrest "healthy male Jews." "Particular care must be taken that Jews arrested on the basis of this directive are not mistreated." Now was the moment to put some of Eichmann's methods into practice in the old Reich.

The first acts of hooliganism occurred in Munich itself, where a drunken band of members of the Stosstrupp Hitler went on the rampage and wrecked the synagogue in the Herzog-Rudolf-Strasse. Goebbels claimed that he tried to stop it going up in smoke, but that he had not succeeded. The city's gauleiter, Adolf Wagner, had to be egged on, as his heart was not in it. Goebbels was obliged to transmit the order personally to destroy the synagogue in the Fasanenstrasse in Berlin. In Munich, he smugly noted the "blood red sky." "In the future, the dear Jews will think twice before they go about shooting German diplomats." Before he turned in that night he parodied *Hamlet* in his diary: "Continue to wield our arms, or bring it to a halt? That is the question."

The 9th was the most important feast day in the Nazi calendar; many of the men were drunk. The SA men had a difficult time starting fires, as no one had laid down stocks of incendiary material. In Rüdesheim the SA men managed to set fire to themselves rather than the synagogue. Some were mere boys—big on destruction but often small in courage. In Feldafing on the Starnberg Lake, the youths were armed with bricks. Nor did everything happen as Heydrich had foreseen, for some of the gangs had accounts to settle too. In Erfurt, the baptized lawyer Flesch was tortured because he had appeared against an SA man in a divorce case. In Aschaffenburg the killing of Jewish businessmen had all the hallmarks of settling scores.

Heydrich's commands about sacred documents were not heeded in Frankfurt, where rioters tore up the old books in a Jewish library. In Vienna they arrested all the Jews lining up for visas outside the British consulate. They demolished the Jewish hospital in Nuremberg and the Jewish children's home in Caputh, near Potsdam. Five Jews were shot in Bremen (Goebbels called them "unlovely excesses").

In Munich the "demonstrators" made straight for Schloss Planegg, the home of the Jewish Baron von Hirsch, and destroyed it. Five hundred Jews were arrested in the city, and the banker Emil Kraemer apparently committed suicide by hurling himself out of the window of his apartment, although he had been unable to walk for two years. The archbishop, Cardinal Faulhaber, lent the Rabbi Leo Baerwald a truck so that he might rescue the contents of his synagogue.

The destruction was generally the work of the SA, occasionally encouraged by regional party officials and carried out by local boys who knew the Jews they were attacking. In some rural parts of Germany the purge was halfhearted. The Jews were too well-known, and the locals did not want to be seen joining in the destruction. It was often necessary to bus the thugs in from elsewhere. Although Jew-baiting was as old as Adam in the German countryside, the disparities between religious and racial antisemitism were shown in stark relief. You were supposed to love your neighbor. There was also a fear that the Catholics would be the next victims, and in some instances thugs destroyed church property when nothing Jewish was to hand.

In Buttenhausen in Württemberg, for example, the synagogue was torched by boys from nearby Münsingen, but the local fire brigade put the blaze out and rescued the contents of the building. The Münsingen thugs came again the next day and set the building alight again. This time they locked the mayor in his office to stop him from getting in the way. The wreckers who came to Oberdorf issued from Ellwangen. When they told the local SA chief, Böss, to set fire to the synagogue, he refused: "I can't do this in Oberdorf, because I've grown up with these people, gone to school with them and seen active service with them on the battlefield." The Ellwangen SA returned the next day, but Böss was adamant. He was stripped of his command but later restored to it because they could find no one else prepared to do the job. When the Ellwangen SA finally got the fire going, local people arrived to put it out. The SA nonetheless managed to take some Jews away and kill one.

In Würzburg the caretaker of a Jewish teachers' training college came to tell the girls to flee. He had appeared in a full, brown Party uniform for the first time. The synagogue in Bayreuth was spared because it was next to the lovely Baroque opera house. Both the police and the fire chief stood by to protect it, even if they could not prevent the SA from wrecking the interior. In Fulda, the Jews were put in prison to protect them from being sent to a concentration camp, and released when the coast was clear. A uniform also came in handy in Schirwindt in East Prussia. The Landrat, Wichard von Bredow, was informed that he had to issue the orders to burn down the synagogue. Bredow put on his army fatigues and went to the place where the Nazis were awaiting his orders. He stood before the building and loaded his revolver. The Nazis fled. He was not punished.

It is easy to exaggerate the efficiency of the operation; the orders had been quickly issued and often only half understood. There is also a danger in believing the many accounts of self-glorification, in which righteous Gentiles chased away Nazi thugs who were terrorizing Jewish citizens, but they cannot all be dismissed out of hand. The German journalist Bernt Engelmann remembered the events in Düsseldorf. He had just finished his labor service and was due to join the Luftwaffe. On the night of November 9–10 he was summoned from his bed by the din coming from downstairs, where some Jews lived. The Nazis were playing the song "Bei der blonden Kathrein" full blast to cover up the noise of their handiwork as they smashed glass and lanced paintings—apparently one was a Chagall.

He told a neighbor to call the police, but she informed him the police were right outside. His mother finally goaded him to act. Like Zuckmayer, Engelmann found the most effective way was to shout at the boys in his best Komissdeutsch or parade ground German. The destruction ceased while one of the thugs called for his superior. Engelmann continued in a commanding tone, implying that his underlings were indulging in theft. He gave the SA man the impression that he was a bigger Nazi than he was. The squad dispersed and went on its way. Later he witnessed the killing of a Jewish ophthalmologist who had put up a fight against the vandals. He seems to have taken one of the thugs with him.

In Berlin children looted a Jewish toy shop. When Gentile women remonstrated with them, they were spat upon and manhandled by the mob. Over thirty synagogues were wrecked. The author Erich Kästner witnessed the destruction of the city's best-known shops on the Tauenzienstrasse. He could see the looters' SS jackboots under their "civilian" clothes. They went about their work systematically, and he reckoned that they had each been allotted five shops. Each time he tried to get out of his taxi to remonstrate with them, a man came up and said, "Criminal Police!" and slammed the door shut. On the last occasion the driver verbally restrained him: "What's the point . . . and apart from everything else it constitutes resistance to the power of the state!"

The fifteen-year-old Peter Fröhlich rode that way too a few hours later. Facades on the Tauenzienstrasse had "been effectively reduced to rubble, their huge display windows shattered, their mannequins and merchandise scattered on the pavement. Evidently more Jewish-owned shops had survived the government's efforts to 'Aryanise' them than I had imagined." Much worse was to follow: His uncle's shop, Fröhlich, the milliner on the Olivaer Platz, had been similarly trashed. For Gerhard Beck the destruction was revelatory. He had not always known which shops in the Badstrasse were Jewish-owned—now it was clear. When he went to work on the 10th, the facades of Hemdenmatz, Bata, Etam, and Salamander had been wrecked. He was working for a furrier in the same street. All the furs had been smeared with excrement. As one Jewish shop assistant exclaimed in disgust, "What did the SA eat to shit like that?"

It was not rare for Gentiles to deplore what was happening. There is even an instance of a member of a Gestapo saving a Jew, while the Nazi authorities had placed sentries outside a Jewish seminary run by a rabbi who had rendered Germany valuable service in the Great War. Klepper went through the Bayrischer Viertel in Schöneberg and noted that the population had not supported the action. His Jewish wife received gestures of support from virtually everyone. The philo-Semitic Maria von Maltzan said the same. She was driving around that night with friends, upset by the burning synagogues and the sight of laughing SA men throwing the Talmud scrolls onto bonfires and beating up rabbis. "The actual private citizen was not involved in it at all." Most of the synagogues went up in flames, but the SA merely wrecked the one in the Heidereutergasse, as it had recently rented space to the post office. It carried on holding services until 1940. The city's most famous synagogue in the Oranienburgerstrasse was saved by the timely intervention of the head of the local police, who informed the arsonists it was a historic building.

The pogrom in Vienna was predictably the most savage of all. It was organized on the ground by the head of the Jewish department of the Gestapo, Dr. Lange. The SA dirty-tricks specialist Skorzeny was commissioned to destroy the remaining synagogues, tasting blood for the first time. Despite the damage inflicted in October, a further forty-two prayer houses were burned to the ground or blown up with hand-grenades, together with the halls in the Central and New Cemeteries. The efficiency of the operation is clear from the report of the fire brigade, which had to be present in case the flames spread to Aryan properties.

The action started at 8:00 AM on the morning of the 10th. By 9:30 they had destroyed the synagogue at Neue Weltgasse 7 in Hietzing, inflicting 100,000 RM worth of damage, but ensured that the neighboring buildings were safe. Half an hour later, the fire brigade was in the Jewish Leopoldstadt. The damage at the synagogue was only half as great. Half an hour later, in the Untere Viakduktgasse, a mere 3,000 RM; a minute later another synagogue went up in the Sixth District, 10,000 RM; half an hour later in the Fifth, 150,000 RM, the biggest prize to date. It had continued to burn, although it had been made safe. Fifteen minutes later it was the turn of the Grosse Schiffgasse in the Second: 100,000 RM; similar damage was done to the synagogue in the Fifteenth half an hour later. It took the fire brigade nearly an hour to reach the Eighteenth, and by that time the arsonists had notched up 80,000 RM worth of damage. The synagogue in the Seitenstettengasse in the First Bezirk was not to be torched. The Gestapo feared for the valuable archive material housed in the neighboring buildings of the IKG.

The Sophiensäle concert halls were turned into a temporary prison. The violence was followed by 680 suicides in Vienna on November 10 or later. There was dancing on the Torah rolls, and in prisons like the Karajangasse eighty-eight Jews were badly hurt and twenty-seven killed. For the first time women were the targets of violence. They were locked in cells with whores and forced to perform orgiastic acts. In Brigitenau two hundred Jewish women were obliged to perform a goosestep march in the nude. One who refused was strapped to a table, and the others had to spit in her face.

Using violence to accelerate the tempo of emigration was not particularly popular in Vienna either. From Styria the SD reports showed that the people preferred "legal" persecution. The same report showed how counterproductive the destruction had been. Papers had been incinerated that would now have to be reissued, and that meant that the targets for emigration would not be met. In at least one instance the thugs destroyed a restaurant that had already been transferred to the ownership of a Party member. In Innsbruck, four prominent Jews were murdered, three of them in front of their families. The anti-Jewish measures had been popular up to now, but in the wake of the pogrom, citizens openly expressed their sympathy for the Jews. Similar sentiments were expressed in Vienna. The jails were filled with Jews. Eichmann addressed the prisoners in the Karajangasse, issuing dark warnings: If the emigration could not be speeded up, he would find other means. The pogrom was followed by a wave of confiscations. Nearly 2,000 Jewish homes were seized, and their inhabitants were forced to find shelter either in *Judenhäuser* or with their relatives.

———

Hitler and Goebbels had met for lunch on the 10th at the Führer's favorite restaurant, the Osteria Bavaria in Munich's Schellingstrasse. Goebbels gave Hitler a report on the night: "He approves of everything. His views are wholly radical and aggressive. The measure itself went off without a hitch." Hitler now wanted the Jewish businesses appropriated. There was no question of their claiming for the damage on their insurance policies. Hitler continued to keep his role a secret, but some people realized that he was involved. When the Prussian minister of finance, Popitz, complained to Göring, he told him the perpetrators should be punished and tried to resign. Göring replied, "My dear Popitz, do you wish to punish the Führer?"

Hitler and Goebbels were alone in seeing the pogrom as a universal success.

The economics minister, Funk, was one of the angriest of his critics, calling the riots a shambles. Ribbentrop called the propaganda minister a little beast: "Goebbels smashes the windows and I have to mend the foreign situation." Hefty criticism from all around moved Goebbels to make an announcement at 5 PM on the 10th, calling the party to an end. Exhausted looters and arsonists went home, often carrying baskets filled with food, wine, and valuables. Goebbels was disappointed at the outcome and thought the number of people who had participated in the vandalism had been miserably small.

Göring didn't like Goebbels, and he was furious about the destruction. Hitler nonetheless mediated between his two princes. In a telephone conversation with Hitler, Göring was won over with the idea of a fine: 1 billion marks for his Four Year Plan. Göring was strapped for cash and may well have been the one who suggested it. Besides a huge armaments program and no money to pay his civil service, there was a near total lack of reserves of foreign currency. Even if he could make some money from it, the effect on foreign trade was disastrous—this would not make international Jewry call off its boycott. Göring managed to win an assurance from Hitler that such methods would not be used again.

Of the 7,800 Jews arrested in Vienna, 1,226 were already in the process of effecting their departure through the Central Office for Jewish Emigration. There were 4,083 businesses closed down and 1,950 buildings confiscated. Jews who were still in the possession of their apartments and houses were obliged to hand over the keys. They were given no time to pack up their belongings. Their remaining valuables were predictably stolen. It provided another chance for some informal plunder, and the police had to step in again to dampen the ardor of the Viennese Gentiles.

Across the Reich, official figures listed 76 synagogues destroyed and a further 191 set on fire. Twenty-nine Jewish-owned department stores had also been demolished, including the provocatively named Nathan Israel in Berlin, which had been protected until then. At a conservative estimate, the thugs had also destroyed a further 815 shops and 117 private houses. The real figure is probably far higher. Even the Party condemned the action, calling it destructive, expensive, and misguided. The SD reports spoke of Party members saying, "This is no longer anything to do with culture or decency." They wanted to know if the perpetrators of the destruction were to be punished too. That Sunday there was a tellingly small amount contributed to the boxes that collected money for the Nazi Winterhilfe (Winter Aid) charity. No one seems to have been too concerned for the Jews themselves, although 200 of them were beaten up, and (officially) 35 killed. The tally is more likely to have been between 100 and 200. The approximately 30,000 who had been rounded up were taken to Dachau, Buchenwald, and Sachsenhausen, where they were encouraged to think about emigration.

The SS promulgated new measures as soon as vom Rath's death was announced. In Buchenwald the prisoners were deprived of food, and there was no more talk of early release. The *Manchester Guardian* said as many as seventy Jewish prisoners had been executed. Bruno Heilig, who was there at the time, reported a number of deaths from savage punishment. Some of the Aryan prisoners saved their food and hid it in the woods for the Jews. Buchenwald was so full that there was no more room, and the transports had to be stopped. Himmler gave orders for the release of all Jews over the age of fifty to accommodate new arrivals. On November 14 more room was secured by Heydrich's order releasing all Jews in possession of papers, allowing them to emigrate. They were to leave within three weeks.

ON THE night of November 9–10 Eichmann received a summons to Berlin by telegram. The Nazi leadership took stock of what they had achieved or destroyed through Goebbels's "spontaneous" demonstrations. Heydrich insisted on Eichmann being there to "communicate his experiences of practical procedure." Eichmann was to tell them how things *should* be done. This was the background to the conference on the progress of the "Jewish question" that took place in the Air Ministry in Berlin on November 12. There were over a hundred persons present, including Göring, Goebbels, and Heydrich. Himmler was absent; he had taken himself to Italy for a five-week break.

Hitler had requested a coordinated solution to the Jewish question. As such the meeting was the forerunner to the better-known Wannsee Conference. The host, Göring, was unimpressed. He feared for his own credibility, as he had exhorted the German people to hang on to every scrap of material for the Four Year Plan, and now this wanton destruction had come. He wanted to know who was going to pay for the damage, particularly insurance bills of between 6 and 10 million RM for the

7,500 businesses destroyed. The Berlin jeweler Margraf in Unter den Linden was presenting a reckoning for 1.7 million RM; the bill for the glass alone came to 6 million RM. The replacements had to be brought in from Belgium, meaning a payout of 3 million RM in foreign exchange— the loss amounting to half of Belgium's annual production in plate glass. The total bill was estimated at 220 million RM. "I have had enough of these demonstrations," Göring told the meeting. "In the end they don't damage the Jews, they damage me, as in the last resort, I am the economy." "I would be happier if you had beaten 200 Jews to death and not destroyed so much of value." Göring issued orders to catch the pillagers and some 800 others. No charges were brought against the men who murdered Jews that night, but four who assaulted women were expelled from the Party and handed over to the courts.

Instead of "spontaneous demonstrations," Heydrich argued that the most important thing was to get rid of the Jews; he drew the others' attention to Eichmann's success. Eichmann's Viennese model was recommended for the Altreich, "where they had yet to achieve so much" and where emigration had stagnated to 20,000 Jews a year. The Reich could not afford to finance the transfer of Jewish assets, and the taxes they had imposed on the Jews were failing to bring in enough money. Heydrich then had a brain wave: The insurers should pay the Jews, and at that point the money would be confiscated. There was discussion as to what to do with the damaged synagogues. Goebbels suggested that the Jews should demolish them themselves. He seemed much exercised by the question of Jews sharing cinemas, theaters, and circuses or even breathing the same open air as Gentiles in public parks and woods. Jews had been seen freely walking around the Grunewald in Berlin. The Reichs' master of hunts, Göring, clearly saw it as a matter of little importance and made light of it. He would have reservations made for the Jews, and all those animals that resembled them—for example, elks, which had similarly hooked noses— could come and join them there.

In his diary, Goebbels interpreted his role in a heroic light and failed to mention Göring's ribbing (on November 22 he claimed that he and Göring were wholly of the same mind when it came to the Jews): "a hot debate over the solution. I represent the radical point of view." He dismissed Funk as "soft" and claimed, "I work splendidly with Göring," and "the radical opinion won the day." He did not mention the fact that he had Hitler's blessing and they did not.

In six months that year, Eichmann had produced a tally of emigration from Austria that was two and a half times as great as that of the Altreich. He explained that the rich Jews had to pay for the poor: "The problem was not getting the rich out, but the Jewish mob." Göring expressed his fear that they would take their money with them. Heydrich was able to reassure him: "In Vienna the dough stayed in the country." By contrast, Goebbels's pogrom had actually slowed down the process of emigration. Heydrich had every reason to be angry with the propaganda chief. Once Göring had been shown the color of the money he could hope to receive, he conferred with the Austrian economics minister Fischböck about the fate of 17,000 Jewish businesses in Vienna. It was decided that only between 3,000 and 3,500 would stay open, and the rest would be either closed or taken over by the state and awarded to trustees.

In the aftermath of the pogrom in Vienna, the police had instructions to arrest the richest Jews. A total of 6,547 were taken into custody, and 3,700 were shipped out to Dachau. At the end of the year the Gestapo totted up their figures and estimated that they had packed 20,793 Austrians off to concentration camps since March 13. When the Jews arrived in Dachau, the guards were delighted to find that they had a number of rabbis under their roofs and singled them out for special punishments. Urns filled with ashes began to arrive a few days later: 350 of the Jews detained after Reichskristallnacht died in Buchenwald that winter, and the combined total for the three camps—Buchenwald, Sachsenhausen, and Dachau—exceeded 5,000, of whom nearly 3,000 were Austrian. Sachsenhausen had the reputation of being the mildest of the three, Buchenwald the worst. After the "Rath-Aktion" the oldest inmate was ninety, the youngest, twelve.

Many of the Jews in Dachau and Buchenwald were released before June 1939. The former frontline soldiers were the first to be liberated. A large number of those were allowed to go as a celebration of Hitler's fiftieth birthday on April 20. The condition imposed on all of them was that they should leave the Reich and never return. They had also to promise that they would say nothing of their experiences in the camps. Even Jews who had not been through this mill were advised to keep quiet about what they had seen and heard. When Arnold Schoenberg's son-in-law, Felix Greissle, arrived in the United States, the composer told him, "Don't say anything you don't have to say about your experiences of the last few weeks. Especially not to newspapermen or to people who might pass it on to them. You know the Nazis take revenge on relatives and friends still in their power. So be very reserved and don't get mixed up in politics. I have kept to this strictly, always refusing to tell any stories, out of consideration for my friends and relatives in Germany. And people completely understand this."

In Dresden, Victor Klemperer was lucky. On November 11 two gendarmes appeared at his door to search his house for weapons. He had the impression that the search was pure torture to one of them. They eventually found the saber he carried as an officer in the First World War. They took him down to the police station, but he was quickly released. Stubborn though he was, he decided it was high time to emigrate, and on November 28 he visited the Advice Bureau for Emigration in the Pragerstrasse. A very humane Major Stübel told him that if he sold his house, he would be able to leave Germany naked, with 7 1/2 percent of its value. Even then he would have had to obtain a berth on a ship, and all the places were taken. Klemperer decided to stay put.

FOLLOWING THE pogrom there were audible rumbles from abroad. The former kaiser in exile in the Dutch town of Doorn echoed the feelings of many members of the old military caste: "What is going on at home is certainly a scandal. It is now high time that the army showed its hand; they have let a lot of things happen. . . . All the older officers and all decent Germans must protest." Of course he was hoping that an army coup would place him back on his throne. His son, August Wilhelm, or "Auwi," who had been an early and enthusiastic member of the SA, took the opposite line, incensing his father with his support for the pogrom. "When I told him that any decent man would describe these actions as gangsterism, he appeared totally indifferent."

The pogrom took away the regime's last vestiges of credibility. Hitler and Goebbels had "unconditional" support from the Duce, who worked himself up into a lather against the Jews, but elsewhere they found little sympathy. In many places the embargo on German goods was reinforced, and doors were shut to German trade. The *Manchester Guardian* in England was not taken in by Goebbels's "spontaneous demonstrations" and attributed the action to Hitler's "old guard." Goebbels's own newspaper, *Angriff*, riposted by making out that the assassination of vom Rath had been instigated by Churchill and Attlee. *Der Stürmer* presented a gallery of "Jewlovers": Mayor [*sic*] Attlee, Anthony Eden (who, they had already pointed out, had Jewish cousins), Winston Churchill, Lloyd-George, Duff Cooper, Stalin, and Roosevelt. The weekly left it to Fips to celebrate the actions that night. In one cartoon a Jew is complaining of the cold draught; in another he runs into the arms of the Church, the Nazis' other bugbear.

The United States was particularly virulent in its condemnation. Hitler and his men saw all too quickly that it was not the 20 million German Americans who led public opinion. There were formal protests made in Britain and France, and in Rome the pope spoke out against racialism and the destruction of lives and property. This led to a demonstration against Jews *and* Catholics in Munich, when the gauleiter, Adolf Wagner, warned Cardinal Faulhaber that his utterances constituted an incitement to the Jews to agitate against the Germans. The cardinal's palace was wrecked as a response to his kindness toward the rabbi on the 10th. Pius XI was not to be put off and continued to attack the Nazis, challenging their claim to racial superiority. There was, he said, just one human race. He wanted to break diplomatic ties with Germany but was dissuaded by Eugenio Pacelli, the former German nuncio and the man who would succeed him as Pius XII three months later.

Archbishop Lang wrote to the *Times* to express his disgust: "Whatever provocation may have been given by the deplorable act of a single irresponsible Jewish youth, reprisals on such a scale, so fierce, cruel, and vindictive, cannot possibly be justified. A sinister significance is added to them by the fact that the police seem either to have acquiesced in them or to have been powerless to restrain them." The letter annoyed Goebbels so much he had the *Times* withdrawn from sale. In Germany the pogrom proved a watershed: The Church of England would now be united in its desire for the British government to assert itself in Germany.

Even within Germany the pogrom marked a change of course. It is said that among the conservative elite there was a fear that the Left was now back in the saddle with the end of Goebbels's disgrace, and that they could now expect an attack on the churches as well as on the capitalists, not to mention the nobility. Certainly Hitler appeared to have forgiven Goebbels.

On November 16, the gauleiter was proud to note that "the Führer wholly approves my and our policies." Hitler showed his solidarity by coming to stay with the Goebbelses in Schwanenwerder after a performance of Schiller's *Kabale und Liebe*. The next day Uncle Adolf played with the children before heading off to Düsseldorf for vom Rath's state funeral.

There were numerous small acts of personal courage in which Germans showed their sympathy for the Jews. The industrialist Robert Bosch in Stuttgart put half a million RM in a Dutch bank to help out Jews lacking funds to continue their journeys to freedom. For Peter and Christabel Bielenberg in Hamburg, it made up their minds for them that they were going to leave Germany and go and live in Ireland. It was only their friend Adam von Trott who held them back. He argued that the evil needed to be fought from within.

For many Germans there was an all-pervading sense of shame. Major Groscurth said, "You have to feel ashamed to remain German," but thought Göring and Hitler innocent of the outrage. Another who disapproved was Heydrich, who believed it had been "the heaviest blow against the state and Party since 1934." Klepper noted there was a desire to emigrate among rich Gentiles and that both churches were muzzled by flagrant attacks on them in the Nazi organs—they were not to speak out for non-Aryan Christians. Eleanor von Trott, the widow of a former imperial minister and mother of Adam, went into Bebra, where one of the "spontaneous" demonstrations had occurred before those unleashed by Goebbels. Leaving her driver at a safe distance, she went into each Jewish shop in turn and personally apologized for the damage to their property. Robert Smallbones, the British consul in Frankfurt, talked of "passionate resentment" among Christian Germans and in the army and civil service, while Vansittart's informant, Group Captain Christie, overheard similar views expressed in Berlin and Essen, talking of "universal horror" and "general abhorrence."

In Württemberg, reactions ranged from dismissing the action as "childish" or inhumane. In Stuttgart glaziers sold glass at a reduced rate "because it was not the Jews who had caused the damage." A Party member sent flowers to a Jew to show his support. Another Nazi in Creglingen helped an arrested Jew to escape with the support of the local leader of the Nazi War Veterans' Association. The ordinary clergy were especially vocal in their condemnation, particularly the Protestants. The Catholics tended to be more cowed after the expulsion of Bishop Sproll.

In Nuremberg the public outcry was so great that Julius Streicher had to make a speech to protest against sympathy being shown for the Jews. Pity for the Jews might have induced relative silence from *Der Stürmer*, which did not formally celebrate the pogrom until issue 48 came out at the end of the month. On the other hand, the more likely cause was Goebbels, who had once again muzzled the press. Ernst Hiemer wrote *Der Stürmer's* cover story, entitled, "Has the Jewish Question Been Solved?" The previous issue, number 47, did include a poignant image by Fips entitled "November Storms" and showing a Jew being leveled by a huge fist.

THE ROUNDING up of the Jews had proved an excellent source of wealth for corrupt German officials. Göring did not see all of it by any means. In Nuremberg the Jews had to sign away the rights to their property before they went into concentration camps. The taxable value of the estate was calibrated at 10 percent of its real worth. In Vienna the corruption was so flagrant that Bürckel was obliged to pack a number of Aryan administrators off to Dachau to join their victims.

In response Jews north of the Inn laid siege to the consulates to obtain visas to leave. Few found what they wanted. Of three hundred who lined up at the Argentinian and Paraguayan consulates in Berlin, only two were able to proceed to making a formal application. On the 19th it was decreed that no one could leave until the billion mark fine or "Atonement Contribution" had been paid.

The Contribution was based on the data accumulated since the enforced registration of Jewish property after April 26. The sum total for Jewish property was set at 7,538,500,000 RM, of which nearly two-thirds was estimated to be in the form of liquid assets. Every Jew liable had to make over 20 percent of his property in four installments. The first fell on December 15, and thereafter every three months, until August 15, 1939. Together with the Emigration Tax, the Atonement Contribution yielded a neat two billion RM. Using the Jews as a cash cow to fund rearmament and other projects was shortsighted. They had already given away so much, and their milk was soon to dry up altogether; income from the beleaguered Jews amounted to some 5 percent of tax revenue. Even the assumption of

Jewish businesses only altered German economic life in small areas such as textiles and department stores. There was still no alleviation of the Reich's finances, which continued to cause grave concern.

On November 18 Göring met members of the Defense Council and explained the parlous state of the nation's coffers and the fear of renewed inflation. The rearmament program was in itself inflationary, as it failed to expand consumer sales. In the New Year the Reichsbank sent Hitler a letter requesting restraint in government spending. Hitler's response was to sack Schacht—although there may have been other reasons. The national debt had increased threefold since Hitler's takeover. Autarky prevented Germany from indulging in conventional foreign trade.

Göring was aware that he was not getting his hands on all the money and that he still lacked buying power abroad. On November 14 Fischböck came to him with the first of several schemes to make the Jews sponsor German exports, an idea that had been aired before Kristallnacht. It came about as a result of a meeting between George Rublee's wife and the German air attaché in London, Ralph Wenninger. Wenninger had introduced her to Theo Kordt, which had eventually resulted in a direct channel opening up between Göring and Rublee. Once again it was necessary to keep Ribbentrop in the dark, especially as the RAM had gotten it into his head that Rublee was a Jew. The international boycott was starving Germany of foreign currency. The chemical giant IG Farben's foreign orders were down by 40 percent, for example. Göring wanted the Jews to be allowed to remain in the export trade: "The business point of view must prevail. . . . Every concession involving ideological principles is possible." Under the scheme, Germany would relieve the richer Jews of 200 million RM and allow them to emigrate; in return, after thirty years Germany would pay 3 percent to the governments participating in the scheme.

The opposition had a new straw to grasp at. Goerdeler relayed the contents of a speech made by the minister of state and vice president of the Reichsbank, Dr. Rudolf Brinckmann, to an audience of industrialists in Cologne. The news was bleak: All the money sucked out of Austria since the Anschluss was now spent. The luxury and high cost of Party functions and the state were to blame. There was no foreign currency and a dearth of raw materials. The annual state budget needed to be reduced by 6,000 million RM straight away. There was only a short time before Germany suffered complete economic collapse. Brinckmann later went insane, although it is not clear whether this resulted from the shambles in the Nazi economy or some other cause.

Within Germany it was clear that the Nazi state was anything but efficient. A further report by Goerdeler showed that the railway system had broken down because it was being bled in the interests of free transport for Party members, road building, and compulsory contributions to various Party funds. They were short of 3,000 locomotives and 30,000 coaches. Goods from Hamburg to Vienna had to go via Trieste to make use of Italian trains. The opportunities for working in the arms industries and in other related trades had led to a huge desertion of the land, with drastic results when it came to food production. There had been a 16 percent drop in the number of farm laborers, which would eventually require migrant labor, chiefly from Poland. It was not just the farms that lacked workers. In the mines of the Ruhr, they were 30,000 men short. Overall Germany needed another million men. The temptation to grab them from elsewhere was obvious.

EVEN BEFORE Reichskristallnacht there was a growing awareness of the urgency of finding homes for the Jews. At the beginning of November, one of the busiest of the Quakers, Howard Elkington, was prepared to stump up £100 to "to help suitable people to emigrate to Australia." A month later he was obtaining visas in bulk from the Foreign Office in London. Norman Bentwich was also keen to explore the chances of upping the quotas for Australia, and he looked into the possibility of sending some to Ceylon. Four hundred Austrian Jews were on the water, ostensibly on their way to Liberia. They had left from Galata in Romania on the steamship *Minerva*.

After the pogrom, parents understood that even if they could not make it themselves, it was imperative to get their children out. On November 15 the leading Zionist Chaim Weizmann (later the first president of Israel) went to see Neville Chamberlain and asked for action to save them. Weizmann set a figure of 10,000 to be found homes in Britain. Pressure was also put on Malcolm Macdonald, the minister for the colonies. It was agreed that a further 5,000 Jews could enter Britain, providing they left again within three years. The idea of the kindertransports had been an informal one at first. It was believed that they should be allowed to recover in lands like Switzerland and Norway before returning to their parents. Jews in Britain were particularly active in arranging the transports. One of these was Wilfred Israel, the model for Gustav Landauer in Christopher Isherwood's novel *Goodbye to Berlin*. Israel's colleague in Youth Aliya was Lola Hahn-Warburg. The pro-Zionist MP Josiah Wedgwood also sponsored 222 refugees.

Diana Hopkinson worked for the Movement for the Care of Children from Germany. In her book *The Incense Tree* she describes the "steady stream of Jews who had been trying to leave Germany," who became

> a torrent which almost overwhelmed the organisations who were work-
> ing for them. In the large blocks of Bloomsbury offices we were invaded
> by a throng of bewildered and anguished people. We were busy not only
> interviewing those who had arrived but with correspondence about
> those who still hoped to escape. We battled with the Home Office for
> the necessary permits and sought financial guarantors; interviewed En-
> glish relations and friends. They wrung their hands and wept and of-
> fered bribes or threats in their efforts to free those still in Germany or
> Austria. If one became a little hardened it was only in the attempt to
> keep one's balance and help more effectively. One could not forget that
> the case numbers concealed suffering human beings, but they themselves
> hated those "case" numbers. None of us knew that a number on their file
> might save them from a number branded on their body in an extermi-
> nation camp later.

Diana's office had been issued with a block permit for 10,000 Jewish children, but that was not enough. She and her colleagues could only take twelve from every thirty applicants. "I was in despair over the hopeless task of assessing those whose claims were the strongest, trying not to choose the most attractive or the most pathetic looking, I was haunted by the thought of what would happen to those left behind."

Once the children arrived in Britain, Jews were concerned about their retaining their faith. Of the 9,000 children who arrived unaccompanied in Britain between 1933 and 1939, only 1,000 were placed with Jewish foster parents. The British Board of Deputies was at pains to stress that even nonreligious children were Jews and that *Konfessionslos* did not generally mean Christian, but rather that "the parents were not members of the Jewish Kultus Gemeinde, for political reasons or because they wish to avoid paying the taxes of the KG." As it was, only a small percentage submitted to baptism while in the care of Christian foster parents.

MEASURES AGAINST the Jews were redoubled. On November 11, they were banned from possessing weapons. By the end of the year they were to be excluded from economic and social life, theaters, German schools (November 15) and universities (December 8). The Zionistische Rundschau was closed and very briefly replaced by the Judisches Nachrichtenblatt. On November 16 they lost the right to serve or wear a military uniform. Their driving licenses were revoked, and their assets, property, and jewelry, with the exception of wedding rings, had to be handed in. All Jewish businesses were to close down on November 23. At the end of the month Victor Klemperer found that he was banned from the library and effectively cut off from new literature.

In Franconia, the gauleiter, Streicher, decided that the time had come to relieve the Jews of all their property. In Fürth the Jews filed in one by one, ceding their rights for a few peppercorns. Some court officers refused to enter the compulsory sales in the land register. Jews were now banned from cafés and restaurants. One victim was the writer and former ladies' man John Höxter, who was wont to cadge money in the Romanisches Café in Berlin. When his friends offered him a coffee, he said he would rather have the fifty pfennigs. They usually gave him that and more, in the understanding he could not earn a living anymore. After Reichskristallnacht he could no longer enter the building. Realizing he would now starve, he hanged himself from a tree in the Grunewald.

One or two things improved. With the closing of the Gildemeester charity for nonreligious Jews in Vienna, the whole machinery for emigration was brought under the roof of the Palais Rothschild. Jews no longer had to look for passports in their own districts. The seriousness of the situation was now clear. In Württemberg, the number of Jews dropped from around 7,000 to nearer 6,000 by March 1939. In Britain a total of £250,000 was raised for non-Aryan Christians by means of an appeal in the parishes; more substantial contributions were made by Jewish peers.

Some of the Jews in Dachau, Sachsenhausen, and Buchenwald, who had papers for Palestine, were out by the end of the month. Others would have to apply to the Jewish agencies or find places on the Perl transports. After the British had closed the Greek door, Italy was the most promising alternative, despite the racial laws. Long lines of women gathered outside Passport Control Officer Foley's office in Berlin, seeking to have their menfolk released from concentration camps. Foley had requested fresh supplies of blank visas for Palestine as well as Youth Aliya certificates that allowed young Jews to go to Palestine without their parents. He also asked for more staff to deal with the workload.

Sworn to secrecy about their treatment in the camps, Jews for the most part did not wish to talk about it anyway. Bernt Engelmann came across a man who simply had to get it off his chest when he visited a hotelier relative. His aunt had hidden a Jew who was waiting for a passport to take him to Sweden. It was no longer legal for Jews to share hotels with Gentiles. She had hidden him in the hunting lodge, where no one would see him. Engelmann noted that the man—Herr Kahn—had evidently lost a good deal of weight, as his clothes no longer fitted him. He had been in Buchenwald for only twenty days and told Engelmann of the treatment that had been meted out to the Jews who had arrived after Kristallnacht.

He had been shaved and inspected by a doctor. He had to swear that any cuts and bruises had been inflicted prior to his arrest. A superior SS officer gave the prisoners a lecture, telling them they had been rehabilitated, and encouraged them to make a donation to the Nazi Winter Aid. They were then led past the boxes, and another myrmidon made sure they contributed. Next they had to pay for the use of their eating utensils. There was another levy, and anyone who had no money to pay had to be covered by those who did. It was a five-mile walk to the railway station in Weimar. Another SS man was collecting money for taxis because the old and infirm would not have made it.

Engelmann and Kahn shared a room in the hunting lodge, and several times he was woken in the night by the other man's groans. Once he shouted, "Don't hit me!" When in the morning a motorcar drove up, Kahn became agitated and asked where he might hide. It was a false alarm: It was Engelmann's aunt with his passport emblazoned with a J.

ON OCTOBER 27, Bishop Batty had left England on a pastoral mission to Austria. He needed to appoint someone to take over from Grimes and make sure that the baptismal business had been properly halted. A month after his trip to Vienna to clear up after Grimes and Collard, he was hauled over the coals for his efforts to aid the Jews by his fellow bishops. The first to take a shot at him was none other than Bishop Bell of Chichester. He wrote to Alan Don on November 30: "I am really very much perturbed at getting the enclosed letter from Mrs Baker about the baptism of Jews in Vienna! I thought from what the Bishop of Fulham told me at the moment on relations with foreign churches that, though there had been a great scandal, it was now over. You see, however, that this complaint is dated 22 November, and baptising at the rate of some fifty a day is really shocking!"

Mrs. Baker was not the only one to blow the whistle. Less than a week later Alan Don wrote to Batty himself:

I think you ought to know that it has come to the knowledge of the Archbishop that a Church of Scotland chaplain at Budapest, the Rev. G. A. Knighton by name, states in a letter dated November 22nd that trouble is being caused in Hungary by the action of the Anglican chaplain in Vienna, who, it is stated, is continuing to baptise a large number of Jews. The actual words are as follows: "All summer the chaplain has accepted Jews and baptised them, without any preparation whatsoever, and baptised them in batches of fifty a day. Several eye-witnesses told me as much." Seeing as you have recently been in Vienna, you may be able to judge as to whether this statement is in accordance with facts or not. If it is you will doubtless consider what action should be taken as this practice, if continued, is likely to cause a good deal of scandal.

Don had forwarded the correspondence to the archbishop. Batty replied the following day:

The matter to which you refer was first brought to my notice by an article in a German paper which attacks all Christian institutions and leaders. It appeared to me to be a matter for investigation on the spot and I went out to Vienna.

The position is as follows—

1. We have our mission to the Jews and it is difficult for a priest to refuse to deal with a Jew who wishes to become a Christian, but at the moment on political grounds the greatest care is necessary and instructions
were issued to the chaplain at Vienna to this effect.

2. It is a fact that a number of Jews were baptised but the statement that
they were baptised without any preparation is *absolutely untrue*. The
preparation given was carefully thought out and I was assured that it covered all that was essential.

3. The chaplain responsible in the summer when this occurred was the
Revd. C. H. D. Grimes, a scholar and a gentleman in whom I have con-
fidence. I think it must be admitted that his intense sympathy with these
poor people in their terrible suffering led him to a greater belief in their
sincerity than an outsider would have done.

4. Mr Grimes resigned the chaplaincy and left over three months ago.
He had been succeeded temporarily by the Revd. F. A. Evelyn who is an
experienced priest. He has been instructed that the greatest care must be
taken in these cases and long preparation given. Also that if there is the
slightest ground for believing that baptism is wanted on political grounds,
it must be refused.

The situation has therefore been dealt with directly it was brought to
my notice, but I must protest against the statement of the Scotch minister that no preparation was given.

Don was satisfied with Batty's letter and also wrote to assuage Bell on
December 7.

Batty may have felt he had successfully concealed Collard and his own
role in the conversions, but he still had not heard the last of it. On January 12, 1939, a Mrs. Elsie Ludovici of Upper Norwood in the south London suburbs wrote to Lang. The wording of the letter would suggest she
was probably a convert herself:

I was . . . horrified to hear that mass baptisms had been taking place in Vienna, that they were being admitted at the rate of as many as 900 a day
into the Anglican Church, that the whole process of conversion was carried out in four days, and that the Jewesses who knew a little English were
present to prompt the converts to say "yes" and "no" at the right moments

in reply to the questions put to them during the ceremony because the converts did not know English or understand what they were being asked. You may imagine my confusion with such allegations which amount to charging the refugees with being converted to the Anglican communion merely for the purpose of benefiting from the charities organised for the help of Christians.

Lang asked Don what he knew about this, and Don assured the archbishop that it was "grotesquely untrue." Mrs. Ludovici seems to have heard about the mass conversions from the Mosleyite Lane-Fox Pitt-Rivers.

CHAPTER TEN

DECEMBER

By the end of the year the national conservatives and the Nazis had finally parted ways. "National" government had been abandoned in favor of an ideologically correct Nazi one. At first Hitler's causes had also been theirs, but there were clear indications in 1938 that this was no longer so. Hitler had already dropped the nationalists from his ranks with the January crisis. The Prussian generals were no longer leading the army; the old school diplomats had ceased to control the Wilhelmstrasse; the voices for a sensibly managed economy had been thrust out into the cold. Göring, a Nazi with national credentials, was increasingly sidelined as the year went on.

Apart from a few diehard Prussians like Kleist-Schmenzin, no one objected to the merger with Austria or the redemption of the Sudetenländer much. They were national causes that signified the end of the Versailles settlement and Germany's return to glory. A liberal German like Peter Bielenberg affirmed this. Czech security, the maintenance of their efficient chains of forts—such arguments meant very little. The Sudetenländer had been given a rough deal, and they were better off in the bosom of the Reich. People at the time did not possess the benefit of hindsight; they did not know what we know now: that Chamberlain's choosing not to fight—although utterly practical—was a disaster for the world.

Many of Hitler's decisions in 1938 were purely pragmatic and neglected to take stock of the national view: like the abandonment of 250,000 German South Tyroleans to Italy to gain Italian support, or the failure to come to a deal with the Poles to revise the border in return for a common stance against Bolshevik Russia. The fact that Vansittart was suspicious of Goerdeler's demand for the return of Danzig and the Polish Corridor is a sign that the diplomat was also incapable of telling the difference between Nazism and nationalism.

On the domestic side, the Reichskristallnacht was no crowd-pleaser, and for many Germans it was either an embarrassment or a reason for distancing themselves from a regime they had tolerated up to then. The conspiracy around Goerdeler, Weizsäcker, Canaris, Witzleben, and Halder is the clearest indication that Hitler had now gone too far, but the opposition was increasingly distant from the source of power and had problems removing him.

It had lost its chance after the failure of the putsch in September, but there was a new generation in the wings that would eventually join forces with the older men and get the ball rolling again. Adam von Trott went to Berlin in November and stayed with Wilfred Israel in his apartment in the Bendlerstrasse. He learned of the attempt to remove Hitler from Schacht. Schacht would keep him and others informed of moves within the Nazi elite. Through mutual friends, Trott was also able to meet some of the military leaders of the opposition: Beck, whom he encountered at the house of the former chief of staff, Kurt von Hammerstein-Equord; Alexander von Falkenhausen; and Fritsch.

DURING THE year the balance of power within the party and its organizations had shifted as well. Himmler and Heydrich gained influence, touting a state based on a racial model too radical for nationalists. Eichmann's "Viennese model" was copied for the Altreich, as Heydrich intended when Eichmann went to Berlin in February 1939 to accelerate the emigration of the Jews there. His solution was increasingly restricted by the decreasing number of countries ready to take in Jews. When the war started in September, most of these lands were no longer an option. When America joined the Allies in 1941, the last haven disappeared. By that time the Nazis had adopted the "final solution."

As for the Führer himself, Hitler's style of despotism had become increasingly oriental. He rose at lunchtime and spent much of the day reading thrillers, watching films, and delivering rambling monologues to his secretaries and adjutants. Cabinet meetings had ended in February 1938, and now only the closest members of his clique had the right of access to their Führer. His satraps were there to interpret the All Highest's will.

At the end of the year, Hitler's new Chancellery was well enough advanced for him to invite the press to revel in his glory. It was as if Hitler was now Wotan in the final bars of *Das Rheingold,* inviting his gods into the new Valhalla. The man who had made the dream come true was Albert Speer, who had been appointed general inspector for the Reich capital on January 30, 1937. He had been given a mere nine months to build the Führer's new palace. In November he had summoned the sculptor Breker to the Prussian Academy on the Pariser Platz and told him to make two three-meter-high heroic figures to flank the entrance from the courtyard: "The subject is up to you, we'll meet again in a week." The meeting had taken all of five minutes.

Money was no object. He later commissioned five bronzes and two life-sized reliefs for the circular saloon that was created by the slight bend in the Vossstrasse. The Mosaic [*sic*] Saloon was decorated with work by Hermann Kaspar. As Hitler told one of his adjutants, "when these gentlemen [the press] enter the Mosaic Hall they must immediately sense the whole sublime nature of the Greater German Reich. The long corridors will reduce my visitors to humility." Beyond the granite hall with its cupola stretched a hall of mirrors lined with red marble and modeled on that of Louis XIV at Versailles, except that at 146 meters it was a little under twice as long. The goal of the visitor was Hitler's study. Its proportions were just as generous: 27 meters by 14.5, and nearly 10 meters high. At one end a portrait of Bismarck hung over a massive fireplace, while on the white marble table rode a statue of Frederick the Great on horseback. The whole edifice had cost just under 90 million marks. The wraps would come off the new palace on January 12, 1939—Göring's birthday.

———

With the imprisonment of thousands of Jewish men following Reichskristallnacht, the Nazis had thrown down the gauntlet to the relief organizations.

Their message was clear: The Jews needed to be bought out, either using their own assets or by finding money from interested parties abroad. It was going to be a long, grueling winter for those who had been sent to concentration camps, but most of the Jewish prisoners were released by the following spring, having sworn they would leave Germany by the next available train or transport.

The Philadelphia-based industrialist Robert Yarnall was in Vienna in December looking specifically to help non-Aryans and *Mischlinge* who counted as Jews under the Nuremberg Laws. The IKG was still in funds and continuing the work of getting Jews out. Engel told him that 55,000 Jews had left to date, out of the total of 165,000, and 20,000 of a supposed figure of 120,000 nonconfessional Jews. Yarnall paid a call on Gildemeester, "the mystery man of Vienna": "He has a Gestapo man at his side all the time to check his work." Yarnall acknowledged, however, that Gildemeester was good at getting children out and Jews released from Dachau and other camps. Yarnall saw some of Heydrich's staff in Berlin and was granted authority to continue in his own task.

The first kindertransport left on December 2; another was dispatched from Vienna on the 10th. There were seven hundred children under fourteen on the train, including a third non-Aryan Christians, who had been assembled by the Quakers and Gildemeester. The children had been tested, medically examined, and issued with passports. Their luggage had been examined. Eichmann bent the rules to allow collective passports for children under the age of eighteen. They left Vienna from Hütteldorf railway station. The scene was predictably tearful. In general only the mothers were there to see them off, as the fathers were often already in concentration camps.

That same month the Quakers in Vienna successfully dispatched 300 non-Aryan children as part of a 1,000-strong transport, and 900 more were to follow. Of these 711 went straight to London and 55 to Sweden. Another 83 stopped in Holland, and 33 remained in Belgium. Priority was given to those with parents who were already dead or in concentration camps, or who were manifestly in danger themselves. When war broke out, 650 cases had yet to be placed on transports. The children were looked after in Britain by the Movement for the Care of Children from Germany, run by Lola Hahn Warburg. The honorary president was Bentwich. A "children's market" was established in London. Gentile foster parents mopped them up with alacrity.

For non-IKG Jews, one-third of the places on the trains was managed by the Quakers and another by Gildemeester. The last third was divided in two and managed by the Swedes and Caritas. Jewish emigration had been self-funded from the first. This had been Eichmann's aim all along. When the Quakers Ethel Houghton and David Hodgkin went to see Emil Engel at the IKG in February 1939, he explained "that, since the money . . . obtained from the sale of foreign currency was used either for emigrating Jews or for giving them material relief, the government benefited in the first instance by getting rid of some undesirables and in the second by being saved from having itself to give relief to starving people since it is by law bound to relieve even Jews when they are absolutely destitute."

The 4th was the Day of German Solidarity, and a curfew was imposed on the Jews between midday and eight that evening. The leading Nazis were out on the streets shaking their Winterhilfe boxes. Goebbels and some of his children took up position in front of the Adlon Hotel on Unter den Linden. There was another campaign occupying their minds: elections in the Sudetenland. Hitler had been in the region on the 2nd. Maybe the incorporation of many pious Catholics led Hitler to issue instructions to postpone the attack on the churches until after a solution had been found for the Jews. By the end of the day they had collected 15 million RM. Later, results came in from the Sudetenland: 99 percent were in favor of joining the Reich.

Some Jewish businesses had contrived to function, despite the various statutes issued in Berlin, but a last nail was driven into the coffin when it was announced that all Jewish firms were to be taken over by trustees prior to sale. The trustees in these cases were named by the Ministry of Economics. The decree also allowed the government to force the sale of Jewish property. All stocks, bonds, and securities had to be deposited at the regional offices of the ministry. It was the culmination of the "economic solution" to the Jewish problem. By the end of the year, the Jews had been removed from business life throughout the Reich. There were still exceptions; the decree was not yet applicable in Bohemia and Moravia, nor did it apply to foreign nationals. When an attempt had been made to register the fortunes of foreign Jews on April 26, it led to a storm of protest from abroad, and the government was forced to step down. Now every acquisition was to be made to enrich the state, rather than the purchaser. A tax was levied on buyers equal to the difference between the price paid and the value of the business. The Jewish names and trademarks were also to be removed—a considerable disincentive to the purchaser. One Aryanized company that complained vigorously was Rosenthal porcelain, which had a significant export business. The Justice Ministry was prepared to make an exception, as there were no Jews left in the business.

NAZI DIPLOMACY was still sending out contradictory signals to its neighbors. On December 6 Ribbentrop went to Paris to sign the Franco-German Declaration guaranteeing the present frontiers. The French were ready to massage the Germans for the time being, as there was no knowing where they would spring next. Ribbentrop, for his part, was pursuing his own dream of driving a wedge between the hated British and the French. There was a comic scene in the Gare des Invalides, when Ribbentrop stuck his nose so high in the air he all but fell backwards onto the tracks.

At the beginning of December the Nazi leaders were forced to admit that, although they wanted the Jews to go, they could find nowhere that would take them. On December 9 the RAM and the French foreign minister, Bonnet, had another meeting in which Bonnet brought up the question of the Jews. France did not want any more. They were about to promulgate measures to keep them out and had plans to shift 10,000 of them to Madagascar. Ribbentrop conceded that no one wanted the Jews. Extreme violence between Jews and Arabs made Palestine less and less tempting, and the other doors were shut and bolted. In mid-November the German Foreign Office had decided to arrange a meeting with George Rublee to work on the idea of creating a fund that would promote German exports. In exchange a degree more protection was to be accorded to the Jews. Under direct orders from Hitler, Hjalmar Schacht arrived in Britain as the guest of Montagu Norman, the governor of the Bank of England. He met Rublee, Lord Winterton, and Sir Frederick Leith-Ross in London on the 14th. The following day he saw Halifax and also had a meeting with Chamberlain. Schacht rightly saw that his days were numbered. In the event of his losing his plenipotentiary powers, he urged them to make contact with Funk.

Schacht's scheme provided for the export of 150,000 Jews over the next three years. In exchange German Jews would create a fund amounting to 1.5 billion RM to be matched by the same sum invested by Jews outside the Reich. This was to be used as credit for the purchase of German exports. The Germans would pay an annual interest of 4 percent and amortize the sum at 2 percent annually. The persecution of the Jews would cease during that period. Schacht was still prepared to run errands for Hitler to find a way back into his favor. Both Hitler and Göring had endorsed this scheme, the so-called Warburg Plan. Schacht reported back to Hitler on January 2, 1939.

The project did not find much favor among the Jews themselves—particularly in America. Secretary of State Cordell Hull pointed out that the boycott was not official, and the Jews preferred the idea of a loan that was not linked to German exports. Rublee still hoped to be able to do a deal, and for that reason he went to Berlin on January 13. A week later, Schacht was relieved of his duties. It seems that a jealous Ribbentrop had finally had his way. Rublee was able to see Göring, who thought it would be possible to continue negotiations through Wohltat. German acceptance of the scheme remained conditional on a relaxation of the boycott.

The Nazi leaders might have found solace in the news from Memelland, where local elections on December 14 showed as much as 87.1 percent in favor of a return to Germany. In Britain, a debate in the House of Lords revealed the extent of Jewish immigration to date. There was concern about the transit of refugees and children in particular. Tallies were limited by the number of voluntary workers prepared to deal with them. Some 15,000 to 16,000 had landed in Britain, but 4,000 to 5,000 had left again. There were around 1,000 children under eighteen who were granted right of asylum. Equally, people over the age of sixty were allowed to stay. There was evidence of a softer attitude: Refugees were allowed to apply for visas in Britain and remain there for two years without papers, provided they had some means of support. Those between the ages of sixteen and thirty-five could submit to further training with a view to finding work in another country. Employment was only to be granted in the case of no Briton wanting to do the work.

The United States had already taken in 40,000; there were 45,000 German refugees in France, 25,000 in Holland (8,000 had already moved on), and 100,000 in Czechoslovakia. It was not apparent at the time, but all those remaining on the Continent were at great risk. There were even 94 Austrian refugees in Albania. The British government was exerting pressure on the colonies to except more immigrants. The Australian government was still claiming it would take 15,000. One S. C. Leslie of the Gas, Light and Coke Company was to go to Austria to interview candidates to work in Australia on December 28. Tanganyika and British Guiana were seen as good bets.

At the same time the Italian government was turning up the heat: on December 7 Jewish refugees were told they had until March 12 to leave, or face imprisonment. The Dutch closed their borders to Jews on December 17, but sent no children back if they had been placed in the carriages by their parents. The Swiss, too, were being increasingly pettifogging in their attitude to the tide of refugees, many of whom had made their way over the green border from the Austrian Vorarlberg. On December 17 the Swiss tally was estimated to be between 10,000 and 12,000. "Permission to enter Switzerland will be given to near relatives of Swiss if in danger and if their onward journey is certain within a reasonable time. Elderly persons will be admitted and arrangements are being made to take about 300 children temporarily." That very day Hitler issued a *Führerbefehl*: rump Czechoslovakia was to be liquidated as quickly as possible.

The British Legation in Berne reported directly to Foreign Secretary Halifax. Jews required visas to enter Switzerland, in direct response to the Austrians: "In the course of July there was a great influx of Austrian Jews, mainly from Vienna." The German attitude was largely one of "good riddance." "German frontier authorities . . . facilitated this illegal crossing of the Swiss frontier. This had, however, been stopped, on diplomatic representations being made to the German government." The policy now was to send Jews who had entered illegally back. Germans had no need of visas to cross the frontier: "The federal government has entered into communication with the German government. The latter announce that all passports would in future bear a special sign (a large J)." Since October 4, German non-Aryans had to possess a visa, too, so only racially pure Germans were allowed to enter Switzerland freely.

It was not just the Jews that were feeling the rough end of the stick. On December 8 Himmler decided he would clamp down on gypsies, issuing a "Decree for the Struggle against the Gypsy Plague." Henceforth gypsies were to be issued with papers for easier identification: brown for purebred, light blue for *Mischlinge*, and grey for Aryan nomads. The aim was to prevent any congress between gypsies and Aryan folk. The text darkly hints at the "final solution of the gypsy problem."

The knives were also out for the Church. A cartoon in *Der Stürmer* showed a priest pelting the regime with muck, but succeeding only in fouling the Cross. For extreme Nazis, the SS, and members of Himmler's circle, Christmas was already a dead letter anyway. *Stürmer* mocked the idea of the Feast of Christmas in the ruins of Bethlehem and showed Father Christmas with a sack of Jews that no one wanted in their stockings. The Nazis wanted Germans to celebrate the winter solstice on the 21st instead.

On December 10 the Nazis once again showed their fangs toward the churches. The singing of carols and school Christmas concerts were banned that year. The Christmas tree—being German—was permissible, but only when shorn of its Christian fetters. Klemperer noted that the newspapers had been muzzled for the first time. Christ had been banished from Christmas. The feast celebrated the great German soul, the rebirth of the light, and the reawakening of the German Reich. "The Jew Jesus, everything spiritual as well as anything generally human has been thrown out." All traditions were under attack, and that included those held by conservative-minded Germans. On December 21 Keitel emitted an ukase that no officers might congratulate the ex-kaiser on his eightieth birthday. "This was signed by a former Imperial officer," wrote Groscurth. "God forbid! And my, how little certain of itself this regime is."

The execution laid on in Buchenwald that Yuletide was not just a warning—it was a gift. Peter Forster had managed the unimaginable: He had escaped from the camp, killed a guard, and crossed the Czech border, but the Czechs had handed him back. His execution was to be a lesson to them all. As was the Nazi custom, the senior prisoner performed the role of executioner. The entire camp was assembled by night. Spotlights lit up the scaffold, as well as the prisoners. No one was allowed to avert his sight. The executioner appeared before the prisoner, twisting the rope. To what end they couldn't say.

Then Forster was strung up, but when this happened, the senior prisoner jumped up and grasped him by the knees. The extra weight broke

Forster's neck. The executioner jumped down, and it was then that the spectators realized why the rope had been twisted: The corpse proceeded to spin faster and faster on the rope lit up by the spotlights. It was a grotesque scene. Only then were the men allowed to return to their huts. A few days later, guards discovered that alcohol had been smuggled into the camp for a New Year's party. Fifty men were made an example. They were stripped, tied to wooden horses, and beaten until the flesh hung from their backs. A drunken Commandant Rödl meandered around, and the Buchenwald band was on hand to play the camp song.

———

Many of the men and women mentioned in these pages died violent deaths. The Nazis either were killed in action, committed suicide, or were hanged after the war. Most of those who resisted their power suffered a similar fate in the last stages of the conflict. Those Jews who failed to leave mainland Europe generally perished as well. Fred Richter's later history makes sad reading. He appeared before a magistrate at the Landgericht on January 20, 1939. He seems to have successfully argued that he was only a messenger and had no idea what he was involved in. He later complained that the magistrate had been rough with him, and he recanted everything he said. He had no idea that espionage was involved.

On September 15, 1939, he was tried before the notorious Peoples' Court in Berlin. Tucek was naturally a model witness. Kriminalrat Preiss appeared for the prosecution: He had interrogated Kendrick and was able to produce his testimony. Preiss informed the court that Richter had tried on several occasions to interest Kendrick in agents. The court concluded that Richter had been lying. Kendrick's testimony was in keeping with Tucek's. Richter was therefore convicted of acting as an accomplice to Kendrick. He was sentenced to twelve years' imprisonment and to pay a fine of 1,000 RM for wasting the court's time. He was released into captivity in Austria. He remained in Stein prison until June 15, 1942. He wrote his last letter to Maud from there in May that year, before he was moved to Marburg in present-day Slovenia; in September that year he was moved to Graz. He left Graz in February 1943 for Auschwitz, dying at 8:22 AM the day after his arrival, allegedly from heart disease. He had not survived the infamous ramp at the railway siding.

Tucek appears to have been working for the Gestapo. A man of that name was active in tracking down and torturing Austrian Communists in Paris during the war, and the French requested his extradition once he had been spotted on the streets of Vienna. He was sentenced to five years' imprisonment by a military court in Paris.

The pogrom of November 9–10 had destroyed Chamberlain's policy of appeasement in Germany. The shock felt by many Britons after the events of the Reichskristallnacht made it untenable. It was now quite clear that Hitler would push for war and that dangling trifles at him, such as the return of the German colonies, would not satisfy him in the long run. Although "J'aime Berlin" (as some were now calling Chamberlain) was unaware of it then, Hitler had already given instructions to OKH on October 21 to draw up plans for the invasion both of rump Czechoslovakia and Memelland.

Foreign boycotts of German goods were slowly strangling the regime. The new enemy was the "Jewish State"—the United States, which for Hitler meant "world Jewry." If the United States were to stop importing German goods, then Germany would institute a policy of expansion to the east. It would mean the conquest of *Lebensraum*. That the die was cast is evident from Hitler's speech in the Reichstag of January 30, 1939: "I want today to be a prophet again: if international finance Jewry inside and outside Europe should succeed in plunging the nations once more into a world war, the result will not be the bolshevisation of the earth and thereby the victory of Jewry, but the annihilation of the Jewish race in Europe." In Goebbels's interpretation, the two-and-a-half-hour speech was a "tough polemic against America." Others have seen the "prophecy" as a green light to his hard-line supporters, who would begin to implement the "Final Solution" in the last weeks of 1941.

ON CHRISTMAS DAY, Kurt von Schuschnigg was still in the Metropole, but he had the solace of a small radio furnished after Himmler's visit on December 11. He could listen to the Coronation Mass from the Steffl. He took solace in the *Agnus Dei*. On December 31, 1938, Austrian passports became invalid. Now Austrians had to seek new papers and face fresh humiliations along the way. On December 30, Helmuth Groscurth recorded a story about Goebbels, who had attempted to rape a young actress in Schwanenwerder. She was able to flee with the help of her fiancé. The Gestapo had learned of the incident and sent the girl a bunch of flowers with the message: "for the brave little lady." This may have explained the minister's mood as he donned his pajamas that night: "and so to bed. A new year! It is spine-chilling! The best thing to do would be to hang myself."

AFTERWORD

The history of Central Europe in 1938 is, to some extent, the history of my own family. That year my maternal grandfather's family scattered to the four winds. The Zirners and the Zwiebacks had come to Vienna from Baja and Bonyhad in Hungary two generations before, when, following defeat in the Austro-Prussian War, the emperor finally allowed Jews to settle in the capital. The cloth merchant Ludwig Zwieback promptly bought the stock exchange building housed in the old Palais Arnstein-Pereira in the Weihburggasse and opened a department store around the corner in the Kärntnerstrasse. His brothers opened a more down-market version in the Mariahilferstrasse. When Ludwig died at his home on the Morzinplatz in 1906, he left each of his three daughters a third share in a fortune of some 2.2 million gold crowns, at a time when a genteel retirement might have been eked out on 3,000 a year.

The daughters were my great-grandmother Gisela; Ella, who inherited the business; and Malwine, who married the lawyer Josef Kranz. My great-grandmother married Marton Zirner, who had succeeded his father, Max, as court jeweler. They had four children: Josef, Katharina, Walther, and Felix. Josef died an "aspirant" in the K & K dragoons near Warsaw in 1915. In civilian life he had been co-répétiteur in the opera houses in Hamburg and Breslau, having abandoned the law for music. He was hoping to become a conductor.

On March 11, 1938, Great-Uncle Josef's wife, Gina Kaus, the feminist novelist and later screenwriter, was the first of my relatives to make the decision to run. She was another sparkling example of old Viennese Jewry: the half-sister of Princess Stephanie zu Hohenlohe, Hitler's Jewish spy. Her books had been burned in Berlin in 1933, and she had made her way home to Vienna. Referring in her autobiography to the flames that engulfed the works of Heine, Thomas Mann, and Sigmund Freud, she said, "Never have I been in such good company."

After Josef's death Great-Aunt Gina married the Trieste-born Gentile Otto Kaus, but that marriage ended in separation. She left Vienna in 1938 with her latest lover, and third and last husband, Eddy Frischauer, the brother of the journalist and writer Willi, who was already based in Britain. As Kaus's wife, she had an Italian passport. When they were detrained in Feldkirch in the Vorarlberg and asked to show their papers, Frischauer flourished his baptismal certificate, prudently issued to him shortly after his birth by his Catholic, assimilated Jewish parents. It worked. He and Gina found safety in Switzerland. His parents, however, were gassed. Gina eventually started a new career in Hollywood. She wrote no more novels, however: She had lost her language and her audience in Germany. She died in Los Angeles at age ninety-two.

Great-Aunt Kathi died in Darjeeling in 1927, shortly after giving birth to a boy called Martin. Martin was bitten by a venomous fly and developed brain damage. Kathi's husband, the Latvian Jew Dr. Rudolf Rapaport, demanded my aunt's dowry, and my great-grandmother had to sell her last properties—the villa in Hietzing and country house on the Mondsee near Salzburg and the heavily mortgaged shop in the Graben—to pay him off. After escaping the Nazis from the south of France, Rapaport achieved fame as the painter Rudolf Ray in Mexico and the United States. Kathi may have had a second child called Bonifacius, the fruit of a liaison in Paris during her student years. He was secretly lodged in an orphanage in Klosterneuburg. The fate of Bonifacius is unknown.

My grandfather and my great-uncle Walther had started up a small business after the *déroute* caused by Rudolf Rapaport demanding my great-aunt's portion. They naturally had no future in Vienna after March 1938. My great-uncle Walther was arrested in June, along with all the Viennese jewelers. He was sent to Dachau before being transferred to Buchenwald. He was eventually released. His Protestant, Bavarian wife had divorced him. Whether she had bought him out, or whether he was released for

Hitler's fiftieth birthday, no one seems to know now. He died a broken man in Central America in 1963, where he ran a coffee plantation.

My grandfather Felix Zirner had married Katharine Bacon. She was an English Catholic, the daughter of the Royal Academician John Henry Bacon. They had a daughter—my mother. The marriage broke up soon after, and Katharine Zirner returned to England, where she died of tuberculosis in a nursing home in Haselmere, Surrey, in 1938. Felix was refused entry into Britain, where he might have joined his daughter. He left for Argentina from Genoa in September. His admission was presumably engineered by the pressure exerted by Rublee on the backtracking Argentinians. He made his way to Bolivia—"the Rolls Royce of emigrations"—and established a small firm restoring churches. It is not known how he financed the journey and visa. A member of his wife's family probably obtained the latter for him in London or Washington. He died of heart failure in 1943 at the age of just thirty-eight.

Gisela Zirner died in 1930. Her sister Ella was still running the family department store in the Kärntnerstrasse with her son Ludwig as managing director. Ella was one of the most prominent women in Vienna. She led a fabulous life, took many lovers, and had an estate in Yugoslavia where guests were collected from the station by a carriage drawn by a team of white horses. In 1933 the Zirners rented out the department store's former canteen to three Hungarian noblemen who turned it into the famous restaurant Zu den Drei Husaren. In 1938 the owner, Count Paul Pallfy, decided that he no longer wished to operate a restaurant in a Nazi Vienna and sold the lease to Otto Horcher, the restaurant tsar of the Third Reich. During the war years its banquettes groaned under the weight of Hermann Göring and other Nazi luminaries. Ella had married my great-grandfather's brother, Alexander, who sat on the board of the Jewish congregation with my great-grandfather. He was not only a pillar of the community but one of the most prominent industrialists in the city. Ella and Alexander went their separate ways before the First World War, and Alexander lived in a suite in the Imperial Hotel. When he died in 1924, several hundred people accompanied his coffin to the Central Cemetery.

Ella had three children. Renée married a diplomat, the scion of a Hungarian magnate family with the sonorous name of Hugo Erös von Bethlenfalva. Erich fled to Monaco when the Germans attacked France and was still there in the fifties. The third child, Ludwig, however, was not Alexander's son but the result of a long-standing affair between Ella and the composer Franz Schmidt, the disciple of Bruckner who had known her since her time at the Academy of Music, where Ella had won first prize for piano.

Schmidt had wanted to marry Ella, but my great-great-grandfather felt the impecunious musician lacked prospects. Schmidt dedicated his First Symphony to Ella and later made a present to her of the score of his opera *Notre Dame*, which was also inscribed to her. At around the time he was writing *Notre Dame*, Schmidt was a constant presence in Ella's apartment next to the Bristol Hotel on the Ring. Schmidt and Ella used to play duets together. A form of synthesis was achieved when Ludwig was born in February 1906. Ludwig also studied privately and at the Academy under his natural father, but his mother refused to allow him to become a professional musician. The Nazis greatly revered Schmidt and were presumably blissfully unaware that he had a Jewish son.

They commissioned a new work from him, *Eine Deutsche Auferstehung* (German Resurrection), which he was halfhearted about and failed to finish by the time he died in February 1939. Shortly before Ludwig left Vienna, a Gestapo man came to see him and confiscated the score of *Notre Dame*. He never learned for certain who had informed them that he had it in his possession, but he suspected that it was Schmidt's pupil, the pianist Friedrich Wührer. Wührer was the first to tell Ludwig that he was Schmidt's son. That was in America after the war; his mother had never discussed his paternity.

On April 6, 1938, Horcher became the owner of the walls of the restaurant as well, when Ella's property was Aryanized. The Nazis swiped half her wealth, her creditors the other—principally the Zentralsparkasse der Stadt Wien. A large sum was paid into a closed account, of which Ella and her son Ludwig naturally saw nothing. After Ella and Ludwig were forced to relinquish their property, they made their way via Cherbourg to New York, Ella on the arm of her new beau, the painter Viktor Krausz. Ella died in 1970. She had wanted to return to Vienna and become involved with the department store again, but Ludwig would not hear of it. Having been given a part of her property back in 1951, she sold it again in 1957. When Krausz died, she took a younger lover who ran off with all that remained of the family fortune.

Ludwig was free at last. After serving as a musician in the American army, he cast off the fetters of commerce, sat numerous exams, and submitted a doctoral dissertation on American piano music. He finally achieved complete metamorphosis, becoming a professor of piano at the University of Illinois at Urbana-Champaign. Assisted by his Viennese-born wife, Laura, he began the opera courses that were later to distinguish the school of music at Urbana, preparing and translating scores and conducting a wide range of operas. He was also the life and soul of the famous Tanglewood Music Festival. As Schmidt's son, he was the heir to the purest Viennese musical tradition.

At his invitation, Stravinsky, Britten, Milhaud, Kubelik, Hindemith, and Beecham all visited Urbana. He was so successful that he was invited to take over the opera school at the Academy of Music in Berlin. He eventually realized his dream of building a proper opera house in Urbana, and although he was already a very sick man, shortly before his death he put on a performance of *Rheingold* there, with Wagner's great-grandson, Wolf Siegfried or "Wummi" Wagner, at his side. After he died in 1971, Laura returned to Vienna to join their teenage son, August, who was training to be an actor. August is now an Austrian citizen and celebrated for his theatre and cinema performances in the German-speaking world.

The Zirners and the Zwiebacks were lucky. They were rich and well-connected and were able to escape from Austria before it was too late. Only one of my close relatives perished. The painter Rudolf Rapaport abandoned his mentally retarded son when he fled to America. Martin Rapp was gassed at Hartheim in 1944.

Acknowledgments

Many people have given me helpful suggestions and references or have delved deep into their memories of a now-distant time: Rupert Allison, John Aycoth, Melanie Barber, Richard Bassett, Angela Bohrer, Ann Bone, the late Gerhard Bronner, Professor Michael Burleigh, Professor Andrew Chandler, the late George Clare, Tim Clarke, Venerable Patrick Curran, Wolf-Erich Eckstein, the late Sir Dudley Forwood Bt, Georg Gaugusch, the late Litzi Gedye, Lydia Hall, Gerhard Heilig, Uwe Kohl, the late Peter Leighton-Langer, Mairin Lodle, Celia Male, Patricia Meehan, Professor Lucien Meysels, Fritz Miesbauer, Gisela Müller, Stefan Popper, Professor Munro Price, Lorli Rudov, the late Arnold Sayers, Professor Hans Schneider, Father Franz Schuster OSB, Henry Wellisch, August Zirner, and Ed Zwieback.

Particular thanks are due to people who lent or sent books and papers, such as my friends Christopher Wentworth-Stanley and Sebastian Cody in Vienna. Sebastian also read the typescript and made a number of important points. Michael Smith of the *Daily Telegraph* gave me a copy of an interview with the deputy Viennese MI6 chief Kenneth Benton before Benton's death. Peter Ede very kindly sent me his manuscript translation of Gräfin Maltzan's memoirs and other helpful suggestions.

I should also like to thank the staffs of the DÖW archive and the Staatsbibliothek in Vienna, the Bundesarchiv in Koblenz, and the library at Swarthmore College in Pennsylvania for providing me with copies of the Corder Catchpool papers. In London I received wonderful support from a number of institutions: the Public Record Office, Friends House Library, the London Metropolitan Archive for the papers of the British Board of

Deputies, the Guildhall Library for the Anglican Church abroad, the Lambeth Palace Library, the Newspaper Library in Colindale, the British Library, the Wiener Library, and the German Historical Institute.

Thanks too to my agent, Georgina Capel, and her staff; to Lara Heimert and Leo Hollis, my editors in New York and London, respectively; to my wife, Candida, who read the manuscript; and to the rest of my family, for giving me a few moments of peace and quiet.

Notes

INTRODUCTION

ix   **Their consumption of strong alcohol doubled:** Richard Grunberger, *A Social History of the Third Reich* (Harmondsworth, 1974), 269.

PROLOGUE

1   **No notes were to be taken:** Hermann Foertsch, *Schuld und Verhängnis: Die Fritsch-Krise im Fruehjahr 1938 als Wendepunkt in der Geschichte der national-sozialistischen Zeit* (Stuttgart, 1951), 75–76. All texts quoted from German sources are the author's translation.

1   **Blomberg's adjutant, Colonel Friedrich Hossbach:** Ian Kershaw, *Hitler*, vol. 2, *1936–1945: Nemesis* (London, 2000), 47.

2   **Blomberg and Fritsch were the first:** Foertsch, *Schuld und Verhängnis*, 77–79.

2   **There was much discussion:** Joseph Goebbels, *Die Tagebücher von Joseph Goebbels, Tel I, Band 5, Dezember 1937–Juli 1938*, ed. Elke Fröhlich (Munich, 2000), 29.

3   **The German railway network:** See Adam Tooze, *The Wages of Destruction: The Making and Breaking of the Nazi Economy* (London, 2006), xxiii–xxiv, 239–243.

3   **Goebbels came out with a typically Nazi:** Goebbels, *Tagebücher I, V*, 95, 96.

3   **Halifax let it be known:** Andrew Roberts, *The Holy Fox: The Life of Lord Halifax*, 2nd ed. (London, 1997), 71.

3   **In December, Prime Minister:** Michael Bloch, *Ribbentrop*, rev. ed. (London, 1992), 159–160.

3   **"The hour approaches:** Fyodor Parparov, *The Hitler Book: The Secret Dossier Prepared for Stalin from the Interrogations of Hitler's Personal Aides*, trans. Giles MacDonogh, ed. Henrik Eberle and Matthias Uhl (London, 2005), 25.

Chapter 1

The epigraph to this chapter is drawn from Jochen Klepper, *Unter dem Schatten deiner Flügel: Aus den Tagebüchern der Jahre 1932–1942* (Stuttgart, 1955), 542.

6 **foreign Jews in Germany:** Victor Klemperer, *Ich will Zeugnis ablegen bis zum letzten: Tagebücher 1933–1941*, ed. Walther Nowojski and Hadwig Klemperer (Berlin, 1995), 391; Goebbels, *Tagebücher I, V*, 82.

6 **"The Jewish question has become a global problem:** Goebbels, *Tagebücher I, V*, 97.

6 **a Jew arriving at an Austrian hotel:** *Der Stürmer* 3, January 1938.

6 **He had been one of the first:** *Der Stürmer* 1, January 1938.

6 **In January 1938 it was Jews:** Klemperer, *Tagebücher*, 395.

7 **The Führer was in complete raptures:** Goebbels, *Tagebücher I, V*, 96.

7 **As commander of the air force:** David Irving, *Göring: A Biography* (London, 1989), 194.

7 **As he left the festivities:** Irving, *Göring*, 196.

7 **Now he saw his chance:** R. J. Overy, *Goering: The "Iron Man"* (London, 1984), 69.

8 **he liked Eva so much:** Jochen von Lang, *Der Adjutant: Karl Wolff–der Mann zwischen Hitler und Himmler* (Munich, 1985), 80.

8 **He even went so far as to confess:** Goebbels, *Tagebücher I, V*, 54.

8 **She had only just been granted:** André Brissaud, *Canaris: Le "petit amiral," prince de l'espionage allemand (1887–1945)* (Paris, 1970), 161; Goebbels, *Tagebücher I, V*, 117.

8 **Blomberg had been a stickler:** T. P. Conwell-Evans, *None So Blind: A Study of the Crisis Years, 1930–1939, Based on the Private Papers of Group-Captain M. G. Christie* (London, 1947), 115.

8 **Blomberg finally told Hitler:** Foertsch, *Schuld und Verhängnis*, 86.

8 **departed for their honeymoon:** Peter Padfield, *Himmler: Reichsführer-SS* (London, 1990), 212.

8 **the honeymoon couple:** Wilhelm Keitel, *Mein Leben: Pflichterfüllung bis zum Untergang* (Berlin, 1998), 201–204.

8 **a "fine fellow":** Goebbels, *Tagebücher I, V*, 103, 105.

9 **"Tell the general that Field Marshal:** Anthony Read, *The Devil's Disciples: The Lives and Times of Hitler's Inner Circle* (London, 2003), 449.

9 **The policeman had looked up:** Lang, *Wolff*, 80.

9 **At the Gestapa:** Thomas Mang, *"Gestapo-Leitstelle Wien—mein Name ist Huber": Wer trug die locale Verantwortung für den Mord an der Wiener Juden* (Münster, 2004), 118.

10 **Over the next few weeks:** Lang, *Wolff*, 81–82.

10 **he had named Walter Funk:** Goebbels recorded rumors of Funk's homosexuality on December 31, 1937. Even Streicher's *Stürmer* alluded to it. See Goebbels, *Die Tagebücher I, V*, 77. Hitler was also aware of it; see Overy, *Goering*, 71.

10 **a Graf von Wedel, who was police president:** A Graf Edgard Wedel or *Hofwedel* ("Court Wedel") had been heavily implicated in the homosexual scandals at the kaiser's court.

10 **Schmidt told Meisinger:** Mang, *Mein Name ist Huber*, 119; Lang, *Wolff*, 82. Foertsch, *Schuld und Verhängnis*, 94.

10 **It is not clear who:** Lang, *Wolff*, 82.

11 **He seems to have made little attempt:** Foertsch, *Schuld und Verhängnis*, 88.

11 **"the worst crisis for the regime:** Goebbels, *Tagebücher I, V*, 117; Read, *Devil's Disciples*, 450.

11 **Göring was the man for the job:** Overy, *Goering*, 70.

11 **"a case of mistaken identity or slander":** Keitel, *Mein Leben*, 207.

11 **Brauchitsch would have to do:** Keitel, *Mein Leben*, 207.

12 **Jochen von Both:** Geyr von Schweppenburg, *The Critical Years* (London, 1952), 171–172.

12 **Göring had Fritsch tailed:** Overy, *Goering*, 70.

12 **Fritsch was a calf fetishist:** Padfield, *Himmler*, 217, who does not disclose his source, which was probably Lang, *Wolff*, 84.

12 **a reactionary general like himself:** Foertsch, *Schuld und Verhängnis*, 91.

12 **"I really want to look at this pig!":** Foertsch, *Schuld und Verhängnis*, 93.

12 **quite tearful the next day:** Goebbels, *Tagebücher I, V*, 124.

12 **"You get the impression:** Alfred Jodl, diary, quoted in Foertsch, *Schuld und Verhängnis*, 89.

13 **he had stumbled across a conspiracy:** Mang, *Mein Name ist Huber*, 120.

13 **stooped so low:** Goebbels, *Tagebücher I, V*, 132.

13 **interrogation by Best:** Goebbels, *Tagebücher I, V*, 122.

13 **under Article 175:** Lang, *Wolff*, 83.

13 **"not a woman's man":** Foertsch, *Schuld und Verhängnis*, 95.

14 **pro-monarchist celebrations:** André François-Poncet, *Souvenirs d'une ambassade à Berlin* (Paris, 1946), 285.

14 **the traditional officer corps:** Goebbels, *Tagebücher I, V*, 119.

15 **on the verge of mutiny:** Detlef Graf von Schwerin, *"Dann sind's die besten Köpfe, die man henkt": Die junge Generation im deutschen Widerstand* (Munich, 1994), 139.

15 **"sullen and touchy":** Franz von Papen, *Memoirs*, trans. Brian Connell (London, 1952), 404.

15 **Beck didn't want the job:** Foertsch, *Schuld und Verhängnis*, 94.

15   (he came to regret it later): See Reinhard Spitzy, *So haben wir das Reich verspielt: Bekenntnisse eines Illegalen*, 2nd ed. (1987), 222.

15   **He wanted to surround himself:** Spitzy, *So haben wir das Reich verspielt*, 218.

15   **"I consider Ribbentrop:** Bloch, *Ribbentrop*, 165–166; Goebbels, *Tagebücher I, V*, 127.

CHAPTER 2

17   **Hitler finally came to a decision:** Goebbels, *Tagebücher I, V*, 131. Fritsch was exonerated by the court on March 18, but he was not given another role. He volunteered to lead his regiment in the Polish Campaign and died before Warsaw on September 22, 1939. It has been suggested that he intentionally sought death.

17   **a "rejuvenation":** Goebbels, *Tagebücher I, V*, 132.

17   **Hitler's sights:** Kershaw, *Nemesis*, 58.

17   **"he ought to be quaking:** Foertsch, *Schuld und Verhängnis*, 103.

17   **Keitel's nominee, Walther von Brauchitsch:** Keitel, *Mein Leben*, 209.

17   **"God-fearing":** Jochen Klepper, *Unter dem Schatten deiner Flügel: Aus den Tagebüchern der Jahre 1932–1942* (Stuttgart, 1955), 553.

18   **German-Japanese alliance:** Bloch, *Ribbentrop*, 161–162.

18   **"a prodigious ignorance:** François-Poncet, *Souvenirs*, 291.

18   **He had spent all of December concocting:** Erich Kordt, *Nicht aus den Akten . . . Die Wilhelmstrasse in Frieden und Krieg: Erlebnisse, Begegnungen und Eindrücke 1928–1945* (Stuttgart, 1950), 172.

18   **His former Anglophilia turned:** Stefan Kley, *Hitler, Ribbentrop und die Entfesselung des Zweiten Weltkriegs* (Padeborn, 1996), 10; Spitzy, *So haben wir das Reich verspielt*, 228.

18   **ordered a whisky:** Possibly a Johnny Walker. Ribbentrop was a close friend of Alexander Walker, the descendant of the original Johnny. See Giles MacDonogh, "Walking Tall: From Grocer to Whisky Powerhouse," *Cigar Aficionado* (Winter 1996).

18   **called his wife:** Bloch, *Ribbentrop*, 171.

18   **(generally contracted to RAM):** Ribbentrop was known as Groraz behind his back—*größte Reichsaußenminister aller Zeiten* (the Greatest Imperial Foreign Minister of All Time). Hitler was Grofaz—*größte Führer aller Zeiten* (the Greatest Leader of All Time).

18   **"My good fellow:** Spitzy, *So haben wir das Reich verspielt*, 219.

19   **"I distrust foreigners who know Dante":** Galeazzo Ciano, *Ciano's Diary 1937–1943*, trans. Andreas Mayor (London, 1952), 61, 62, 81.

19   **Hitler told his closest retinue:** Kershaw, *Nemesis*, 59.

19   **"This is completely unexpected:** Klepper, *Tagebücher*, 551.

20   Austria was his home too: Parparov, *Hitler Book*, 24.

20   Hitler was beginning to fear: Goebbels, *Tagebücher I*, V, 65, 122.

21   Hitler had been wanting to get rid: Kley, *Hitler, Ribbentrop*, 46.

21   "a man of winning appearance: Willi Frischauer, *Twilight in Vienna*, trans. E. O. Lorimer (London, 1938), 291.

21   Schuschnigg himself had once told: Ray Moseley, *Mussolini's Shadow: The Double Life of Count Galeazzo Ciano* (New Haven, 1999), 41.

22   His departure came as a relief: *Der Stürmer* 1, January 1938.

22   He was looking around: Conwell-Evans, *None So Blind*, 124.

22   Göring's gaze turned greedily: Tooze, *Wages*, 243–246.

23   following his dismissal: Bloch, *Ribbentrop*, 176.

23   Papen had visited Hitler: Papen, *Memoirs*, 406–408.

23   He gave orders that the border: G. E. R. Gedye, *Fallen Bastions: The Central European Tragedy* (London, 1939), 224; George E. Berkley, *Vienna and Its Jews: The Tragedy of Success, 1880s–1980s* (Cambridge, 1988), 249.

23   When they arrived in the Führer's: Parparov, *Hitler Book*, 26.

23   Hitler threatened to invade Salzburg: Ciano, *Ciano's Diary*, 82.

23   He told Schuschnigg: Kurt von Schuschnigg, *Austrian Requiem*, trans. Franz von Hildebrand (New York, 1946), 13.

23   Arthur Seyss-Inquart: Seyss had been born Arthur Zaytich to a Bohemian schoolmaster and his German wife in Moravia. When the family moved to Vienna, the father changed his name to one with a more Germanic allure. Goebbels thought him "no Nazi in our sense of the word" and a "great dud." *Tagebücher I*, V, 170, 181.

23   Hitler also demanded the dismissal: Hubert Wingelbauer, "Das Österreichische Bundesheer," in Verein für Geschichte der Stadt Wien (hereinafter Stadt Wien), *Wien 1938* (Vienna, 1978), 39.

23   During the meal Schuschnigg: Spitzy, *So haben wir das Reich verspielt*, 226.

24   wholly unbriefed Ribbentrop: Bloch, *Ribbentrop*, 178.

24   whose one contribution to the debate: Joachim von Ribbentrop, *The Ribbentrop Memoirs*, trans. Oliver Watson (London, 1954), 84.

24   the Austrian economy was to be integrated: Papen, *Memoirs*, 415–417.

24   This settlement was based on: Kley, *Hitler, Ribbentrop*, 49.

24   According to one account: Keitel, *Mein Leben*, 218.

24   "There are no orders.: Papen, *Memoirs*, 417. This may well have been his sole appearance as the god of war.

24   "Not worth mentioning: Parparov, *Hitler Book*, 26.

25   "That is a long time: Schuschnigg, *Requiem*, 25.

25   "In tanks, planes and motorised vehicles: Schuschnigg, *Requiem*, 26.

25   According to Papen: Hanns Haas, "Der Anschluss," in *NS-Herrschaft in Österreich: Ein Handbuch*, ed. Emmerich Talos, Ernst Hanisch, Wolfgang Neugebauer, and Reinhard Sieder (Vienna, 2001), 40–41.

25   arriving in Berchtesgaden: Papen, *Memoirs*, 420.

25   Other sources suggest: Bloch, *Ribbentrop*, 172.

25   "Now you have some idea: Kershaw, *Nemesis*, 71, quoting Papen, *Memoirs*, 420.

25   campaign of sabotage: Brissaud, *Canaris*, 185.

25   Tuesday the 15th: Jodl diary, also quoted in Ian Colvin, *Chief of Intelligence* (London, 1951), 47.

25   Despite reservations: Haas, "Der Anschluss," 40.

26   Mussolini thought much the same: Ciano, *Ciano's Diary*, 74, 77.

26   "We looked at Jewish civil servants: Rudolf Aschenauer, ed., *Ich Adolf Eichmann* (Starnbergersee, 1980), 84–85.

26   Keppler was also in touch: Padfield, *Himmler*, 219.

26   The two men had already hatched: Mang, *Mein Name ist Huber*, 57.

26   When the two Germans: Hans Safrian, *Die Eichmann Männer* (Vienna, 1993), 27; Theodor Venus and Alexandra-Eileen Wenck, *Die Entziehung jüdischen Vermögens im Rahmen der Aktion Gildemeester* (Vienna, 2004), 89; David Cesarani, *Eichmann: His Life and Crimes* (London, 2004), 54.

26   The district commissioner for Galilee: John Mendelsohn and Donald S. Detwiler, eds., *The Holocaust: Selected Documents in Eighteen Volumes* (New York, 1982), 6:69.

27   "that he has been his own: Klemperer, *Tagebücher*, 397.

27   Hossbach memorandum: Hans Roos, *Polen und Europa: Studien zur polnischen Aussenpolitik 1931–1939* (Tübingen, 1957), 300.

27   "The German Reich is no longer: Schuschnigg, *Requiem*, 32.

27   a "cheeky speech": Goebbels, *Tagebücher I, V*, 168, 155, 174, 100.

27   "Austria was being spoken: Klepper, *Tagebücher*, 559.

27   "This is good for us: Goebbels, *Tagebücher I, V*, 178.

27   The British Foreign Office had already: Roberts, *Holy Fox*, 87.

28   Eventually Henderson reappeared: Goebbels, *Tagebücher I, V*, 169, 188, 194.

28   "In the end we are: Goebbels, *Tagebücher I V*, 181.

28   In Berlin, Goebbels noted: Goebbels, *Tagebücher I, V*, 166.

28   The musical director of the Vienna: Berta Geissmar, *The Baton and the Jackboot: Recollections of Musical Life* (London, 1944), 325.

29   Still, he did not feel that: Goebbels, *Tagebücher I, V*, 181–182.

29   Goebbels was particularly livid: Goebbels, *Tagebücher I, V*, 143, 146.

29   Fritsch protested: Schwerin, *Junge Generation*, 140.

CHAPTER 3

31   "They have no sense: Klemperer, *Tagebücher*, 398.

31   "cowardice, fear and hypocrisy": Goebbels, *Tagebücher I, V*, 183.

31   "no longer decent: Goebbels, *Tagebücher I, V*, 183, 192.

32   **bugging his telephone:** Schwerin, *Junge Generation*, 141.

32   **"Colonel-General," said Goltz:** Schwerin, *Junge Generation*, 141.

32   **He almost certainly made contact:** Schwerin, *Junge Generation*, 141.

32   **"Yes, I was lying.":** Lang, *Wolff*, 85.

32   **Goebbels rightly called it:** Goebbels, *Tagebücher I, V*, 241.

33   **He summoned his parliament:** Schuschnigg, *Requiem*, 33.

33   **"The Duce is now strongly critical.":** Ciano, *Ciano's Diary*, 84.

33   **interpretation of Bruckner:** Ernst Lothar, *Das Wunder des Überlebens: Erin-nerungen und Ergebnisse* (Hamburg, 1960), 103.

33   **storm troopers of the Ostmark:** Ostmark was also the name awarded to Austria after Hitler reduced it to a province of the Greater German Reich.

33   **merely shrugged his shoulders:** Lothar, *Erinnerungen*, 104.

34   **Schuschnigg was getting brave:** Kordt, *Nicht aus den Akten*, 192–193.

34   **"*C'è un errore*":** Ciano, *Ciano's Diary*, 79.

34   **"foolish and provocative.":** Roberts, *Holy Fox*, 89.

34   **He had sent Ribbentrop to London:** Kordt, *Nicht aus den Akten*, 195.

34   **"Listen to me.:** Spitzy, *So haben wir das Reich verspielt*, 234.

34   **Hitler realized that:** Goebbels, *Tagebücher I, V*, 198–199.

34   **General Alfred Jodl noted:** Jodl, *Diary*.

34   **"The Nazis are rising:** Ciano, *Ciano's Diary*, 87.

34   **preserve Austrian independence:** Papen, *Memoirs*, 424.

34   **In the end they did nothing:** See Richard Lamb, *The Ghosts of Peace, 1935–1945* (Wilton, 1987), 56; Goebbels, *Tagebücher I, V*, 199.

35   **the Austrian *Kruckenkreuz*:** A Greek cross with long flat tops to the arms. It was not the only Nazi-style trapping of the Corporate State. Schuschnigg ended his speeches with a rousing "*Front-Heil!*" The equivalent of Kraft-durch-Freude was Neue Leben, and Jungvolk mirrored the Nazi youth organizations.

35   **Austrians were better Germans:** See Isabella Ackerl, "Die Propaganda der Vaterländischen Front für die geplante Volksfragung vom 13 März 1938," in Stadt Wien, *Wien 1938*, 18–23.

35   **"Devious and shabby":** Spitzy, *So haben wir das Reich verspielt*, 231.

35   **Göring later gleefully pointed out:** Georg Stefan Troller, *Das fidele Grab an der Donau: Mein Wien 1918–1938* (Düsseldorf, 2004), 239–240.

35   **The leader of the Austrian Legion:** Goebbels, *Tagebücher I, V*, 200.

35   **A boy who shouted:** Lothar, *Erinnerungen*, 105.

36   **German-Japanese alliance:** Bloch, *Ribbentrop*, 194–195.

36   **The RAM learned of the Anschluss:** Viscount Templewood, *Nine Troubled Years* (London, 1954), 282.

36   **another for 300,000:** Jonny Moser, "Das Schicksal der Wiener Juden in März- und Apriltagen 1938," in Stadt Wien, *Wien 1938*, 173.

36   **"but we were worried:** Gina Kaus, *Und was für ein Leben—mit Liebe und Lit-eratur, Theater und Film* (Hamburg, 1979), 198.

37   "a precise declaration about: Ciano, *Ciano's Diary*, 87.

37   the system established by the Germans in the Saar: The Versailles Treaty had awarded the Saar region on Germany's western border to the French for a period of fifteen years, after which its destiny would be decided by a plebiscite. In January 1935, over 90 percent of the Saarländer voted to return to Germany.

38   "Yes, he should act!": Parparov, *Hitler Book*, 27.

38   "The situation can only be saved: Schuschnigg, *Requiem*, 46.

38   In Berlin it was still not certain: Goebbels, *Tagebücher I, V*, 203.

38   In Austria, public loudspeakers told men: Wingelbauer, "Das Österreichische Bundesheer," 41.

38   By 6 pm the troops: Haas, "Der Anschluss," 43; Wingelbauer, "Das Österreichische Bundesheer," 42.

38   "We left Vienna to avoid bloodshed: Lothar, *Erinnerungen*, 108–109.

38   The idea was to make him: Kershaw, *Nemesis*, 77.

38   The Italians had already washed their hands: Ciano, *Ciano's Diary*, 87.

39   "most of them with heavy sabre scars: Schuschnigg, *Requiem*, 48.

39   One was Gauleiter Joseph Bürckel: Kordt, *Nicht aus den Akten*, 191.

39   Hess came by train: Maximilian Liebmann, *Theodor Innitzer und der Anschluss: Österreichs Kirche 1938* (Graz, 1988), 65.

39   "I can't see a thing, nothing at all: Troller, *Fidele Grab*, 242.

39   *Stammlokal*: Like a local pub to an Englishman, an extension to his home.

39   "Seyss ordered only soup: Troller, *Fidele Grab*, 242.

40   "We leave tomorrow.": Kaus, *Und was für ein Leben*, 200.

40   he gave the order for his troops: Haas, "Der Anschluss," 45.

40   The Nazis also captured: Gerhart Botz, *Nationalsozialismus in Wien: Machtübernahme, Herrschaftssicherung, Radikalisierung 1938–1939* (Vienna, 2008), 62–63.

41   Göring called Seyss to tell him: Irving, *Göring*, 209.

41   When listeners heard: Geissmar, *The Baton and the Jackboot*, 327.

41   the end of "Jewish rule.": Goebbels, *Tagebücher I, V*, 203; *Stürmer* 12, March 1938.

42   "All right, but not with any: Willi Frischauer, *Goering* (London, 1951), 153.

42   This was nevertheless risky: Herbert Rosenkranz, *Verfolgung und Selbstbehauptung: Die Juden in Österreich 1938–1945* (Vienna, 1978), 9.

42   "I feel as if I were looking: Andrew Chandler, "Lambeth Palace, the Church of England and the Jews of Germany and Austria in 1938," *Leo Baeck Institute Year Book* 40 (1995): 227.

43   Another significant Jewish body: Sylvia Maderegger, *Die Juden im österreichischen Ständestaat 1934–1938* (Salzburg, 1973), 47–48, 56.

43   They were greatly resented in Germany and Austria: Alexander A. Bankier, "' . . . Auch nicht von der Frau Hinterhuber': Zu den ökonomischen Aspek-

ten des Novemberpogroms in Wien," in Historisches Museum der Stadt Wien (hereinafter Historisches Museum), *Der Novemberpogrom 1938* (Vienna, 1988), 71.

43   Jewish "dictatorship.": Troller, *Fidele Grab*, 66–67.

44   The law was more in keeping: Rosenkranz, *Verfolgung*, 32.

44   It was believed that Schuschnigg: Nina Scholz and Heiko Heinisch, " . . . *Alles werden sich die Christen nicht gefallen lassen": Wiener Pfarrer und die Juden in der Zwischenkriegszeit* (Vienna, 2001), 56–57.

44   The Ostjuden, lately come from the shtetls: E-mail from Henry Wellisch of Toronto, November 22, 2007.

44   With the *Taufschein*: Georg Fischer in Elfriede Schmidt, *1938 . . . und was dann? Fragen und Reaktionen* (Thaur bei Innsbruck, 1988), 31.

44   a third of the Jews in Dachau: Bruno Heilig, *Men Crucified* (London, 1941), 94.

44   Tarrel had converted: Lambeth Palace, file LR 1CC21, report by Hugh Grimes, February 1, 1937.

45   20 percent of potential refugees: Lambeth Palace, Bell Papers 35.

45   estimated their numbers at 60,000: Sheila Spielhofer, *Stemming the Dark Tide: Quakers in Vienna 1919–1942* (York, 2001), 111; Florian Freund and Hans Safrian, "Die Verfolgung der österreichischen Juden," in Talos et al., *NS-Herrschaft*, 789.

45   The philosopher Karl Popper: Karl Popper, *Unended Quest: An Intellectual Autobiography* (London, 1982), 105.

45   In the first half of 1934: Maderegger, *Ständestaat*, 60.

45   300,000 chiefly young Viennese: See Gerhard Botz, *Wien vom Anschluss zum Weltkrieg* (Vienna, 1978).

45   As one contemporary put it: Maximilian and Emilie Reich, *Zweier Zeugen Mund: Verschollene Manuskripte aus 1938: Wien–Dachau–Buchenwald* (Vienna, 2007), 200.

45   Hitlerites were already out: British Board of Deputies (archives; hereafter BBD), C11/8/1/1.

45   Hitler Youth members: Reich and Reich, *Zweier Zeugen Mund*, 36.

45   "The Jews here are very much worried: Friends' Library Archive (London; hereafter FLA), Germany Files, GE9, Emma Cadbury to Alice Nike, March 11, 1938.

46   "It is the heartless, grinning, soberly dressed: Gedye, *Fallen Bastions*, 18.

46   The Czechs prudently sealed their borders: George Clare, *The Last Waltz in Vienna* (London, 1994), 200.

46   only those with the appropriate: Botz, *Nationalsozialismus*, 71.

46   They were happier to see: François-Poncet, *Souvenirs*, 317.

46   Other Jews boarded trains to Romania: Rosenkranz, *Verfolgung*, 31.

46   Once in Czechoslovakia: Gedye, *Fallen Bastions*, 363.

47   He was in the theatre all day: Carl Zuckmayer, *Als wär's ein Stück von mir* (Frankfurt, 2006), 83.

47   "It was the witches' Sabbath: Zuckmayer, *Stück von Mir*, 84.

47   "The air was filled with the cacophony: Zuckmayer, *Stück von mir*, 90.

47   promptly negotiated an exit visa: Lothar, *Erinnerungen*, 110–112.

48   Fortunately the border official was a fan: Lothar, *Erinnerungen*, 120–126.

48   she felt like hugging: Kaus, *Und was für ein Leben*, 205–208.

48   Franz Theodor Csokor: Troller, *Fidele Grab*, 226.

49   The Gustav Mahlerstrasse: Geissmar, *The Baton and the Jackboot*, 329–331.

49   There were two days of "wild" persecution: Reichsgesetzblatt (law, in published form) I, 1938, 237.

49   Later the Deutsche Bank: Michael Smith, *Foley: The Spy Who Saved 10,000 Jews* (London, 1999), 107.

50   They called themselves *Araber*: Rosenkranz, *Verfolgung*, 23.

50   it was the Fatherland Front that had: Troller, *Fidele Grab*, 245.

50   He got them out: Interview with Sir Dudley Forwood, June 12, 2000.

50   No one attempted: Wingelbauer, "Das Österreichische Bundesheer," 46.

50   It did not work twice: Rosenkranz, *Verfolgung*, 33.

51   "Nobody who knew the average Viennese: Safrian, *Eichmann*, 31; Lauterbach, in BBD Acc 3121/c11/12/2/1938. When the Austrian authorities sought to atone for the violence after 1945, the Viennese were found to be suffering from collective amnesia. In Erdberg they tracked down the chief perpetrator, Josef Breitschneider. Despite the almost total lack of witnesses for the prosecution, he was sentenced to eighteen months and released after six.

51   "*Arisches Schwein geht*: Elisabeth Klamper, "Der schlechte Ort zu Wien: Zur Situation der Wiener Juden vom 'Anschluss' bis zum Novemberpogrom 1938," in Historisches Museum, *Novemberpogrom*, 34–35.

51   Once the torturers had been paid off: Emilie Reich in Reich and Reich, *Zweier Zeugen Mund*, 268.

51   Since the police and the SA: Botz, *Nationalsozialismus*, 74.

51   The emptying of the Schiffmann stores: Hans Witek, "'Arisieren' in Wien: Aspekte nationalsozialistischer Enteignungspolitik 1938–1940," in Talos et al., *NS-Herrschaft*, 795.

52   "*Darr Jud muss weg und sein*: Safrian, *Eichmann*, 34.

52   Of assets totaling 9 million marks: Rosenkranz, *Verfolgung*, 30.

52   signs banning Jews: Rosenkranz, *Verfolgung*, 28.

52   His wife, Lilly, was murdered: Sophie Lillie, *Was einmal war: Handbuch der enteigneten Kunstsammlungen Wiens* (Vienna, 2003), 429–430.

52   He was summoned before the head: Elfriede Schmidt, *1938 . . . Und was dann? Fragen und Reaktionen* (Thaur bei Innsbruck, 1988), 2.

52   The physiologist Otto Loewi: Schmidt, *Und was dann?* 18.

52   "The chap didn't want to come: Reich and Reich, *Zweier Zeugen Mund*, 61.

53   in the tradition of good *Adabeis*: From *auch dabei*, the traditional Viennese gawper, but with a malicious implication.

53   Friedell's arrest: Troller, *Fidele Grab*, 253.

53   Friedell had jumped to conclusions: Berkley, *Vienna and Its Jews*, 274.

53   Freud's four sisters were all murdered: Lydia Marinelli, ed., *Freuds verschwundener Nachbarn* (exhibition catalogue), Vienna, 2003, 28.

53   He was murdered by the SS man: Schwerin, *Junge Generation*, 145.

55   Only Party members wore swastikas: Emilie Reich, in Reich and Reich, *Zweier Zeugen Mund*, 262–263, 267.

55   the price had risen: Robert Young, *A Young Man Looks at Europe* (London, 1938), 327.

57   Captain von Köpenick from his own play: In *Der Hauptmann, von Köpenick*, an unemployed cobbler and petty crook, dresses up as a Prussian officer and manages to commandeer the petty cash in the town hall of Köpenick near Berlin. It was based on a true story, and particularly loathed by the Nazis.

57   Only when Swiss guards entered: Zuckmayer, *Stück von mir*, 94–107.

57   Zuckmayer records that aristocrats: Zuckmayer, *Stück von mir*, 90.

58   twenty-three bullet holes: Gedye, *Fallen Bastions*, 54.

58   Many of them were arrested: Herta Maria von Kubinzky in Schmidt, *Und was dann?* 120–121.

58   There were only tiny pockets: Rosenkranz, *Verfolgung*, 13.

58   In Rechnitz there were: BBD Acc 3121/c11/12/2/1938; Rosenkranz, *Verfolgung*, 45.

59   "We have never seen anything: BBD, C11A/7, April 6, 1938.

59   "The Situation in Austria is even worse: BBD, C11A/7, April 6, 1938.

59   Lang's secretary, Alan Don: Chandler, "Church of England," 230.

59   They were eventually allowed to go: http://oesterreich-2005.at/projekte/1143303416/1143309027.

59   an exception was made for Alphons Barb: Barb was the author's godfather. In Britain he found work in a bicycle factory in Leeds.

60   He was allowed to continue to live: Rosenkranz, *Verfolgung*, 153; private information.

60   Very few wriggled through the net: Ludwig Reichhold, "Die Liquidierung der Vaterländischen Front," in Stadt Wien, *Wien 1938*, 25; Wolfgang Neugebauer, introduction to Reich and Reich, *Zweier Zeugen Mund*, 14; Lang, *Wolff*, 87.

60   Most of them were released: Jonny Moser, *Die Juden Verfolgung in Österreich 1938–1945* (Vienna, 1966), 5; Marianne Engel, "Archive des Grauens," *Profil*, July 23, 2001.

61   He was to get fresh furniture: Padfield, *Himmler*, 222, from Lang, *Wolff*, 89–90.

61   The desecration of the sign: Lang, *Wolff*, 91.

61   "with all means": Safrian, *Eichmann*, 27.

61   "crush the assimilatory organisations.": Safrian, *Eichmann*, 27

62   little love lost between them: Venus and Wenck, *Die Entziehung jüdischen Vermögens*, 21.

62   "penniless vagabond.": Frischauer, *Goering*, 154.

62   "Otherwise these scenes of brotherhood: Klepper, *Tagebücher*, 564.

62   the Hotel Weinzinger: The hotel was pulled down in the 1960s.

62   "Italy was not at all opposed.": *Der Stürmer* 12, March 1938.

62   The enthusiasm that Hitler observed: Kershaw, *Nemesis*, 80.

62   He had originally planned: Haas, "Der Anschluss," 47.

63   Under him served a small group: Emmerich Talos, "Die Etablierung der Reichsgaue der 'Ostmark,'" in Talos et al., *NS-Herrschaft*, 59.

63   Theodor Habicht: Gerard Jagschitz, "Von der 'Bewegung' zum Apparat," in Talos et al., *NS-Herrschaft*, 98.

63   Hitler did not trust Austrians: In the directorate of finance in Hitler's hometown of Linz, for example, thirty of the sixty-five staff were from across the border. Jagschitz, "Von der 'Bewegung' zum Apparat," 101.

64   On March 17, the spokesman: Helene Maimann, "Die Reaktionen der Auslandspresse auf den 'Anschluss' Österreichs an das Deutsche Reich," in Stadt Wien, *Wien 1938*, 116–117.

64   Once upon a time he had earned: Lang, *Wolff*, 88.

64   There was no denying the enthusiasm: Young, *A Young Man*, 336.

64   "apart from the Jews in Vienna: Frischauer, *Goering*, 154.

65   his "delight at the old dream of German unity": Liebmann, *Innitzer*, 66–67.

65   Elsewhere the abbot Ambros Minarz: Sebastian Bock, *Österreichs Stifte unter dem Hackenkreuz: Zeugnisse und Dokumente aus der Zeit des Nationalsozialismus 1938–1945* (Vienna, 1995), 54.

65   He took no notice of Hitler's: Liebmann, *Innitzer*, 66–67.

65   Everyone in the Church feared a new *Kulturkampf*: During the first *Kulturkampf* Chancellor Bismarck tried to break the Catholics after the creation of the Second Reich.

65   On March 13, the bishop: Rosenkranz, *Verfolgung*, 23–24.

65   Papen believed that Austria: Papen, *Memoirs*, 432.

66   Hitler reassured Innitzer: Erika Weinzierl, "Kirche und Nationalsozialismus in Wien im März 1938," in Stadt Wien, *Wien 1938*, 168–169.

66   The SS scattered: Liebmann, *Innitzer*, 71 and 264 n156. Hitler's adjutant, Gerhard Engel, was witness to the blessing.

66   "breach of loyalty and treason": Goebbels, *Tagebücher I, V*, 242.

66   Certain Evangelicals had been hoping: Walter Sauer, "Loyalität, Konkurrenz oder Widerstand?" in Talos et al., *NS-Herrschaft*, 162–163.

66   "a popular uprising: Goebbels, *Tagebücher I, V*, 209.

66   but to some extent he had connived: Botz, *Nationalsozialismus*, 95.

66 On returning to the airport: Spitzy, *So haben wir das Reich verspielt*, 249.

66 "such as the capital: Patricia Meehan, *The Unnecessary War: Whitehall and the German Resistance to Hitler* (London, 1992), 51.

67 a "completely undisciplined manner.": Safrian, *Eichmann*, 31.

67 At the time of the plebiscite: Klamper, "Der schlechte Ort zu Wien," 37.

67 The next day Berlin reaffirmed: Reichsgesetzblatt I, 1938, 262.

67 "Germany is governed by the rule: Safrian, *Eichmann*, 32.

67 "There will be no organised pogroms: Later certain Nazis would ignore this, particularly Goebbels.

67 "Frau Hintenhuber: A typically Aryan Austrian or South German name.

67 They were to be arrested: Gerhard Jagschitz, "Von der 'Bewegung' zum Apparat," in Talos et al., *NS-Herrschaft*, 94.

67 Once again the Nazis: Botz, *Nationalsozialismus*, 133.

67 "Then we'll throw away: Goebbels, *Tagebücher I, V*, 216.

67 The policy of Beck: Goebbels, *Tagebücher I, V*, 228.

67 For Hitler, the Teschen pocket: Roos, *Polen und Europa*, 301, 305, 307–308.

68 In the meantime any German: Roos, *Polen und Europa*, 319.

68 "First comes Czecho: Goebbels, *Tagebücher I, V*, 222.

68 "as Germans to recognise: Printed in Schmidt, *Und was dann?* 296.

68 Austrian priests had already suffered: Haas, "Der Anschluss," 46.

68 Waitz wrote of his astonishment: Liebmann, *Innitzer*, 76, 78, 93–94.

68 Eichmann slapped Löwenherz: Cesarani, *Eichmann*, 63.

69 The IKG was asked to raise: Safrian, *Eichmann*, 37.

69 The Gestapo provided: Mang, *Mein Name ist Huber*, 21.

69 The father of writer Erich Fried: Tina Walzer and Stephan Templ, *Unser Wien: 'Arisierung' auf Oesterreichisch* (Berlin, 2001), 30.

69 He was also one of the three: Engel, "Archive des Grauens."

70 "soft and spineless.": Wolfgang Neugebauer, "Der NS-Terrorapparat," in Talos et al., *NS-Herrschaft*, 730.

70 There was a mythical Viennese: Troller, *Fidele Grab*, 224.

70 They even reported the assistant: Engel, "Archive des Grauens."

70 the decommissioned Northwest Station: Goebbels spoke for three hours there three days later. In his own account, he was received with "storms of excitement." (*Tagebücher I, V*, 238).

71 The federal reserves would provide: Tooze, *Wages*, 246.

71 Jewish businesses were to be: Walzer and Templ, *Unser Wien*, 38.

71 Göring had had a letter from Queen Mary: Irving, *Göring*, 218.

71 Baron Louis was being held: Raul Hilberg, *The Destruction of the European Jews*, 3 vols., 3rd. ed. (New Haven, 2003), 1:100–101.

72 The business was eventually split: Hilberg, *Destruction*, 1:118–119.

72 It was important that the state: Walzer and Templ, *Unser Wien*, 39–40.

72   **From now on the Nazi:** Walzer and Templ, *Unser Wien*, 40.

72   **This is borne out by the figures:** Rosenkranz, *Verfolgung*, 40–41.

73   **"I cannot take responsibility:** Reich and Reich, *Zweier Zeugen Mund*, 201.

73   **Jobs were to be created:** Gerhard Botz, "Beseitigung der Arbeitslosigkeit in Wien 1938/1939," in Stadt Wien, *Wien 1938*, 190.

73   **Giving them work would make:** Botz, *Nationalsozialismus*, 172.

73   **Beneš was opposed to:** Goebbels, *Tagebücher I, V*, 159.

74   **He did not want the Yugoslavs:** Kley, *Hitler, Ribbentrop*, 72, 79.

74   **The most they could do:** Roberts, *Holy Fox*, 93.

74   **This Czech "führer" was a gym:** Lang, *Wolff*, 101.

74   **The Nazis hoped for:** Conwell-Evans, *None So Blind*, 135.

75   **"Just wait!":** Goebbels, *Tagebücher I, V*, 221, 237.

75   **"You may not, under any:** Quoted in Roger Moorhouse, *Killing Hitler: The Third Reich and the Plots Against the Führer* (London, 2006), 68.

75   **Dohnányi was also instrumental:** Klemens Von Klemperer, *German Resistance Against Hitler: The Search for Allies Abroad, 1938–1945* (Oxford, 1992), 24–25.

76   **Two of his most trusted:** Meehan, *Unnecessary War*, 36.

76   **He served the Third Reich as:** Klemperer, *German Resistance*, 20.

76   **The gaffe threatened:** Meehan, *Unnecessary War*, 121–122.

77   **he informed officers of the limits to their oath of obedience:** Even the most blinkered Wehrmacht officer of the Third Reich had come round to Beck's point of view in the end. At his trial in Nuremberg Wilhelm Keitel regretted "that he had not seen that there were limits to a soldier's sense of duty." Keitel was hanged.

77   **"for the Führer, against war:** Schwerin, *Junge Generation*, 147.

77   **Schacht's impatience can't:** Bella Fromm, *Blood and Banquets: A Berlin Diary, 1930–38* (New York, 1992), 267.

77   **He was connected:** Bodo Scheurig, *Ewald von Kleist-Schmenzin, ein Konservativer gegen Hitler* (Frankfurt am Main, 1994), 153.

78   **By the time Kleist:** Klemperer, *German Resistance*, 97–98.

78   **Hitler had made it plain:** Ian Kershaw, *Hitler, the Germans, and the Final Solution* (New Haven, 2008), 55.

78   **Personal belongings could also be removed:** When the author spoke on the telephone to Emeritus Professor Hans Schneider in his Milwaukee home, he was informed that Schneider was surrounded by furniture from his parents' Viennese flat. The professor had no idea how they had got it out.

79   **There were various schemes:** Hilberg, *Destruction*, 1:138–142.

79   **On March 26, the IKG in Vienna:** Reichsgesetzblatt I, 1938, 338.

79   **among the Jews "who were besieging:** BBD, C11A/7, April 6, 1938; Clare, *Last Waltz*, 199.

79 **In December, Gertrude Löwenhek:** Public Record Office (London; hereafter PRO) TI 5833 580, December 14, 1938, 607–609.

79 **"They knew every back door:** Clare, *Last Waltz*, 206.

80 **When they reached the front:** Clare, *Last Waltz*, 205.

80 **On average people waited:** Safrian, *Eichmann*, 35.

80 **"The only foreign exchange:** Clare, *Last Waltz*, 211.

81 **By the end of September:** Safrian, *Eichmann*, 44–45.

81 **There was even a suggestion:** Louise London, *Whitehall and the Jews, 1933–1948: British Immigration Policy, Jewish Refugees, and the Holocaust* (New York, 2000), 60.

81 **There were accusations of favoritism:** London, *Whitehall and the Jews*, 66.

81 **The distrust might have been:** PRO T1 5833 580, December 17, 1938, 624–625.

81 **"a totally obedient:** Safrian, *Eichmann*, 15.

82 **The Ha'avara Agreement:** Venus and Wenck, *Die Entziehung jüdischen Vermögens*, 16.

82 **50,000 found their way to Palestine:** Safrian, *Eichmann*, 24–25.

82 **taking their home comforts with them:** Freund and Safrian, "Die Verfolgung der österreichischen Juden," 769.

82 **"centres of crime.":** Rosenkranz, *Verfolgung*, 108–109.

82 **With time Eichmann:** Wolfgang von Weisl, "Illegale Transporte," in *The Jews of Austria: Essays on Their Life, History and Destruction*, ed. Josef Fraenkel (London, 1967), 169–170.

83 **"systematically foster illegal:** BBD, Acc 3121 C11/12/2, Norman Bentwich, Report, August 17, 1939.

83 **"There is a class, for example:** BBD, Acc 3121 C11/12/2, Norman Bentwich, Report, August 17, 1939.

83 **The Home Secretary was determined to "treat each case:** B4/I/34 BBD, Acc/3121/CO2/01/006, March 23, May 3, July 4, 1938.

84 **But the British didn't:** BBD Acc 3121/C11/12/2/1938.

84 **"strong Arab demands:** PRO W1 6579/3. Extracts from the House of Lords Debate, December 14, 1938, 40–41.

84 **"They used to fill up the courtyard:** Smith, *Foley*, 106, quoting an interview with Benton made shortly before his death. Interview generously communicated to the author by Michael Smith.

85 **"climatically unsuitable.":** PRO FO 371 329, 335–336.

85 **The new policy was as leaky:** Paul Bartrop, introduction to *False Havens: The British Empire and the Holocaust*, ed. Paul R. Bartrop (Lanham, 1995), 7–8, 13.

85 **"On the evening of 11 March we knew:** Professor Lucian Meysels, note to Christopher Wentworth-Stanley, March 2, 2003.

86   **In the first three months:** Damien McElroy, "Family Fights to Clear Stigma that Haunted China's 'Schindler,'" *Sunday Telegraph*, April 10, 2001.

86   **Only 350 had found work:** BBD, LMA, B4/1/5.; BBD, C11/7/1/4, June 21, 1939.

87   **In many cases it was simply:** Walter Gardner in Schmidt, *Und was dann?* 41.

87   **He reported that there were already:** BBD, Acc/3121/BO4/WE/24.

87   **Some Jews got stuck in India:** BBD, LMA, B4/1/5.

87   **Paraguay appeared to encourage:** BBD Acc 3121/12/2/1938.

87   **The first to arrive landed:** Paul R. Bartrop, *Australia and the Holocaust, 1933–45* (Melbourne, 1994), 44, 56, 85.

87   **Australia looked to be the only:** PRO FO 336.

87   **In 1938 the Foreign Office:** PRO FO 371 323 December 14, 1938.

87   **It was ready to provide:** Lambeth Palace, Bell Papers 35/144–145.

87   **the Christian "number was as great:** Lambeth Palace, Bell Papers, Church of England Committee for Non-Aryan Christians, Annual Report 1937–38.

88   **"clever, malicious and untruthful:** Lambeth Palace, Headlam Papers 58, to Dowson, October 27, 1933. On the other hand Headlam was capable of ticking off the Nazi ideologue Alfred Rosenberg: "We find by experience that a strain of Jewish blood may strengthen a race."

88   **"I am asking for further:** Lambeth Palace, Lang Papers, 38/1, March 12, 1933.

88   **"My own opinion is that a protest:** Lambeth Palace, Lang Papers 38, 14–15, March 31, 1933.

88   **"She was silent when she should have:** Quoted in Klemperer, *German Resistance*, 40.

88   **"The Confessional Church deserves:** Lambeth Palace, Headlam Papers, Batty to Headlam, November 27, 1935.

88   **Jews had been turned back:** Lambeth Palace, Lang Papers, 38, 152, March 22, 1938.

88   **"for an alteration of the laws.":** Quoted in Chandler, "Church of England," 228.

89   **The statement was interpreted:** Goebbels, *Tagebücher I, V*, 239.

89   **That last line caused him:** Chandler, "Church of England," 228–229.

89   **Bishop Batty was naturally:** Chandler, "Church of England," 233; Lambeth Palace, Lang Papers, 38, 178, Batty to Lang, July 21, 1938.

89   **"standing up for Jewish assassins.":** *Der Stürmer* 52, December 1938.

89   **The Quakers succeeded in getting as many:** Spielhofer, *Stemming the Dark Tide*, 115–116.

89   **Of these 60 percent went:** Lawrence Darton, *An Account of the Work of the Friends' Committee for Refugees and Aliens, First Known as the Germany Committee of the Society of Friends* (London [?], 1954), 46–47; FLA, Germany Files, GE9.

90   **Catchpool had been in touch:** Catchpool Papers, letter to Sir Robert Vansit-
     tart, May 16, 1938.
90   **"I can only help non-Aryans:** HNN to Emma Cadbury, FLA, Germany Files
     GE9.
90   **They included Anton Rintelen:** Venus and Wenck, *Die Entziehung jüdischen
     Vermögens*, 122–123.
90   **although Catchpool annoyed:** Catchpool Papers, letter to Lotte Leonhardt,
     August 26, 1938.
91   **"under the cloak of charity.":** Peter Berger, "The Gildemeester Organisation
     for Assistance to Emigrants and the Expulsion of the Jews from Vienna, 1938–
     1942," in *Business and Politics in Europe, 1900–1970: Essays in Honour of Alice
     Teichova*, ed. Terry Gourvish (Cambridge, 2003), 215.
91   **Somehow Rintelen's son-in-law:** Venus and Wenck, *Die Entziehung jüdischen
     Vermögens*, 124–125.
91   **Rajakowitsch was an "ambitious Nazi,":** William R. Perl, *Operation Action:
     Rescue from the Holocaust*, rev. and enl. ed. (New York, 1983), 45.
91   **Professor D. Cohen:** BBD, C11/12/2, Letter from Prof. Dr. D. Cohen, May
     31, 1938.
91   **"whether Mr Gildemeester:** Henry Friedlander and Sybil Milton, eds.,
     Archives of the Holocaust: An International Collection of Selected Documents
     (New York, 1990), 300, 346.
91   **"well-meaning but eccentric:** Norman Bentwich, "The Destruction of the
     Jewish Community in Austria," in Fraenkel, ed., *The Jews of Austria*, 469.
91   **One woman who worked:** Gertrude Scholz in Elfriede Schmidt, *Und was
     dann?* 199.
91   **he remained in touch with the Quakers:** FLA, Germany Files, GE9, Friends'
     House; B. G. Lawson to Alec Marsh in Vienna, December 14, 1938. See also
     Berger, "The Gildemeester Organisation," 217.
91   **"a Christian who was truly:** Perl, *Operation Action*, 43.
92   **All but one of the rich Jewish families:** Berger, "The Gildemeester Organisa-
     tion," 225.
92   **By the time the scheme:** Berger, "The Gildemeester Organisation," 221.
93   **about 30,000 Jews:** Berger, "The Gildemeester Organisation," 227–228,
     230–231.
93   **he told them he would not part with:** Moseley, *Mussolini's Shadow*, 46.
93   **Not everyone by any means:** Douglas Reed, *Disgrace Abounding* (London,
     1939), 228–229.
93   **"Some, a few":** Reed, *Disgrace*, 234–235.
94   **"Only if the Jews:** *Der Stürmer* 7, February 1938.
94   **Balner survived the war:** Scholz and Heinisch, *Wiener Pfarrer*, 65.
94   **Such gallantry did not:** Reed, *Disgrace*, 235–236.
94   **Alois Rothenberg was appointed:** Rosenkranz, *Verfolgung*, 51–52.

94   **"I believe that it was also God's:** Michael Burleigh, *Third Reich: A New History* (London, 2000), 276–277.

94   **Germans remember hearing:** See, for example, Bernt Engelmann, *In Hitler's Germany: Everyday Life in the Third Reich*, trans. Krishna Winton (London, 1988), 109.

94   **There is a suggestion that his decision:** Botz, *Nationalsozialismus*, 186–187.

95   **"a shameful blot:** Goebbels, *Tagebücher I, V*, 245.

CHAPTER 4

97   **It was organized by:** Neugebauer in Reich and Reich, *Zweier Zeugen Mund*, 16.

97   **It contained 151 persons:** The full list is printed in Verein für Geschichte der Stadt Wien, *Wien 1938*, Vienna 1978, 16–17.

97   **"Take off your spectacles:** Reich and Reich, *Zweier Zeugen Mund*, 66.

98   **The Austrians proved a great:** Fritz Bock, "Einleitung," in Stadt Wien, *1938*, 12–13.

98   **"Lazy, Jew-infested:** Neugebauer in Reich and Reich, *Zweier Zeugen Mund*, 21.

98   **"Amongst them were two ambassadors:** Heilig, *Men Crucified*, 78.

98   **"Looking at you one:** Bock in Stadt Wien, *1938*, 12.

98   **Colonel Walter Adam:** "A repellant fellow! It will be good when he comes adrift." Goebbels, *Tagebücher I, V,* February 14, 1938, 154.

99   **Major Alexander von Eifler, chief of staff:** He had previously seen the inside of a Corporate State cell, having been sent there by General Vaugoin, minister of war. They were reunited in Dachau. Eifler was to die there in January 1945.

99   **including Friedmann, Ehrlich, and Stricker from the IKG:** Ehrlich was kicked to death by a capo in Dachau; Stricker and Friedmann were killed in Auschwitz in 1944.

100   **(he hanged himself in the camp):** Moser, *Juden Verfolgung*, 6.

100   **Pictures of their "healthy" life:** Neugebauer in Reich and Reich, *Zweier Zeugen Mund*, 20.

100   **Others dispute this:** Benedikt Kautsky, *Teufel und Verdamte: Erfahrungen und Erkenntnisse aus sieben Jahren in deutschen Konzentrationslagern* (Zurich, 1946), 193.

100   **he wrote the camp song:** "*O Buchenwald, Ich kann Dich nicht vergessen, / weil Du mein Schicksal bist. / Wer Dich verliess, der kann es erst ermessen, / wie wundervoll die Freiheit ist!*" (O Buchenwald, how can I forget you? / As you have been my lot. / Whoever leaves you will know at once how true / That freedom hits the spot.)

100   **Löhner-Beda was beaten to death in Auschwitz:** If that was not bad enough, after Löhner-Beda left for Dachau, his wife was pestered remorselessly for the details of his fortune. Walzer and Templ, *Unser Wien*, 29–30.

100 **He had betrayed:** Neugebauer in Reich and Reich, *Zweier Zeugen Mund*, 20.

100 **"You know that from now on:** Reich and Reich, *Zweier Zeugen Mund*, 96.

101 **"Herr Reichsführer, I would:** Neugebauer in Reich and Reich, *Zweier Zeugen Mund*, 24.

101 **"There was one thing:** Gedye, *Fallen Bastions*, 169.

101 **The Communists were often left:** Wolfgang Neugebauer, "Der NS-Terrorapparat," in Talos et al., *NS-Herrschaft*, 725.

102 **There had been eighty:** Catchpool Papers, to W. Arnold Foster, January 1, 1938.

102 **Of course this did not include:** Catchpool Papers, to Dr. Margery Fry, February 7, 1938.

102 **In the course of 1938:** Kautsky, *Teufel und Verdamte*, 27.

102 **The SS needed labor:** Burleigh, *Third Reich*, 375–376.

103 **Beck's family soon came:** Gad Beck with Frank Heibert, *An Underground Life: Memoirs of a Gay Jew in Nazi Berlin*, trans. Allison Brown (Madison, 1999), 132.

103 **the cultural historian Peter Gay:** "Gay" is the translation of the German word *Fröhlich*, but as the writer is quick to point out, "merriness" was the sole meaning current at the time he adopted it.

103 **With a little flourish of Prussian:** Peter Gay, *My German Question: Growing Up in Nazi Berlin* (New Haven, 1998), 120–121.

104 **"Kosher snack":** *Der Stürmer* 13, April 1938.

104 **Others crossed the border:** Rosenkranz, *Verfolgung*, 56–57.

104 **The quickest method:** Rosenkranz, *Verfolgung*, 59.

105 **A particular sticking point:** Liebmann, *Innitzer*, 136, 139.

105 **The Roman declaration:** Liebmann, *Innitzer*, 142.

105 **Hitler and his propaganda minister:** Goebbels, *Tagebücher I, V*, 254–256.

105 **Hitler and Goebbels had also:** Goebbels, *Tagebücher I, V*, 258.

105 **The plebiscite had been marginally:** Botz, *Nationalsozialismus*, 236.

106 **the dreaded "Piefke" or Prussian:** In practice, the Piefke is rarely a Prussian but generally just a German from north of the river Main. Even Catholic South Germans are occasionally branded with the name, although Bavarians are thought to be honorary Austrians.

106 **"I can now prove that:** Friedrich Percyval Reck-Malleczewen, *Diary of a Man in Despair*, trans. Paul Rubens (London, 2000), 76.

106 **"Half an hour after:** Ernst Wiechert, *Der Totenwald* (Erlangen, 1946), 23.

106 **Sproll's eviction established:** Goebbels, *Tagebücher I, V*, 280; Jill Stephenson, *Hitler's Home Front: Württemberg under the Nazis* (London, 2006), 60–61.

107 **"These Berlin potato-faces fill:** Reck-Malleczewen, *Diary*, 67.

107 **He acquired the country place:** Lillie, *Was einmal war*, 292.

107   The former owner, von Remnitz: John Weitz, *Hitler's Diplomat: Joachim von Ribbentrop* (London, 1992), 152.

107   Any person (not just Jews): BBD, Acc/3121/BO4/WE/24, Weisl to Waldman, June 2, 1938.

107   It is a measure of the success: Hilberg, *Destruction*, 1:133.

107   Smuggling was rife: London, *Whitehall and the Jews*, 80–81.

107   The Nazis had coined: Walzer and Templ, *Unser Wien*, 11.

108   He announced that he was also: Communication from Hans Schneider, September 11, 2003.

108   Some companies were robbed: Rosenkranz, *Verfolgung*, 65.

108   There was no recourse: Rosenkranz, *Verfolgung*, 66

108   The dismissal of the Jewish textile workers: Rosenkranz, *Verfolgung*, 30.

109   If one of these had 25 percent: Rosenkranz, *Verfolgung*, 128.

109   The Hungarians complained: Rosenkranz, *Verfolgung*, 130–131.

109   Two weeks before: Klemperer, *Tagebücher*, 401.

109   Some of the designs: Peter Adam, *The Arts of the Third Reich* (London, 1992), 263.

109   The Third Reich also celebrated: Geissmar, *The Baton and the Jackboot*, 331; Klepper, *Tagebücher*, 583; *Stürmer* 16, April 1938.

110   After the festivities: Keitel, *Mein Leben*, 222.

110   he had given the ambassador, Mastny, his word: Not that it always counted for much. He told the blackmailer Otto Schmidt no harm would come to him, then authorized his execution. He could, on the other hand, be induced to save a well-heeled Jew and even found a job for Schuschnigg's brother Arthur.

110   On April 28 Goebbels noted: Goebbels, *Tagebücher I, V*, 276.

110   Goebbels wrote, "access forbidden: Goebbels, *Tagebücher I, V*, 269–270.

111   "It won't be long: Goebbels, *Tagebücher I, V*, 277.

111   Near the Reichsbrücke over the Danube: Rosenkranz, *Verfolgung*, 43; Berkley, *Vienna and Its Jews*, 260.

111   The Jewish General Sommer appeared: Lambeth Palace, LR 1, reports from Czech Consul-General and "The Sack of Vienna."

111   The café acted: Rosenkranz, *Verfolgung*, 86.

112   In Austria the fortunes: Erika Weinzierl, *Zu wenig Gerechte: Österreich und Judenverfolgung 1938–1945* (Graz, 1969), 34.

112   He was concerned: BBD Acc 3121/C11/12/2/1938.

112   Deedes paid similar calls: Leo Lauterbach, "The Jewish Situation in Austria," BBD Acc 3121/C11/12/2/1938.

113   By the time they had: Letter from Lorli Rudov to the author, October 20, 2001.

113   "We are trying to get her a permit: FLA Germany Files, GE9, July 8, 1938.

113   Many went because it was seen: Darton, *Friends' Committee*, 48.

113   The baptismal certificate *might* work: E-mail from and telephone conversation with George Clare, January 16, 2001.

113   The British Empire let in a smattering: PRO T15833 580 of December 14, 1938.

113   St. Helena allowed: Bartrop in Bartrop, *False Havens*, 5–6.

113   "in spite of the government's best efforts": Bartrop in Bartrop, *False Havens*, xi.

113   South Africa took virtually none: Bartrop, *False Havens*, 189; see also Ann Beaglehole, "Jewish Refugee Immigration to New Zealand, 1933–52," in Bartrop, *False Havens*; Popper, *Unended Quest*, 105.

114   "You would have got on the back: Conversation with George Clare, January 16, 2001.

114   Later there were speeches: Goebbels, *Tagebücher I*, V, 282–283.

115   "You look just like the porter: Spitzy, *So haben wir das Reich verspielt*, 260.

115   "Oy! Look at that!: Kordt, *Nicht aus den Akten*, 210.

115   As it was, the party traveled: Paul Schmidt, *Hitler's Interpreter* (London, 1950), 80.

115   There were baskets of fruit: Schmidt, *Hitler's Interpreter*, 82.

115   It would be up to the Nazis: Goebbels, *Tagebücher I*, V, 286.

115   although Ciano thought they only had eyes: Ciano, *Ciano's Diary*, 113.

115   Even Mussolini told Ciano: Moseley, *Mussolini's Shadow*, 42; Ciano, *Ciano's Diary*, 113.

116   Only recently Mussolini had decided: Klemperer, *Tagebücher*, 412.

116   Intelligent Germans in his party: See Klepper, *Tagebücher*, 589.

116   Goebbels looked out of the train: Goebbels, *Tagebücher I*, V, 285.

116   According to Paul Schmidt, they showed: Schmidt, *Hitler's Interpreter*, 81.

116   There was no sympathy: Ciano, *Ciano's Diary*, 96.

116   Some Nazis who had been agitating: Kordt, *Nicht aus den Akten*, 211.

116   "He belongs to a category: Ciano, *Ciano's Diary*, 112.

117   Hess agreed with Goebbels: Goebbels, *Tagebücher I*, V, 287.

117   "despicable democratic leader.": Kordt, *Nicht aus den Akten*, 218.

117   Bülow-Schwante was summarily: Schmidt, *Hitler's Interpreter*, 82.

117   Hitler expressed his anger: Brigitte Hamann, *Winifred Wagner: A Life at the Heart of Hitler's Bayreuth*, trans. Alan Bance (London, 2005), 284.

117   His gaffes caused chortling: Spitzy, *So haben wir das Reich verspielt*, 271.

117   "liquidate the monarchy for ever.": Ciano, *Ciano's Diary*, 112.

117   "The nobility is international: Goebbels, *Tagebücher I*, V, 288–291.

117   Mussolini had to find: Denis Mack Smith, *Modern Italy: A Political History* (Ann Arbor, 1997), 396.

117   "[the] *Osservatore Romano*: BBD, B4/WE/24 May 11 1938.

118   *Der Stürmer* celebrated: *Der Stürmer 18*, May 1938.

118   Some Jews were tempted to hang on: Hilberg, *Destruction*, 1:98–100.

118   **Twenty-five issues appeared:** Rosenkranz, *Verfolgung*, 75.

118   **The physical pressure was to be:** *The Attorney-General of the Government of Israel v. Adolf Eichmann*, Minutes of Session No. 18, Jerusalem 1961.

119   **For Palestine there was:** Rosenkranz, *Verfolgung*, 71.

119   **"I was no Jew-hater:** Safrian, *Eichmann*, 44.

119   **"I learn from a reliable but indirect:** BBD, Acc/3121/BO4/WE/24.

119   **"Practically every European country:** BBD, Acc/3121/BO4/WE/24.

120   **"Most of the victims being converted:** "News from Austria and Germany" in BBD, Acc/3121/BO4/WE/24.

120   **As far as they were concerned:** Office of the Chief Rabbi, report March 1944, BBD, 3121 C2/2/4/1.

120   **He wanted to achieve his mission:** Kershaw, *Nemesis*, 92.

120   **"increasing diplomatic controversies:** Quoted in Alan Bullock, *Hitler: A Study in Tyranny*, rev. ed. (Harmondsworth, 1962), 446.

121   **Germans felt certain:** Klemperer, *Tagebücher*, 409.

122   **"I am utterly determined that Czechoslovakia:** Quoted in Bullock, *Hitler*, 447.

122   **"He who wants to sit:** Quoted in Bullock, *Hitler*, 449.

122   **Hitler already believed:** Kershaw, *Nemesis*, 98.

123   **On July 12 a New Military:** Tooze, *Wages*, 249–253.

123   **Even the timing of Operation Green:** Tooze, *Wages*, 264.

123   **Goebbels thought this would be:** Goebbels, *Tagebücher I, V*, 345; *I, VI*, 41.

124   **"The Commander in Chief:** Peter Hoffmann, *The History of the German Resistance 1933–1945*, trans. Richard Barry, 3rd ed. (London, 1977), 77.

125   **In another account he was tortured:** Reich and Reich, *Zweier Zeugen Mund*, 91–92.

125   **The assistant refused:** Heilig, *Men Crucified*, 90.

125   **"Comrades around me were:** Heilig, *Men Crucified*, 93.

125   **"There is only rabble.:** Goebbels, *Tagebücher I, V*, 323.

125   **Naturally suicides in Austria:** Rosenkranz, *Verfolgung*, 87.

125   **The purpose of these shipments:** Moser, *Juden Verfolgung*, 7–8.

126   **Fortunately four years of service:** Schuschnigg, *Requiem*, 77.

126   **But if he was in deep water:** Schuschnigg, *Requiem*, 75.

127   **"You little bureaucrat!":** Schwerin, *Junge Generation*, 166; information for Angela Bohrer, Schulenburg's daughter. Her mother witnessed the telephone call.

127   **"I was livid.:** Goebbels, *Tagebücher I, V*, 329.

128   **At the time of the Fritsch crisis:** Helldorf was hanged after the failed plot of July 20, 1944.

128   **He later lied to Goebbels:** Goebbels, *Tagebücher I, V*, 331.

128   **The "eyesore" came down:** Klemperer, *Tagebücher*, 417; *Der Stürmer* 29, July 1938.

128 **The child was named Edda:** Emmy Göring claimed that she was named after a friend, not Mussolini's daughter and wife of Count Ciano. Emmy Goering, *My Life with Goering* (London, 1972), 76. Willi Frischauer (*Goering*, 158– 159) scoffs at this and says that she invented the story after Ciano's "treachery." The Görings' daughter was originally named Ebba. It was Hermann Göring who changed it to Edda.

128 **In Nuremberg, Streicher put it about:** Overy, *Goering*, 73.

128 **There were naturally rumors:** Bella Fromm, *Diary*, 272.

128 **They went directly to show the baby:** Goering, *My Life with Goering*, 81.

129 **There had to be no history:** Burleigh, *The Third Reich*, 230–231.

129 **The crosses were to be worn:** Grunberger, *Social History*, 108.

129 **A cartoon by Fips:** *Der Stürmer* 20, June 1938.

129 **"Most of the Jews:** BBD, Acc/3121/BO4/WE/24, Weisl to Waldman, June 2, 1938.

129 **Jews had been forced:** BBD, Acc/3121/BO4/WE/24, Weisl to Waldman, June 2, 1938.

130 **"The authorities are encouraging:** Perl, *Operation Action*, 75.

130 **In his reply Wiley suggested:** Mendelsohn and Detwiler, *Holocaust*, 5:222– 225.

130 **A year before, Hitler had declared:** Hilberg, *Destruction*, 1:123.

131 **"what had been a secure middle class:** Communication from Hans Schneider, September 11, 2003.

131 **"He asked the first reliable looking man:** Communication from Hans Schneider, September 11, 2003.

131 **"A large number of pastors:** Goebbels, *Tagebücher I, V*, 339.

132 **"indescribably romantic.":** Goebbels, *Tagebücher I, V*, 337, 342–343.

132 **"How paltry others:** Goebbels, *Tagebücher I, V*, 344.

132 **"Obviously such declarations:** Lambeth Palace, Bell Papers, 428/27 of October 22, 1935.

132 **"Baptism alters nothing.":** Lambeth Palace, Bell Papers, 428/118.

133 **Grimes baptized 8 Jews:** Baptismal Register in the Anglican Chaplaincy in Vienna.

133 **Some might have believed:** E-mail from Peter Henried, October 14, 2002.

134 **Weisl was at a loss:** BBD, Acc/3121/BO4/WE/24, Weisl to Waldman, June 15, 1938.

134 **On the one hand, Jews were being:** BBD, C11A/8.

134 **George Clare remembered:** Clare, *Last Waltz*, 230.

134 **"the persecutions were carried out:** BBD, Acc/3121/BO4/WE/24, Unsigned, undated document in German.

134 **the gauleiter reported "lots of arrests:** Goebbels, *Tagebücher I, V*, 352.

134 **Together with Helldorf he made:** Goebbels, *Tagebücher I, V*, 366.

134 **He was to use these methods:** Goebbels, *Tagebücher I, V*, 333, 335.

135   **On June 22 the German prizefighter:** John Exshaw, "Max Schmeling" (obituary), *Independent*, February 5, 2005; Goebbels, *Tagebücher I, V*, 306, 358.

135   **German sprinters had proved no match for Americans:** Only the sprinters— Germany won the 1936 Olympiad with a third more medals than its nearest rival, the United States.

135   **The fastidious Reck-Malleczewen:** Reck-Malleczewen, *Diary*, 72.

135   **The next day the municipality:** Bella Fromm, *Diary*, 274–275.

135   **"For the rest, the fight:** Goebbels, *Tagebücher I, V*, 358.

135   **Confiscations yielded:** Rosenkranz, *Verfolgung*, 67.

CHAPTER 5

137   **he did not have a chance:** *Prager Presse*, July 22, 1938.

137   **Hitler's Austrian Legion mutinied:** Goebbels, *Tagebücher I, V*, 366.

137   **"This is a revolution.:** *Daily Telegraph*, July 1, 1938.

137   **"overfilled with Jews:** *Daily Telegraph*, July 2, 1938.

138   **"I don't want this.":** Goebbels, *Tagebücher I, V*, 372.

138   **warned Goebbels:** Goebbels, *Tagebücher I, V*, 375.

138   **"He looked very small":** Goebbels, *Tagebücher I, V*, 377.

138   **The following day, July 5, Goebbels:** On July 2 Malcolm Christie had reported to the Foreign Office in London that Hitler intended to attack Czechoslovakia in the autumn. The following day Chamberlain had delivered a speech at Kettering in which he had voiced his reluctance to go to war.

138   **"I promised him:** Goebbels, *Tagebücher I, V*, 369–370.

138   **"We as a nation of:** Quoted in Padfield, *Himmler*, 224.

139   **He was laughing:** *Der Stürmer* 30, July 1938.

139   **That July, Munich hosted:** Klemperer, *Tagebücher*, 415.

139   **cited the fact that 85 percent:** *Der Stürmer, Sondernummer: Der Jude in Oesterreich* (special issue), July 1938.

139   **In Vienna it was announced:** *Prager Presse*, July 22, 1938.

139   **Jews were now being cleared:** Rosenkranz, *Verfolgung*, 154.

139   **"Jews are hardly ever seen:** *Daily Telegraph*, July 6, 1938.

139   **Gentiles could also justify not paying:** *Times*, July 6, 1938.

140   **381 illegal immigrants had arrived in Palestine:** Weisl later gave this figure as 385, and the cost as £16. See von Weisl, "Illegale Transporte," 166, 172.

140   **It transpired that the British:** Weisl, "Illegale Transporte," 172.

140   **Eichmann voiced his pleasure:** Geoffrey Wheatcroft, "No Fairy Tale: The History of Zionism: Vladimir Jabotinsky's Difficult Legacy, and Its Powerful Supporters and Opponents," *Times Literary Supplement*, February 22, 2008.

140   **At the South Station:** Rosenkranz, *Verfolgung*, 111.

140   **He showed understanding:** Rosenkranz, *Verfolgung*, 112–113.

141   **it must have meant Miss Stamper:** Conversation with Eric Sanders, the former Ignaz Erich Schwarz, November 8, 2001. Sanders remembered a kindly woman at the PCO who suggested the best means of getting to Britain. In his case it was to apply for a full-time course in higher education.

141   **She resigned soon after:** London, *Whitehall and the Jews*, 68.

141   **"We should need a staff:** Christopher Andrew, *Secret Service: The Making of the British Intelligence Community* (London, 1986), 535–536, quoting Sherman, *Island Refuge* (London, 1973).

141   **"It gets under your skin:** Smith, *Foley*, 148.

141   **At the end of July the Greeks:** Klepper, *Tagebücher*, 619.

141   **Some 850 despairing Jews:** In his later account, Weisl says there were only 750 Jews. See Weisl, "Illegale Transporte," 173.

142   **It was on its seventh journey:** Rosenkranz, *Verfolgung*, 170.

142   **"I try to console them:** Rosenkranz, *Verfolgung*, 94.

142   **It appears that food parcels:** FLA, Germany Files, GE9, Ethel Houghton to Alice Nike, July 9, 1938.

143   **"Why are the borders closed to poor Jews?":** *Daily Telegraph*, July 16, 1938.

143   **"degrading reproach:** Quoted in Gedye, *Fallen Bastions*, 350.

143   **He reported that even ministers:** Chandler, "Church of England," 234.

143   **The Jews had first to find backers:** Rosenkranz, *Verfolgung*, 97.

143   **Later that small tally:** Mendelsohn and Detwiler, *Holocaust*, 5:242–243.

143   **He felt the Americans:** Mendelsohn and Detwiler, *Holocaust*, 5:242–243, 250–252, 258.

143   **he refused to accept:** Marc Eric McClure, *Earnest Endeavors: The Life and Public Work of George Rublee* (Westport, 2003), 248.

143   **The Viennese-born Dr. Henry I. Wachtel:** Rosenkranz, *Verfolgung*, 104.

144   **They also pointed out:** McClure, *Rublee*, 248–249.

144   **Those taking medical degrees:** Rosenkranz, *Verfolgung*, 98, 102.

144   **Cuba wanted $500 dollars a head:** Rosenkranz, *Verfolgung*, 101.

144   **Northern Rhodesia:** Mendelsohn and Detwiler, *Holocaust*, 5:152–156.

145   **Kenya seemed particularly open:** Rosenkranz, *Verfolgung*, 102. A Jewish acquaintance told the author recently that he had spent his early years in Kenya, where his father had a farm after training in Britain. His parents had emigrated from western Germany.

145   **As one Australian said:** Amy Zahl Gottlieb, *Men of Vision: Anglo-Jewry's Aid to Victims of the Nazi Regime, 1933–1945* (London, 1998), 86.

145   **"conditions of exodus:** T120/3183/E523535-E523542 in Mendelsohn and Detwiler, *Holocaust*, 5:00.

145   **"a catastrophic setback.":** FLA, Germany Files, GE9. Corder Catchpool to Wilfred Israel, August 31, 1938.

145   **The Jew was mocked:** *Der Stürmer* 30, July 1938.

145 "I'm afraid we were too hopeful: FLA Germany Files, GE9.HNN/IB to Emma Cadbury, August 27, 1938.

146 **Argentina admitted Jews:** Author's conversation with Gerhard Bronner in Vienna; FLA, Germany Files, GE9, Emma Cadbury to Hermia Neild, August 27, 1938.

146 **The conference closed more doors:** McClure, *Rublee*, 249.

146 **To some extent the Americans:** McClure, *Rublee*, 253–254.

146 **They were offering similar ideas:** Berger, "The Gildemeester Organisation," 220.

146 **The pope did not desist:** Goebbels, *Tagebücher I, V*, 385.

146 **Sometimes the Gestapo simply pushed:** BBD, E3/282.

147 **There were eighty-three former Austrians:** BBD, C11/7/1/4.

147 **The Dutch and Belgians were showing:** Rosenkranz, *Verfolgung*, 106.

147 **The doubtful morality of a few monks:** Stefan Spevak, *NS Vermögensentzug, Restitution und Entschädigung in der Diözese St Pölten* (Vienna, 2004), 15.

147 **Schuschnigg cried out:** Schuschnigg, *Requiem*, 69.

148 **On July 24 Hitler's secretary:** Bock, *Österreichs Stifte*, 12.

148 **A NAPOLA was established:** Spevak, *St Pölten*, 31–32, 35.

148 **The compensation was in the form:** Irving, *Göring*, 222.

148 **He was back at the grindstone:** Irving, *Göring*, 223.

148 **As early as June 16, Hitler had reiterated:** Goebbels, *Tagebücher I, V*, 349.

149 **Wiedemann was a succession:** Martha Schad, *Hitlers Spionin* (Munich, 2002), 96.

149 **Princess Stephanie survived the storm:** Schad, *Hitlers Spionin*, 98–102.

150 **Not so long ago he had to take:** Lang, *Wolff*, 96.

150 **There were the usual works by Ziegler:** Grunberger, *Social History*, 537–538.

150 **Hitler lent huge support:** Adam, *Arts of the Third Reich*, 115.

150 **They were exhibited at:** Arno Breker, *Im Strahlungsfeld der Ereignisse* (Preussisch Oldendorf, 1972), 109.

150 **The Munichois were quick:** Hellmut Lehmann-Haupt, *Art Under a Dictatorship* (New York, 1954), 114.

151 **The sculptor Arno Breker:** Grunberger, *Social History*, 540, 543.

151 **"We are hoping in this way:** Goebbels, *Tagebücher I, V*, 97, 399.

151 **What failed to sell:** Hildegard Brenner, *Die Kunstpolitik des Nationalsozialismus* (Munich, 1963).

151 **the original idea had been Stefan Zweig's:** The libretto was eventually written by Joseph Gregor.

151 **Hitler did not attend:** Grunberger, *Social History*, 522; Michael Kennedy, *Richard Strauss* (Oxford, 1995), 95–97.

151 **In the village he met people:** Goebbels, *Tagebücher I, V*, 390.

152 **He had lost his librettist to Buchenwald:** Goebbels, *Tagebücher I, V*, 366.

152 **The fruit of the discussion:** Goebbels, *Tagebücher I, V*, 393.

152 "the struggle towards a life: Grunberger, *Social History*, 519.

152 Goebbels thought the sets for *Parsifal*: Goebbels, *Tagebücher I, V*, 394–395.

152 Goebbels thought it useful propaganda: Frederick S. Potts, *Bayreuth: A History of the Wagner Festival* (New Haven, 1994), 165.

153 Wagner's father, Ludwig Geyer, might have been a Jew: *"Ein Geyer ist beinahe schon ein Adler"* ("A vulture—Geyer—is almost an eagle—Adler"). The rumor was first put about by Nietzsche, who pointed out that Geyer was almost as Jewish a name as Adler. *Der Fall Wagner*, Taschen Ausgabe (Leipzig, n.d.), 2:213.

153 Goebbels had no patience: Goebbels, *Tagebücher I, V*, 366.

153 Winifred was able to invoke: Hamann, *Winifred Wagner*, 289.

153 He also boasted: Hamann, *Winifred Wagner*, 291–292.

153 In June she was allegedly insulted: Goebbels, *Tagebücher I, V*, 331.

153 In Breslau Hitler and Goebbels: Lang, *Wolff*, 99.

153 "The hatred between the Czechs and the Germans: Goebbels, *Tagebücher I, V*, 401.

153 "What are we going to do: Goebbels, *Tagebücher, Teil 1, Band VI–August 1938–Juni 1939*, 29–30.

154 Hitler indulged in one: Hamann, *Winifred Wagner*, 293.

154 The report also signaled: Rosenkranz, *Verfolgung*, 67.

154 "The doors slammed shut: Wiechert tells his story in the third person.

155 He estimated that 117 prisoners: Reich and Reich, *Zweier Zeugen Mund*, 209.

155 In July alone, 103 prisoners: Wiechert, *Totenwald*, 108–109, 114.

155 Very few of those who indulged: Kautsky, *Teufel und Verdamte*, 146, 196.

155 One way he found of dealing: Wiechert, *Totenwald*, 119.

155 On August 3, the minister wrote: Goebbels, *Tagebücher I, VI*, 32.

156 "Jews, fear this devil not!: Reich and Reich, *Zweier Zeugen Mund*, 224.

156 He spent a year: Kautsky, *Teufel und Verdamte*, 137.

156 "Jews and Christians, united: Reich and Reich, *Zweier Zeugen Mund*, 185.

CHAPTER 6

157 "The loveliest holidays of my life!": Goebbels, *Tagebücher I, V*, 367.

157 "It is so good to possess a person: Goebbels, *Tagebücher I, VI*, 32.

157 "Let us hope: Goebbels, *Tagebücher I, VI*, 34, 38.

158 "The Führer is like a father: Goebbels, *Tagebücher I, VI*, 44.

158 even angrier with Goebbels: Hassell, *Diary*, 11.

158 "A very long and very sad telephone: Goebbels, *Tagebücher I, VI*, 44.

159 "repulsive caricatures of Jewish individuals: *Daily Telegraph*, August 3, 1938.

159 There was space given to the Goldschmidts: *Daily Telegraph*, August 6, 1938.

159   The show had been put on first in Munich: *Neue Freie Presse*, August 3, 1938.

160   The organizers nonetheless asked: Rosenkranz, *Verfolgung*, 153.

160   "the same as in Vienna: FLA, Germany Files, FSC/GE/5, Factual Notes on a German Trip by D. Robert Yarnall, December 7, 1938.

160   The London *Times* claimed: *Times*, August 5, 1938.

160   could only add to their despair: *Daily Telegraph*, August 15, 1938.

160   On August 17, the Party forced Jews: *Prager Presse*, August 26, 1938; Hilberg, *Destruction*, 1:175–176.

160   Three days later, the various Jewish: *Neue Wiener Presse*, August 22, 1938.

160   The jumpy Swiss: *Wiener Zeitung*, August 19, 1938.

160   The next day the British press: *Daily Telegraph*, August 6, 8, 9, 1938.

160   Another showed a Jew: *Der Stürmer* 34, August 1938.

161   He was sent to prison: *Daily Telegraph*, August 13, 1938.

161   "We don't want these people: Goebbels, *Tagebücher I, VI*, 54.

162   Meanwhile ordinary Germans: Klepper, *Tagebücher*, 627.

162   "We must aim for surprise: Goebbels, *Tagebücher I, VI*, 48.

162   It was Göring's first peace feeler: Irving, *Göring*, 224–225.

162   His plea fell on deaf ears: Meehan, *Unnecessary War*, 140.

163   "Probably Anschluss,": Catchpool Papers, letter from Sir Robert Vansittart, August 8, 1938.

163   Colvin needed to tell the British: Colvin, *Intelligence*, 55.

163   "An open pledge to assist: Colvin, *Intelligence*, 62.

164   Lord Lloyd, chairman of the British Council: Lloyd was to come into his own as secretary for the colonies under Churchill.

164   Hitler was "Revenge for Königgrätz.": In the battle of Königgrätz in 1866, the Prussians defeated the Austrian army and established hegemony over north Germany.

164   Deny him Sudetenland: Scheurig, *Kleist-Schmenzin*, 154, 158, 164–165.

164   "utterly and terribly defeated.": Colvin, *Intelligence*, 67. Colvin was a friend and confidant of Kleist's.

164   "We must discount: Meehan, *Unnecessary War*, 144.

165   On the 27th, the Sudeten leader: Helmuth Groscurth, *Tagebücher eines Abwehroffiziers 1938–1940* (Stuttgart, 1970), 104.

165   "a lot of treason.": Klemperer, *German Resistance*, 103–104.

165   "I must warn you against: Colvin, *Intelligence*, 54.

166   The British ambassador in Berlin: PRO FO C3401 254.

166   Siegfried or "Fred" Richter: His own family called him Onkel Siegl.

166   Once, in a tram, he pressed a wad of cash: Conversation with Mrs. Chapman, Richter's niece, September 13, 2000.

168   He proved obdurate: All these details in Richter's trial before the Volksgerichthof: 1 J 172/38g 3 L 46/39.

170 **No reason had been given so far:** *Daily Express,* August 13, 15, 17, 19, 20; *Daily Telegraph,* August 20, 1938.

170 **On August 22 it was revealed that Kendrick:** *Neue Freie Presse,* August 23, 1938; *Daily Telegraph,* August 22, 1938.

170 **Kendrick had been running:** *Prager Presse,* August 19, 1938.

170 **"Kendrick's attempted departure:** PRO FO C8453/261.

170 **Kendrick was released at midday:** *Times,* August 22, 1938.

170 **He left for Budapest after lunch:** PRO FO C8533/270.

170 **It appeared that Ribbentrop was angry:** PRO FO C8454/263.

170 **The Anglophobe Ribbentrop:** *Prager Presse,* August 21, 1938.

170 **His second-in-command, Kenneth Benton:** Peggie Benton, *Baltic Countdown* (Pontwell, 1984), 11.

170 **Mary Holmes and Betty Hodgson:** Nigel West, *MI6* (London, 1983), 58.

170 **Eric Gedye, the *Morning Chronicle*'s correspondent:** Conversation with Mrs. Litzi Gedye, June 14, 2000; West, *MI6,* 115.

170 **The vice consul, Walker, elected:** PRO FO 8564/274.

170 **Frank Foley and his entire staff:** Smith, *Foley,* 116.

170 **"It is altogether a most unfortunate:** PRO FO C8982/241/18.

171 **A temporary incumbent, the Reverend:** Guildhall Library, Uncatalogued, Cologne Chaplaincy, File 1936, 1950–7, Rev. F. E. Collard letter to Mr. Williams of April 7, 1950.

171 **Possibly Batty ordained him in 1936:** Mrs. Collard, daughter-in-law of Fred Collard, remembers attending his ordination in Saint Paul's Cathedral. Telephone conversation, August 15, 2000.

171 **The Gestapo drove the crowd away:** PRO FO C85264/309–310; PRO FO C8756.

171 **Collard was taken to the Metropole:** Conversation with Mrs. Collard, August 15, 2000. She said he was proud of what he had done for the Jews, and while he remained in Cologne, he used to tell them, "Get out, and go as far as you can."

172 **"few hundred refugees:** BBD Acc/3121/BO4/WE24, Weisl to Waldman, August 29, 1938.

172 **"In recent days the emigration:** Rosenkranz, *Verfolgung,* 89.

172 **"Approaches to the British consulate in Vienna:** George Lane-Fox Pitt-Rivers, *The Czech Conspiracy* (London, 1938), 73–74.

173 **Batty must have lost heart:** PRO FO C8673/321–323.

174 **The Swedish pastor:** Weinzierl, *Zu wenig Gerechte,* 103, 111.

174 **Younger members of the mission:** Ulrich Trinks, "Die schwedische Mission in der Seegasse," *Dialog-Du Siach* 43, June 2001.

174 **Sir Geoffrey Mander tabled:** Communicated by Professor Munro Price.

174 **Grimes contacted the Foreign Office:** PRO FO C8564/274.

174 **Grimes possibly objected:** PRO FO C8673/286.

175 **He insisted that the British would not move a muscle:** Ribbentrop's diplomacy has been rightly condemned for its crassness, but in this evaluation he was correct.

176 **"The English [*sic*] will do anything:** Ciano, *Ciano's Diary*, 148.

176 **"None of these all-too-polite Englishmen:** Meehan, *Unnecessary War*, 154.

CHAPTER 7

177 **It had been the ambassador's idea:** Kley, *Hitler, Ribbentrop*, 122.

177 **the British premier didn't tell his "Inner Cabinet":** Meehan, *Unnecessary War*, 156.

178 **His more reasoned tone:** Goebbels, *Tagebücher I, VI*, 61, 66, 70.

178 **"That's impossible—Czechoslovakia:** Gedye, *Fallen Bastions*, 440.

179 **"only a man lacking:** Quoted in Grunberger, *Social History*, 515.

179 **Goebbels was thrilled:** Goebbels, *Tagebücher I, VI*, 76, 79.

179 **"vain, stupid prima donna.":** Martha Schad, *Hitlers Spionin*, 89–92; Goebbels, *Tagebücher I, VI*, 80.

179 **"He faces danger:** Goebbels, *Tagebücher I, VI*, 75.

180 **"We have to have Prague,":** Goebbels, *Tagebücher I, VI*, 78.

180 **the outgoing French ambassador:** Spitzy, *So haben wir das Reich verspielt*, 305.

180 **All eyes turned to Hitler:** François-Poncet, *Souvenirs*, 322.

180 **the usual son et lumière:** Goebbels, *Tagebücher I, VI*, 81.

180 **He didn't even attempt:** Conwell-Evans, *None So Blind*, 141.

180 **"That would be disappointing:** Goebbels, *Tagebücher I, VI*, 84.

181 **"He is already onto the next step:** Groscurth, *Tagebücher*, 117.

181 **"I greet a hundred:** Goebbels, *Tagebücher I, VI*, 85.

181 **Goebbels adorned the cards:** Meehan, *Unnecessary War*, 167.

181 **It had an "indescribable" effect:** Goebbels, *Tagebücher I, VI*, 88.

181 **Hitler's liaison with the Wilhelmstrasse:** Parparov, *Hitler Book*, 29.

181 **a hunting party at Rominten:** The hunting lodge in East Prussia that Göring had bought from the former kaiser.

182 **"Keep your mind quite clear:** Schmidt, *Hitler's Interpreter*, 90.

182 **Chamberlain waved his hat:** Parparov, *Hitler Book*, 29.

182 **The German-Polish cooperation:** Goebbels, *Tagebücher I, VI*, 90.

183 **Many Poles thought Beck's policy:** Roos, *Polen und Europa*, 338–339.

183 **"If that is so, why did you:** Schmidt, *Hitler's Interpreter*, 93.

183 **He had not brought an interpreter:** Spitzy, *So haben wir das Reich verspielt*, 307.

183 **"the old man took an aeroplane:** Parparov, *Hitler Book*, 30.

183 **had expressed the fear that:** Groscurth, *Tagebücher*, 120.

183 "the commonest little dog: Lamb, *The Ghosts of Peace*, 80.

184 Goebbels consoled himself: Goebbels, *Tagebücher I, VI*, 97.

184 Wilson as "the Sow.": PRO FO C11001.

184 "the Lord who wrote the mad: PRO FO C11001.

184 "dangerous, mendacious, sly and scheming.": Goebbels, *Tagebücher I, VI*, 103.

184 The former Foreign Secretary Eden: PRO FO C10929.

184 Bonnet as "the Swine.": PRO FO C11001.

185 In ten years he would have managed: Goebbels, *Tagebücher I, VI*, 98.

185 the Führer "a genius.": Goebbels, *Tagebücher I, VI*, 102.

185 He did not know how they could: Ulrich von Hassell, *The von Hassell Diaries, 1938–1944* (London, 1948), 11.

185 A camp was built: Klepper, *Tagebücher*, 645.

186 The Reich would win: Klemperer, *Tagebücher*, 424.

186 The chief fear: Groscurth, *Tagebücher*, 124.

186 On September 22 he hurriedly dispatched: Schwerin, *Junge Generation*, 158.

186 "the Old Man will soon be: PRO FO C11001.

186 The generals plied him with memos: Goebbels, *Tagebücher I, VI*, 105–106.

187 the Germans had carved out a very large slice of the Czech cake: Chamberlain had been prepared for the cession of all areas more than 50 percent German, but Hitler wanted to remove the votes of Czechs planted in German-speaking areas after 1918, while any German who had left after that date would be allowed to make his views known.

187 vigorously denied by Masaryk on the 28th: PRO FO C11001.

187 They were calculated to make: Kordt, *Nicht aus den Akten*, 261.

187 "Oh, Mr Prime Minister, I am: Bullock, *Hitler*, 458.

187 fortified with "the right stuff,": Schmidt, *Hitler's Interpreter*, 99.

188 There was a final discussion: PRO FO C11001.

188 the drunkard Hoffmann: The father-in-law of Baldur von Schirach and the discoverer of Eva Braun.

188 the French were woefully unprepared: Roberts, *Holy Fox*, 115.

188 who was "shitting himself.": Goebbels, *Tagebücher, I, VI*, 111.

189 "The Germans are being treated like niggers: The Czech language was apparently remarkably similar. Officials at the Czech foreign office told Eric Gedye, "The Chamberlain government . . . is treating our head of state as though he were a nigger chieftain ruling some troublesome colonial tribe." Gedye, *Fallen Bastions*, 410.

189 He told Goebbels: Goebbels, *Tagebücher I, VI*, 117.

189 "Now we have arrived: Klepper, *Tagebücher*, 653.

189 It was his idea that Hitler: Goebbels, *Tagebücher I, VI*, 111.

189 "audience should represent the people: Goebbels, *Tagebücher I, VI*, 113.

189 "Now let Herr Beneš make his choice.": Bullock, *Hitler*, 463.

189   "a horrible, undignified rant.": Groscurth, *Tagebücher*, 124.

190   President Roosevelt was alarmed: PRO FO C10931.

190   lip service to international opinion or law: Reich and Reich, *Zweier Zeugen Mund*, 211.

190   "So—next week we'll all find: Schmidt, *Hitler's Interpreter*, 105.

190   "one of the first business leaders: Hassell, *Diaries*, 13.

190   It seemed certain that Hitler: Schwerin, *Junge Generation*, 160.

191   open criticism was heard: Meehan, *Unnecessary War*, 52–53.

191   "frigid silence.": Klepper, *Tagebücher*, 656; Conwell-Evans, *None So Blind*, 148; Spitzy, *So haben wir das Reich verspielt*, 313.

191   "Look at the people's faces: Kordt, *Nicht aus den Akten*, 267.

191   hid behind a curtain: Conwell-Evans, *None So Blind*, 148.

191   "Everywhere the most profound impression: *Tagebücher, I, VI*, 117.

191   "complained about the generals: Goebbels, *Tagebücher I, VI*, 115.

191   foot-and-mouth disease: Jill Stephenson, *Home Front*, 62.

191   the Germans were ready for change: Schwerin, *Junge Generation*, 162.

191   "calm and dignified.": Groscurth, *Tagebücher*, 125.

192   He found tables set for lunch: François-Poncet, *Souvenirs*, 327.

192   "Why should you take the risk: Schmidt, *Hitler's Interpreter*, 106.

192   "liquidation of English prestige,": Ciano, *Ciano's Diary*, 154, 156, 162.

192   Chamberlain also offered to fly: PRO FO C10883/1941/18.

192   anti-Nazi Bernardo Attolico: Moseley, *Mussolini's Shadow*, 37.

192   The country was already "done for.": Hassell, *Diaries*, 15.

193   There was never any love lost: Goebbels, *Tagebücher I, VI*, 119; Spitzy, *So haben wir das Reich verspielt*, 316.

193   "We'll carry on fortifying ourselves: Goebbels, *Tagebücher I, VI*, 120.

193   "indescribable enthusiasm.": Kershaw, *Nemesis*, 121.

194   "young and full of vigour.": Ciano, *Ciano's Diary*, 166.

194   Mussolini was to be the focus: Bullock, *Hitler*, 468.

194   The RAM was still shouting for war: Groscurth, *Tagebücher*, 128.

194   "like a petulant child": Bloch, *Ribbentrop*, 213–214.

194   He was particularly furious: Kley, *Hitler, Ribbentrop*, 140.

194   Even Winifred Wagner thought: Hamann, *Winifred Wagner*, 295.

194   There was occasional rearguard action: François-Poncet, *Souvenirs*, 331.

194   expressed his liking of the French premier: Schmidt, *Hitler's Interpreter*, 109.

194   the frigid, vulpine Chamberlain: Goebbels, *Tagebücher I, VI*, 125–126.

195   In the end he had not even been able: Schmidt, *Hitler's Interpreter*, 110.

195   "modest apartment": *Ciano's Diary*, 167.

195   Hitler's peaceable intentions: François-Poncet, *Souvenirs*, 334.

195   That night the Munichois celebrated: Schmidt, *Hitler's Interpreter*, 114.

195   Even *Der Stürmer* congratulated: *Der Stürmer* 44, November 1938.

196   Hitler did not join them: Bullock, *Hitler*, 471.

196   "Foreign Policy Committee unanimous: Meehan, *Unnecessary War*, 132.

196   "exhausted and happy": Klepper, *Tagebücher*, 657, 658.

196   they sang the "Leuthen Chorale": So-called because the wounded soldiers
       sang it spontaneously on the battlefield at Leuthen on December 5, 1757,
       once Frederick the Great's victory was assured.

196   "as happy as a child.": Goebbels, *Tagebücher I, VI*, 121.

196   "He fought bravely: Goebbels, *Tagebücher I, VI*, 124.

196   "Now, there's going to be: Irving, *Göring*, 229.

197   "I confess that I failed: Klemens von Klemperer, ed., *A Noble Combat: The
       Letters of Shiela Grant Duff and Adam von Trott zu Solz 1932–1939* (Oxford:
       Clarendon, 1988), 327 and 329–330; quoted in Giles MacDonogh, *A Good
       German: Adam von Trott zu Solz* (London, 1989), 118.

197   "Brauchitsch would hear no more: Colvin, *Intelligence*, 70.

197   On September 3 they were evicted: *Prager Presse*, September 2, 1938; An-
       drew McFadyean, Report on Italy, January 25, 1939, BBD, C2/2/2.

198   "Antisemitism is not compatible: Quoted in Gilbert, *Kristallnacht*, 136.

198   It would put pressure: Chandler, "Church of England," 234–235.

198   If anything, the camp was: Heilig, *Men Crucified*, 113.

198   Weisl predicted that 6 million: BBD Acc/3121/B04/WE24, Wolfgang von
       Weisl to Mr. Waldman, September 21, 1938.

198   Eichmann sought the fastest emigration: Rosenkranz, *Verfolgung*, 94, 96.

198   Poland had another 3.2 million: BBD Acc/3121/BO4/WE24, Weisl to Wald-
       man, September 20, 1938.

199   Latvia was now the sole European country: Clare, *Last Waltz*, 213.

199   In the autumn of 1938 there were an estimated: BBD, C11/2/33, Joint For-
       eign Committee.

199   At the beginning of October, however: BBD, E3/282, N. Laski to George
       Rublee, October 4, 1938.

199   The Dutch, too, were showing: BBD, E3/282.

199   30 to 40 fresh refugees: BBD, E1/37, Philip Vos KC, September 7, 1938.

199   In the wake of Evian he noted: BBD Acc/3121/BO4/WE24, Weisl to Wald-
       man, September 21, 1938.

199   The court ruled in Sacher's favor: Leo Mazakarini and Andreas Augustin,
       Hotel Sacher Wien (Singapore, 1994), 72–74; A. A. Löwenthal, *Sammtliche
       Schriften*, Band VII (Stuttgart, 1959), 56–59.

Chapter 8

201   *Der Stürmer* reckoned: *Der Stürmer* 47, November 1938.

201   Although the Munich Agreement had laid down: Livia Rothkirchen, *The
       Jews of Bohemia and Moravia: Facing the Holocaust* (Lincoln, 2005), 79; Lon-
       don, *Whitehall and the Jews*, 143; Gedye, *Fallen Bastions*, 489.

202   This failed to prevent: London, *Whitehall and the Jews*, 146–147.

202   On October 11, Mastny assured: See, for example, Melissa Müller and Reinhard Piechocki, *A Garden of Eden in Hell: The Life of Alice Herz-Sommer*, trans. Giles MacDonogh (London, 2007), 106–107, for the plight of a Jewish doctor from the Sudetenland; Irving, *Göring*, 241.

202   Those half million Germans: *Documents on German Foreign Policy 1918–1945* (Washington, 1951), D IV, 82, 152, 183; hereafter DGFP.

202   "And he will make it happen: Goebbels, *Tagebücher I, VI*, 127.

202   He did not wish: Groscurth, *Tagebücher*, 135.

202   "No general dares show: Groscurth, *Tagebücher*, 130.

202   "There is a marked contrast: Groscurth, *Tagebücher*, 131.

203   "lots of gold.": Groscurth, *Tagebücher*, 132.

203   Groscurth remarked that this was: Groscurth, *Tagebücher*, 134.

203   "Canaris, how long do we: Groscurth, *Tagebücher*, 135.

203   In a fish factory he was greeted: Groscurth, *Tagebücher*, 146.

203   He was still sulking: Donald Cameron Watt, *How War Came: The Immediate Origins of the Second World War, 1938–1939* (London, 1989), 30.

204   George Rublee, who had been: McClure, *Rublee*, 256.

204   This was the final stage: Klepper, *Tagebücher*, 660.

204   The Swiss authorities had: BBD, E3/282, Letter from Saly Mayer, August 15, 1938.

204   The Polish government: Weinzierl, *Zu wenig Gerechte*, 37.

204   They had to hand over: Yad Vashem Archives, 0–5/1–2; Rosenkranz, *Verfolgung*, 157.

205   "It is reliably reported: *Times*, October 7, 1938.

205   Religious symbols: Evan Burr Bukey, "Die Stimmung in der Bevölkerung während der Nazizeit," in Talos et al., *NS-Herrschaft*, 78–79.

205   "cheeky homily": In Schmidt, *Und was dann?* 297; Goebbels, *Tagebücher I, VI*, 312.

205   The youths also cried: Botz, *Nationalsozialismus*, 486.

205   The storming of the archbishop's: Scholz and Heinisch, *Wiener Pfarrer*, 95.

206   They also defenestrated: Liebmann, *Innitzer*, 198.

206   "String up the priests!": Liebmann, *Innitzer*, 204.

206   "You have Innitzer: Bock, *Stifte unter dem Hackenkreuz*, 90.

206   A formal prohibition: Stephenson, *Home Front*, 140.

206   He accused his British critics: DGFP, D IV, 303.

206   "It wasn't at all aggressive: Goebbels, *Tagebücher I, VI*, 141.

207   "and we will swallow: Goebbels, *Tagebücher I, VI*, 139.

207   The German Foreign Office was: DGFP, D IV, 54, 56.

207   "I submit and arrange: Goebbels, *Tagebücher I, VI*, 158.

207   Only Hitler was smiling: Roger Manvell and Heinrich Fraenkel, *Doctor Goebbels: His Life and Death* (London, 1959), 170–172.

207   "In the distant future: Goebbels, *Tagebücher I, VI*, 158.

207   "Only the ten thousand: Hassell, *Diaries*, 18.

207   François-Poncet was struck: François-Poncet, *Souvenirs*, 342–343; Goebbels, *Tagebücher I, VI*, 131.

208   Stojadinovich was also "acclaimed.": Groscurth, *Tagebücher*, 151.

208   He realized that it was true: Reich and Reich, *Zweier Zeugen Mund*, 231–233.

208   She had a shirt and a suit: Henriette Mandl, in Reich and Reich, *Zweier Zeugen Mund*, 300.

209   The destruction continued: Rosenkranz, *Verfolgung*, 158.

209   A total of 444: BBD, C11/12/2/1938.

209   The Belgian government had decided: Quoted in BBD, E3/282.

209   "Every means adopted for: Edward Crankshaw, *Gestapo: Instrument of Tyranny* (London, 1956), 89.

210   Camps were established: Sybil Milton, "Menschen zwischen Grenzen: Die Polenausweisung 1938," in Historisches Museum, *Novemberpogrom*, 48–49.

210   Mutual antipathy to Jews: Roos, *Polen und Europa*, 371.

210   "The Polish Corridor is: Ciano, *Ciano's Diary*, 113.

211   Indeed, there had been cries: Roos, *Polen und Europa*, 356.

212   "You only have to look: Quoted in Read, *Devil's Disciples*, 507.

212   "vain, lightweight: Moseley, *Mussolini's Shadow*, 45; Ciano, *Ciano's Diary*, 185.

212   A memo from Best: Hans-Jürgen Döscher, *Reichskristallnacht: Die Novemberpogrome* (Frankfurt am Main, 1988), 51.

212   The Gestapo entered schools: Klepper, *Tagebücher*, 669.

213   It was packed, and many: Marcel Reich-Ranicki, *The Author of Himself: The Life of Marcel Reich-Ranicki*, trans. Ewald Osers (London, 2001), 107–108.

213   Later the expulsions: See Trude Maurer, "Abschiebung und Attentat: die Ausweisung der polnischen Juden und der Vorwand für die 'Kristallnacht,'" in *Der Judenpogrom: Von der 'Reichskristallnact' zum Völkermord*, ed. Walter Pehle (Frankfurt am Main, 1988).

213   "Three simple questions: *Der Stürmer* 44, November 1938.

213   When Canaris met: Groscurth, *Tagebücher*, 158–159.

CHAPTER 9

215   "a slight suggestion of Al Capone.": Ciano, *Ciano's Diary*, 188.

215   "in compensation for the damage: Klepper, *Tagebücher*, 673.

216   Hitler put the matter right: Irving, *Göring*, 230–231.

216   "He goes his own way: Goebbels, *Tagebücher I, VI*, 174.

216   He needed to find a way: Goebbels, *Tagebücher I, VI*, 166.

216   Cesar Bresgen and Heinrich Spitha's: Grunberger, *Social History*, 518.

217   Grynszpan admitted killing: Döscher, *Kristallnacht*, 58–64.

217   One of the men who claimed: Kate Connolly, "Historian Says Jewish Boy Killed His Nazi Lover," *Guardian*, October 31, 2001.

218   He was officially declared dead: Elisabeth Klamper, "Herschel," in Historisches Museum, *Judenpogrom*, 58.

218   There were reports that the hue: George Lane-Fox Pitt-Rivers, *The Czech Conspiracy: A Phase in the World-War Plot*, 2nd enl. ed. (London, 1938), 13.

218   "It is clear that the German: Wolfgang Benz, "Der Ruckfall in der Barbarei," in Pehle, ed., *Judenpogrom*, 15.

218   "We must be clear that in the next: Also quoted in Padfield, *Himmler*, 238–239.

219   Himmler fairly accurately: See Giles MacDonogh, *After the Reich: From the Fall of Vienna to the Berlin Airlift* (London, 2007).

219   "Now we want to be blunt: Goebbels, *Tagebücher I, VI*, 178.

220   "Now the dish is: Goebbels, *Tagebücher I, VI*, 180.

220   It has been suggested: Lang, *Wolff*, 104, 106.

221   When her children asked him: Hamann, *Winifred Wagner*, 298.

221   Wolff believed to the end: Lang, *Wolff*, 105.

221   "Find out immediately: Lang, *Wolff*, 105.

221   The Party (Goebbels) was told: Uwe Dietrich Adam, "Wie spontan war der Pogrom?" In Pehle, ed., *Judenpogrom*, 79; Hilberg, *Destruction*, 1:38–39.

222   Goebbels claimed that he tried: Goebbels, *Tagebücher I, VI*, 180.

222   "Continue to wield our arms: Goebbels, *Tagebücher I, VI*, 181.

222   In Rüdesheim the SA men: Benz, "Der Ruckfall," 22.

222   In Feldafing on the Starnberg Lake: Hassell, *Diaries*, 20.

222   In Erfurt, the baptized lawyer: Benz, "Der Ruckfall," 40.

223   In Aschaffenburg the killing: Gilbert, *Kristallnacht*, 31.

223   In Vienna they arrested all the Jews: *Manchester Guardian*, November 11, 1938.

223   "unlovely excesses": Goebbels, *Tagebücher I, VI*, 182.

223   In Munich the "demonstrators": Adam, "Wie spontan war der Pogrom?" 78.

223   There was also a fear: Burleigh, *Third Reich*, 332.

224   Both the police and the fire chief: Hamann, *Winifred Wagner*, 297.

224   In Fulda, the Jews were put: Gilbert, *Kristallnacht*, 109.

224   He was not punished: Gilbert, *Kristallnacht*, 94–95.

225   He seems to have taken one: Engelmann, *Hitler's Germany*, 121.

225   When Gentile women: Gilbert, *Kristallnacht*, 42.

225   "What's the point: Quoted in Giles MacDonogh, *Berlin* (London, 1997), 433.

225   His uncle's shop: Gay, *German Question*, 134–135.

225   the facades of Hemdenmatz: He was possibly wrong about Hemdenmatz, or the owners were cunning—they advertised in *Der Stürmer*.

225 "What did the SA eat: Beck, *Underground Life*, 36–37.

225 There is even an instance: Gilbert, *Kristallnacht*, 46.

225 "The actual private citizen: Gräfin von Maltzan, *Memoirs*, trans. Peter Ede (unpublished ms.), 57.

226 Most of the synagogues: Beck, *Underground Life*, 36.

226 The city's most famous synagogue: Gilbert, *Kristallnacht*, 44, 48–49.

226 the synagogue at Neue Weltgasse 7: Incidentally, opposite the family house where the author's mother was born in 1927.

226 The Gestapo feared for the valuable: Jonny Moser, "Die 'Reichskristallnacht' in Wien," in Historisches Museum, *Judenpogrom*, 61.

226 The violence was followed: Weinzierl, *Zu wenig Gerechte*, 65.

227 In at least one instance: Gilbert, *Kristallnacht*, 64–65.

227 Similar sentiments were: Rosenkranz, *Verfolgung*, 161–162.

227 If the emigration could not be: Rosenkranz, *Verfolgung*, 159.

227 the Osteria Bavaria in Munich's Schellingstrasse: It is still there and looks much the same, except that it is now called the Osteria Italiana.

227 "He approves of everything: Goebbels, *Tagebücher I, VI*, 182.

227 "My dear Popitz: Burleigh, *Third Reich*, 326, quoting Hassell, *Diaries*, 28.

227 The economics minister, Funk: Hilberg, *Destruction*, 1:39.

228 "Goebbels smashes the windows: Bloch, *Ribbentrop*, 222.

228 moved Goebbels to make an announcement: Some say this was Göring. See Martin Gilbert, *Kristallnacht: Prelude to Destruction* (London, 2006), 46.

228 Goebbels was disappointed: Manvell and Fraenkel, *Doctor Goebbels*, 157.

228 Göring managed to win: Hilberg, *Destruction*, 1:40.

228 It provided another chance: Walzer and Templ, *Unser Wien*, 32; Moser, "'Reichskristallnacht,'" in Historisches Museum, *Judenpogrom*, 62.

228 The real figure: Gilbert, *Kristallnacht*, 118.

228 Even the Party condemned: See Benz, "Der Ruckfall."

228 "This is no longer anything: Benz, "Der Ruckfall," 47.

229 Bruno Heilig, who was: Heilig, *Men Crucified*, 154; Gilbert, *Kristallnacht*, 26.

229 This was the background: Safrian, *Eichmann*, 23.

230 Berlin jeweler Margraf in Unter den Linden: Goebbels later had a brilliant idea: He was going to issue a statement that the jeweler had been plundered by a Jew. Hitler was delighted. *Tagebücher I, VI*, 199.

230 The total bill was: Tooze, *Wages*, 277.

230 "I have had enough of these: Quoted in Bankier, in Historisches Museum, *Judenpogrom*, 79.

230 No charges were brought: Hilberg, *Destruction*, 1:45.

230 He would have reservations: Bankier, in Historisches Museum, *Judenpogrom*, 81.

230 (on November 22 he claimed: Goebbels, *Tagebücher I, VI*, 198.

230 dismissed Funk as "soft" and claimed: Goebbels, *Tagebücher I, VI*, 185.

231 "In Vienna the dough: Safrian, *Eichmann*, 47–48.

231 It was decided that only: Walzer and Templ, *Unser Wien*, 57.

231 At the end of the year the Gestapo: Engel, "Archive des Grauens."

231 When the Jews arrived in Dachau: Gilbert, *Kristallnacht*, 179.

231 Urns filled with ashes began: Gilbert, *Kristallnacht*, 183.

231 Sachsenhausen had the reputation: Klepper, *Tagebücher*, 688.

231 After the "Rath-Aktion": Kautsky, *Teufel und Verdamte*, 29.

231 They had also to promise: Moser, *Juden Verfolgung*, 9.

232 "Don't say anything you don't have to: Arnold Schoenberg, *Arnold Schoenberg: Letters*, trans. Eithne Wilkins and Ernst Kaiser, ed. Erwin Stein (London, 1964), 205.

232 Klemperer decided to stay put: Klemperer, *Tagebücher*, 435.

232 "When I told him that any decent: Giles MacDonogh, *The Last Kaiser: William the Impetuous* (London, 2000), 456.

232 Hitler and Goebbels had "unconditional" support: Ciano, *Ciano's Diary*, 193.

233 Goebbels's own newspaper: *Daily Herald*, November 9, 1938.

233 *Der Stürmer* presented a gallery: *Der Stürmer* 46, November 1938.

233 In one cartoon a Jew is: *Der Stürmer* 45, November 1938.

233 The cardinal's palace was wrecked: Gilbert, *Kristallnacht*, 143.

233 He wanted to break diplomatic: Gilbert, *Kristallnacht*, 172.

233 "Whatever provocation may have been: Chandler, "Church of England," 237.

233 It is said that among the conservative elite: See, for example, Heinemann, *Konservativer Rebell*, 93–94.

234 The next day Uncle Adolf: Goebbels, *Tagebücher I, VI*, 189.

234 The industrialist Robert Bosch: Burleigh, *Third Reich*, 333.

234 He argued that the evil: Jamie Bulloch and Katharina Bielenberg, *Peter Bielenberg* (privately printed memoir) (2001), 80–81.

234 "You have to feel ashamed: Groscurth, *Tagebücher*, 157.

234 "the heaviest blow: Groscurth, *Tagebücher*, 162.

234 Klepper noted there was a desire: Klepper, *Tagebücher*, 682.

234 Leaving her driver at a safe: MacDonogh, *Good German*, 118–119.

234 talking of "universal horror": Meehan, *Unnecessary War*, 55–56.

235 The Catholics tended to be more: Stephenson, *Home Front*, 144.

235 On the other hand, the more likely: Kershaw, *Final Solution*, 175.

235 In Vienna the corruption was: Grumberger, *Social History*, 138–139.

235 Of three hundred who lined up: Gilbert, *Kristallnacht*, 151–152.

235 The first fell on December 15: Hilberg, *Destruction*, 1:134–135.

235 income from the beleaguered Jews: Tooze, *Wages*, 277–279.

236 On November 18 Göring met: Goebbels, *Tagebücher I, VI*, 219.

236 **Wenninger had introduced:** Mendelsohn and Detwiler, *The Holocaust: Jewish Emigration 1938–1940*, vol. 6: *Rublee Negotiations and Intergovernmental Committee* (New York, 1982), 5; McClure, *Rublee*, 260.

236 **The international boycott:** McClure, *Rublee*, 262.

236 **"The business point of view:** McClure, *Rublee*, 266–267.

236 **Under the scheme, Germany would:** Mendelsohn and Detwiler, *Holocaust*, 5:149.

236 **There was only a short time:** Meehan, *Unnecessary War*, 98–99.

237 **Goods from Hamburg:** Meehan, *Unnecessary War*, 99.

237 **A month later he was obtaining:** FLA Germany Files GE9.

237 **They had left from Galata:** BBD E3/282.

237 **It was agreed that a further 5,000:** Rosenkranz, *Verfolgung*.

238 **The pro-Zionist MP:** Naomi Shepherd, *Wilfred Israel* (London, 1984), 146–147, 149.

238 **"steady stream of Jews:** Diana Hopkinson, *The Incense Tree: An Autobiography* (London, 1968), 163.

238 **"I was in despair over:** Hopkinson, *Incense Tree*, 163.

239 **As it was, only a small percentage:** BBD, Acc 3121 C2/2/4/1, Ruth Horowitz to Dr. B. Homa, July 21, 1950.

239 **Some court officers:** Hilberg, *Destruction*, 1:127.

239 **Realizing he would now starve:** Maltzan, *Memoirs*, 58; MacDonogh, *Berlin*, 380.

239 **In Württemberg, the number of Jews:** Stephenson, *Home Front*, 145.

240 **He also asked for more staff:** Smith, *Foley*, 133.

240 **It was Engelmann's aunt:** Engelmann, *Hitler's Germany*, 128–131.

241 **On October 27, Bishop Batty had left:** *Times*, October 27, 1938.

241 **"I am really very much perturbed:** Lambeth Palace, Lang Papers, 38/255, Bell to Alan Don, November 30, 1938. Mrs. Baker's letter is missing.

241 **I think you ought to know:** Lambeth Palace, Lang Papers, 38/260, Alan Don to Batty, December 5, 1938.

241 **Batty replied the following day:** Lambeth Palace, Lang Papers, 38/264, 265, 266, December 6–7, 1938.

243 **Mrs. Ludovici seems to have heard:** Lambeth Palace, Lang Papers, 38/311, 313, 322.

CHAPTER 10

245 **A liberal German like Peter Bielenberg:** Conversation with Peter Bielenberg, summer 1988.

246 **Through mutual friends, Trott was also:** MacDonogh, *Good German*, 122–123.

247 **"The subject is up to you:** Breker, *Strahlungsfeld*, 93.

247   The Mosaic [*sic*] Saloon was decorated: Breker, *Strahlungsfeld*, 93, 98; Wolters, *Neue deutsche Baukunst*, 12.

247   "when these gentlemen: Parparov, *Hitler Book*, 36.

248   Yarnall saw some of Heydrich's staff: FLA Yarnall, "Factual Notes," in FSC/GE/5.

248   In general only the mothers were there: Gertrude Scholz says that no parents were present; she was there. See Elfriede Schmidt, *1938 . . . Und was dann?* (Thaur bei Innsbruck, 1988), 201.

248   When war broke out, 650 cases: Darton, *Friends Committee*, 50–51.

249   Gentile foster parents: Rosenkranz, *Verfolgung*, 182.

249   he explained "that, since the money: FLA Germany Files, GE9, Ethel Houghton to Bernard Lawson, February 4, 1939.

249   By the end of the year, the Jews: Hilberg, *Destruction*, 1:125–126.

250   Ribbentrop, for his part: Conwell-Evans, *None So Blind*, 116.

250   There was a comic scene: Bloch, *Ribbentrop*, 229.

250   Ribbentrop conceded that no one: DGFP, D IV, 481.

250   He met Rublee: Mendelsohn and Detwiler, *Holocaust*, 6:22; DGFP, D IV, 351.

250   In the event of his losing: Sir Frederick Leith-Ross, *Money Talks: Fifty Years of International Finance* (London, 1958), 254.

251   German acceptance of the scheme: McClure, *Rublee*, 269–274.

251   Employment was only to be granted: PRO W16643, December 17, 1938. Hoare to Josiah Wedgwood, *Bulletin of the Co-ordinating Committee for Refugees*, February 1939.

252   It was not apparent: PRO 371, House of Lords Debates, December 14, 1938.

252   One S. C. Leslie: PRO W16614/48, December 16, 1938.

252   Tanganyika and British Guiana: PRO W16580 45.

252   on December 7 Jewish refugees: PRO T15833 580 635, December 7, 1938.

252   The Dutch closed their borders: Rosenkranz, *Verfolgung*, 186.

252   "Permission to enter Switzerland: PRO W1 6645/94, December 17, 1938.

252   "In the course of July there was: PRO W1 6645, December 17, 1938.

252   Since October 4, German non-Aryans: PRO W1 6645, December 17, 1938.

253   The aim was to prevent any congress: Jeremy Noakes, "Social Outcasts in the Third Reich," in *Life in the Third Reich*, ed. Richard Bessel (Oxford, 1987), 90.

253   The text darkly hints: Michael Burleigh and Wolfgang Wipperman, *The Racial State: Germany 1933–1945* (Cambridge, 1991), 120–121.

253   A cartoon in *Der Stürmer*: Der Stürmer 50, December 1938.

253   "The Jew Jesus, everything spiritual: Klemperer, *Tagebücher*, 448.

253   "This was signed by a former Imperial: Groscurth, *Tagebücher*, 164.

254   A drunken Commandant Rödl: Reich and Reich, *Zweier Zeugen Mund*, 253–255.

254 He left Graz in February 1943: Döw–Akten 20000/R244. Judgment of the Volksgericht, Berlin, September 15, 1939, 1 J 172/38g; Auschwitz Sterbe-Index Nr 10163/1943.

255 He was sentenced: Judith Fels-Margulies, *Anmerkungen*, in an otherwise untitled and undated document.

255 It would mean the conquest: Tooze, *Wages*, 283.

255 "tough polemic against America.": Goebbels, *Tagebücher I, VI*, 245.

255 Others have seen the "prophecy": Kershaw, *Final Solution*, 109.

255 He took solace: Schuschnigg, *Requiem*, 85.

256 "for the brave little lady.": Groscurth, *Tagebücher*, 163.

256 "and so to bed: Goebbels, *Tagebücher I, VI*, 226.

AFTERWORD

258 the half-sister of Princess Stephanie: Stephanie was the result of a liaison between Gina's father and Stephanie's mother. Stephanie's father was in prison at the time.

258 "Never have I been in such: Kaus, *Und was für ein Leben*, 184.

258 the Trieste-born Gentile Otto Kaus: Kaus was killed in an air raid on Berlin.

258 My grandfather and my great-uncle Walther: Information from Gisela Müller.

259 "the Rolls Royce of emigrations": The phrase belongs to the late cabaret artist Gerhard Bronner.

259 During the war years its banquettes: See my article "Otto Horcher, Caterer to the Third Reich," *Gastronomica 7*, no. 1 (Winter 2007). Also "The Reichs-marschall's Table," BBC Radio 4, first broadcast March 14, 2005.

259 When he died in 1924: Laura Wärndorfer, *Meine einhundertzwanzig Jahre*, MS autobiography, n.d., 50.

260 Ludwig was born in February 1906: To celebrate Schmidt's Second Symphony Ella had the painter Adalbert Franz Seligmann decorate her music room with eight panels with various bacchanalia.

260 Wührer was the first to tell Ludwig: "Do I thank him or punch him?" Ludwig had asked his wife, Laura, at the revelation.

260 A large sum was paid: Walzer and Templ, *Unser Wien*, 42–43.

260 the painter Viktor Krausz: Krausz's rich Jewish wife, Marianne, had committed suicide in 1938. The Krausz collection passed into the hands of the Nazi authorities. The old masters must have pleased them, Krausz's own paintings rather less.

Index

Page numbers listed as "Ins" indicate photograph inserts.